Things We Wish We Had Said

Also by Anthony Campolo
Partly Right
A Reasonable Faith
It's Friday, but Sunday's Comin'
You Can Make a Difference
Who Switched the Price Tags?
20 Hot Potatoes Christians Are Afraid to Touch

Things We Wish We Had Said

Reflections of a Father and His Grown Son

TONY & BART CAMPOLO

WORD PUBLISHING
Dallas · London · Sydney · Singapore

ISBN 0–8499–0685–7

9 8 0 1 2 3 9 AGF 9 8 7 6 5 4 3 2 1

Printed in the United States of America

To Marty

. . . the best reason I ever had for growing up at all
B.C.

. . . the kind of daughter-in-law who makes parents believe
that marriages are made in heaven
A.C.

Contents

Acknowledgments

We are indebted to some very special people for their help in putting this book together. Without Dad's executive associate, Mary Noël Keough, and my wife, Marty, it would never have been typed. Without my Mom, it would not have been edited. Pat Carroll, Sue Dahlstrom, and Sarah Thorpe also helped us turn out the manuscript. To all of these wonderful people, Dad and I say "Thank you" from the bottom of our hearts, and "thanks" to you, too, for letting us share our lives with you.

Bart Campolo

Foreword

There are four of us in the Campolo family. Peggy and I met at Eastern College when she was a freshman and I was a senior. Two years later, in June 1958, we were married. Lisa was born in 1960, followed by Bart three years later. Today, Lisa is a successful lawyer in Boston, and Bart is based in Philadelphia. He and his wife, Marty, are the founders of Kingdom Builders Supply, a nonprofit organization helping urban churches to reach out to neighborhood youth.

Our kids were, for the most part, fun to raise. If we had it to do over again, there are a lot of things we would do the same, but there also are a lot of things we would do differently. Nobody raises kids without having some regrets, and I, personally, have a lot of them. There are things I did that I shouldn't have done, and there are things I said that I shouldn't have said. In retrospect, it is the things that I should have done and said and didn't that are far more troublesome to me. I know now that I did not deal with a lot of important stuff. Last year, Bart and I had the opportunity to share speaking responsibilities at a large youth conference. We did a lot of remembering and reflecting and shared our sometimes very different perceptions of times past. We answered some questions for the young people, but we raised even more questions for ourselves.

Bart is twenty-six years old now, and I wonder just how well we knew each other when he was growing up and how well we know each other now. I wonder just how much he understood the motivations that lay behind my actions, and I wonder how much I understood about his. Did I have any real grasp of what he was going through as he grew up? Did he have any sense of what I was thinking or that trying to be a good father was sometimes hard for me?

Looking back on those years, we sense that there was a lot concealed on both sides. That is part of what lies behind the writing of this book. In reality, Bart and I are opening up a lot of things with each other that we have not covered before. There were things I should have said to Bart that would have helped him understand me better, and, undoubtedly, there were a lot of things that he might have told me that would have helped me to do better by him as a father.

The other reason for writing this book is that I do believe there were many things that Bart and I did right during his growing up years, and I hope those things can be of some help to others who are trying to figure out the father–son thing. Perhaps our evaluation of what we did and did not do in our relationship with each other can help others to think through how they ought to raise their sons.

It also occurs to me that, in this age when so many single mothers are left with teenage sons to raise, there is much of this material that could be useful to them. Single mothers may get some help in understanding what a son needs from a father and what a father ought to be giving to his son. A knowledge of what is missing is required before a single mother can consider how to compensate for a father who isn't there.

A book like this one could be written by my daughter and me, or, for that matter, by my son and his mother, but this time it's Bart and me. If at times we seem to leave Peggy and Lisa out of it, it's only because we don't presume to speak for them. Bart and I hope that what we have to say to each other in these letters will prove useful to anyone who is trying to be a good parent to a boy who is trying to become an adult—and we also hope that this book will be of help to young people who have to work at both growing up *and* figuring out their parents at the same time.

Tony Campolo

One

Meeting My Father's Son

Dear Dad,

You are an incredibly tough act to follow. Whenever I compare myself to you, I come out the loser, Dad, and yet, more and more as I get older, I can't stop myself from doing it all the same.

I think you are a great father. Having said that, though, I still need to answer the question of what it means to be your son. I have to answer it for myself, the same way you had to answer it about your father and he had to answer it about his. You may not be "Tony Campolo, Christian leader" to me, but you are my Dad, and that is enough for anyone to come to terms with. It's not a matter of what you did right or what you did wrong in raising me as much as it's the standard you set just by being who you are.

Perhaps the best way I can describe it to you is to use our basketball games as an example, because for me those games have always reflected our relationship and personalities better than anything else. From the very first time you took me down to the gym at Eastern College to teach me how to shoot, I realized that basketball was something you really cared about. It was fun, to be sure, but it was also important to you that I learn to play the game the right way, and because it was important to you, it became important to me as well, right from the start. After that, I spent a lot of time with a basketball in my hands, practicing the fundamentals and imagining myself as a star player with you in the stands cheering me on. Fortunately, I had some natural ability to go along with my intense desire to please you, and by the time I was ten years old I was good enough to play with you in the pick-up games you were always finding wherever we happened to be.

It was a hustle, really, except that we didn't play people for money. We would walk onto the court as though we had never seen one before and begin to shoot the ball awkwardly, cheering wildly whenever we managed to hit the rim. The college guys at the other end of the court would watch our act for a while and then go on with their game. They were always surprised when you walked over and asked them if they wanted to take us on, and nine times out of ten they declined, not wanting to show up a klutzy father in front of his adoring son. Somehow, though, you usually managed to embarrass them into it. "What's the matter?" you'd jeer, "Are you guys afraid you can't keep up with an old man and a little kid?" They'd go easy on us at first, so that by the time they figured out how good we really were, we usually had a pretty big lead. Then they'd bear down on us, but most times it was a case of too little too late.

I always got a kick out of those games, even though my job was mainly to throw the ball to you and watch you beat both of the other guys singlehanded. Oh, I'd shoot a few baskets to keep them honest, but it was definitely your show. Even when they were better, we usually won anyway because you simply refused to let us lose. I've seen a lot of basketball players, Dad, but I've never seen anyone as hard-nosed as you are in a game. You would dive after loose balls, smash into guys twice your size, and run over anyone who got in your way. I asked you about it once, and you told me that when you were growing up in the city, the playground courts were always crowded with guys waiting to play. The team that won kept playing while the losers went to the end of the line, so everyone hated to lose. Kids in the city play basketball for blood. You had to be tough, you told me, and after watching you play I didn't doubt it.

Later on, we began to play against each other, one-on-one, and you always won. I got bigger and stronger and more skillful every year, but you won anyway, even after I had clearly become the better player. I could beat players who could in turn beat you, but somehow that never translated when we matched up together. No matter how big a lead I managed to build, you always caught me in the end with a clutch steal or an impossible shot.

"You'll never beat me," you used to rib me between baskets, "because you're not tough enough. You don't want it bad enough. Face it, kid, you're soft."

You were kidding, of course, but we both knew that you were right, too. I was not tough. I'm still not tough. Even though I made the varsity team like you had, I was always a finesse player, relying on my skills and shying away from heavy contact. I was talented enough, but I lacked the "killer instinct" that makes a talented player a winner. You, however, were a scrapper without great height or dazzling speed and without my ball-handling abilities, but you were armed with an aggressiveness I'll never have.

One time, at a Bible conference where you were speaking, I thought I was finally going to beat you. We were in a five-on-five game that day, but guarding each other made it one-on-one between us, and I was outdoing you in a big way at both ends of the court. Toward the end we started really banging each other around, both of us intent on winning the game. We were having fun, but the other players probably thought we were trying to kill each other (you certainly weren't "turning the other cheek" the way you had preached about that morning!). On the last point, I took the ball and drove hard for the winning basket. You appeared out of nowhere and knocked both me and the ball to the ground. You not only blocked my shot, you bloodied my nose as well. The other men looked embarrassed as I got up, but you and I just laughed. "You should know better than to try something like that, kid," you said with a sly grin, and the game went on. My team lost—again.

I never could win. I had to wait until age slowed you down before I ever took a game from you, and when it finally happened we both knew that it wasn't really me who had beaten you after all. Even when I won, I lost. That's the way it is for me with you. I have every advantage, but you win on character.

5

And if, perchance, you don't, well, anyone can see that I have all the advantages. It's never a real victory! And make no mistake—I'm not just thinking about basketball anymore. It's the way our lives are.

You see, I know all about your life. I know because I remember all those stories you told me about growing up on the streets of West Philadelphia, the youngest son of an immigrant family too poor to buy you your opportunities. I know that you got the same toy truck three Christmases in a row, except that every year it was painted a different color so you'd think it was new. (Frankly, I've always wondered how such an intelligent man could have been such a stupid kid.) I know that you lived in a tiny row house with rooms the size of closets—you even showed me the house once. I know about fighting to keep from being robbed . . . about having to share the weekly bottle of soda pop with your two older sisters . . . about hitchhiking because you didn't have bus fare . . . and I know your father died partly because he was too poor to have a good doctor until it was too late.

I also know that you worked for your family as a kid and gave the money you earned to your parents. I know that you worked your way through college, too, and then seminary. Even if you hadn't told me about it all yourself, I would still know because Mom-Mom Campolo told those same stories about you, over and over again. She was so proud of you and of what you had accomplished, and she wanted me to be proud, too. She wanted me to understand that it is a great thing to come from a poor Italian family in the inner city and earn a Ph.D. and become a college professor and a famous preacher as well. She wanted me to see you as a great man, not because of your gifts and abilities, but because you overcame so many obstacles to become a scholar and a servant of God by the sheer force of your own will. "Your father," she'd tell me, "went over the top for Jesus."

I guess every kid has heard a slew of those often-repeated when-I-was-your-age stories. They are our parent's way of letting us know that no matter what we happen to be going through at the time, they had it worse. They are a kind of oral tradition, too, a family history that's passed down from one generation to the next. I always liked listening to those stories because they told me that I was part of a larger tradition. Mom-Mom Campolo told them all the time, but Grandmom and Grandpop Davidson waited to be asked, I think because they thought I would be bored. On the contrary, I love knowing about who and where we come from as a family, except when I know you're using one of those when-I-was-your-age stories to manipulate me into doing something.

To a well-heeled suburban kid like me, though, being poor didn't always sound all that horrible. The way you described it, your childhood seemed like one adventure after another—a constant battle against anything that tried to hold you back. "We were poor," you'd say, "but boy, did we know how to have fun." I can remember thinking that stickball in the streets sounded a whole lot more exciting than my Little League with all its fancy uniforms and coaches and practice sessions, and that hitching across the city by yourself sounded a whole lot better than getting driven to school in Mom's station wagon. My life was surely more comfortable than yours, but it was just as surely more boring, too. Besides, you made it very clear to me that it was the hardships you had to overcome, the sacrifices you had to make, and especially the hard work you had to do that made you into the person you are today. I could tell you were proud of your childhood. You had to fight to survive, you said, and it made a man out of you.

So now, after all of the years of wondering, I must finally ask you the obvious question: Why did you let me grow up without all of those things that made such a difference in your life? How could you raise me in the lap of luxury and expect me to develop character, when you had already fought all of my character-building battles for me when you were becoming a man? Didn't it occur to you that by sparing me from the hardships, the sacrifices, the hard work, and the fights you were robbing me of the chance to become the kind of man you are?

Take a good look at me. What have I accomplished? What have I achieved? I'm a White, Anglo-Saxon, Protestant male raised by two highly educated parents in an affluent suburban community in the richest country in the world. I've never been beaten, hungry, discriminated against, or too poor for anything, including an Ivy League education. I worked at summer jobs when I was in school, of course, but the money I earned was my own, to buy things I wanted, because you bought everything I needed. You would be hard pressed to find anyone in the world who has had any more advantages than I have had. The problem is that I didn't do anything to earn all those things, except manage to be born in the right place at the right time. You are the one who earned it, not me. Because of that, you know a lot of things about yourself that I'll never be able to know about myself. You know that you're tough and that you have character. You know that you can make a way for yourself and that you deserve to be where you are in the world. Those are important things, Dad.

I remember during the '88 election, they said that George Bush was "someone who was born on third base and thought he'd hit a triple." I don't know about George Bush, but I'm well aware that I didn't overcome anything to put myself where I am. I never had that chance.

So how can I measure up to you, Dad? How can I accomplish anything that will compare to your Horatio Alger rags-to-riches story? We both know the answer to those questions: I can't. The game was over before it started. I have begun to understand why so many children of successful people rebel against their parents' value system altogether: they know that they can't make it work. When you start at the top, there really isn't any direction you can go except down. Maybe that sounds like self-pity to you, but surely there's some truth to it. You never had to think about that, of course, because your situation was precisely the opposite of mine—you had nowhere to go but up. You weren't born on third base, or even on second. Consequently, there was no pressure on you to achieve any particular degree of success. By the time you were graduated from high school, you had already gone farther than your parents ever could have dreamed of going themselves. You could take chances with your life, secure in the knowledge that wherever you ended up you were already a winner. You had nothing to lose and everything to gain, whereas my situation is exactly the reverse.

You see, Dad, it's not just that I started out with so much. The rules of the game have changed as well.

For the first time in history, economists tell us, the generation presently coming of age cannot expect to achieve a higher standard of living than their parents. Certainly there are more and better opportunities than ever before, but there's also more competition as well. There are more people, for one thing. The rewards of success are higher than ever, but then so is the price. Take education, for example. I've always felt guilty that you put me through college because I know that you worked yourself through without any help from your parents. But even if I had tried to work my way through school, how could I have earned the $10,000–$15,000 a year that a private education costs nowadays? That's more than I make in a year now, working full time. (If college students could make $15,000 a year in part-time jobs, they might wonder if it made sense to be in college in the first place or if they wouldn't be better off making careers out of whatever it was they were already doing so successfully.) The point is that things are different now from what they were when you were my age. The odds are stacked even more heavily against a kid on his own than they were only ten years ago, let alone twenty-five. Yet even knowing all that doesn't really quell my self-doubts, because somehow I sense you could find a way to make it today if you had to, and somehow I worry that I wouldn't have been able to do the same if I had been in your shoes during the fifties.

I think that kind of feeling is often a big factor in why kids rebel against their parents. Convinced that they will lose if they play "the game" and try to live up to their parents' standard of success, they opt not to try at all. They look for another game, another way to establish themselves in the world. Unfortunately that isn't always as easy as it seems because of the way heredity can limit options.

Years ago I watched an interview with Joe Frazier, the heavyweight boxing champion of the world at the time. His son, Marvis, was no more than ten years old, and I remember Joe telling the interviewer that he did not want Marvis to become a boxer. "He should be a doctor or a lawyer or something like that, where you use your head for something other than getting hit," Joe said earnestly. I thought it was great that he wasn't pressuring his son to follow in his footsteps, because clearly Joe's shoes would be nearly impossible to fill. But I wasn't surprised eight years later to find Marvis Frazier boxing professionally on television. Whether he liked it or not, Marvis Frazier had the body of a boxer, just like his dad. Besides, he had practically been raised in Joe's North Philadelphia gym, surrounded by other fighters. That he would become a boxer was almost inevitable. He wasn't as good as his dad though, and something he said after he lost the fight badly summed up the tragedy of that fact: "I'm not my Dad," he said, "but I'm going to keep boxing anyway because that's what I do best."

I can relate to that one myself, because all of the things I do best are the things you do best as well. You do them better than I do, of course, but they are still my strengths. What makes it worse for me is that, as a Christian, I feel bound to utilize my gifts and abilities as best I can for the Kingdom of God—even though that means leaving myself open to comparison with you. I've tried doing a lot of other things, but I've always come back to speaking and teaching because, for better or for worse, those are the things I am gifted to do, just like you. But you're more than just gifted as a speaker. You're aggressive, the same way you were in basketball. To other people it may seem as though you're talking off the top of your head (and I'll just skip the obvious jokes, because I inherited your pitiful hair genes along with some of the good ones), but I know how much work goes into those sermons. I've watched you study for hours to master a difficult idea just so you can make it seem easy to the people you'll explain it to later. There are no easy ways to find new things to say or new ways to say old things, but you keep doing it year after year. You push yourself hard before you even stand up to speak, let alone once you're doing your thing. You know how to "read" audiences, too, with a wisdom that comes from having preached a hundred times to every kind of group as you worked your way up the ladder to become a top speaker. You are a gifted speaker, Dad, but you are a workman as well.

I'm a speaker, too, but I didn't have to work very hard to become one. I had you as an example and as a teacher, for one thing, which is a serious head start. I also have your last name as well, which helps more than you can imagine. People are always giving me opportunities to speak, sometimes at places where you had to wait twenty years to win a hearing, simply because I'm your son. I don't try to kid myself that I've earned my chances, and I don't pretend that I have the same drive and ability that keeps you on top of the game. I do my very best—make no mistake about that—but, like Marvis Frazier, I have to admit that I'm not my Dad, even though speaking is what I do best. The chances come because of whose son I am.

Think about this book that I'm writing at the tender age of twenty-six. Neither of us is foolish enough to think that anyone would publish my writing if my name were Bart Smith. It's you, Dad. We both know that. Of course, I take those opportunities just the same, and I put everything I have into making the most of them. I don't like admitting it sometimes, but the way I've resolved all of this speaking stuff is to treat being your son and having your last name the same way I would treat any other spiritual gift: as something to be used to serve God and His people. So many doors open for me because of you that I seldom feel like I've earned my position, but I'm ready and willing to trade that sense of accomplishment for the opportunity to share the Gospel and the chance to challenge people to live their lives for the love of God and the love of His people. I may not say things as well as you do, but that has nothing to do with what the Holy Spirit can or cannot do through me, so I've learned to depend on God and not worry about everything else. It may be a rationalization, but as long as I can preach the Gospel, organize ministries in the inner city, and invite young people to commit themselves to Christian service, it's a rationalization with which I can live.

But that still doesn't resolve the larger issue between you and me. Maybe nothing really can. You didn't choose your environment, and neither did I. Your parents weren't able to give you all of the things they'd have liked to have given you, and you became a fine man. You gave me everything, but even as you gave it, you took something away from me that I know you wouldn't want taken from you. You kept me from making it on my own. Perhaps I sound like the most horribly ungrateful person you could ever imagine, but I'm counting on you to know better than that. The most important thing in the world is love, and we both had plenty of that growing up. It's just that when I look at the world around me and see all of the suffering and need, I feel guilty about everything I've received. More and more I get angry when people talk about prosperity as though it were a reward for godliness, because I know that, in my case, it has a lot more to do with family background and because most of the finest Christians I know are poor. They love and depend on God in ways I'll never understand, and it offends me to hear people suggest otherwise in order to justify their own wealth or the way they spend it.

No words in all the world frighten me like those of Jesus: "From everyone who has been given much, much will be demanded, and from the one who has been entrusted with much, much more will be asked" (Luke 12:48). That verse haunts me through all of this, and it may be why I sometimes long for someone else's beginning. For God has much to say to those to whom He has given talents, wealth, education, opportunities, and, above all, grace. In this country we often fail to listen, but one day we'll have no choice. When I was a boy, the worst thing in the world wasn't to anger you, Dad, but to disappoint you. I feel the same way about my Heavenly Father. I don't fear for my salvation, but I worry about what I'll say when I stand before God and must tell Him what I did with everything He gave me. Sometimes it keeps me up at night. I worry about our entire nation and especially about American Christians, and I wonder what account we'll offer for our lifestyles of excess while our brothers and sisters went hungry and died. I think the day of judgment may not be our favorite part of eternity, for what could be more unhappy than to have disappointed the most wonderful Loved One we'll ever have by wasting His treasures and allowing His children to suffer? There is grace, to be sure, and there is forgiveness, but what account will we ever give, as individuals and as a nation, if we do not begin to listen to the voice of God?

As for me, I worry about my character as well, and I fear that in missing the struggles that you overcame, I've also missed the chance to become strong. You're a fine man, Dad, and I'm very grateful for that—I just wonder sometimes how I'm ever going to become the same kind of man myself.

Love,
Bart

Dear Bart,

If, according to Freud, the resolution of the Oedipus complex is brought about because a boy makes a positive identification with his father, then you were well on your way to resolving that complex in your preadolescent years. You always made me aware of your admiration for me, even when you were a little kid.

When you were about nine years old, the whole family went along with me to a speaking engagement at a small rural church. As we drove into the parking lot of the church, we saw only four cars, indicating that the church would be far from filled. Sizing up the situation, you exclaimed, "Dad! This is a disgrace! Hardly anybody has come to hear you speak—and you're so famous!"

Lisa, who has always had a knack for seeing things as they really are, responded, "Well, Bart, if he's so famous, where are all the people?"

You, in your usual cavalier manner, answered, "Knock it off, Lisa—it's pretty tough being famous when nobody knows who you are!"

You were always like that. Your mind was made up about your Dad, and you weren't about to be confused with the facts. You gave me what I'm sure almost every father wants from his son—admiration. I must say, however, that at times I've felt that your admiration was undeserved and at other times frightening. The hero worship that a son can give a father sometimes ignores many flaws and failures. You certainly were blinded to many of my failures and made me out to be bigger than life. Let me note some things you should consider.

In my drive for success, I worked too hard and too long and too often exhausted myself physically. Consequently, I was often irritable and short with people. You and Lisa were usually spared my nastiness, but Mom on too many occasions had to bear the brunt of how I felt. I don't know how much of that unfair meanness toward Mom you observed. I know that you saw some. I look back on my behavior at such times with shame and feel guilt. The Lord never willed for me to work so long and hard as to be that strung out.

Jesus Himself set the example for recognizing the limits of physical endurance and for stopping even godly service before exhaustion could lead to falling into sinful behavior. In Matt. 8:16–18, we read about His ministering to people. When He became exhausted, He told His disciples that He was worn out and that it was time for Him to stop and to pull Himself together. The disciples weren't very understanding, and they pressed Him by saying that there were scores of people who were still waiting to be healed and served. Jesus asserted Himself at that point and demanded to be put into a boat and taken to the other side of the Sea of Galilee.

Jesus knew how to say when enough was enough—but, then, He *was* the Messiah, while some of the rest of us only have messiah *complexes*. We act as though we should never stop working as long as there are people out there asking for our help. We're motivated more out of egotism than love, and we kid ourselves if we pretend otherwise. We end up pushing too hard and then taking it out on those who are closest to us, who love us, and who have gotten far less of our time than they had a right to expect.

As you admire ambition, take a second look at it in my life. I think that there will be a lot about my ambition and what it has done to those I love—and to myself—that is deserving of your criticism.

I think that my ambition was in large measure built into me by my poor Italian parents. My Mother was a first-generation

American, and my Dad immigrated here as a boy. They bought into the American Dream in a much bigger way than most WASPs who accept it as their inheritance. My parents saw being American not as a given, but rather as something to be achieved. In such a family, I grew up as a marginal person, not fully belonging to the "American" way of life, but also not having any sense of real at-homeness in the Italian subculture of my extended family. People like me work desperately to be accepted, and part of my drive, I am sure, stems from the sense that my personal achievements somehow earn me a place in the dominant culture. This kind of a background made me ambitious, but it also conditioned me to live on tiptoe for most of my life. I *need* to be accepted.

You may not have the kind of drive that sometimes goes with being a first-generation ethnic, but there is a positive side to not having it that I don't want you to ignore or take for granted. You are so much more relaxed about life. You enjoy life more. You seem to be able to stop and smell the roses. You come across as someone who *knows* that he belongs and doesn't have to "show off" to earn a place in this world. Count your blessings, kid.

I concur with your assessment that you may not have that inner sense of drivenness to do as much as I feel driven to do, but don't be so sure that your talent will not be enough to make you a much greater achiever. In your letter you mentioned what you learned from me on the basketball court—but do you remember that, even without my knock-down-sock-it-to-'em style, you were a good high-school basketball player?

In your very first regular-season game as a varsity basketball player, you came off the bench and scored a team-high nineteen points to lead your team to victory. Your smooth moves and natural style led to an array of floating jump shots that had the fans on their feet. You may not have been a blood-and-guts guy under the boards, but on that day your sheer talent made your team a winner. You never did become the star player I thought you could have been, but I always admired the way you kept things in perspective. There's something wrong with wanting to be a winner at all costs.

It's true that I've had to work my head off to overcome some of the limitations of my background, but that doesn't mean that what I produce is better than what you produce. For instance, anybody who reads this book will become aware of the fact that you are a good writer. You may not have had to work very hard to become a good writer, and you probably would be an even better writer if you drove yourself a little harder, but your talent enables you to accomplish much, much more than I could have ever dreamed of doing at your age. You write better than I do already. It is only that I have more life experiences to draw from that keeps me in the same league with you.

Bart, you often have heard me say that *being* is more important than *doing*. I sometimes preach a sermon that strongly declares that what a person *is* is more important than what a person *does*. As far as I'm concerned, you, more than anyone else I know, validate that sermon. You have learned how to *be*, and this is more important than learning how to do.

Sometimes I'm so busy in programs and projects that I forget people. Too often, those who work in sacrificial commitment to the visions of ministry that I've given them tell me how their feelings have been hurt because of my inattentiveness to them as persons. I'm always crushed when my failure to feel for people like I should is pointed out to me, and I long to be a more sensitive person. Caring for people is one area in which I wish I were like you. I admire you for your relationships and your awareness of how other people are feeling.

A good example of what I'm talking about comes to mind as I remember the summer of 1985. I had asked one of my friends, Jim Burns, who was then director of youth ministries at South Coast Community Church in Newport Beach, California, to take you on as an intern. In previous years you had chosen to work in my youth programs among the poor kids of Philadelphia. That year, though, I thought that the time had come for you to recognize that rich kids have their problems, too. So Jim set it up for you to join him as a summer intern to work with the church young people. My friend was well aware that you didn't need any "up front" experience as a speaker, so he minimized that particular role for you in your work with him. Instead, your job was to address the personal, spiritual, and psychological needs of the kids in the youth group as a support person and counselor.

Jim's reports to me at the end of that summer were filled with superlatives. He told me how your ability to empathize with teenagers made them eager to accept you as their friend, how your concern for them as individuals made you ever ready to provide long hours of listening for them. Jim talked glowingly about the kind of person you *were* and of the way in which you related to people who hurt. I was proud of you.

When I heard about your ministry out there in Newport Beach, I knew for sure that you had something that was far more precious than drive in your keen sensitivity for people. Sometimes those of us who have plans to change the world fail to feel for the needs of individuals who are hurting. Sometimes we're blind to the emotional needs of those who are staring us in the face. Not so with you, Bart! Not so with you!

There was, however, something that you mentioned about your upbringing in your letter which bothered me, and that was your questioning me about having raised you in the suburbs. The suburbs are "dangerous" places for kids, and your reflections on growing up there have me second guessing and wondering what would have been best for you.

Suburbs are, for the most part, plastic enclaves where kids can grow up separated from the realities that torture most of the world. Poverty is unknown. The old and the decrepit are carefully removed. The ugly side of life remains out of sight. Pimps, whores, and street people all live "downtown." Suburban kids live in a never-never land of narcissistic self-indulgence where nothing is ever asked of them except that they be constantly happy. Psychologists, like Harvard's Robert Coles, point out that kids in such environments lack any real purpose for living and often become depressed and bored with life because they can find no significant reason for their existence.

I tried to keep you from these maladies of suburban life by regularly taking you to places where there was suffering and involving you in work that would serve the needs of the poor.

Remember when I took you with me up to Wilkes-Barre, Pennsylvania, after a flood had devastated that city? Do you remember working side by side with me as we shoveled mud out of basements and cleaned up homes for desperate people? Remember our trips to Haiti and the Dominican Republic, where you were forced to look on the pain of the poor of the Third World? Remember being taken by Mom to visit elderly shut-ins who were lonely and sad? We tried to compensate for your "impoverished" life in the suburbs, but I still think you're right. It wasn't enough to overcome all that the suburbs do to kids.

Now you have Kingdom Builders Supply, your own inner-city mission outreach program. You'll be recruiting scores of college kids who have grown up in suburbia to come and join you in your ministry. You and these collegians will be working out of inner-city churches to reach some of the most oppressed and disadvantaged kids of America. I know that the parents of these college kids will be telling you of their concerns regarding the safety of their children in the city. They will be worried about what might happen in the city to suburban-bred young people who are in no way streetwise, and they are right to be concerned, because there is real danger on the city streets.

If those parents could understand what I've been talking about here, they would be even more concerned about what will happen to their children if they *don't* come to work with you and simply live out their lives in the "dangerous" suburbs. These parents should be worried about children who never escape from the stifling world of the "good life," where all appears to be well, but really isn't. They ought to be asking what will happen to kids who live where there is nothing at all about which to concern themselves—except for their own personal happiness. Parents ought to be begging you to take their children on as volunteers instead of just worrying about their safety.

Your letter shows me that you understand the liabilities of suburban living all too well. Maybe in your ministry you can make others understand this, too.

Love,
Dad

Two

How Do You Share Your Faith with Your Kid?

Dear Bart,

One of the most difficult problems for any Christian father is how to tell his kids about Christ and lead them into a personal relationship with Him. This was no less of a problem for a father who happened to be on the preaching circuit as a speaker for evangelical gatherings. As a matter of fact, Bart, I sometimes felt that it was harder for me to talk to you about a vital personal faith in Christ *because* I was a preacher. I felt that way for a number of good reasons.

First, there was always the concern that, growing up in a Christian home and having the gospel thrown at you so many times and in so many ways, you might become indifferent to it all. I was afraid that hearing the message of Christ over and over again might keep you from taking it seriously. I feared that daily exposure might inoculate you with Christianity and render you immune to the real disease. This was a real possibility. I've seen a good number of kids from Christian families (and not just preachers' families) who seemed to have developed the capacity to turn off the claims of Christ because of the years of practice they got in doing it as they grew up. Sometimes a guy like you can be told something so many times that he just doesn't hear it anymore. Overexposure can be a real turnoff, and I always harbored the fear that you might have been overexposed.

In addition to the fact that you heard me articulate the way of salvation from the pulpit on innumerable occasions, I made special efforts to outline the gospel story for you on a one-to-one basis.

You may not remember this, but once I took you with me to a men's Bible conference at Keuka College in upper New York State. After a lot of prayerful preparation, during which I asked God to give me the right words to say to you, we started out on the five-hour drive to the conference. I had planned for us to have this long time together so that I could talk to you in an unrushed and relaxed manner. I figured that, during the trip, I could get the discussion going in a casual way, entertain questions, and then resolve the matter of your making a decision for Christ.

Everything started out as I had hoped that it would. We got to discussing who Jesus was and is and what being a Christian is all about. You asked questions and engaged in a lively exchange with me for more than an hour.

The one thing I did not do was to press you to make a decision. Both of us now agree that it is not enough for a person to believe in what Jesus did on the cross and what He is presently doing in the world. We know that, in addition to believing the right things, a person must make a decision to allow the resurrected Jesus to be *Lord.* That involves a commitment to do what Jesus would do if He were in your place and facing your options. Being a Christian requires a commitment to obey the will of God as revealed in Scripture and as discovered through both prayer and the help of other Christians in the church.

I guess I failed to press you to make a decision that day because the way you talked to me led me to believe that you had already made your commitment to Christ. Looking back on it now, I think that I made a mistake at that point. Too often we take things for granted when talking with loved ones—particularly those in our own family.

I am convinced that when a person believes in what Christ accomplished through His death and resurrection and chooses to surrender fully to the will of God, such a person will be born-again. By that I mean that the presence of Christ will be "felt."

With full surrender comes the consciousness that Christ is close at hand and even within. It's like being aware of a friend who is ever present. It's the good feeling that He is always there for you to lean on for help and direction. I wanted you to have that kind of relationship with Christ. I wanted you to know the aliveness that comes from being in Christ and from having Christ be in you. I suppose I should have pressed you that day to yield yourself to Christ's lordship, but I didn't. Once again, my fear was of putting you on some kind of spiritual overload that might set off a negative reaction that would have moved you away from Christianity.

Second, I often wondered if seeing the inconsistencies between what I preached and what I practiced would make you cynical about my own professions of Christianity and even about the gospel itself. I don't think any of us are as good as the message we preach. I know that the Christ I declare is much more than can be seen in the way I live from day to day. As best I can, I try to let my listeners know that, in this respect, I am like the Apostle Paul who wrote: "I press toward the mark for the prize of the high calling of God in Christ Jesus" (Phil. 3:14). I try not to pretend that I'm an actualized or completed Christian. Instead, I endeavor to communicate the fact that I am still very much involved in the process of being transformed into the likeness of Christ and to invite those who listen to join me in the lifelong struggle to overcome the darkness that is in all of us.

Regardless of my qualifying statements, I think you expected more of me, and I worried that my failure to live up to what I called for from the pulpit (for people to become) would lead you to think that Christian leaders were phonies whose messages were not to be taken seriously.

The point at which I was most concerned was in respect to my lifestyle. There is no question in my mind that being a Christian requires a commitment to a radical lifestyle that I myself have failed to approximate. Along with Deitrich Bonhoeffer, I believe that "When Jesus calls a man, He bids him come and die." But if there's anything I haven't done, it is to die to the affluent American lifestyle.

On the basis of my preaching, some people are led to think that I live in a hovel and never spend any money on worldly pleasures. I've declared that Christians ought to live simply so that others might simply live. I've pointed out in sermon after sermon that there's something drastically wrong when Christians think that they can be followers of Jesus, yet ignore what He tells the rich to do about the poor and the oppressed of the world. After all the rationalizations for an affluent lifestyle are given, all of us must face what is written in 1 John 3:17–18.

But whoso hath this world's good, and seeth his brother have need, and shutteth up his bowels of compassion from him, how dwelleth the love of God in him? My little children, let us not love in word, neither in tongue; but in deed and truth.

There is no way of escaping the almost six hundred passages in the Bible that call us to work out our commitment to God by sacrificially serving the poor with the resources He has placed in our hands. If there is anything that has marked my preaching, it has been the declaration that Christians should look and act more like Francis of Assisi and Mother Teresa. I don't believe that good works for the poor will save us, but I do believe that being a Christian is having your heart broken by the things that break the heart of Jesus and that having the mind of Christ (Phil. 2:5) means we will inevitably think like He would think and act like He would act—particularly toward the downtrodden people who cross our paths.

The excuse I usually give to those who inquire about my lifestyle is that my wife does not agree with me as to how we ought to live. The simple lifestyle principles are not part of what she considers to be essential to Christianity. I tell myself that I've made concessions to her as part of maintaining a good marriage. There is some truth to this argument.

I think you know me well enough to know that if I had had my way, I certainly would have opted for living in the inner city where I could have had direct contact with the urban poor. I grew up among the poor and went to school with oppressed minority people, and I identify with their plight. The cries of those inner-city people who receive only the short end of society's opportunities are very much a part of what I have carried to the middle-class audiences to whom I speak.

While it is true that where we live is in large measure determined by the fact that Mom did not and does not feel called to live among the poor, I know you are aware that, in a host of ways, I've bought into a great deal of the affluent lifestyle quite apart from her influence. I may drive an old car, I may not spend a lot of money on clothes, and I shy away from the symbols of wealth and status which are so much a part of American bourgeois society. Nevertheless, I have my own particular splurges with which you are all-too-well acquainted. For instance, I love to travel and end up spending more that a frugal Christian should on holiday vacations. Also, when I travel in connection with my speaking engagements, I usually end up being entertained in first-class ways. Staying at the best hotels is not exactly what the people who hear me preach think of me as doing. I can live high while spending very little because those who invite me to speak pay the bills. I sometimes feel a bit uncomfortable about all of this, but not enough to put my foot down and demand more simple living.

Perhaps the point at which I feel the greatest discomfort is when people visit our home. We bought the house at a price that in today's market would be a fantastic bargain, and we chose to buy it because it was located within walking distance of my office and in a very safe neighborhood. Since my work was going to keep me on the road so much of the time, I agreed with Mom that she should live in a safe community. It wouldn't have been fair to ask her to live in a place where she felt she didn't belong, especially when I wouldn't be there much of the time.

Yet, when all the pros and cons have been given, I still have a sense of guilt about having such a lovely (and now expensive) house. There's much more room in it than we use, and it costs too much to maintain it. When I think of people squeezed into huts in Haiti or into ghetto tenements, it doesn't seem fair that I should have so much extra space. From time to time we've helped out students by having them live with us, but all in all I feel uneasy about all the room we have and really do not share.

In the end, it is probably having been socialized into loving privacy that has conditioned my housing habits. In this, I share with all Americans the tendency to have more housing space than I need. Bart, I know you share this uneasiness of mine, and I hope that the way Mom and I have lived has not led you to think me hypocritical.

Third, I've worried about how much my failure to conduct regular family devotions could have adversely influenced your willingness to become a Christian. From time to time I initiated special times for Bible reading and prayer, but it was hard for me to maintain consistency in these spiritual disciplines since my personal schedule was so helter-skelter. With evening meetings on more weekdays than not, I wasn't home at suppertime often enough to make a relaxed devotional time a regular part of our family life. Breakfast time always seemed to be too filled with anxious anticipation to permit me to take time for sacred reflection. I wish now that I had put more creative energy and time into planning family devotions. I suppose if I had worked at it, or even if I had been more demanding, I could have made it work—but I didn't. I sensed resistance and just gave up.

In those early days of your life, Mom wasn't on the kind of spiritual wavelength that would have led her to view family devotions as being of great significance. I know because she says so herself, and if she had it to do over again, things would be different. Since her Christian experience a few years ago, she has put us all to shame with her spiritual concerns. Back then, however, Mom just didn't see the need for family devotions, and I never made it a bone of contention between us.

Even if my Christian commitment failed to compel me to make regular devotions a part of our lives, my knowledge of sociology should have caused me to make them a family ritual. You have heard me give numerous lectures on the positive influences that rituals can have on individuals and particularly on children. Rituals (like family devotions) have been proven to be a primary factor in building loyalty and cohesiveness among family members. "The family that prays together stays together" is not simply a cliché; it is an articulation of a sound sociological principle.

Ever since sociologist Emile Durkheim first outlined the role that rituals can have in building group solidarity and inculcating values into children, people in my discipline have known that practices like regular family devotions are more important in Christian education than all of the Sunday school lessons that could ever be taught. I'm sure that the reason Jesus instituted holy communion was to turn every meal into a ritual that would renew the memory of His death and resurrection and revitalize the faith of His disciples. I do not think that His command that we should remember His death and resurrection whenever we eat or drink until He comes again was meant to be something occasionally observed at church worship services. Consider exactly what He said when He instituted this sacrament/ordinance:

And when he had given thanks, he brake it, and said, Take, eat: this is my body, which is broken for you: this do in remembrance of me. After the same manner also he took the cup, when he had supped, saying This cup is the new testament in my blood: this do ye, as oft as ye drink it, in remembrance of me.

1 Cor. 11:24–25

Jesus distinctly wanted to make every meal into a ritual in which His saving work for us would be remembered. It seems to me that Jesus wanted every meal to be a devotional time. I believe that if we followed what I read as His mandate on this, our lives would be consistently holier and our tendencies to fail or waver spiritually would be dramatically diminished.

Both my understanding of sociology and my reading of the Bible should have compelled me to treat the matter of having family devotions on a daily basis with a sense of urgency. It seems to me that parents who fail in this Christian discipline ought not be surprised if their children fail to become committed to Christ as they grow older. I know that I should have been a better father in this respect, particularly in the face of the indifference Mom had to such matters back then. Forgive me.

Last of all, Bart, I think that I may have failed you by not letting you know about my own doubts and times of spiritual dryness. It's difficult for any parent to know what to do about these matters. On the one hand, I think it's a mistake to communicate to kids that Christians experience an uninterrupted life of confident faith and spiritual joy. For all who follow Christ, there are times of painful depression and times of questioning. Jesus Himself had such times. As I read about His prayer in Gethsemane, I am convinced that at that point in His life He was going through such a "down time" that He struggled with what being an obedient Son of God was all about. In Matt. 26:37–39, we read:

And he took with him Peter and the two sons of Zebedee, and began to be sorrowful and very heavy. Then saith he unto them, My soul is exceeding sorrowful, even unto death: tarry ye here, and watch with me. And he went a little farther, and fell on his face, and prayed, saying, O my Father, if it be possible, let this cup pass from me: nevertheless not as I will, but as thou wilt.

On the cross, as He bore the sins of the world, Jesus experienced doubts and cried out to His father: "My God, my God, why hast thou forsaken me?" (Matt. 27:46). I'm sure that in His cry to His Father He was using the opening words of Psalm 22, and, like the Psalmist, overcame those torturous doubts in a way that enabled Him to declare triumphantly to the world, "It is finished!" Throughout the entire passion story, however, I see a Savior who was willing to display His doubts and depressing struggles. He makes it clear that one need not be in sin to fall into such painful states of being. His example makes it easier for me to work through my spiritual down times and doubts and to grasp that living out the will of God is not some kind of easy joyride without any depressions. Perhaps I should have tried to do for you what Jesus did for all of us.

I don't want you to get the impression from what I've written thus far that Mom and I think we blew our chance to lead you into a relationship with Christ and a commitment to the work of His kingdom here on earth. Actually both of us did a lot of things of which, upon reflection, we're quite proud. Mom went out of her way to make you into a caring person. Both by word and example, she taught you the kind of religion that the Apostle James so much admired in his epistle.

Pure religion and undefiled before God and the Father is this, To visit the fatherless and widows in their affliction, and to keep himself unspotted from the world.

James 1:27

Mom always made it her special mission in life to visit and give special attention to older ladies whom everyone else seemed to have forgotten or left behind. Wherever she traveled, she made sure to send postcards to her special elderly friends. She visited them faithfully and often took you along with her. There was Mrs. Henry who served as a housekeeper for the family next door to us and was also a member of our church in Philadelphia. Whenever possible, Mom used to drive her to and from church. Mom also took her to lunch and gave her little gifts from time to time. Once she spent Christmas Eve with us.

When Mrs. Henry was hospitalized, Mom may have been her only regular visitor. She took you along on some of those visits, and I remember that you and Mom were the ones who packed up Mrs. Henry's things when she had to move. I'm sure that something of what it means to be a Christian in ministry to others rubbed off on you as you helped Mom to help her friend.

Mom also visited Mrs. Rue, a widow who, in the end, had nobody in the world but your Mom to look after her. Her only relatives were in Texas and too far away to do very much. So Mom took over and became Mrs. Rue's family. Mrs. Rue was a chain smoker, and your Mom hated smoking, but she loved Helen Rue. She was an interesting old woman who read a lot and listened well, so visiting her always made for an interesting time. Mom got you involved with Mrs. Rue, who had never had any children, and she enjoyed you very much. You visited her on your own from time to time, and I remember one Christmas Day when you took dinner to her and visited while she ate it. Your visits to Mrs. Rue were far more frequent than one might have expected from a high school or college kid. Mom's unselfish giving of herself and her ongoing concern for Mrs. Rue were beautiful things for you to see. In the end, it was Mom who looked after Mrs. Rue during her dying days in the hospital. That had to have had an impact on you. I don't know of anybody who looks after lonely old ladies like your mother does.

Most of all, Mom must have patterned for you the biblical admonition to honor one's mother and father. She always made sure to be close at hand to respond to her parents whenever they had any needs. As Grandmom and Grandpop grow older, Mom has always been there for them. She is ready to drop everything at a moment's notice if one of them has to be driven to the doctor. She is willing to give up her much-needed vacations, as she did on at least two occasions when one of them happened to be hospitalized. The way she calls, visits, and writes to her parents would be a Christian model for any kid growing up. You had to have been impressed. If someday you look after Mom and me when we're old, I'll have to attribute your good Christian character in these matters to what you learned from your mother.

I did some things, too, that were designed to influence you for Christ. I was constantly trying to figure out how to impact your life in such a way that you would become a solid Christian and make the crucial decisions of your life under the leading of the Holy Spirit. Among the ways Mom and I decided that I might make this happen was for me to take you along as a traveling companion. Since my work required that I travel a lot, we decided that you should go along with me as often as possible. This was not an easy decision to make, because, when you were growing up, we could not easily afford the cost of those extra plane tickets. As Mom and I both look back on your growing up years, however, we always say that the cost of those trips was some of our best spent money. I would strongly recommend what we did to any parent who is torn between the need to be with his or her children, on the one hand, and extensive travel demands, on the other.

Taking you on the road with me allowed us some of the best quality time we ever had together. Because you were in school, most of our trips took us away from home over weekends. On a typical trip, you and I would be together for twenty-four hours a day, for two and a half days. We did a lot of talking and getting to know each other during those times. We talked about lots of things, and I had the chance to share my values and viewpoints on everything from sports to race relations. By the time your sports activities at school put an end to most of those excursions, I am sure that you had picked up a pretty comprehensive image of what I was all about and what I believed about God and the world in which we live.

Once, when the two of us were up in New York, we came upon a demonstration against a porno movie that was being shown at one of those skin-flick theaters just off Times Square. This particular movie, entitled *Snuff,* was undoubtedly one of the most obscene, dehumanizing movies ever made. Its climactic scene was reported to be one in which the prostitute (the main character) is slashed to death by two of her psychotic patrons. In order to create realistic panic in the death scene so as to provide the optimum "pleasure" for the sick kind of male sadists who would pay to see such horror, word had it that the film's producers had had the woman who played the part actually murdered in front of the cameras. The film was advertised as having been made in Brazil, "where life is cheap."

There was a crowd of ardent feminists picketing the show. As they marched in a circle in front of the theater, I decided that it would be a good thing for us to join with them. They were chanting in opposition to the film, "Life is never cheap! Life is never cheap!" We picked up on their chant and demonstrated with them. To my surprise, one of the women participating in the demonstration began to yell at us. "What are you doing here? You're just like them!" she shouted, indicating the men in line to buy tickets. "All men are sadistic animals that ought to be castrated!" I yelled back, "All men are not the same, and we have a right to be here! You've got no corner on opposition to the brutalization of women!"

After it was over, a couple of hours later, we went to a burger place and had a long talk about what the demonstration meant. I tried to make you understand that what those women were doing in that demonstration was very Christian and that my big regret was that the church was not visibly represented. I pointed out that Christianity is not just about getting people into heaven when they die, but also about creating a just and loving society in this world. I tried to get you to realize that the kind of just society that Jesus wants us to create in His name is one in which women can enjoy their God-given dignity. I told you that the church too often ignores what men do to women, particularly if those women are their wives. I pointed out to you that being a Christian requires that you champion the rights of women. In our long discussion I also had the chance to explain that a lot of men who are psychologically sick get some kind of perverted enjoyment out of humiliating and hurting women; that this happened often enough so that some women ended up being suspicious of all men; and that the woman who had tried to get us to leave the demonstration was, in all likelihood, one of them. In that discussion I think we got into a lot of stuff that fathers and sons don't often get into.

Another time we went to Fort Wayne, Indiana, on a trip that proved to be memorable for what didn't happen. Most of the weekend we sat in boring meetings and had little of interest to keep us entertained. You got a pretty good look at the tedious and dull side of my life. After that, whenever people alluded to how interesting my job must be, you would jokingly say to me under your breath, "There's always Fort Wayne," and we would laugh. It was our secret "in" joke.

I think that every kid should have a clear idea about what his father does for a living, and there's little doubt that you knew what was involved in my job long before you were twelve years old. Whether or not you realized it, your going along with me on those trips helped *me*. You constantly asked the "whys" and the "wherefores" about everything I did. You asked me a lot of questions that I should have been regularly asking myself but probably would not have had you not been there. Those questions forced me into a lot of healthy self-examination and helped me to ask questions about my integrity and about the validity of what I believed was my Christian calling.

Also, you may have kept me out of trouble. Traveling as I do to various religious gatherings, I see a lot of preachers and Christian musicians get themselves into compromising and morally dangerous situations that they would never have gotten into if they had had one of their kids along. It is a difficult thing to keep your guard up when you are all alone—which is probably why the early church sent its evangelists out in pairs. If you have to do extensive traveling in your chosen vocation, I hope that you remember our many trips together. I hope that you deem those times of sufficient importance in molding your character and helping you to become a Christian that you will plan to take your kid along with you. There's nothing you can ever do to make up for time you might have—but didn't—spend with your kid during those precious formative years.

The thing that I consider to be the most important single effort I made to instill within you a Christian value system was taking you to Haiti and the Dominican Republic. I figured that if you could see for yourself the way that most poor people live in Third World countries, you would understand how privileged you were by comparison. I wanted to explain to you the responsibilities that go with privilege. I longed for you to understand the biblical declaration that "to whom much is given, from him much is expected" (Luke 12:48).

The first trip was when you were just twelve years old. I had to go to the Dominican Republic to check on some of the missionary work sponsored by the Evangelical Association for the Promotion of Education, the organization that Mom and I helped to create in order to implement our vision for service to the hurting, hungry people of the world.

I vividly recall watching your reactions as you stood on the roof of one of our clinics, overlooking the river-edge slums of Santo Domingo. You stood there motionless with an almost blank expression on your face as you surveyed the horror of what lay stretched out before you. There were an estimated forty thousand people squeezed into that deplorable squalor, without any fresh water or sanitary facilities. There were kids walking barefoot through slimy paths where excrement mixed with mud. Dirty children, dressed in rags or just plain naked, seemed to be standing in front of every shack. Not even the hot noonday sun could make that dismal scene seem bright.

You stood there taking in the sight for almost five minutes. I think you would have stayed longer if I hadn't tapped your little head and told you that it was time to go. I can't be sure about how that scene affected you, but I sensed that you were shaken in ways that would make a lasting impression.

When you were twenty, I took you with me to Haiti. We were to participate in the dedication of a school and an orphanage which had been constructed with funds that we had raised. I'm sure that whatever horrors you saw in the Dominican Republic must have seemed mild compared to the agonies you witnessed on that trip. You were older then, a "cool" Ivy-league university student, and probably more ready for what you experienced. I wanted you to be there anyway, because I knew that you were near the time when you would be making a decision about your life's work. Perhaps, I thought, if you could once again feel the pulse of a suffering people, you would want to commit yourself to meeting human need.

How could you help but be impressed by what our limited efforts for the Haitian people had accomplished? There, among the dirty, depressed conditions of that Haitian town, were the shining bright smiles of the hundreds of kids who were in our school and orphanage. You must have seen that we had made a difference. There's no reward for hard work and sacrifice that can compare with the joy that comes from sensing you have made life better for some hitherto hopeless children.

Whenever I talk to parents who want to know something they can do to influence their children in such a way as to turn them away from the materialistic values of our society and turn them on to Christian living, I always tell them about our trips to the Dominican Republic and Haiti. I contend that a few weeks in the context of social and economic oppression can utterly change a youngster's world-view and cause the kid to rethink what life is all about. That's why I have my office work so hard at arranging such trips for parents and their kids. I believe that kids from middle-class American homes need that kind of experience.

When you reflect on how Mom and I tried to channel your life, I hope you will think well of us. Undoubtedly, we made mistakes, but we tried hard to do the best we could. In the end, I don't think that parents play the determinative role that they think they do in what their children become. Kids have wills of their own. We parents can provide experiences and training as best we know how, but young people decide for themselves what to do with what parents give them. I think parents take far too much credit when their kids turn out great and far too much blame when their kids mess up their lives. After all, God created two perfect children in Adam and Eve. He placed them in a perfect environment, yet both of them rebelled and did evil. Such can be the consequences of having children with wills of their own. I can only pray that you will continue to will the will of God.

Love,
Dad

Dear Dad,

People are often surprised when I tell them that I didn't accept Christ until I was a sophomore in high school, as if being your son should have guaranteed my salvation from birth. They're even more surprised when they discover that it was a kid on my high-school soccer team and not my evangelist father who led me to make that decision.

For some reason, it's difficult for those people to understand that while there're a lot of things that parents can give to their children, a relationship with God isn't one of them—even if one of those parents is a big-time preacher. All of the things you talked about doing for me in your letter were important, but at best they brought me to the place where Christianity was a real possibility. Only God can do the actual work of salvation. Paul says in Eph. 2:8–9: "For it is by grace you have been saved, through faith—and this not from yourselves, it is the gift of God—not by works, so that no one can boast. For we are God's workmanship, created in Christ Jesus to do good works, which God prepared in advance for us to do."

As you pointed out, though, some of the things you did made it harder, not easier, for me to take Christianity seriously. In fact, I still think you underestimate the problems your failure to "practice what you preach" have caused for me over the years. I'm glad that you are uncomfortable with yourself in light of the things that you proclaim about Jesus and the simple lifestyle, because I am convinced that your proclamation is right. Beyond being right though, you speak God's truth with passionate intensity. The people who assume that you live in a modest home and deny yourself in order to provide for the needs of others have every right to expect that of you at this point, never mind that you might responsibly choose a safe community or maintain high expenses related to your work. You have taken a stand out there.

No one except God can rightly judge another person's spending, and no one should try. But as your son, I think I can ask you to ask yourself one important question: Relative to no one else's, since every situation is unique, how does your lifestyle reflect the self-denial of Jesus? That clears away all the special circumstances and the problem of deceptive appearances. I'm not asking how much you give, but how much you *give up*—for isn't that the real meaning of Jesus' story of the widow's mite? You don't have to answer to anyone but yourself and God, but until you tell me that you are at peace with your lifestyle, why should I or anyone else let you off the hook of your own demands? And please don't try to convince me that your sacrifice comes in the form of the incredible amount of time you spend preaching and teaching and doing the work of the Kingdom, either. It is in your use of time, even more than in your use of money, that I think you have failed to live up to the things you say.

You used to have a great sermon called "The Protestant Work Ethic and the Spirit of Capitalism" that used Max Weber's classic text as a starting point. I don't remember all the twists and turns, but the basic theme was that somehow Martin Luther and John Calvin had fully convinced Protestants that prosperity and achievement were the marks of salvation, with the result being an incredible obsession with work. This work ethic was the driving force behind the rise of American capitalism to worldwide preeminence, you said, but it also created a nation of people who confused what they did with who they were. You explained that Jesus cared more about the heart and soul of people than about what they accomplished in the world. The fruit of the Spirit was not property, but rather "love, joy, peace, patience, kindness, goodness, faithfulness, gentleness, and self-control" (Gal. 5:22–23). "What you are," you concluded, "is far more important than what you do." It was a good sermon, Dad. I wish you had been there to hear it.

Because of all the people I know, you derive your sense of value from what you do more than anyone. How else can you explain the ridiculous schedule you maintain, which keeps you from developing normal friendships or staying healthy or even seeing your darling son as much as you should? To everyone else you preach that to have a close relationship with God is the most important thing in the world, yet you drive yourself as though God would rather have you work for Him than be with Him. You say you sometimes wonder why you don't take personal retreats more often, but you know the answer already—you are too busy. You are too busy for your support group, too busy for your family, too busy for exercise, too busy to develop friendships with non-Christians, too busy to disciple younger believers, and, by your own admission, too busy to spend a day with God. You're so caught up with doing for God that you have no time to be with Him. I know that people are constantly after you to speak more and write more and raise more money for missions and every-thing else, and those are all good things, but isn't the point of serving God to get to know Him in a more intimate way? If by serving Him, you are hurting yourself and failing to develop a more Christlike character, can that really be God's will? Maybe you think I'm way off base in all of this, but at least I want to pose the question: Is your lifestyle really causing you to grow closer to Jesus? And if it isn't, do you really think Jesus has called you to sacrifice your own faith for the sake of everyone else's?

Dad, please don't get me wrong; I don't think you're some sort of stubborn, willful hypocrite. Nobody ever resolves these things perfectly or once and for all; certainly not me. The reason I'm so aware of them in the first place is that I have the same problems myself. I don't live the way you do, of course, but I'm not in the same demand, either. Even so, I struggle with my lifestyle and keep asking myself what Jesus calls for and how I will respond. I'm often consumed with "doing" myself, as if there were some way I could earn God's love by accomplishing great things on His behalf. A friend of mine once asked me this simple question: "If you were locked in an empty room for the rest of your life and could not do anything at all, do you think God would love you as much as He does when you are preaching the Gospel and working with inner-city kids?" My head says yes, of course, but my life says that I'm not so sure. Christian service is supposed to be our grateful response to God's grace, not our attempt to merit it. Sometimes I run so fast telling people about it that I forget to experience that grace for myself. I have picked up a lot of good things from you, Dad, but you and I both are probably going to have to deal with accepting our self-value apart from our accomplishments for as long as we are alive. Value comes from God, and that value is infinite for all people. So, as far as I'm concerned, and I know as far as God is concerned, you are the most wonderful man imaginable even if you never speak or write or achieve anything ever again. You are not what you do. You are what you are, and I love you.

Before you worry too much about how your own shortcomings affected my openness to the faith, though, let me tell you that you were and are the best argument I have ever known for accepting Jesus Christ. What was most remarkable to me as a boy was not that you failed to live up to everything, but that you succeeded in living up to so much. Your relationship with God never seemed to be wrapped up with a set of rules and regulations, but I saw the difference it made in your decisions, and I respected you for trying to make your life into what you sensed God wanted it to be. You were right about the benefits of our trips together and my time visiting shut-ins with Mom, and especially about showing me the realities of Haiti and the Dominican Republic. All of it was important. Yet, as good as all those experiences were for me, I didn't make the connection between the way God worked in your life and the way He wanted to work in mine; I was not even all that sure whether or not I believed in God in the first place. That you and Mom were sincere and kind, I never doubted, but that you were right about God, I did doubt. I dutifully went to church because I didn't want to make a big deal about it, and I enjoyed going places with you because you were fun to watch, but most of the time I don't remember feeling anything at all about God, and in my heart I never considered myself a believer. Besides, I had enough to worry about already as a kid. I didn't need any hassles from on high.

I went through elementary school as a little kid with a big mouth, which meant I got beat up a lot and didn't have many friends. "Don't worry," you said, "when you get to junior high school, there will be soccer and basketball teams, and once you're a star player you'll have more friends than you'll know what to do with." You were correct in your prediction, but to a cynical kid like me, popularity through minor celebrity seemed pretty shallow, and I remained something of a loner even when I became popular.

I didn't let that popularity fool me until I made the varsity soccer team as a high-school sophomore. Suddenly I was running with an older crowd, and I quickly became enamored of all the attention, especially after I became the starting goalkeeper on the team. The other goalie was a senior named Joel Dragelin, and he was expected to beat me out, but I did very well early on, and it became a real battle between the two of us. I was supremely confident, though, and I let Joel know it every chance I got. He was gracious to me, but I tried to psyche him out by treating him badly and showing off in front of the coach. I probably didn't deserve it, but I was the starter when the season opened, and Joel's chance to oust me was ruined when he caught his hand under a lawn mower while trying to remove a stick. The doctors managed to repair his severed middle finger, but there was no way for him to play after that.

If I had been Joel, I feel sure that I would have hated the arrogant punk who had taken my place. I probably would have cheered every time the ball got past him for a goal, if indeed I went to the games at all. Joel, however, was anything but bitter. As a matter of fact, he went out of his way to be nice to me. At the games, he carried my equipment bag and brought towels out to me between halves. When I was beaten by a shot, he stood behind the goal and encouraged me. "You'll get the next one," he would say, while showing me how to correct my mistakes.

Strangely enough, instead of making himself my enemy, he became my biggest supporter throughout the season. That probably would have impressed me more had I not been so caught up in the excitement of being on a winning team and so thrilled by the acceptance of the other players. In fact, I didn't take much notice of Joel at all until after I had blown the big game at the end of the season. Soccer was over, and I was abandoned like a used pop bottle by the rest of the team.

Only Joel stayed interested in me, stopping me in the hall to say hello or telephoning to ask me to go out and do something with him and his friends. I hesitated at first, but after awhile I jumped at his invitations—it wasn't as though I had a lot of options. Besides, Joel impressed me. He was one of the most popular kids at our school, and he had befriended me even though I had treated him badly.

I should have guessed that he was a Christian, but I didn't even think about that until he invited me along to his youth group one night. It was one of those "mega" youth groups, with two hundred kids and a rock-and-roll band, and even though I wasn't very excited by all the God-talk, I liked being there. Joel was a big wheel, and he made sure everyone was nice to me. I decided to go again the next week.

After that, things happened pretty fast. I still didn't believe in God, but Joel did, and he talked to me about it every chance he got. At the same time we were becoming close friends. One Saturday morning he picked me up early, and we went out to breakfast at McDonald's.

"Bart, I can see that you know the basics about Christianity from your folks already, but I don't think you know God yourself at all," he said, after we had finished eating. "You've got head knowledge, but that doesn't matter very much. I guess what I want to know is, have you ever thought about really becoming a Christian?"

I hadn't up until then, Dad, despite everything you had done to try to get me thinking about it. But at that McDonald's I decided that even though I didn't believe in God for sure, I desperately wanted to have the kind of faith and joy that Joel and his friends at that youth group had.

I prayed to accept Christ that day, hoping that somehow, somewhere, I would get the faith to back up my prayer. I wish I could say that it came at that moment, but it didn't. What really happened was that I "faked" my faith for a few months while I waited for something to happen. That's right, Dad, I faked it. I went to youth group, read my Bible, cut out a few big sins, and hung out with Joel a lot, pretending I was experiencing things that I wasn't. I even prayed to a God I wasn't sure of, asking Him to make Himself real to me the way He was real to Joel and to the other kids and the way He was real to you. Some might say I was lying then, but I think "seeking" is a better word because I was in earnest and, in the end, I received what I was after. Somewhere in the midst of going through the motions, my faith became real.

I know so many people who wish they could believe in God, because they're sure that something is missing from their lives, and I sympathize with them. Without God, the universe becomes a harsh, cold reality without meaning or purpose, and most of us don't have the courage to face up to it without despairing.

Believing in God, however, requires more than just a heartfelt desire. Would-be believers must be willing to come to the place in their lives where faith becomes a genuine possibility. An adulterer without faith doesn't need to repent in order to win God's love, but he probably needs to repent in order to be able to believe in that love. Sometimes faith requires stepping out of willful disobedience. Sometimes it requires setting aside enough time to read and think and pray to the God in whose existence you don't yet believe. Sometimes faith requires the seeker to spend time with believers and to experience the love of God secondhand. There are no universal answers, but going through the motions is only a lie if you are not really hoping to find anything, and it may very well be the first step toward genuine faith: "For everyone who asks receives; he who seeks finds; and to him who knocks, the door will be opened" (Matt. 7:8).

You weren't the one who prayed with me when I made my decision to follow Christ, Dad, but I think you had a lot to do with bringing me to the place where faith was a genuine possibility. All those trips and conversations and demonstrations with you and the visits with Mom were part of the way God worked out my relationship with Him.

The assistant coach of our soccer team, Sam Holt, used to make us tuck in our jerseys, polish our cleats, pull up our socks, and anything else that would give us a respectable appearance. "Men!" he would bark like a drill sergeant, "If you *dress* like a soccer team, and if you *act* like a soccer team, and if you *practice* like a soccer team, one of these days when you least expect it, you might actually *play* like a soccer team!"

That same principle applies to a lot of things in life. When I was growing up you walked me through the motions of being a Christian, and you lived like a Christian yourself, and you left it at that. Some of the stuff you did may have confused me, but for the most part I knew what you were all about, and your life helped make faith a genuine possibility for me. What more could I ask of you, Dad? The rest was up to God. It always is.

Love,
Bart

Three

The Pains of Growing Up

Dear Dad,

Fifth grade was a rough year for me. Like a lot of other schools at the time, my school was experimenting with what was known as the "open classroom." Normal classroom structure gave way to an independent study format. Each Monday, a list of assignments appeared on the blackboard which were to be completed by Friday afternoon. We still had periods of instruction, but much of the day was left free so that we could do our work in our own way at our own pace. Or, in my case, so that I could fool around all week and then go crazy on Fridays trying to get it all done. I just was not responsible enough at age eleven to handle all of that mid-1970s openness. To make matters worse, I was on the outside of the most popular group of kids in school and had few prospects for getting in. The only break I got that year was in the friendship of Daniel Keough, the biggest kid in the school. He was no better liked than I was, but he kept me from getting beaten up too often, and for that I was tremendously grateful.

Even though I was rejected by the main group, I always knew what they were doing, and I tried my best to do the same in the hopes that they would change their minds about me. When they began buying Adidas sneakers, I begged Mom for a pair of my own. When it became the style to straddle chairs backwards, I did the same, even though it wasn't all that comfortable. I even strained to overhear their conversations so that I would know the correct slang to use at recess. So it followed that when they began to carry around their People Cards, I did the same.

I don't know if you remember about the People Cards, Dad. In a flash of inspired cruelty, the popular kids that year came up with the ultimate weapon to reinforce their domination over the rest of us. One day I noticed a few kids snickering over the index cards they were passing back and forth. It took me a while, but eventually I discovered that each of those cards was dedicated to one of the kids in our class. They were like some sort of home-made baseball cards. Each card was marked with the kid's name and a crude cartoon drawing of his face. A brief paragraph underneath the caricature described the "pros" and "cons" of that person, which was either glowingly positive or viciously negative, depending on that person's position in the school pecking order. Finally, there was an overall rating on a scale of one to ten.

As I think about it now, I can still remember the fear that those cards inspired in me as each of the popular kids developed his or her own collection. Did they have a card about me, I wondered, and if they did, what did it say? There was no way to find out, of course—People Cards were a private joke—but even though I never saw my card, I immediately knew what it must be like, and it hurt me. Yet, incredible as it seems, what hurt me most was not the hatefulness of those kids but rather the knowledge that I was unacceptable to them.

Rather than seeing their cruelty, I believed them. Instead of being put off, I wanted to fit in all the more. So I began a collection of People Cards myself, thinking that if I showed it to a few of the popular kids and they liked them, I might earn some points and gain their favor. I worked hard on my cards, too, struggling to make them clever enough and mean enough to win me a position among the elite. Strangely enough, that is exactly what happened. My cards were a hit. For a few weeks in the middle of my fifth grade year, I became a full-fledged member of the same group of kids who had, until then, treated me as a complete outsider.

I thought that popularity would be the greatest thing in the world, but when it finally happened to me, I was unsure of what to make of it. I was still insecure, and I was particularly uncomfortable with the way my newfound acceptance affected my friendship with Daniel Keough. It simply wouldn't do for a new insider to have too much contact with a confirmed outsider, and instinctively we both knew that. I drifted away from him, and he let me go without saying very much, which saved me from facing up to my betrayal directly.

Whether I admitted it or not, though, I had a very real sense of uneasiness about my newly won position and my new group of friends as well. For all of their good looks and correct clothes and prestige among the rest of the school, the popular kids weren't all that nice, even to one another. Like it or not, though, I had become one of them, and there was no turning back—until you found my People Cards.

You were waiting for me on a Friday afternoon when I came home from school. As soon as I walked in the door, I knew that something was very wrong. To begin with, Mom was nowhere to be found, neither was Lisa. What made things even more suspicious was the fact that you weren't usually the parent on duty when it came to being home to prepare my after-school snacks. To top it off, you obviously were *not* happy. Still, you waited until after I had had some juice and cookies before asking me to come into the living room for a talk.

"Bart," you began softly, "I wasn't rooting through your stuff at all, but you left some things on the steps today, and when I was moving them I found these . . . ," and you pulled out the cards in their little box, "and I wanted to ask you what they were."

How could I answer you? I had avoided the truth until then, but as soon as I saw those cards in your hands, I knew that I was all wrong. I explained myself half-heartedly. You listened quietly for a while, and even after I had finished you didn't yell at me or tell me what a rotten person I was. You just told me how mean you thought the cards were and that it was wrong to judge people by such shallow standards. You asked me what I thought Jesus would think of such cards, and you told me that you weren't angry, really, but that you were just very disappointed in me. Hearing you say that was worse than a beating.

By that time, I was crying uncontrollably, but you went on talking. Then, just before you left me alone with my miserable self, you said the most liberating words a mixed-up fifth grader who suddenly hated himself could have ever heard: "This really isn't like you at all," you said. "That's why this caught me so off-guard . . . because you're a nice person, Bart, or at least I've always been pretty sure that you were. This just isn't the kind of thing a nice person like you would do."

What perfect words they were for me! Somehow they managed to make me feel both horrible and wonderful at the same time, and, most of all, they gave me the hope that all was not lost. My Dad still loved me, even though I had let him down. I wasn't doomed to a life of cruelty because, blessed thought, that wasn't like me at all. Sitting alone and ashamed of myself in that living room, I realized something absolutely crucial. My actions may have been lousy, but I was still a nice person in your eyes. Or at least I could be.

As important as that final affirmation was, though, it was just as important that you helped me to understand exactly why the People Cards were such a terrible thing. Deep down I had been uncomfortable with them all along, but as a fifth grader I didn't have the critical capacity to articulate exactly why they were so wrong. I needed some kind of rationale to go along with my instinctive inclinations, and that is exactly what you gave me. Now I had an explanation, both for myself and for anyone else who cared to ask, and that explanation was the weapon in my hand that gave me the courage to take my stand.

Kids are pressured into so many things they know are wrong because they aren't able to give themselves or each other honest and good reasons not to do them. It isn't enough to tell young people to "just say no" or to "just do" anything for that matter. Parents can yell and scream about disobedient kids, but unless they're willing to help those kids understand the "whys" behind the rights and wrongs, all the noise in the world will accomplish nothing except create a lot of tension. In that particular situation, you didn't make me do anything at all, but I was grateful because you gave me all the justification I needed to do what I had secretly wanted to do all along.

When I renounced the entire institution of People Cards the following Monday, I went back to being an outsider at school, but I also got back together with Daniel Keough, who was as loyal and affirming a friend as I've ever had. More importantly, I had had my first significant experience of moral crisis and had been shown the way out. That Friday-afternoon conversation was an inspired piece of parenting, Dad, and it left an indelible mark on my life.

Of course, elementary school is only the beginning of the peer pressure cooker for a kid, not the end. It gets even worse in junior high, because suddenly there are so many different peer groups from which to choose. It didn't take me very long to figure out that I couldn't just be a kid anymore—I had to be a jock or a brain or a druggie or a preppie or a criminal or . . . something, or else I would be deemed a nothing by default. My problem was that I really didn't know what any of those stereotypes meant as far as my life was concerned. None of those rapidly emerging peer groups was handing out pamphlets outlining the basic assumptions and underlying values of its lifestyle, and there were no introductory lectures or orientation sessions either.

The only way I could find out what one of those peer groups was like was to get inside of it and do whatever the members were doing, to try the group on and see how it fit. So that is exactly what I did, all the way through junior high school and for the better part of senior high school as well. I experimented with different possibilities. You couldn't have missed what was happening with me then, Dad, because every peer group I tried meant that I took on a new identity altogether.

As my groups of friends changed, so did my clothes, my hair, my speech, my music, my taste in girls, my use of time and money, and sometimes my grades as well. I won't bother to review the whole series of "new-look" Barts because there were so many of them. None of them was really *me* and yet every one of them affected who I became in the end. In one sense you really had no reason to take them seriously, which is why I'm glad that you didn't make a big deal out of a lot of superficial issues that had nothing to do with what was really going on in terms of my personality.

In another sense, each one of those peer groups had the potential to alter radically the person I was going to become and what my life was going to be about, and both of us knew it. Even though a lot of times I was only playing the part of a jock or a preppy or a little criminal, there was always the chance that I would "lose myself" in my character or that I would simply do something that I would have to live with for the rest of my life.

I first saw *Rebel without a Cause* when I was in high school. My youth pastor, who was wise enough to know that sometimes secular films are the most Christian films of all, showed it at church one Sunday night because he wanted to talk to us about the way everybody needs to belong to something. He knew that a group of teenagers would understand and identify with the confusion and desperation portrayed by James Dean, Natalie Wood, and Sal Mineo, and he wanted us all to see that we weren't the only ones who had ever felt alienated, that we weren't alone in feeling alone.

In the movie, James Dean's parents are so weak-willed that they do anything he wants them to and give him whatever he asks from them. He has money and nice clothes, a new car, and those drop-dead good looks to top it off. What he doesn't have, though, is a clear sense of his own identity, and as the new kid in school that quickly gets him into trouble.

He gets mixed up with a gang of tough guys whose respect he feels he absolutely must earn, no matter what the cost. The night of his big showdown with the leader of that group, Dean realizes that he's in over his head, and he begs his father to stand up to him, to stop him, to save him from his own decisions. But his father can't do it, and Dean storms out of the house on his way to ruining his own life.

It's a powerful scene, full of pathos and adolescent agony, and it moved me when I first saw it. I couldn't have explained it then, but I perfectly understood the way Dean's character was struggling with the overpowering weight of his own free will because I was doing the same thing myself.

Free will is a difficult concept however you approach it. Theologians assert that it is God's greatest gift to humanity and the most significant element of His creation, because without free will it would be impossible for us to love either God or one another. Genuine love, by definition, is the free choice of a free individual. Certainly God could have made Himself a collection of talking robots that would forever speak of their "love" for Him, but He wanted something infinitely higher than that. So, instead, he created human beings and gave us the potential to accept or reject His will. Our freedom is what sets us apart from every other living thing as human beings—it is the essence of being made in the image of God. A person has to be free, in order to have the ability to love or to understand being loved.

Although God's gift of free will established the possibility of love, so, too, did it create the possibility of sin—and, with sin, every other evil, including death. Truly free people may decide to live in a way that is contrary to the will of God. That is the theme of the story of Adam and Eve, and that is the cause of the terrible injustice and suffering that dominates our world. It is surely not God's will that we hurt and destroy others or that we ourselves be hurt and destroyed, but we are not bound by God's perfect will, and we can do that which He does not want us to do.

Every evil in this world, as well as in our own lives, is rooted in free decisions against God's will—ours or someone else's. Not only are we fallen because of sin—all Creation is fallen as well. While our sins can surely be forgiven, they still have very real consequences for the sinner and those who have been sinned against. When God forgives a convicted murderer and restores that person to righteousness, it is a miracle indeed, but that doesn't mean the person is automatically freed from prison, and it certainly doesn't bring the victim back from the dead or put an end to the suffering of the grieving family. In some sense, what is done simply cannot be undone, and it is for that reason that we can never take our own decisions lightly just because we are sure of the grace of God.

What we do matters, and our choices make a difference, both in our own lives and in the lives of other people. It is when we understand that truth—when we recognize that the decisions we freely make have real and sometimes enormous consequences —that our freedom threatens to become a gift too burdensome to bear. To be free means to be responsible for our own lives and for the choices that we must make, and such responsibility can be a frightening prospect indeed—especially to a young person. It can crush a kid to consider the realities of his own life. For who has more options than a kid in today's youth-oriented society? Who has more choices and decisions to make than a child of modern America? Who has more of that burdensome gift called freedom? No one, Dad. No one at all.

As a kid, though, I learned to know better than to complain to an adult about having too much freedom. Freedom is a burden if you have more than you can handle, but it is the world's most coveted commodity when you don't have enough of it. Adults, more often than not, don't have nearly as much freedom as they would like. I felt as though most of the adults I knew envied my freedom when I was growing up.

In fact, some of the most frustrating experiences of my life were when I came to you with my problems and crises only to find that to you they weren't problems and crises at all, but rather blessings in disguise. "Man, oh, man," you would say, "I only wish I had opportunities like the ones you're talking about." What made it worse was that I knew you really meant what you were saying, that you really did envy my opportunities. Nothing is more alienating than having someone tell you how lucky you are when you feel absolutely miserable about your life.

Looking back, though, I can see why you might have reacted the way you did to my situation. In that respect, I am old now. Even though I am only twenty-six, I can't escape the fact that a lot of my big decisions are behind me. Already I find myself asking whether I've made the right choices and wondering what things would be like if I had made those choices differently. There is something ironic about the way kids are always wishing they were grown-ups while so many adults long, and sometimes even pretend, to be kids all over again. For the kids, it's usually just a case of imagining adulthood as being able to do whatever you want and having a lot more money with which to do it. The adults are not misled in the same way. They know exactly what they are wishing for: the seemingly unlimited freedom of youth. Yet to the kid who has that freedom, it doesn't seem like a blessing at all, but rather a curse in disguise. At least that's how it felt to me.

You see, it wasn't just a matter of choosing a few classes or figuring out what skateboard to buy or who to ask to the freshman dance—I was trying to figure out who and what I was going to become, and I was scared to death that I was going to make a mistake. I would have denied it a thousand times under oath, but the truth is that I had my life in my hands, and I didn't know what to do with it.

I think a lot of kids are as confused as I was, even though they won't admit it, even to themselves. On a lot of levels, freedom is a burden to them because even though they have the world at their feet, they don't know what it's for or how to deal with it. Yet everywhere I look, kids are being given more and more freedom and responsibility at earlier ages than ever before—and it is destroying them.

I met Jill at a Bible camp in Wisconsin where I was the speaker. Like James Dean's parents in *Rebel without a Cause*, Jill's mother and father had left her on her own almost from the beginning, their alcoholism having consumed any interest they might have had in their daughter's life or in her decisions. A very attractive girl, Jill began to date at the age of twelve because having a boyfriend told her that she mattered to somebody. Older boys, sensing her desperate need for love and acceptance, used her vulnerabilities against her. Time and time again, she allowed herself to be taken advantage of sexually in exchange for a short-lived sense of security. Physical relationships took over her life, so that by the time she talked to me at the age of fifteen she had become utterly addicted to sexual contact. As she put it, sex was the only "love" she had ever known.

The reason she came to me was that after hearing the good news of God's unconditional love, she desperately wanted to become a Christian but felt powerless to stop herself from doing what she knew God forbade. Jill believed in the forgiveness of sins, but she couldn't believe that God could heal her emotional wounds and change her into a different person. I tried to convince her, but she went away despairing.

"It's my own fault," I remember her saying sadly. "Nobody held a gun to my head and made me become what I am. I made my own decisions and now I'm going to have to live with them forever."

Jill was only fifteen years old when I talked with her, but she had already given up hoping for anything really wonderful in her own life. She had been burdened with the full weight of her freedom at the age of twelve, with no help or guidance whatsoever to help her bear it, and it had crushed her spirit.

There's a time to let kids make their own decisions, to be sure, Dad. I didn't want you to run my life, and I hated it when you reigned me in too tightly. What I did want, though, was for somebody to help me with those tough decisions by making me ask myself the hard questions about them. When you ridiculed my choices, I stuck to them more than ever, even if I knew they were wrong, because I couldn't bear to be humiliated by admitting my mistakes. But when you took the time to help me see the consequences and ramifications of those choices and showed me how they fit in with the better side of my personality, then I felt as though I just might be able to handle things after all.

In order for freedom to be the blessing that God intended for it to be, it must be more than simply having permission to do whatever you want to do so long as you don't encroach on the freedom of anyone else to do the same. That definition of freedom may work well for lawyers and legislators as they manage the government of a city or a nation, but it is sorely inadequate for any of us as individuals. For even after we have liberated ourselves from the bondage of every external force that threatens our ability to do as we please, we find that our own desires can enslave us in a far more unescapable way than we ever imagined possible. It is more obvious in the case of drug addicts and alcoholics, but all of us have to deal with our appetites for things that can destroy us. None of our hearts are pure. When adults look at kids with envy because they can do anything they want to do with themselves and their lives, they forget that what a person wants to do is not always what will make him joyful or satisfied in the end.

One Saturday night when I was about thirteen years old, you came home from a long day on the road to find me in a deep state of depression. Over dinner, while I silently ate my meal, you and Mom talked about the things you had done since breakfast.

"So Bart . . . what did you do all day?" you finally inquired as Mom began to serve dessert.

"Nothing," I replied in a sullen tone of voice. "I did nothing. I sat around and watched television to tell you the truth. It was a lousy, boring day because there's nothing to do in the whole lousy, boring place."

I wasn't looking at you when I said it, which is probably why I didn't stop before I did, but Lisa was, and she quickly asked to be excused. It was too late, though. You were into your tirade before she could even push back her chair.

"Why you ungrateful little kid!" you exploded. "How dare you say there's nothing to do around here when all your mother and I do is work so you can have a nice time. What I wouldn't give for a free day myself! Bored? You were *bored?* Stop feeling sorry for yourself! What's the matter with you that you can't think of anything better to do than watch television all day? Why when I was your age . . . "

I'll spare you the rest. As heartfelt as your lecture was, I'm afraid you missed the point. You yelled at me for doing nothing as though it was my first choice, when the real problem was that I was just not creative enough to fill in the vacuum of an empty day. Kids are not born knowing how to have fun any more than they are born knowing how to work. They need to be taught. You may have thought you were doing me a favor by giving me so much free time, but all you really did was leave me feeling like a loser because I didn't know what to do with myself. You should have been glad I didn't do something worse, actually, because as Sören Kierkegaard once said, boredom is really the root of all evil. G. K. Chesterton had the same idea when he wrote, "At the end of the day, when the children tire of their toys, it is then that they turn to torturing the cat."

You see, Dad, boredom is always the end product of the kind of freedom that is nothing more than being allowed to do whatever you want. Even when it leads to evil, it only finds its way back to boredom again. The writer of the Book of Ecclesiastes had that kind of freedom, and yet, after pursuing every kind of desire known to man to the fullest measure, his conclusion was this:

"Meaningless! Meaningless!" says the Teacher. "Utterly meaningless! Everything is meaningless." What does man gain from all his labor at which he toils under the sun? Generations come and generations go, but the earth remains forever. The sun rises and the sun sets, and hurries back to where it rises. The wind blows to the south and turns to the north; round and round it goes, ever returning on its course. All streams flow into the sea, yet the sea is never full. To the place the streams come from, there they return again. All things are wearisome, more than one can say. The eye never has enough of seeing nor the ear its fill of hearing. What has been will be again, what has been done will be done again; there is nothing new under the sun.

Eccles. 1:2–9

That man had denied himself nothing that he desired, but after he had done it all and experienced everything the world had to offer, he was bored. I see the same phenomenon in so many of the young people I meet. They can do anything they want to do, but they're bored, and because they're so bored they turn to drugs and to sex and to crime and to cars and to music and to video games and even to getting rich and amassing material possessions like their parents. They look everywhere for excitement and new experiences, always reaching for a higher high. Sometimes they follow the group and sometimes they follow their own desires, but in the end there's not much difference. They turn to those things to escape the burden of their freedom, and yet, when everything has been said and done and they have run every possibility all the way through or been crushed and destroyed by the consequences of their own decisions, they come to the awful realization that they are bored all over again. Life to those kids, as to the writer of Ecclesiastes, becomes meaningless because chasing after excitement and fulfillment by doing whatever you please ultimately holds no more promise than trying to catch the wind.

As I said before, in order for freedom to be a blessing instead of a curse, it must be something more than just having nothing that you *have* to do. Real freedom is not simply being allowed to do as *you* please, but rather being liberated from all bondage—including the bondage of peer pressure and the bondage of your own desires—to do what pleases God. Jesus came not only to set the captives free *from* something but also to free them *for* something, and that something was and is to choose to do the will of God.

Freedom was never meant to be a moral vacuum where all decisions are equally valid without any "shoulds" and "should nots" or "musts" and "must nots," for God didn't cease to be when He gave us our free will. Instead, He is the hope and the reality that saves us from the crushing weight of what that free will would otherwise become.

"Come to me, all you who are weary and burdened," Jesus says in Matt. 5:28, "and I will give you rest." The rest Jesus gives is not simply being able to do as we please—it's the call to do His will and to do His work, which He promises will be better for us than anything we could desire ourselves: "For my yoke is easy and my burden is light."

I think you understood that when you liberated me as a boy from those horrible People Cards. I was enslaved to my own desire for acceptance at that point, and to simply have let me do as I pleased would have been the cruelest kind of freedom. What I needed was *real* freedom—the ability to do whatever it was that Jesus wanted me to do—and that's what you gave me. When kids fall prey to peer pressure, they are not the victims of the other kids as much as they are the victims of bondage to their own desires. They need freedom, to be sure, but it must be real freedom—the liberation from anything that keeps them from doing the will of God.

Sometimes that means that kids need help in understanding the consequences or possible consequences of a particular decision, and sometimes that means they need a way of explaining what's right or wrong to themselves or to their friends. Sometimes that means having parents who are willing to play the "heavy" so that their son or daughter can say no to something without losing too much face. That happened a few times for me, and I was glad to be able to say, "My Dad won't let me," when the truth was that I wasn't sure about what to do.

Curfews work that way, I think. I remember picking up a girl at her house for a first date and being very intimidated when her father told me I had better have her home by ten o'clock or there would be trouble. Something in his tone of voice let me know that I didn't want to cross this man.

His daughter and I had a nice time that night, but when it got close to 9:30, I told her we had better start for home even though the movie wasn't yet over. "Oh, don't worry about that," she said. "My real curfew isn't until midnight. I just had my father say that in case things didn't go well and I wanted to get away from you early. He's got that tough-guy act down so well, I never have any trouble with pushy boys anymore."

That was one sharp father, I think. He gave his daughter freedom in the best sense of the word, and she appreciated it.

Mom had a different way of helping me figure things out, and that really helped me when I was trying on all of those different identities as a kid. It was quite simple, really, and it grew out of her characteristically unlimited optimism. No matter what I was into at the time, she always managed to see some marvelous way in which I could use it to do good.

When I was a "jock," she talked with great excitement about how I might become the kind of coach who makes a difference in the lives of his players. When I ran with kids who were in trouble, she used to speculate on what was troubling them and how I could use my influence to get them back on track. As a high-school freshman, I became obsessed with juggling for awhile, which seemed like a pretty neutral thing to me. Not to Mom, though. "Oh Bart!" she bubbled. "Imagine all the joy you could bring to people in old folks homes and hospitals as a juggler. That would be so exciting!" She even bought me a set of special juggling pins and rings to spur me on.

The genius of her enthusiasm was that it never depended on what I was doing—she found glorious possibilities in everything I tried. Her unspoken message was very clear to me at the time: I was free to become anything I chose to be because no matter what I did, it could and must be done for God and for the good of His people.

That's what real freedom is, I think: the understanding that in a world filled with choices and decisions, under tremendous pressure from other people and our own desires, amid the paralyzing fear of mistakes or failure, loving God and loving His people are the only things that really matter, and doing those things is a decision that we genuinely have the ability to make in every situation.

You and Mom didn't let me do whatever I wanted to, Dad, but you gave me my freedom nonetheless. I think I finally appreciate it.

Love,
Bart

Dear Bart,

Your fifth-grade year was an easy one for me to remember. It was a time when the spontaneity that had always been the hallmark of your personality was eclipsed. You were trying to make that shift from defining yourself from what you thought *I* thought of you to defining yourself as what you thought the kids at school thought of you. It was a hard time because you knew you were great as long as your identity was provided by me. Growing up, however, required going beyond your Dad and finding your identity in the messages that came from those significant others called peers. That year, the messages you were getting from your peers weren't very positive.

You were a kid with a lot of natural athletic ability at a time in life when athletic ability was pretty important, and I think some of the kids in school were jealous of you. You had been to a lot of places and done a lot of things that enabled you to play oneupmanship with them and win. Most importantly, you were extremely verbal. Your vocabulary and ability to express yourself allowed you to dominate conversations without your even realizing it. Consequently, you posed a real threat to a lot of those boys in your fifth-grade class. Shutting you out may have been more the result of their defensiveness than the result of your failure to be "cool" in their eyes. Regardless of the cause, you were hurting.

Another reason that year was tough was that up to that time, you and John Baxter had been such close friends that you were really more like brothers. His parents were good friends of ours, and his dad was a professor at Eastern, too. The campus was the "backyard" for both of you, and you did virtually everything together. Fifth grade was a time when you and John each felt the need to widen your horizons, and that translated into the two of you going your separate ways. Sometimes you even fought. Both John's parents and Mom and I believed that we had to stay out of it and let you boys work things out. It was tough for all of us, but it was the right thing to do. In the end, it was as though you guys really were brothers, because it was John who was the best man at your wedding, but in the fifth grade, splitting up with your best friend was an almost unbearable grief.

Parents who care always find that when their kids hurt, they hurt, too. Mom and I talked long and hard on the question about what to do. Mom even made a secret visit to school to get your teacher's perspective on the problem. She found that the teacher was well aware that you were shut out of the "in" clique of boys in that fifth-grade class. She was very much tuned in to the not-too-subtle cruelties that were played out on a daily basis within her classroom. The suggestion was made that you ignore the "in" clique. There were other kids in your class who could be your friends and who weren't playing the kinds of exclusionary games that those mean kids were playing with their People Cards.

First of all, there was your true-blue friend, Daniel Keough. Daniel was a kind of counterculture kid, who, in the best sense, scoffed at what the "in" kids were all about. Then there was Rocky Walker. Rocky, like you, was outside the "in" group, but he didn't seem to care. He was a good-looking guy and a great athlete. Your teacher thought that Mom and I should engineer your getting together with Rocky so that the pain of being excluded from the clique would be forgotten in a new friendship. We tried to do just that, but we learned that parents can't really determine what friendships do and do not work for their kids. You and Rocky did not become best friends that year, but I guess your teacher wasn't too far wrong in her suggestion because you and Rocky did become friends during high school, and he was a groomsman at your wedding.

Finding those People Cards wasn't difficult. You always seemed to carelessly leave things around in full view of everyone. I believe I found them one evening after you had gone to sleep. They were lying on the steps that went up to your third-floor bedroom. They upset me, but they also gave me a chance to do something that I think has served you well ever since. They gave me the opportunity to show you that the group you would have given almost anything to join was not worth joining; that if you did join the "in" clique, it might be at the expense of being the kind of person Jesus would have you be. Such an opportunity was not to be passed up, and, as you recall those painful events, the confrontation over the People Cards was all that I hoped that it would be. I think the thing that really got you away from trying to be like those mean kids was the realization that being like them required things that would never do for a follower of Jesus Christ.

I do not want to give the impression that I think that all peer groups are bad for growing boys. It is just that parents should be sure that the social roles prescribed by any peer group their sons or daughters seek to join allow for living out a commitment to Jesus. Unless a peer group allows a child to do loving things for others, parents must be ready to do everything in their power to get their kids out of it. Being good parents requires discernment with regard to your child's friends.

From what you wrote to me in your last letter, I guess we did help you in your choices of friends. Mom, particularly, helped you to look at the ways in which the various peer groups you joined held possibilities for creative service to other people.

Testing various peer groups is part of every kid's quest for identity. As you properly surmised, each group provides an identity for a kid to try on for size to see if he or she is comfortable in it. Fortunately, you never tried to be a part of certain peer groups that could have destroyed you. For instance, almost every school these days has a drug-using gang on campus, which turns out the kids who are "burn-outs." Your school was no exception.

You just never gravitated to that crowd. For the record, I would have stepped in and interfered with your life dramatically if you had. It is one thing to give a kid the freedom to find himself, but it's something else to let him destroy himself.

There were times when Mom and I didn't like what you were into, but when we saw that the identities you were trying out weren't going to destroy you, we made ourselves sit back and let you do your thing. At times you concerned us with the groups you chose. At times your choices pleased us. Sometimes you entertained us. Except for a brief time when you were in college, you never seriously upset us by your choice of friends.

I don't know what I would have done if you had gotten into a group that was into heavy metal rock music. In some respects, that music is a preference, and kids can always shoot back to their parents that when *they* were teenagers, *their* parents didn't like their music either. It may sound like a valid argument, but I don't think it really sticks.

Today's heavy metal rock is more than a simple matter of musical taste. It is a subculture with its own particular view of life. It is producing too many rebellious, ruined lives to be treated with benign neglect. Its glorification of spontaneous sexual gratification, acceptance of drugs, and fascination with the dark side of life make it an unacceptable social force. When I recognize how much of a role heavy metal rock music plays in unifying kids who thrive on destructive anger and rebellion, I tend to vote for declaring war on it.

I am well aware of the fact that all rock music does not serve such anti-Christian purposes. There are some very positive things going on in modern music. Some contemporary rock and many of those who play it and listen to it give ample evidence to support that case. But when kids are shutting themselves up in their rooms to spend hours immersed in music that glorifies things evil, including Satan, I know that parents should step in.

You may recall that your sister, Lisa, got into all kinds of music when she was a teenager. When that happened, I spent hours listening to her music with her, and we had long discussions on the relative merits of those groups she most admired. As it turned out, there wasn't much to censor in what she had chosen, and in the end she did a lot to educate me about the positive side of rock music.

My appreciation for so much of what the Beatles and Bob Dylan recorded is a direct result of a daughter who educated her father. I did what I think parents must do to protect their kids from self-destruction: I learned what was being put into her head by the music she was into and tried to help her develop a sense of discretion as to what was and was not acceptable.

I really liked what you had to say in your letter about freedom. You showed me that we agree on the subject. Both of us know that freedom can be an incredibly heavy burden for kids and, in most cases, they will try to get rid of the burden by allowing themselves to be controlled by their peer groups. In so many cases, kids who scream for freedom from their parents do so only to become enslaved to the groups they run with both in and out of school.

Erik Erikson, the famous expert on child development, explains that every growing youngster goes through various well-defined stages in the process of becoming an adult. He persuasively argues that there are assigned privileges and responsibilities with each of these stages. It is Erickson's contention that, when a kid is forced to accept the privileges and responsibilities for a stage of development that is beyond him or her, that kid will become disoriented and neurotic. I believe he is absolutely right.

I have often watched with dismay as parents have relinquished all control over their children. Such parents are usually either too confused to give any useful direction to their children's lives or too lazy to put in the time that this kind of help requires. They try to fool themselves into believing that they are really helping their kids to be adults. In reality, most of these parents are copping out of the God-given responsibility of training up their children in the way they should go.

When a pre-teen child is given the privileges and responsibilities that should be reserved for the mid-teen years, that freedom will tax him beyond his ability to handle it. When a kid is an adolescent and is given the privileges and responsibilities that go with being an adult, she often will fall apart. I am sure that a great deal of the not-too-latent hostility that I discern among young people these days is related to their anger over getting what they thought they wanted from their parents— unrestrained freedom.

The seventeen year old who has been given a new car, expensive clothes, and no limitations as to where he can go and what hours he must keep can be the angriest of all kids. He is completely free to do what he wants, but he was given this freedom before he learned to discipline himself as to how to use it.

Obviously, parents can err in the other direction. They can keep their children so restrained that they never have the chance to test their wings. Bart, both you and I can name kids who have been stifled by parents who made too many decisions for them and were overprotective. Parents have to learn how to give the freedom that allows for experimentation with life and, at the same time, keep vigil lest their children burn themselves out.

My own mother was quite adept at maintaining that balance with me. If I demonstrated any sense of equilibrium in dealing with this particular challenge of parenthood, I probably learned it from her. When I was eight years old, my Mom would pay an older girl who lived up the street from us to walk me to school. Crossing Philadelphia streets was dangerous, and my school was several blocks away, so my mother paid the handsome sum of a quarter a week to make sure I got there safely.

From the beginning of this arrangement, I despaired of the vast outlay of money for something that I was convinced was totally unnecessary. After much nagging and begging, my mother finally gave in to my request. She stopped paying my escort and agreed to give me the twenty-five cents each week on the condition that I never run to school and that I look both ways before crossing streets.

Years later, when I was bragging about this example of my early independence at a family gathering, my mom told me the rest of the story. Sure, she got rid of the girl who walked me to school, and she let me set out each morning convinced that I was on my own. I was allowed to assume responsibility and to feel free.

What I didn't know was that each morning my mom had followed me to school herself, making sure to stay out of sight. After school she was always there to follow me home. There were strange people who might mess up a little kid in the city, and she knew it. There were wrong turns a seven-year-old child could take. She wanted me to be free, but she also wanted to keep a watchful eye on me. She figured out a way to do both, even though it took a lot of her time.

When your turn to be a parent comes, Bart, I hope that you, too, learn how to walk that thin line separating the giving of too much freedom from the exercising of too much restraint. That is one of the most important lessons you will ever have to learn.

Allow me to suggest that when your time comes to figure all of this out, you invite the church to help. Get your church to form a Sunday school class or special group for young couples with children so that you, along with other parents, can study together the Christian way to handle your children's need for freedom. It is much too difficult to figure out alone. When parenting becomes difficult, we need the prayers as well as the wisdom and experience of other Christian parents. That's what "bearing one another's burdens" (Gal. 6:2) is all about.

Love,
Dad

Four

Going beyond the Birds and the Bees

Dear Bart,

Every father is supposed to talk to his son about sex. I didn't. That expected discussion about the birds and the bees never occurred between us. This was due in part to neglect and in part to design. Undoubtedly, there were some misunderstandings and confusions that could have been avoided had I taught you what I was supposed to teach you about sex. I did, however, try my very best to give you an adequate education about love. I thought that understanding love was far more important than learning about the "plumbing" of reproduction.

When I was in graduate school studying the sociology of the family, my professors often made the point that good sexual relationships usually came from good interpersonal relationships. I remember one of my favorite teachers, James H. S. Bossard, regularly poking fun at those in the field of family studies to whom he referred as being in the "pure orgasm school of thought." His sarcasm was aimed at those in the field who overemphasized the importance of being well-informed about sex as a prerequisite to successful marriages and healthy psychological adjustment.

Bossard argued convincingly that ours is a society in which people have become experts on how to relate physically but are sadly inept at relating to each other as persons. He went on to contend that if a man and a woman develop a deep love and respect for one another, then all else will follow. It was his belief that if a man and woman develop a profound friendship (that's right—I said "friendship"), a sexual adjustment is likely to follow.

Conversely, Bossard was convinced that sexual problems that occur between husbands and wives are much more likely to be the result of things that have gone wrong with their friendship than because of anything wrong with them physically or any lack of knowledge of the best techniques of foreplay or positioning.

Maybe it was a cop-out, but part of my failure to talk to you about the physical side of sex was a consequence of my not viewing that side of the sexual relationship as anywhere near as important as the emotional and spiritual dimensions of what goes on between a man and a woman.

I did all that I could to let you know that being married was the most fulfilling experience that a person could have. Mom was and is my best friend, and I did my best to make you ever conscious of that reality. Of course, being friends with your mother has always been a very easy thing.

Mom is a great conversationalist. There are those who may not think of that as a crucial trait for being sexy—but to me it is. To be married to a person who has the capacity to make life interesting makes sex incredibly exciting. People who bore each other out of bed quickly prove boring in bed as well. What people talk about when they are together in the dark is really very important to maintaining a sexually fulfilling relationship. Physical attraction is important, but if there is nothing else, even a gorgeous partner soon becomes tiring to be around.

I think you got a good lesson on how unsexy the physical side alone can be the summer you turned fourteen. Remember, you went with me to Vancouver, Canada, when I taught summer school at Regent College on the campus of the University of British Columbia? I'll never forget that day when we accidentally discovered the nude beach behind the dormitory where we were staying.

It was a hot August day, and we asked some of the guys who lived on our floor where there was a good place to swim and cool off. "Sure," they told us, "just run down the hill behind the dorm and on the other side of those trees you'll come out on a great beach." We didn't ask any other questions, because we never suspected what would follow. You and I got into our bathing suits, ran down the hill, and burst out onto a beach littered with reclining, naked couples. Utterly embarrassed, not knowing what to do, our immediate reaction was to run out into the ocean so as to conceal from everyone else on the beach that we were wearing bathing suits.

As soon as we could, we made our way back to the safety of the dormitory, laughing wildly, but also shocked. As soon as we settled down you said, "That was ugly. Those naked ladies didn't look like I thought they would." On that hot August afternoon, you made an important discovery: Most people don't look very glamorous without their clothes. I hasten to add that things only get worse with age!

At fifty-three, I hope I'm still sexually interesting to your Mom. She certainly is to me. Excitement, however, comes more from what we say to each other than from anything else. Sociologists and psychologists have long theorized about the importance of talk in lovemaking, but all of their intuitive knowledge gained empirical validation with the famous Kinsey Report. That study, still the most comprehensive investigation of sexual behavior ever made, gave data gleaned from hundreds of personal interviews and actual tests verifying that women become more sexually excited by talk than by anything they see or touch. As a guy who is getting old, I find that comforting. As a guy in his mid-twenties, you should find that incredibly important.

Tenderness expressed in talk is one of the most underrated aphrodisiacs ever to exist. Thoughtful attention to the other person may be the best form of foreplay, but never wait to be in bed before you evidence that quality. What goes on in the hours before you go to bed is what is most crucial to a gratifying sexual relationship. I experience my most difficult times with Mom when I behave like a selfish clod all evening and then try to get amorous at bedtime. It takes more than a sexual encounter to truly make love. I think a good Bible verse for any married couple who want guidance on how to keep their sex lives alive and fulfilling is Eph. 4:32:

And be ye kind one to another, tenderhearted, forgiving one another, even as God for Christ's sake has forgiven you.

Humor is another trait that is essential for maintaining the joy of sex. One of the more memorable nights I ever had with Mom was spent in the remote little town of Geraldine in New Zealand. The two of us were on vacation, and we were looking for a motel for the night. We found one in Geraldine that had a room with a waterbed. We had always joked about trying one of those things someday, and we decided that the day had come.

When we got into bed, everything became wildly funny. Maybe it was the bed or maybe it was us, but neither of us seemed to be able to move without getting the other to bounce up and down like we were on a trampoline. Once, when I tried to get out of bed, I fell back into the mattress and literally bounced Mom out. We spent hours laughing. We laughed at the bed, we laughed at each other, we laughed at the whole absurd situation—and we felt very close to each other.

Personally, I think that people without a good sense of humor must have a hard time surviving in marriage—or in anything else, for that matter. I consciously tried to let you and your sister know how Mom and I related to each other—that we got along great, cared for each other, had an awful lot of fun together, and that each of us thought the other to be a very special person. Some might ask what all of those things have to do with sex education. In reality, without them, sex becomes little more than a bodily function to relieve tension.

There is something about all of this that *does* concern me. Did Mom and I paint an unrealistic image of marriage? Did we make it seem too easy? Did we leave you with the idea that we never got disgusted with each other—even to the point of wishing we could chuck the whole thing?

Mom and I did our best not to argue in front of you. I'm sure that from time to time you noted irritation and gruffness between us (usually on my part and seldom on hers), but we never let you in on the really serious conflicts. We had the same problems that most couples have, and sometimes those problems became great crises. Mom and I would both tell you now that, if we had not been Christians, we might have ended our marriage at several points along the way.

Religion used to do that for people. It would keep them together when their marriage seemed to be falling apart. It certainly did that for us. I'm sure that there were times for Mom, and there were certainly times for me, when I felt that marriage was a trap. I thank God that, because of our religious moorings, neither of us viewed divorce as an option for getting out of that "trap." Instead, we always believed that the only alternative was to put things together again and make our marriage work. When love seemed to have died, as it did at times, we did not consider walking away from our marriage. Instead, we worked hard to create love and happiness again—and it always worked.

By doing for each other what lovers are supposed to do for each other, even when we didn't feel like it, we eventually experienced the resurrection of what had been killed; what came to life again always seemed richer and deeper than what we had had before. When people don't allow their suffering to kill their love, working through it together is bound to make their love better. It's been thirty years for Mom and me, and in all honesty I love her more now than ever before.

I feel sorry for you and your generation, because in today's world not even religion seems to hold people together. Let it be known that as far as I'm concerned, *true Christianity* still provides the glue that can hold people together in a world that's falling apart.

I don't think you were ever really aware of the hard times Mom and I had, because we thought it would be bad for you to know. A kid faced with the kind of pain and divisiveness that are hallmarks of a marriage in trouble is in great danger of being emotionally and psychologically destroyed. I often wonder what happens inside children who have to witness the knock-down, drag-out confrontations that all too often go on between parents in conflict.

In times of extreme frustration, husbands and wives sometimes say things that are horrible and make threats about leaving that can devastate a kid. Such painful exchanges should never take place, but when they do, there is no excuse for letting the children be party to them. It may be that in a day or two the trouble will pass, and the couple may begin to put their world together again, but the kids who have had to watch and hear their parents' worst times, may never get over it. They may harbor secret fears that will haunt them for years and cloud the way they look at life.

Mom and I had some tough times, but we hid them from you for these reasons. At least I hope we did. Not only did we refuse to argue in front of you; we tried to keep you from knowing we had problems at all. Was that a mistake? Did we leave you with the false impression that people simply get married and live happily ever after? Did we keep you from one of "the facts of life" that is far more important than what is usually written up in books with that title?

Another part of what I considered to be sex education was helping you to come to grips with what it really means to be a man in the deepest Christian sense of the word. In many respects my understanding of manhood was going through a disturbing reevaluation as you were coming of age. Consequently, I hadn't gotten enough of my act together on this matter to do the kind of job I wished I had done in raising you to be a godly husband. My earlier conception of what it meant to be a man was, for the most part, blown away by the feminist movement. The funny thing is that the feminist movement, which fostered my radical reevaluation of my role as a Christian husband and father, is condemned by many Christians as being dangerous to the family. I think that what the feminists taught me has brought me a lot closer to what God wills for me to be as a man than did much of what I got from the pulpit while I was growing up.

The feminists taught me that raising children wasn't ordained to be the woman's job. Raising kids is something that should be mutually shared by parents. Unfortunately, I did not grasp this truth until it was a little too late. When you were a baby, I seldom changed a diaper or, for that matter, even babysat in order to give your Mom some time off.

Somehow I'd grown up believing that such things were a mother's responsibility. If I ever did babysit for you, Mom was surprised, filled with gratitude, and treated me as though I'd gone out of my way to do what was supposed to be her job. The idea that the kids were hers and that my job was to be the bread-winner seemed to me to be legitimized by the church.

Preachers and teachers throughout Christendom erro-neously allowed many of us to think that this was the way God wanted it. Needless to say, many of us males foolishly encour-aged and supported this idea. In Paul's letter to the Ephesians, he writes:

Submitting yourselves one to another in the fear of God. Wives, submit yourselves unto your own husbands, as unto the Lord. For the husband is the head of the wife, even as Christ is the head of the church: and he is the saviour of the body. Therefore as the church is subject unto Christ, so let the wives be to their own husbands in every thing.

Eph. 5:21–24

We took this passage and used it to imply that men had a right to make their wives into people who served them and took care of all the dirty work of keeping house and raising children. Note that we usually didn't go on to fully consider verse 25:

Husbands, love your wives, even as Christ also loved the church, and gave himself for it. . . .

As I look back on those years when you were a baby, I not only regret what my faulty religion did to Mom, but also how it cheated me. I really missed some of the great joys of life. When I see modern fathers carrying babies, changing diapers, and doing all the other things that go with parenting, I realize that I passed up something very precious. Because I thought it was my right as a man to be free from the responsibilities that go with child rearing, I failed to take advantage of some of the greatest privi-leges of fatherhood. I hope you have learned enough to be a different kind of husband and father than I was during your early years.

By the time you were about six years old, my views about marriage and child rearing were being challenged by some of the graduate assistants who worked with me at the University of Pennsylvania. They were well read in the feminist literature that was emerging in those days and most anxious to expose the male chauvinism of their would-be mentor. They challenged the idea that a male should be a "macho man" and began to help me to see that a healthy male was assertive but also tender, strong but also sensitive, a leader but also a servant.

The more they talked about what they thought should be male characteristics, the more I realized that they were describing the traits of Jesus. Jesus was a man who wasn't afraid to let people see Him cry when He saw loved ones in pain. Jesus was not so into the "male" affairs of life that He was unable to consider the loveliness of the lilies or to feel tender about little children and sparrows. Being the "Lion of Judah" did not keep Him from comparing Himself to a mother hen:

O Jerusalem, Jerusalem, which killest the prophets, and stonest them that are sent unto thee; how often would I have gathered thy children together, as a hen doth gather her brood under wings, and ye would not!
Luke 13:34

The more my feminist students taught me about being a man, the more I saw in Jesus qualities I had never noticed before. The more I learned of these qualities, the more I wanted you to have them, too. A full understanding of Jesus reveals what being a whole person is all about.

Somehow you got the message of Christlike manhood in spite of me. There was a precious softness about you that made you into a very special child. When you were in kindergarten, the mother of one of your classmates called to invite you to her daughter's birthday party. She told Mom that you were the only boy invited, but that her little girl wanted you to come more than she wanted anybody else. Mom was curious, did some investigating, and was told by your teacher that this little girl was picked on constantly by the other children in the class. Children can be cruel to one another, and evidently this little girl had become the brunt of everyone's meanness. Everyone, that is, but you. You had become her defender, and the more the other kids picked on her, the more you became her friend. You just couldn't stand to see anybody sad or suffering. You had the kind of sensitivity that might not be considered "macho" but is certainly in character with Jesus.

Being rough and tumble was never a big thing with you even though you had the physique to be so. Despite the fact that you were an all-star goalie and a varsity basketball player, you were never the kind of guy who wanted to be distinguished by toughness. The kind of strength that it takes to be a pacifist was what I found in you. Even when it seemed to others that it would have been right for you to haul off and land a punch or two, you never did.

I remember when you were in the second grade, there was a boy who rode on your school bus who got some perverse delight out of humiliating you by spitting on you. You would come home each day in tears, finding it difficult to handle the way he embarrassed you in front of all your friends. I pointed out that you were much bigger than he was and could easily beat him up. You simply told me that you knew that you could, but didn't want to. When there was no letup in the spitting, I *ordered* you to hit that mean little boy. The spitting stopped, not because you fought back, but rather because you told him, "Bill, if you don't stop, I'm going to have to hit you. I don't want to hit you, but my father told me I have to hit you if you don't stop. I'm really sorry, but I have to do what my father tells me."

Little Bill never messed around with you after that. Once again you had demonstrated what being a Christian man is all about. You got no joy from being tough even though you were strong enough to be tough. You had discovered the strength it takes to avoid using violence. Jesus must have been proud of you—and He must have been disturbed by my "fatherly" advice.

I knew that you had broken out of the stereotypical role prescribed for high-school boys when you joined the high-school chorus. You had already established yourself as one of the most prominent jocks in the high-school when Mom asked you if you would join the chorus. She had loved going to the concerts when your sister was in high school and had been hoping that you would carry on the tradition. You never even blinked. Never mind that the macho men on campus probably thought it a bit uncool. Never mind that none of your close buddies were in the chorus. If that's what your Mom wanted, no more needed to be said.

There was one time that the chorus had a concert scheduled the same night as a basketball game. When you asked how that could happen and what other choir members did in such situations, you were told that your high school had never had a basketball player in the choir before. The night of the concert you sang with the choir. Mom was there, of course, and then she drove you over to the gym in time to join the game that had already started. I thought that was really neat.

Sex education in our home also involved coming down hard on pornography, even though many people expected "real boys" to be into dirty pictures. Back in the 1960s, I had joined the rest of the liberal establishment in contending that pornography was merely an unpleasant sideshow that accompanied freedom of speech. At that time, I found pornography distasteful, but I didn't see it as a threat to your well-being or as an instrument for generating perversion. Fortunately, my ideas about pornography changed before you reached puberty, so that you grew up in a home that was strongly against it. In light of my most recent reflections on the matter, I would be even more outspoken against it than I was when you were growing up.

Today, there is mounting evidence that pornography is addictive. It's not just a naughty thing; according to many authorities, it tends to get a real hold on some people. For reasons that are hard to explain, the addiction is primarily a male problem. The consequences of the addiction, however, should be frightening to both men and women.

Those who become addicted start with the "soft" porn of something like *Playboy* centerfolds. Such photos prove titillating for a while, but they gradually lose their capacity to generate the desired sexual stimulation. Harder forms are then sought and found, but the addict soon finds that even these become inadequate to meet his increasingly perverse hungers. Lust, unlike love, thrives on domination and is fed when the object of lust is helpless and innocent.

People who pride themselves on being open-minded are likely to scoff when radio and television preachers suggest that what begins with *Playboy* may be the first link of a chain that eventually binds men to finding their delight in sadistic child porn. In our home, we even took out after forms of pornography that church people all too often accept. We especially downgraded things like beauty pageants. I have always been a bit perplexed that the feminist movement has been more opposed to the Miss America contests than has the church.

Feminists rightly contend that such beauty contests make women into sexual objects instead of treating them as persons. It cuts no ice with them when the promoters of those pageants argue that the bathing suit competitions are only a "small" part of the contests. The feminists ask why the bathing suit competitions are included at all. In some beauty contests, the measurement of the contestants' hips and bust are announced. The obscenity of that is all too obvious. We would never put up with any contest that advertised the measurements of the private parts of men's bodies. So the feminists rightly ask why we don't protest when the private parts of women's bodies are measured and made public knowledge.

In our home, we condemned those beauty contests as sexist institutions and talked about them as exercises in the denigration of women. We rejected them, along with *Playboy, Penthouse,* and all the rest because they portray women as sexual objects that exist only to satisfy men. The Campolo view is that women must always be viewed as persons to be loved and never as things to be used. If sex education involves helping adolescents understand the perversity of pornography, I think you might give me passing grades in this area of your training.

In the same way, I provided an ample critique of dating, making you aware of the inherent evils of the system. To begin with, I let you know that the facts demonstrate that most teenagers are incapable of handling the sexually pressurized situations that go along with modern dating. Both Mom and I tried to help you see how much psychological strain and hurt is involved in this "game," which most parents seem to view as innocent fun.

Most guys at fourteen and fifteen are not equipped verbally to keep a date going for an entire evening and usually lack the creativity to think of interesting things to do or places to go. Consequently, necking often becomes an escape from the awkwardness of not knowing what to do. Necking allows teenagers to seem sophisticated to each other even in the midst of social ineptness.

With Christian kids, the problems are even more severe because their heavy necking—in which hands go all over the place—leaves them in deep states of guilt. There are always those neo-Freudian psychologists who claim that guilt is a sick reaction to innocent sexual play generated by an overly restrictive church. Maybe there is some justification for this position, but it seldom occurs to these all-too-arrogant critics of religious restrictiveness that the guilt may be a healthy reaction to the violation of the will of God.

I don't know how involved you got in necking and petting, but I have my suspicions. The fact that you found it so difficult to "break off" with some of the girls with whom you went steady, long after you realized that the relationship was going nowhere, used to have me wondering. Guilt can keep a teenager, particularly a Christian teenager, tied into a relationship long after it should have cooled. Somehow teenagers think that if it all happens with people they really love and intend to marry, it will all be OK in the eyes of God. Down deep inside, however, they know better.

Usually, kids who start getting sexually involved turn off to God and the church. Finding it impossible to continue what they're doing and, at the same time, remain close to God, they give up on being close to God. Teenagers often distance themselves from God simply because it's easier for them to do their sexual things that way. I'm not sure how this all worked itself out in your life, but I hope you didn't do yourself or others any harm along the way. In the midst of those turbulent years, I tried to make you ever aware that nothing could separate you from the love of God (Romans 8). I wish that all teenagers who have crossed the lines required for clean sexual relationships would realize that God is still with them and is ready to make them like new again. They should all know 1 John 1:9:

If we confess our sins, he is faithful and just to forgive us our sins, and to cleanse us from all unrighteousness.

Bart, there were other things about dating that I tried to teach you. I tried to make you aware that in the modern American dating system too many teenagers get left out, and those who get left out are often emotionally crushed. More than half of American teenagers graduate from high school without ever having had a date. The thing that is really rotten about this is that in our society kids often feel worthless if they are dateless. Their own parents usually pity them, and their self-concepts are often reduced to zero. I'm sure that our dating system has much to do with the prevalence of depression among contemporary teenagers.

I think you caught that message because during your high school days most of your going out was with "the gang" that included both guys and girls. Group dating is one of the healthiest things that teenagers can do, and I have a hard time figuring out why church youth leaders don't do more to encourage it. Group dating is inclusive, and it gives shy kids a chance to have a good time in nonpressurized situations. Teenagers don't have to worry about whether they will have anything to talk about on group dates because when a gang of kids is together the only problem is to find enough time for all of those who want to talk. Group dating also makes it easy to avoid those situations that can lead to morally compromising sexual behavior.

In today's world, teenagers can never be totally free from the one-on-one kind of dating that has become normative. What was amusing to me was your own awareness of what was wrong with the dating system. It seemed as if many of the one-on-one dates you had were basically an effort on your part to make sure that some really neat girls weren't left dateless on important occasions. The fact that you went to at least three senior proms but didn't go to your own is a case in point. You were well aware of the fact that some of your female friends might be left dateless for this ritual of American high school life, and you were always ready to volunteer to get one of them safely through such a rite of passage. I'm sure you had become aware of the absurdity of what the American dating system does to teenagers simply by recognizing how many personable girls were without dates each year as the night of the prom approached.

When all is said and done, it must still be said that I never really sat you down and gave you specifics about the physiological aspects of sex. I depended on the school to do the job, and that was wrong. Too many parents are like I was and feel that the sex education programs of the public school system will do what they know is really their responsibility.

What is taught at school is OK, I suppose, but, because of the laws requiring separation of church and state, sex education must be given in a "value-free" manner. Of course, that's what's wrong with sex education in the public school system.

God has ordained for the sexual act to be laden with spiritual significance, and to treat it as though it were only a physical act is a great distortion. My gripe is not with the school system, which I think is doing what it must do in our pluralistic society. My gripe is with myself.

I should have explained the biblical significance of sex. I should have helped you to see that if two people come together, not just for sexual pleasure, but to express the kind of love that God wills for a husband and a wife to have between them, then the sexual act can be a sacrament that binds two people together to share a creative life.

And Adam said, This is now bone of my bones, and flesh of my flesh: she shall be called Woman, because she was taken out of Man. Therefore shall a man leave his father and mother, and shall cleave unto his wife: and they shall be one flesh.

Gen. 2:23–24

I should have made clear to you all the biblically prescribed responsibilities that go with the sexual act when it occurs within the confines of marriage.

Like a lot of other Christian parents, I left it up to the secular school system to carry out what was my God-given responsibility as a Christian parent. I wish I had it to do over again. Looking back on your developing years, I realize you must have had a lot of sexual struggles in which I was no help at all. I'm sorry.

Love,
Dad

Dear Dad,

When I read the first few sentences of your letter about sex, I began to load up a heavy dose of guilt to lay on you. It always bothered me that you never talked to me about sex straight out, and I figured this was my chance to let you know how I felt. As I read what you wrote, though, I began to realize that you had indeed taught me a great deal about sex and countless related subjects, even though we never had the "big talk." Still, Dad, I think you ought to know just how ignorant I was about the basics of human sexuality as a result of your approach to the entire subject.

Do you remember the old "I Dream of Jeannie" television show, which starred Barbara Eden and Larry Hagman? It was very popular back in the late sixties, and I watched it every week. Television historians are well aware of "I Dream of Jeannie" because of the great controversy it created when it first came on the air.

The problem was that Barbara Eden's genie costume had a bare midriff that showed her navel, and up to that point a belly button had never been shown on prime-time television. By today's standards, her outfit was positively modest, but the censors of that era refused to permit the show to broadcast until it was altered to cover up her navel.

The whole affair became quite a sensation, and as I read

about it in the newspaper as a boy, I remember wondering what the big deal was all about. It all seemed so silly to me until . . . in a moment of revelation, I grasped the hitherto unthinkable secret of human sexuality: a woman's belly button! So that's where the action is, I thought to myself . . . from that moment until I was thirteen years old! Never mind that everybody had one, that even I had one, I was secure in my understanding. That's right, Dad, until I was a teenager, I thought the belly button was where babies came from—and it was all your fault.

Fortunately for me, you were a social scientist and had an extensive library of textbooks. One time when I was exploring the wonders of your office, I happened upon the then-notorious *Everything You Always Wanted to Know about Sex But Were Afraid to Ask.* As soon as I saw it, I knew it was the book for me, so I smuggled it up to my room and read it cover to cover in one sitting. What a great book that was for a curious teenager, filled with straightforward definitions and matter-of-fact descriptions of everything I could possibly think of—and a lot of things that I hadn't even considered—without either pornographic exaggeration or moralistic value judgments to confuse things. All things considered, it was probably as good an introduction to human sexuality as I could have received. It neither embarrassed me nor turned me on, and it answered my questions without a lot of commotion.

As you pointed out so well in your letter, however, there is a whole lot more involved with understanding our sexuality than simply knowing the physical mechanics of the sexual act, and I relied on you and Mom for most of the rest. I know you think the two of you did a good job, Dad, and I tend to agree with you. The biggest lie the culture tells a kid about sex is that it can be meaningful as an end in itself, that even in the absence of love, two consenting people can use one another for a lot of harmless fun. I may not have understood how it all worked for a long time, but there was never any doubt in my mind that everything from holding hands to sexual intercourse only makes sense when it reflects the emotions and the commitments of a monogamous relationship. I learned that the amount of physical expression should depend on the level of emotional and practical commitment that stands behind it—and on the commandments of God.

Perhaps that doesn't seem like such an earth-shattering truth, but most kids don't learn about it until after they have gone too far. "How far should I go?" is *never* a question that should be answered in the heat of passion. At that point, it's usually too late to make a good decision. Kids need to be encouraged to think about standards and personal limits for physical relationships before a relationship even starts.

Your insistence that physical expression and commitment need to match up didn't keep me from making mistakes, but it did give me a starting point for setting my standards. It also helped me see that the deepest physical expression should be reserved for the deepest commitment, that sex was only for married people. You got me thinking about sex in terms of relationships instead of in terms of self-gratification, and that made it easier for me to understand how feminism, machismo, pornography, dating, and even marriage either fit or didn't fit together into a Christian point of view.

There is one area of sexuality where your silence really did hurt me, I'm afraid: masturbation. You never told me anything about masturbation—whether it was right, whether it was wrong, or even whether it was a normal thing for me to be concerned or confused about. I was completely unprepared for the flood of mixed emotions that hit me at puberty, but there's no question that masturbation was the thing that caught me most off-guard and the thing that caused me the most unhappiness and self-doubt.

It was also the thing that made me feel the most alone. I didn't know that I wasn't the only person in the world who masturbated or that by the time they're eighteen nearly everyone has had the experience of manipulating their own sexual organs to provide a pleasant sensation. The numbers vary from study to study, but nearly everyone agrees that close to three-quarters of all girls have masturbated and that, as it is sometimes said, 90 percent of boys have had the experience and the rest are liars. The problem is that even though masturbation is very common, hardly anyone talks about it in an open manner. The mere mention of the word "masturbation" is enough to make most people uncomfortable, which may be why you never discussed it with me. Whether it gets talked about or not, though, masturbation is a big problem for a lot of young people (and probably a lot of older people, too).

The problem, of course, is whether or not masturbation is wrong. From the moment I first discovered it—quite by accident, I might add—I always assumed that it must be wrong. It wasn't that I thought all sexuality was sinful. I know better than that. But you had taught me that all sexual activity is intended for relationships, that even holding hands or a good-night kiss demands some degree of emotional and practical commitment.

Masturbation is something a person does alone, usually secretly, privately. Like most kids, I was always terribly afraid of being caught or found out (why do you think I was so insistent that you never enter my room without my permission?), and that panicky feeling told me I must be doing something wrong. If it was okay, I reasoned, why was I so ashamed?

Moreover, I felt guilty about the thoughts that ran through my mind when I masturbated, especially after I became a Christian. Surely, nobody who truly loved God would think about things like that, I told myself, especially after reading all of the things the Bible has to say about sexual purity.

Then I heard a youth pastor's offhand comment about masturbation being an "abomination before God," and for a while the issue was settled, at least in my mind. My body, however, had some ideas of its own. Despite all of the confusion, guilt, fear, shame, and even the sense that I was letting God down, I felt helpless to control myself for very long. Sometimes I would hold out for a day or two and sometimes for a week at a time, but even though I believed masturbation was wrong I couldn't stop myself from doing it. Most of the time I even had some of those forbidden *Playboy* magazines hidden in my room.

A pattern emerged in my life—masturbation, guilt, recommitment to abstinence, temptation, failure—that began to have a frightening effect on my self-image. I began to hate myself in a very real way. I felt that I was evil somehow, in the depths of my heart, and that I didn't deserve the grace of God but rather His punishment instead.

Finally, after reading the passage about it being better to cut off one part of your body than for your whole body to be thrown into hell, I resolved to cut into the back of my wrist with a pen knife every time I failed until I either stopped masturbating or lost my hand. That was a terrible time for me.

I wasn't suicidal, but I definitely wanted to hurt myself, and I did. The physical scars I had from that episode are gone now, but I well remember the frustration and the turmoil that brought me to a point of self-mutilation. I see those same feelings in too many kids today, for the same reasons, and it worries me. Somehow we need to bring this issue out in the open and remove the isolation it causes. There are too many people suffering in silence without any help or guidance when it comes to masturbation.

For me, the experience of cutting my wrist was a turning point. I knew I was in trouble. In the midst of my private agony, something told me that God loved me too much just to leave me alone in confusion. I found a passage in James that says, "If any of you lacks wisdom, he should ask God, who gives generously to all without finding fault, and it will be given to him" (1:5). I began to reconsider the whole issue. How could it be that God had given me a healthy sex drive at the age of twelve but forbade me from exploring it until I was married, probably ten years later, if I got married at all? What about wet dreams—how could God require people to control what happened while they were asleep? Furthermore, if everything was so clear-cut, why were there no Bible verses that said "Do not masturbate" the way they said "Do not commit adultery" and "Do not steal"?

I stopped assuming and started looking for answers. Is masturbation always wrong? Exactly what is it that makes it a sin? What I found was that there's a lot of disagreement about masturbation, even among the people who claim to know. Nobody has ever been able to give me the definitive answer to the question of masturbation. However, in the words of Jim Burns, a dedicated Christian author who has since become my close friend and mentor, I found the kind of understanding that many young people are looking for. In his excellent book on youth sexuality, *Handling Your Hormones,* I found this passage:

> If I must be pinned down, I believe that not all masturbation is necessarily sinful. However, you must make up your own mind. You must intelligently work through the decision. And I would suggest that you turn to God for help. Let me give you two opposing viewpoints from two outstanding Christian people to help you arrive at your decision.
>
> First, in his book *This Is Loving?* David Wilkerson says, "Masturbation is not a gift of God for the release of sex drives. Masturbation is not moral behavior and is not condoned in the Scriptures. . . . Masturbation is not harmless fun." On the other hand, Charlie Shedd, a very respected Christian authority on sex and dating, does call masturbation a "gift of God." He claims that masturbation "can be a positive factor in your total development" and goes on to say that "teenage masturbation is preferable to teenage intercourse. It is better to come home hot and bothered than satisfied and worried."
>
> My own view is somewhere in between these two extremes. Masturbation is practically universal. It isn't the gross sin some people think it is, yet at times it can have a negative side to it.

Jim's book goes on to explain that masturbation becomes very negative when it becomes obsessive-compulsive and dominates a person's life and becomes sin when it involves uncontrolled fantasy and especially pornography or the semi-pornography that makes up so much of today's television.

I agree with him completely, especially on the last point. The most destructive things to me were and are the images that I have allowed to fill my mind through magazines, movies, and particularly television.

Beyond the images themselves, the modern media has a pornographic attitude toward sexuality, and women in particular, that reduces people to the status of objects and makes sex into a purely physical act. In the long run, though, television does something far worse than inspiring lust: it creates unrealistic expectations and false standards for young people.

Sex on television and in the movies almost always consists of first-time encounters between young, thin, beautiful people who aren't married to each other. Consequently it comes across as unfailingly intense and exciting. These radiant Greek gods and goddesses never argue, pay bills, tend to screaming children, have a cold, get tired or depressed, or experience anything to cool their passions. They aren't real people, but watching them makes those of us who are married feel inadequate and gives those who are unmarried unrealistic expectations.

Married sex can be intense and exciting to be sure, but for different reasons and in different ways and not all the time. I used to think that parents who locked up the television and VCR were fuddy-duddies, but now I think that parents who don't are insane. Television is not just a problem for children, either. We all need to be aware of the not-so-subtle danger of letting a sick and often evil culture determine what we think about.

Paul said it well in Phil. 4:8: "Finally . . . , whatever is true, whatever is noble, whatever is right, whatever is pure, whatever is lovely, whatever is admirable—if anything is excellent or praiseworthy—think about such things." Everything doesn't need to be "Christian" to fit that criteria, but we had better stop kidding ourselves about the effect of what we read and watch and think.

The point of all this, Dad, is that there was a lot going on with my sexuality that I needed help with, even before I got involved with actual relationships. I was very fortunate to be part of a very strong Christian support group in high school, and the love and trust there eventually allowed me to open up and share my struggles. I worry about people who suffer in silence— no one should have to work out their sexuality alone. I had you and Mom, too, and all of the things you described in your letter. As I said before, Dad, I always thought you neglected my sexual education. Now I see that in teaching me about love and relationships, you were giving me the most important lessons of all.

Love,
Bart

Five

My Friends, My Teachers, and Other Aliens

Dear Dad,

I read a lot of books about parents and kids as I prepared to write these letters, Dad, and, frankly, it was a little discouraging. Ideas that had seemed so unique and creative when you and I discussed them turned out to be practically common knowledge after all, and I suddenly realized that we are not as brilliant as I thought we were (which means that we are *definitely* not as brilliant as *you* thought we were). As good as some of those books are, though, somehow it seems like a lot of them are based on the implicit assumption that if parents simply do their jobs right, their kids will automatically grow up into wonderful people; if they don't, their kids will surely be human disasters.

The general attitude seems to be that the family is some sort of closed system, operating in a vacuum. That kind of unspoken message bothers me because it clearly misunderstands the realities of the world today. The average kid experiences a whole host of teachers, coaches, counselors, babysitters, and grandparents before they are graduated from high school, not to mention the influences of their own friends and siblings, the church, and the mass media.

While I believe that you and Mom have done a terrific job as parents, the inescapable fact is that there are a lot of other people who have had a hand in making me into the person that I am, for better and for worse. Regardless of what anyone thinks of how I turned out, I am undeniably the product of a collaborative up-bringing. You can't take all the credit—and more importantly you can't shoulder all the blame. I've seen it happen too often to deny that a parent can single-handedly destroy a child, but I know that even two parents don't raise their children all by themselves. Too many other people impact our lives to allow it, and, for my money, that's usually a good thing.

Elsewhere in these letters I write about how I became a Christian when I was fifteen years old. It's strange the way we Christians usually speak about becoming a Christian as though it were something we did once and were done with, like getting our tonsils taken out. In reality, accepting Jesus as Lord and Savior is just the first and easiest part of the lifelong task of becoming a Christian.

Even so, there is something very special about that first commitment that makes it a unique blessing. I've experienced some truly amazing things since I became a Christian, but I still don't think I will ever recapture the unbelievable excitement I had in those first weeks of my new life with God. Everything seemed so wonderful to me, and I couldn't believe my good fortune for being alive and full of faith. I can relate to the old hymn, "Amazing Grace" when it says, "How precious did that grace appear the hour I first believed," because I was a lonely, depressed kid looking to escape a life I hated when I was trans-formed by the overwhelming love of God, and becoming a Christian thrilled me.

New Christians are exciting people to be around, I think, because they don't take anything for granted, and they haven't yet learned to tone down their joy. They are often the most authentic Christians, too, because they take Jesus at His word when He says to love God with all your heart, soul, strength, and mind and to love your neighbor as yourself. Unfortunately, we who have been at it longer usually teach them to copy our own compromises instead of following their sense of commit-ment ourselves.

I spoke at a revival service not long ago in Northeast Philadelphia, and had the thrill of watching an older woman give her life to God. I would not have known about it, however, if her distraught daughter had not brought her up to talk with me after the service.

It seems that this woman had already begun to make plans for her new life in God's service and was considering leaving her job to work for a children's shelter downtown. Her daughter was very upset, primarily because she had been counting on her mother's income to finance a new boat. "Would you please tell my Mom that being a Christian doesn't mean she should do everything for God?" the younger woman asked me. "If she quits her job, it's going to spoil everything."

Her mother looked at me with disappointed eyes and said sadly, "I thought she'd be happy for me, but all she keeps saying is that God doesn't expect us to go overboard. But He does, doesn't He?" We talked for fifteen minutes, and I encouraged the mother in her decision to follow God's calling no matter what, while her daughter fumed. I'm thankful that she was so full of excitement, and I can only hope that she got into fellowship with some other committed Christians and ignored the "kill-joy" she had raised.

As exciting as it is, the euphoria of salvation doesn't last forever. For me, it didn't last more than a few months. As my emotional commitment to God gradually subsided and I found myself unable to manufacture new doses of enthusiasm, I began to wonder if I really was a Christian after all or if I had simply gone on some sort of spiritual joyride that was about to end whether I wanted it to or not.

My friend Joel, who had led me to Christ, helped all he could, but he wasn't very much farther along than I was as a disciple. Neither were the rest of my newfound Christian friends, most of whom were "baby" Christians, just as I was. Like the seeds on the shallow soil in Jesus' parable of the sower, we had received the word with joy, but we had no roots. And like those same seeds, we were beginning to wither and die.

It was just about that time that a college student, Phil Thorne, took over our youth group. Although he was only twenty-one years old, Phil was not your average Christian college kid by any measure. He was married, for one thing, and he was also a top student at Haverford College, a highly academic secular school in our area. How he found the time to manage a youth group of well over 180 high school kids, I'll never know, but he did just that for more than a year, until the church hired a full-time youth pastor, and Phil stepped down to become a volunteer leader.

I was a sophomore in high school when Phil arrived, but already I was working hard as a part of the group's student leadership. Because our group was so big and our leaders were all part time, the kids did everything from planning events and recruiting to counseling and leading Bible studies. In a lot of ways it was a great thing for me to be able to jump right in and begin to put my newfound faith into action.

Before I knew it, I was doing a whole lot more than just setting up chairs and being part of a skit or two. By the time Phil arrived, I was clearly in a position of spiritual leadership— but with almost no biblical foundation and a faith that was fading fast. On the outside I probably looked like I had my act together, but on the inside I was one very uncertain young man.

Youth ministers talk a lot about relational ministry, which oftentimes simply means spending time with kids, and there's a lot to be said for being a friend to young people. But Phil approached me in a different way. After he introduced himself, he simply said, "You're Bart Campolo, and I hear you're pretty involved here. I'd like to have you and a few other guys get together with me once a week so I can help you grow in your relationship with God."

No frills. No inducements. He even set the time for our meetings at 6:00 A.M. on Tuesday mornings so as to weed out anyone who wasn't really committed to what he was trying to accomplish. Some people might say that he went about things all wrong, I suppose, but as a new Christian struggling to keep my faith alive, I didn't care much about the strategies of youth ministry. Here was someone who was willing to help me grow. I thought I had died and gone to heaven.

It would be hard to describe what Phil Thorne did for me over the next three years. To be sure, he taught me how to study the Bible and how to pray and how to use my strengths as a person to influence other people for God, but he did more than just introduce me to the basics of Christianity. He made those Tuesday mornings a time when the other guys and I could talk about our lives honestly and work together to figure out what God wanted to do with us.

The conversations we had in Phil's living room were alive with the excitement of a group of boys who had found a man to lead them, and we talked for hours about everything from our girlfriends to predestination (I learned, by the way, that my girl-friend wasn't predestined to "dump" me, but she did anyway). We also grew close as friends because Phil showed us the way that Christians should care for one another in true fellowship. We weren't allowed to put each other down around him, because he knew that even playful put-downs can hurt and establish barriers between friends. We learned to pray for each other and keep each other in line, too.

I've made a lot of friends since that time, but I've never been part of any fellowship that had the kind of intensity and camaraderie that characterized what we ended up simply calling "The Group." When I got married years later, it was those guys— George, John, Rocky, Jeff, and Matthew, along with my college buddy Jerry—who stood up with me. Phil was at my wedding, too, because he was important to all of us, and we had become a part of his life.

Phil was much more than my teacher or even my Christian brother—he was my hero. To me, no one was smarter or hand-somer or nicer or more in touch with God than he was. I tried to hide it from him, unsuccessfully I'm sure, but I wanted Phil's approval more than anything back then, and some of my happi-est times were when he would take me along on an errand or let me help him with his laundry or tell me that I had done or said something well. One time he asked me to help him teach a few Sunday school classes, and I felt so honored that I must have walked on air for a week afterward.

I loved to be with him because of who he was and even more because I knew he cared about me even though he didn't have to. He asked me hard questions about myself, and he wasn't satisfied until I gave him straight answers. In answering Phil, I began to discover who I was and what my life was all about, or at least what I wanted it to be about. And I imitated him in every way I could think of because to me he was the greatest Christian man alive.

As I am writing all of this down and thinking about that time in my life, it occurs to me that it must have been awfully hard on you to see me respond that way to someone else. All of a sudden, another man was at the center of my life, where you had always been. It wasn't just that I devoted so much time to my little support group and to the larger youth group as well. All of a sudden I was full of new ideas and perspectives, and I measured everything, including my family, by the things I was learning from Phil. I'm sure you got tired of hearing "Phil says . . ." or "Well, according to Phil . . ." over and over again, but you never said a word about it to me. Here you were, my own father, preaching and teaching young people all over the country about the Christian life, and your own son was somebody else's disciple, not because you had walked out on me or let me down somehow, but rather because I had turned to Phil instead of you.

I've been a youth worker myself since that time, and sometimes kids respond in that same way to me. It amazes me because I know I'm not half the person my young followers make me out to be, and I try not to let their praise affect my self-concept. It is all too easy for those kids to put me on a pedestal—they only see me in short doses when I'm at my best and in an environment they love. They don't get a chance to see my weaknesses the same way they see those of their parents. Often my only job is to care for their emotional and spiritual needs and give them a good time, while their parents have to deal with all the nitty-gritty stuff of their daily lives. Phil had that same advantage with me, of course, but I didn't know it at the time. So he was my hero, and you were just my Dad, and I feel very sure that I let you know that every chance I could.

Although I know I must have hurt you, Dad, you never did a thing to undermine what was happening in my life. On the contrary, you encouraged it. There was never any battle for my allegiance because you never put up a fight or said a single word against Phil or anything he taught me—even when those things conflicted with your own thinking and beliefs.

If you had wanted to, I feel sure that you could have found a weakness in my Phil-inspired belief system, or in my image of Phil himself, and used it to make me turn away from him, but you didn't do anything like that. You kept quiet, even when I spouted off with the self-righteous judgments that new Christians are so prone to mistake for wisdom, and you supported what was going on in my life even though I almost completely left you out of it. You could have tried to hold onto me or make me feel guilty about leaving you behind, but instead you let me go.

I am fully convinced now that nothing you could have done at that time would have been as good for me as what you didn't do. I was finally growing, and more than anything in the world, I needed to grow on my own just then.

There are a lot of reasons why I left you out, of course. Both as an adolescent and as a new Christian, I was establishing my own identity, and while I wasn't exactly rebelling against you, I didn't want that identity to become nothing more than an extension of your own. Maybe some people would say that I had something to prove, but I think it had more to do with my knowledge that you were too powerful a person for me to handle at that point. You have a way of expressing your opinions that makes them seem like facts, and I knew that I would never be able to stand up to you in a discussion or an argument. Phil was powerful, too, but he was my friend and my choice, so I didn't resent his efforts to shape my personality. You, however, were someone who could have taken away my individuality altogether.

If I let you in, I told myself, I would gradually become just like you and lose myself in the process. I was afraid that your relationship to God would become my relationship to God, and even at that point in my growth I instinctively knew that that kind of thing was the ultimate danger.

Jesus had died so that I could have my own direct relationship with God, even if it was weak and sporadic and filled with doubts and fears. It belonged to me, and I wasn't taking any chances on losing it by mixing it up with you.

Besides, I didn't want you to know about a lot of the stuff I was dealing with just then. Like most boys that age, I was essentially a walking hormone factory, and it immediately became clear to me that my survival as a Christian had a lot to do with sorting out my sexuality. Unfortunately, that wasn't an issue you and I openly discussed. Amazingly enough, the guys in my support group eventually trusted each other enough to talk about our sexual lives, our struggles with pornography and lust and even masturbation, and to hold each other accountable as brothers in Christ. But even when I admitted that stuff to them, Dad, there was no way I was going to admit it to you.

I was also very proud and excited about the things that my support group was accomplishing as a ministry team in our high school. Phil insisted that, while Bible study, prayer, and personal piety (keeping ourselves straight as far as sex, drugs, language, etc., were concerned) were all vital, we could never grow the way God wanted us to if we weren't out in the world acting as His servants. Before long Phil had us sharing the Gospel with our friends, leading prayer groups during lunch at school, inviting people to our youth group, and planning special events that were aimed at sharing the love of God by creating a warm atmosphere of friendship. As we worked together, God used us at our high school to draw people to Him.

It was really exciting for us to be leading some of our friends to Christ and seeing God work in their lives. Next to some of the things that you were involved with, Dad, the work that we were doing seemed pretty insignificant. I would come home from a Bible study all thrilled because one kid had shown an interest in what I'd said, but after I heard about the rally where you had spoken to 10,000 people and had seen 500 give their lives to Jesus, it just didn't seem worth mentioning. You were building orphanages while I was trying to witness to my basketball coach. You were writing theology while I was figuring out who all of Jesus' 12 disciples were. It's not that I resented what you were doing—I was proud then, just as I'm proud now, and excited about the way God was using you—but it made me feel small to think about placing my stories next to yours, so I didn't. I've had variations of that feeling throughout my life, and no doubt will until the day I die. I know that we're not supposed to compare ourselves with other people, but it's awfully hard not to do it just the same.

Lately though I've discovered that God doesn't see things quite the way I do. What impresses Him is not the end result of an action, but the purity of the motives and the quality of faithfulness that go into it. As Mother Teresa put it, "God has not called us to be successful—He has called us to be faithful to Him." By that measure those early efforts were probably my finest because I hadn't yet grown skillful and polished, and I relied solely on the power of God. All of the training seminars and experience I've had since then have certainly made me a more capable and seasoned minister, but I often think I was better off when I hadn't yet developed so much confidence in myself.

Jesus said, "If any man remains in me and I in him he will bear much fruit; apart from me you can do nothing" (John 15:5), but I still find myself trying to do all sorts of things in my own strength. To God, though, the only ministry that really counts is that which is accomplished by His power. When we are willing to empty ourselves of our own desires and motivations and allow Him to do His will through us, then our ministry will have power. The things I did in high school belonged to Him that way, and that means they were very important. I know now that you would have seen them that way if I had shared them with you, Dad. But as exciting as they were to me, I tended to hold them back from you then because—in my mind—they didn't measure up.

I guess I should feel apologetic about having left you out of my spiritual life for so long at that point, but I don't. It was important for me to develop my own relationship with God, and that's exactly what happened. Maybe I would feel differently, though, if you hadn't offered yourself to me all over again when

I began to lose my bearings in college. By then I had developed enough confidence in myself that I didn't fear being overpowered, and it felt good when you began to talk with me as though I were your Christian brother as well as your son. Your spiritual guidance has meant a lot to me since then, and I've come to know you in a way I never could have imagined as a boy. You waited for me, though, and let God use someone else in my life, and that made all the difference in the world.

A lot of new Christians don't last very long because they have no one like Phil to help them put down roots and grow. Clearly that means something has gone very wrong with Christian leadership. I don't mean to sound cynical, but it seems that a lot of evangelism being done today is actually worse for the people we reach than if we had left them alone. Once they make a decision for Christ, that is exactly what we do—leave them alone. It is no wonder that so few of them actually survive as disciples. When the Apostle Peter says of such people that "It would have been better for them not to have known the way of righteousness, then to have known it and then to turn their backs on the sacred command that was passed on to them" (2 Pet. 2:21), we who cavalierly lead others to Christ and then make no provision for their continued growth should shudder with fear. We would be kinder to keep our Good News to ourselves unless we can provide the kind of support that will give a new Christian a fighting chance.

I know so many people who have sprung up quickly as believers only to have their faith wither and die because there was no one to come alongside them and help them put down roots. That's not just a shame; it's a sin. Everywhere I look, and especially in the ghettos where I work, there is a need for mature Christians who will offer themselves as mentors and friends to kids, and especially to Christian kids who are struggling to live for God.

God brought Phil Thorne into my life and used his example and his love to inspire me and to make me strong. I love Phil with my whole heart and am forever thankful for him and to him.

Nothing could have happened, though, Dad, if you hadn't let it happen, and for that I am every bit as thankful. You had to step into the background for a time, and you did it graciously and humbly and unselfishly. I know you loved me then because you did what was best for me instead of what was best for you.

Of course, you didn't let just anyone become my role model unchallenged. The reason I know that you could have undermined Phil in my eyes if you had wanted to is that you did just that to some other people when you felt their influence on me was negative. Like most kids growing up, I was always being impressed by somebody, and my personality changed nearly as quickly as my role models. As with my peers, though, you kept a close eye on my heroes.

A few years before I became a Christian, I had a teacher in school who quickly convinced me that he knew everything in the world worth knowing. He was a quick-witted cynic, and I thought he was the coolest man alive. When I began to parrot his words and ideas the way I did later on with Phil's, however, you weren't so passive. Oh, you knew better than to ridicule or contradict my reigning role model directly, for that would have only increased my loyalty by offending my sense of fair play. Since he was not there to face your attacks, I would have become his defender. So instead of a frontal assault, you and Mom developed a far more effective approach.

Instead of downplaying my hero, both of you became very interested in whatever it was he said each day. But the questions you asked to draw me out were also designed to make me follow my teacher's way of thinking through to its conclusions. For instance, when I repeated a saucy joke that he'd made about women, you didn't get upset. You simply said, "I wonder how you would feel if that had been your mother he was talking about, or your sister?" and left me to figure out the obvious answer. Humor that degrades women never seems so funny when you think about women as real people instead of sexual objects, so I didn't much like the joke when I thought of it that way. It felt wrong.

Another time it was his perspective on the welfare system and another time his statements about the importance of athletics, but always you asked questions that forced me to look beyond my teacher's clever words to the basically selfish attitudes that lay behind them. You didn't put him down exactly, but you didn't let his influence get very far either.

Once you had sown the seeds of doubt, though, it was Mom who finished him off as a role model. He wasn't the kind of man she liked, I knew, but she didn't try to make me dislike him myself. She knew a better way to stop his influence over me. As you began to expose the gaps in my hero's armor, she tried to make me feel sorry for him instead of angry.

"That poor man," she lamented, "he must have had awful trouble in his life to make him feel that way. You should do your best to be kind to him, Bart. I think he needs some kindness to soften his heart." She was right about my teacher, I think, but that was not the only reason she said what she did. You both knew that if I began to pity this man, he was finished as a role model. And so it was that I came to really care for that teacher and yet came to no harm in the process.

It was inevitable that I would look to other people besides you for guidance and examples, and I think you always knew that. But even if you couldn't be my only influence, you saw to it that no one got a clear shot at me unless it was for my good. I've had more than my share of significant adults, some of whom I am convinced you actually coerced into my life to help me, and I've been affected just as profoundly by some of my peers over the years. Each of them has touched my life and my character in some way, and in them I see the hands of God shaping me into the person He wants me to be.

Without a doubt, you and Mom have exerted the greatest influence, though, and one of the most significant ways you have done that is by allowing, encouraging, and interpreting all of those other people in my life. You didn't do all the work on this temple of God, but you had a major role in determining who did.

All of this writing about role models and teachers reminds me of one of the last things Phil showed me in the Bible before I graduated from high school. In 2 Tim. 2:1–2, the Apostle Paul gives a specific charge to his disciple Timothy. "You therefore, my son, be strong in the grace that is in Christ Jesus. And the things you have heard me say in the presence of many witnesses, entrust to reliable men who will also be qualified to teach others." After Phil read that passage aloud, he looked at me and said, "Bart, I've put a lot of myself into you, and I love you. Now I expect you to do the same for someone else. That is the way of Christ, and that must be our way as well."

He was right, of course; personal discipleship is the way of Christ. I suppose there's a place for television evangelism and video Bible studies, and I enjoy Christian concerts and festivals a great deal, but those are not the ways that Jesus made His disciples. Disciples are made through an intentional relationship with a mature Christian—someone who celebrates our victories and points out our areas of weakness—someone who sometimes gives us the answers and at other times makes us ask the questions—someone who prays for us and with us—and someone who ultimately refuses to let us slip away from God without a fight. All of those other things that make up the Christian subculture are fine, so long as buildings, programs, and paraphernalia don't get in the way or become so important to us that we fail to establish the kinds of personal relationships that bring about true Christian growth. What's the use of all our churches, choirs, evangelistic outreaches, books of theology, and everything else if we are only making believers—and not disciples—out of all men and women?

Don't get me wrong, Dad. You know that I'm not some radical who's out to undermine organized Christianity. I believe in the Church. I moved back to Philadelphia and started Kingdom Builders Supply specifically to work with inner-city churches.

KBS brings solid inner-city churches that are committed to neighborhood ministry together with Christian college students and adults who need vision and the chance to make a difference with their lives. We help those churches design effective summer outreach programs, and then we recruit teams of full-time summer volunteers from around the country to make those programs happen. The organization is based on a fairly simple premise: inner-city churches are the last, best hope for people in our nation's ghettos. What we're doing, though, is more than just empowering those churches for the work God has called them to do. By using college students as volunteers, we're also inspiring a new generation of young people to service and discipleship among the poor.

A typical KBS summer program includes things like day camps for children, evening youth groups, community clean-up days, neighborhood Bible studies, Christian block parties, and lots of visitation. It's hard, but it's a lot of fun, too. Volunteers don't experience only poverty and injustice; they also feel the joy of being used by God to meet needs. That's the kind of experience that changed my life, and it can change their lives as well. The real goal of KBS is to challenge people not only to a summer, but to a whole lifetime of service. Inner-city churches need more than short-term volunteers to build the Kingdom of God amid the desperation and desolation of their neighborhoods. They need committed Christian disciples who are dedicated to nurturing more committed Christian disciples.

That's what churches everywhere need, I think. We can't simply offer people the Gospel and expect them to survive unless we also offer them relationships with mature Christians who will help them to grow. That really is the way of Christ, and it must be our way as well. I guess I got a little carried away there, Dad, but I know that you'll understand. This stuff is important to me.

Every child, every person is sacred because he or she is made in the image of God and is a place where God desires to dwell. I want to do all I can to see to it that more kids, and especially poor kids, have a chance to have relationships that can help them to grow in their relationships to God and become the people He intends for them to be.

I'm glad that you let me have the kind of relationship I had with Phil. I'm glad I have that same kind of relationship with you now. I hope that throughout my life, and especially in my work with Kingdom Builders Supply, I'll be able to provide those kinds of relationships for other people. The world doesn't need any more nominal believers, but it desperately needs more disciples of Jesus Christ.

Love,
Bart

Dear Bart,

Thanks for your letter. It very much confirmed the old cliché that if you want to hold onto somebody, you must learn to let them go. When you moved into your teens I was well aware of what every parent must know, and that is that an adolescent boy must establish his identity over and against that of his father. The same thing is true for mothers and daughters. Every normal kid comes to that point when he or she has to say, "I'm not you! I'm me!" That statement can best be made when there is somebody other than a parent who can provide a model of what that kid would like to be. The time came when you knew you had to be your own self. There was that psychological need to construct an identity different from mine. Even as you faced that task, you were well aware that you could not construct this new identity out of nothing. It was only natural that you should look around and try to construct the new you out of building materials that were readily available in your social world.

Thank God that Phil Thorne was there when you were doing all of this. He was not me, but he was committed to the same Jesus that I love. He had a different kind of personality and a different perspective on how the Christian life should be lived. Nevertheless, he loved you and wanted you to be all that Jesus had called you to be. That you found Phil, or that he found you, was a great relief to me. In the end, I feel sure it was God who arranged for you to meet each other as an answer to my prayers that you would be protected from Satan and his workers. I am thankful to God that you did not resist the relationship with Phil, which I know is largely responsible for your stance in Christ today.

Of course, it was a little hard on me to have a theology and lifestyle prescribed by someone else become dominant for you. Certainly there was some mild irritation on my part at being judged by whatever came out of Phil's mouth. I remember the day you questioned my devotional life because I wasn't reading my Bible and praying with the kind of faithfulness that Phil had prescribed. What was even worse was that Phil was right, and I had to stand corrected by his judgment coming from you. There was even some jealousy associated with seeing how your new-found hero was impacting your life. I suppose if a man can't handle such things, he is far too insecure to be a good father, and he ought to get some counseling on how to be an adult.

What you didn't mention in your letter was that Phil was the youth leader in a church that was different from the one attended by the rest of our family. Getting involved with him and with his youth group meant that on Sundays you went to church without us. Looking back on your high school years, I'm glad that we had the sense to let you go. I think Mom was most affected by your decision. She often wondered if it was OK to split up the family like that. There was even some consideration given to the whole family changing churches. Other families whose kids had been reached by Phil's ministry and whose kids wanted to be a part of his youth group had made that kind of move.

Personally, I think parents are crazy if they don't identify with a church that turns their kids on spiritually. I could never quite figure out how in some parents' minds denominational loyalty takes precedence over the spiritual well-being of their children. Providing a meaningful church experience for kids may be one of the most important tasks for parents of teenagers.

In our case we didn't change churches, but we let you change. We figured that being in a church apart from ours would be a good thing for a kid like you. Too often you had to labor under the weight of being Tony Campolo's son, and being in a church outside of my sphere of influence gave you a chance to develop as a Christian and become a leader without having my shadow looming over you.

As a teenager, you chose Phil, but earlier in your life I often chose those who would act as role models for you and who would exercise influence over you. When you were a little boy, I gave very careful consideration to whom our family would visit and who would be invited to visit us in our home.

At the top of the list was my mother. We visited her often, and you had lots of fun times at her house. My mom was a great storyteller, and most of all she was great at relating the history of the Campolo family. I could count on her to relate the exploits of my youth and to make me look bigger than life. It always surprises me that more grandparents don't grasp that helping their grandchildren to understand their roots and background is one of their primary responsibilities. Your Mom-Mom Campolo was committed to making you sense that you were part of a great family tradition and that it was your responsibility to carry on with honor.

Mom-Mom knew that telling a good story required a certain degree of embellishment and that the reality was never quite as dramatic as she made it out to be. Oral tradition is never pure history; it is far more important than that. The story of a family should always be a glorious tale that is left unfinished so as to invite the young to write new chapters that are worthy of what has gone before. There ought to be a law that prohibits grandparents from running away to Florida in retirement! They should not be allowed to escape from their responsibility to build a sense of family continuity and tradition into their grandchildren. There also ought to be a law that requires parents to regularly take their children to see grandparents so that those who are old can tell those who are young the story of the family! This is crucial if children are to know who they are and what they ought to be.

Both Mom and I put a lot of thought into deciding whom we would invite into our home when you and Lisa were young, being well aware of how impressionable kids are. I was on the faculty of the University of Pennsylvania during the time that Penn had a nationally ranked basketball team. You and all your classmates looked up to these players as superstars. I had some members of the team as students in one of my seminar classes and had come to know them as friends outside of class, so I made sure to invite them to visit us. They were neat guys who treated me with respect and made it clear that there was more to life than basketball. The fact that people you admired thought highly of your parents may have had a lot to do with how you came to view us.

Sociologists in the field of the family have long known of the influence of visitors on the character formation of children, and prominent scholars among them have urged that parents give more attention to who comes and does not come into a child's home. I often recall the story of the way in which a missionary who visited in the home of George Seagraves when he was a boy altered the future of his life. His parents had invited the missionary to have dinner with their family on a Sunday afternoon. After the meal was over, the missionary played with young George for several hours and climaxed their pleasant afternoon by drinking a glass of water while standing on his head. Seeing this "awesome feat" left the boy with an inescapable desire to be a missionary, too. Years later, George Seagraves became a world-famous missionary in Burma, saved countless lives, and led many to know Christ. Such are the consequences of outside influences on children. Parents may not provide all of the major influences that work themselves out in the lives of their children, but they can certainly help to determine who does provide them. In the end that may be the most important influence of all.

Love,
Dad

Six

College: Where It All Comes Together or It All Falls Apart

Dear Bart,

I really tried to get you to go to a Christian college rather than a secular school. Having been a professor of sociology in both kinds of colleges, I was acutely aware of what can happen to impressionable students during four years of higher education. It was one of my greatest fears that some awe-inspiring professor, whose cynicism would make him seem all the more worldly wise, would make Christianity seem like an archaic folk religion to you.

When I was on the faculty of the University of Pennsylvania, I had the chance to observe firsthand several students who started their college training as believers, only to turn into cynics who scoffed at the Christian faith and derided those who held onto their beliefs, as though they belonged to the Flat Earth Society. One day I was discussing religion with one of those students, and I was stunned by the bitter contempt she had toward anything Christian. I can still hear her saying, "I don't know how my parents could have drilled all of that crap into my head."

"Maybe it was because they loved you," I responded. "And maybe it was because they wanted you to know the truth."

"Don't tell me that you believe all of that stuff!" she inquired with an air of heightened disbelief. "How can you accept all those wild Bible stories? How can a person smart enough to know better believe in the Bible?"

My answer to her was simple and direct: "I decided to! And

why *don't* you believe in the Bible and its message of salvation? Isn't it because you decided to reject it? Don't tell me that somebody *proved* to you that the Bible was a pack of fairy tales or that Jesus was never crucified and resurrected from the grave to provide us with salvation. I know better than that. Isn't the real reason that you have decided to turn your back on the Christian faith tied up in the fact that it's not cool to be a believer in academia? Isn't your real reason for turning your back on Jesus due to your fear that your profs might think you a bit quaint and that your fellow students might consider you somewhat unsophisticated?

"Come on," I said to her, "tell the truth. Honest doubt I respect, but when a person turns away from Jesus primarily because being a Christian doesn't go with the version of open-mindedness that has come to be considered the mark of having been educated, I can only bite my tongue and try not to sneer."

In retrospect, I think I was a bit cruel with her, but I do hope that I got her thinking about the real reasons why she said that she no longer believed in the biblical revelation. College professors are often worshiped by students, especially if those students are endeavoring to establish distance between themselves and their parents in the process of going through some kind of late adolescent rebellion. A charismatic professor can provide legitimation for rejecting what religious parents are all about. Identifying with some academic gadfly who makes Christianity seem like a cross between superstition and militaristic racism can enable such young people to think of themselves as superior to old mom and dad and to believe that they have moved beyond the seeming naiveté of their parents.

When I taught at a secular university, I became very aware of how powerful an influence a professor can have over students. In my case, I was able to make having faith appear as a brave and courageous thing. I could set up the arguments in classroom discussions so that not to believe in God made life totally absurd and without any moral basis. I doubt if I made many converts, but to my students Christianity usually became a viable option for a legitimate world-view.

120

A couple of years ago I was walking down the Avenue of the Americas in New York City when a young woman came running up to me exclaiming, "Dr. Campolo! Dr. Campolo! Do you remember me? I had you for Intro to Sociology at Penn. I want you to know," she went on to say, "that the course you taught was an incredible experience for me. That whole year I really believed in God." Such is the power of some of the men and women who serve as college profs. No wonder James the apostle wrote:

Not many of you should presume to be teachers, my brothers, because you know that we who teach will be judged more strictly.

James 3:1, NIV

For those who use the position of academic leadership to destroy faith while playing games that feed their own egos, I can only mention the words of Jesus:

But whoso shall offend one of these little ones which believe in me, it were better for him that a millstone were hanged about his neck and that he were drowned in the depth of the sea.

Matt. 18:6

A Christian college can do much more than just provide professors who can be role models for faith. This is not to minimize the fact that having Christian teachers in some of your most formative years can play a major part in your faith formation, but there is another important reason for taking your college training at a Christian college; namely, the development of a Christian world-view. There are some who still argue that information is neutral and that truth is objective. But ever since scholars began probing the phenomenology of knowledge, there has been an increasingly accepted postulate that information is always selected and arranged to support a particular point of view. There is a growing awareness that the subjective commitments of the knower determine how reality is understood and what truth appears to be. It is not that objective truth does not exist, but rather that the personal convictions of the knower determine how that objective truth is handled and understood.

What all this means is that what a college student is taught is inevitably made to support a particular point of view. At a Christian college, you would have learned to look at things the way Christians do. You would have learned biology in a way that would have affirmed belief in a Creator. You would have learned psychology in a way that would have had you view human beings as moral creatures, responsible for their actions and ultimately answerable to God. In the arts you would have been focused on the religious concerns that gave birth to the music of Bach and the paintings of Michelangelo. You would have discovered that even the existential concerns of secular artists probe ultimate questions that can only be resolved in faith. In short, your entire approach to the world would have been shaped by the Christian faith so that what you learned and what the Bible teaches would be integrated into a unified system of knowledge.

In Christian colleges that remain true to their original purposes, all education supports the theme that Christ is Lord of all. Therefore, in the study of sociology, economics, and political science, there should be an underlying commitment to social justice. The task is not simply to understand the world, but to figure out how to transform it into the kind of world that Jesus wants it to be—in other words, into the Kingdom of God. At its best, the Christian college is not a greenhouse for the safe growth of kids who need protection from the big, bad world, but a boot camp for those who would join a movement that will triumph in history.

Secular universities no longer seem to me to have any real commitment to answering the ultimate questions of human existence such as "Where did we come from?" "Where are we going?" "Why are we here?" As Allan Bloom so strongly contends in his book, *The Closing of the American Mind,* secular universities no longer have any sense of mission or purpose other than that of providing vocational training for those who want to climb the ladders of economic and social success. They have been transformed into the ideal incubators for would-be Yuppies. Bart, the last thing in the world I wanted for you to be was a Yuppie. They seem so boring!

There is one other concern that I had about the college you would attend. A large percentage of those who attend college find their mates there. I wanted you to marry a Christian woman, and I knew that if you attended a Christian school your chances of marrying a Christian would be greatly enhanced. This might seem a bit devious, but it is the hidden agenda for many of us who have tried to guide our kids to Christian colleges—and, what's more, it's a strategy that often works.

But you didn't fall in line with what I wanted you to do. I guess I can't blame you. For years we lived on the campus of Eastern College, where I teach, and I realized long before you made your decision about college that you wanted to sample a different environment. Nevertheless, I did what a parent is supposed to do when trying to get a kid like you turned on to a Christian college: I had you visit the ones I thought would interest you. I sent you to Wheaton, because I felt that there you would find the smartest student body. I sent you to Calvin College because I thought that there you would find the sharpest faculty. I sent you to Furman University because I believed that there you would find a Christian atmosphere which transcended the legalisms that often haunt Christian schools. In the end, you chose Haverford College, a secular school with a Quaker tradition and extremely high academic expectations.

It was interesting to learn why you chose Haverford. You told me that it was because of what the students there talked about during their off hours. The conversations in the dining hall and the student lounges seemed to you to be filled with exciting discussions about world concerns and the urgent issues of the day. In your observations, the talk among students on Christian college campuses seemed trivial by comparison. Regretfully, I have to agree with you. I, too, have noticed the difference, but I think you were judging Christian college students against students of the highest academic caliber that secular schools had to offer. If you had visited most of the state universities and community colleges that I have visited on my speaking tours, you might have thought better of Christian colleges. Nonetheless, it does seem a bit strange to me that students at Christian colleges don't seem more mature. There is a high-schoolish quality in the dispositions of many of them when it comes to academic affairs and social concerns. Perhaps it's because those of us who run Christian colleges tend to treat our students as something less than adults. In any case, I found it difficult to argue with you.

Still, I wish you had gone to a Christian college because I am convinced that there is much more to a college education than academics. At Eastern, for instance, there is a concerted effort to get students involved in ministry. Tutoring programs for ghetto kids, prison ministries, and a variety of Christian groups like Evangelicals for Social Action are aimed at getting our undergraduates involved in meeting the needs of the poor and oppressed. Most other Christian colleges make similar efforts to get their students off campus and into the kind of transforming experiences that privileged kids can have only when they reach out to minister to those who suffer. I believe that college students can only have good minds if they have "dirty hands"—and I wanted you to have "dirty hands" as you worked in the kinds of difficult places where good Christian colleges try to place their students.

The first year at Haverford College didn't seem to go well for you. You failed to be the flashy soccer star you had been in high school; you and the coach never hit it off very well. While most of your classes went well, your work in science courses and your failure to master computers made you something less than a complete success. I think that a lot of kids who are accustomed to easy triumphs in high school experience something of a psychological shock when they discover that they are rather average at a first-rate college. While I know it happens to a lot of kids, it was a particularly painful thing for me to see my own kid going through this adjustment. You didn't seem to handle it all that well. You became strange and difficult to talk to. The old happy-go-lucky Bart was gradually slipping away, and a rather morose new kid seemed to be taking his place.

You were no longer in close contact with the gang you ran with in high school. Those church kids who had formed a close-knit fellowship built on mutual concern and support were no longer part of your daily experience. You were cut off from the kind of spiritual renewal that comes from intimate Christian friends who are there to keep you spiritually faithful and morally straight. The loss of this influence on your life was fairly obvious, and I prayed long hours that the Lord would provide some new means of renewing and sustaining your faith in Christ.

Then came one of my biggest frights. There seemed to me to be some hints that you might be homosexual. Looking back on it now, the whole set of circumstances seems ridiculous. But Haverford College had an attraction for homosexuals. The Quaker tradition of the school had generated an openness and acceptance of people whom society had long persecuted. The administration and faculty of the college had worked hard to overcome the homophobia that seems so rampant in our society. As a consequence of these attitudes and actions, Haverford had become a place where homosexuals could feel at home. You talked about the homosexual behavior of some of the guys in your dorm and how you had unintentionally walked in on some embarrassing and intimate situations in the normal course of your dorm living. The new sullenness that was very uncharacteristic of the old you suggested that something was troubling you. Then you started to wear an earring, which in some circles is interpreted as a sign of a homosexual identity. One day when you were home, you wanted to borrow Mom's nail polish remover. We didn't know what for, but when parents are filled with fear every little thing gets misinterpreted.

I had always tried to teach you that for most people sexual orientation is not a choice. I had tried to explain to you as you were growing up that those who persecute homosexuals—sometimes under religious auspices—are often ignorant of the fact that, in the overwhelming number of cases, whatever biological and sociological factors have imprinted our homosexual brothers and sisters occurred long before there was any self-awareness of what was going on in their lives. Furthermore, I had pointed out that many homosexuals who become Christians still maintain their homosexual orientations and choose lives of celibacy as the primary way to continue life in the evangelical community. I had tried to teach you to respect and love those people who have suffered so much at the hands of uninformed and cruel people. I had preached compassion and understanding of homosexuals. Now, however, the issue was no longer hypothetical for me. It was existential.

Was my kid a homosexual? If so, how would I react? What if I found out you had a homosexual lover? Would I continue to love you as I had told so many parents of homosexual kids to do? Would I be able, in any way, to accept your homosexual lover— even if I believed intellectually that as a Christian I *should* love him regardless of what my religious upbringing had taught me on this matter? You'll never know the hours I walked the floors alone, praying and thinking and working through all of these questions.

In spite of knowing better, I did all the things a typical parent in my place would do. I frequently inquired about your dating life and probably would have welcomed the news that you had gotten sexually involved with some young woman. That's how crazy a so-called enlightened parent can be driven by latent homophobia. Perhaps you remember that I finally had to ask you outright—and I will never forget you answering—"Dad, I'm too heterosexual for my own good!" I sighed a sigh of relief— and then I began to worry about what was implied in that statement. Such are the worries of fathers!

During your second year at Haverford, I felt that I had to do something to rescue you from what I interpreted as spiritual slippage. I wondered whether the liberal theologies you were learning in your religion classes were taking their toll on you. I wondered if, as a consequence, you were becoming cold toward Christianity with all of its moral expectations. Regardless of what might be going on, I was aware that something precious was dying inside you and that something needed to be done to revive you spiritually.

About that time, Glenn Welch, the pastor of a small Methodist church near your college, contacted me and asked if I knew of anybody who would be interested in working with his youth group, and I recommended you. You decided to take the job, and you were great! You got right into your ministry with renewed zeal, and in no time at all you seemed to once again be alive in Christ. I am convinced that getting involved in Christian service is one sure way to foster spiritual renewal in a college kid. I know it worked with you. Between your ministry with youth and the wise counsel of Glenn, a bright and confident Bart once again began to emerge.

Still, all was not well. At the end of your sophomore year at Haverford, you asked if you could take some time off from school. Part of your reasoning had to do with your renewed commitment to ministry. It bothered you that we were spending so much money on your education when there were so many needs out there in the world. You realized that, like so many college students, you were in college only because you couldn't think of anything better to do. Your awareness of the staggering needs in places like Haiti, the Dominican Republic, and Camden, New Jersey, made you think it would be best if you got right to work.

It took some persuading, but you finally convinced me that this would be a good thing. A lot of parents get scared when their kids want to take time off from college and fear that they might never return to finish their education. Looking back on it now, I think that taking time off was a very good thing for you. A lot of college kids haven't the slightest clue as to what they are supposed to be getting out of college. They graduate from high school and are expected to go to college—and so they do. It might have been a good idea if we had given you the chance to take some time off after high school so that you could catch your breath and try to figure out what your life was supposed to be all about. We parents sometimes rush our kids through stages of growth and development when they would be better off passing through them at their own pace. There are times when it is a good thing to let kids come up for air and get their bearings.

It was the end of the summer when we decided that you should take some time off from school. We were fortunate in that it was possible for you to travel and work along with me for a few months. You even enrolled in one of my classes at Eastern. Day in and day out we were together. We talked, exchanged ideas, and learned a lot about each other. You were battling your way to your own identity, and it was a good thing to watch. That was a precious time for me because it was a rare opportunity to get to know my son as the emerging adult who was gradually becoming a partner in ministry.

When you decided to return to school, you had two reasons: you realized that there were some things you needed to know that you could learn in college and you understood that to be able to best help the poor and disadvantaged, you would need the kind of credentials that would merit respect from those who could provide support for your ministry.

You decided that you would take your last two years at Brown University. I wondered how you would ever be accepted because at that time Brown was the hardest school in the country to get into, and its attitude toward transfer students was less than inviting. I thought that if they gave you an interview and looked at your high SAT scores, you would have a pretty good chance. Fortunately, we had a friend with enough influence to get you the interview, and the rest is, as they say, history. Influence can't make a person a success, but it can certainly position that person to take advantage of a chance for success if he or she has what it takes.

I often wonder about all the great kids who have what it takes but never get positioned to show their stuff. In a truly just society, everybody would have the chance to be all that they could be—but it's not a fair world, and it wasn't fair with you. You had some extra things going for you that a lot of other kids don't.

From the beginning, life at Brown went well for you. It wasn't but a few days after you arrived on campus that you made contact with some fellow students who were in Campus Crusade for Christ, a Christian organization that was in high gear on Brown's campus. They swept you into their fellowship, and before long you were leading Bible study groups and sharing your convictions about Christ with others. There was marked growth in your Christian character. When your involvements with Christians led to your getting involved with a ministry in the ghetto of Providence, Rhode Island, I knew that things would be all right for you. I felt relieved. My prayers were being answered.

What I learned from all of this is that attending a secular school can be a time of spiritual growth and service, providing the right contacts are made with fellow students. You never seemed to find the Christian fellowship you needed at Haverford. I know there were good Christians on campus, but for reasons that I do not know, you never seemed to jell with them.

Becoming a vital part of a circle of Christian friends at Brown, however, made all the difference in the world for you. I think that when parents look at the secular schools that their children might attend, they should give special attention to whether or not there is a dynamic Christian group on campus that could provide spiritual nurturance and challenges. There is no guarantee that their children will plug into such groups, but being sure that they exist is the least that parents should consider.

Organizations like InterVarsity Christian Fellowship, Navigators, and Campus Crusade for Christ have chapters on many secular campuses. At some colleges, like Duke University, the chaplain has put together relational groups that keep students alive and growing. Sometimes denominational programs (like the Wesley Foundation at Texas Tech) provide the context for Christian life and witness. After seeing what happened to you at Brown, I wish I had done more investigating as to who was doing what for Christ on campus before the decision was made as to where you would do your college work.

All in all, you came through college in pretty good shape. You took good courses and did a lot of thinking and an awful lot of growing. If I have any real criticism to lend it is that I don't think you took enough advantage of extracurricular activities.

When you were at Haverford, you could have made the basketball team, but you didn't even try out. Perhaps you were afraid to or perhaps you were overreacting to me and my wishes for you. I don't know, but I wish you had. I wish you had gone out for the school paper or student government or something. Nevertheless, you came through college a Christian—and a better one at that. So I had better count my blessings and be proud of what you did become by God's grace and through a lot of hard work on your part.

Love,
Dad

Dear Dad,

You and I will probably never agree about all of this college stuff, but for the record I think I had better register my version of the story even though I don't expect to change your mind. On the one hand, you have taught at a Christian college for more than twenty years now, so it would be pretty disappointing to me if you didn't take that side of the argument. On the other hand, it just may be that your loyalty to Christian higher education keeps you from seeing the other side as clearly as you might. As your loving son, I'll do my best to "enlighten" you and to defend my own choices as well.

You are right, of course, when you point out the dangers of secular colleges and universities for Christian young people. I watched too many of my classmates change from committed Christians to confirmed agnostics during college to pretend that both the academic content and the general lifestyle of such schools are not potentially devastating. As you well know, I almost fell apart at a secular college myself.

But you make it seem as though the major reason Christian students give up their faith has to do with their fear of being scoffed at or dismissed as unsophisticated by the evil hordes of secular humanists waiting to devour the Children of God. I think there definitely are professors out there who love to "deprogram" Christians, but I also think that there is usually a lot more at stake in the battle for the mind than academic coolness or acceptance. Every student who encounters radical doubts as a result of his or her academic pursuits is not impressionable or naive, Dad, and I think you know that. An intelligent person armed with a developing critical perspective cannot help but encounter very real problems with mainstream Christianity, no matter how strong their relationship with God may be. Unless, of course, they refuse to examine anything that is not already preinterpreted into the Christian tradition and deemed safe to consider.

When I was at Haverford, and especially when I was at Brown, I had to face not only the great Christian thinkers of history, but the great secular thinkers as well. What is more, my professors were not predisposed to magnify the strengths of the former or the weaknesses of the latter in order to maintain the delicate workings of a particular theological system. They had their biases to be sure—some were even Christians—but as scholars they sought to focus on the merits of the idea in question, instead of on making sure that it would fit into some specific world-view. You say that was a danger, and I must agree with you.

Regardless of what some people believe, everyone who is not a Christian is not an utter fool. Evolution is not absurd. The Bible is not without ambiguity, and its origins are not above being seriously questioned. Everything in other religions is not godless fabrication and foolishness, and Christians have no corner on faith or sincerity or love. People who are pro-choice are not evil, and abortion is not a simple issue with a simple answer.

The secular world is not all wrong, Dad. That is what your book, *Partly Right,* is all about. In college, I had to face an array of new ideas, some of which were very compelling. Instead of accepting somebody else's entire system, I had to judge things on their own merits and decide for myself what was true. I had to work out my own salvation with fear and trembling because there was no one there to work it out for me. It was scary sometimes. While there was tremendous risk in that process, there was also tremendous potential for growth.

132

You told that student of yours who said, "I don't know how my parents could have drilled all that crap into my head," that it might have been because her parents wanted her to know the truth. But how did you know what her parents had taught her in the name of Christianity?

I shudder when I think of some of the things I picked up from other people in my early days as a Christian. I heard prejudices and preferences that were turned into doctrines and interpretations of Scripture that justified sin instead of inspiring repentance. I was once told that everything that happened was God's will—just before I went to Haiti and saw little twelve-year-old girls being sold into prostitution to feed their starving brothers and sisters. I often heard it said that God prospered the people who loved Him—even though I know many rich sinners and have seen beautiful, obedient Christians dying in poverty.

Now that stuff really *is* crap, Dad, but to me it was Christianity, too, until I learned different. Maybe at Eastern, someone would have set me straight, but at some other Christian colleges, maybe not. There was no question, though, that in the glare of secular academia such "truths" could not conceal their falsehood. College is dangerous to be sure. It forced me to question everything I had blindly accepted up until then, but what was ultimately rejected was not the Truth at all. And the faith that emerged in me was strong, because I had done what Paul says to do in 1 Thess. 5:19–22, "Do not put out the Spirit's fire; do not treat prophecies with contempt. Test everything. Hold onto the good."

The difference between almost losing my faith at Haverford and thriving as a Christian at Brown wasn't that I stopped testing everything. The difference was that at Brown I kept the Spirit's fire burning in my life. Your letter talked about the fellowship at Brown in glowing terms, and there was a lot happening there, but to tell you the truth, Dad, I wasn't as involved with those groups as you thought I was. They are great for some people, but they were a little too rigid in their beliefs for me.

As I have said, I was not taking anything for granted in college, so I was not very comfortable with people whom I perceived as having made up their minds before they knew all the facts. Still, I didn't need to agree with them about everything to appreciate their sincere faith and excitement, so I went to their meetings once in a while to share the joy of praising God together.

What really kept me going at Brown, though, was my friendship with Jerry White. How we got to be friends is a long story involving a girl whom both of us liked and neither of us wound up with in the end, but what emerged from our rivalry was a strong bond. Like me, Jerry was encountering the doubts and confusion that often go along with sincere thinking, but he didn't seem to be in danger of slipping away from God. We would talk for hours, or study and debate all day long, but he always made sure that we did it from inside our faith. Uncertain as we sometimes were, he made sure we read our Bibles (as listeners—not as students), went to church, and even shared our faith. He got me to pray with him, too, more than I have ever prayed before or since, and as we prayed, God became wonderfully present even in my doubts. We encountered ideas that shook us to our foundations and changed the way we thought about everything. But together we worked out a faith that made sense to us. Deep down I think God put Jerry at Brown just for me, because more than anyone else, he kept my thinking from putting out the Spirit's fire. When college was over, by the grace of God, I had held onto the good.

I did not think enough about how I was going to face the dangers of attending a secular college, which is why it almost did me in. As you said in your letter, there was a lot more going on there than what happened in the classroom and the library, and I didn't handle any of it very well at first.

The lifestyle of a college student is selfish by its very nature. You eat, sleep, read, work, go to class, and do everything else on your own schedule, concerned only with your own grades and your own welfare. At a secular school that selfishness can very quickly turn into decadence as well. The academic demands at Haverford and Brown were intense, but somehow that didn't keep students from doing a lot of drinking and a lot of sleeping around. People seldom dated steadily, but there were a lot of one-night stands. Drugs and alcohol were abused with impunity. If fact, there was a generally permissive attitude toward anything that did not adversely affect your GPA.

Anytime you find yourself in an atmosphere without limits there is great potential for trouble. Frankly, the lifestyle issues of college were much more dangerous to me than anything I encountered in my classes because, cut off from all the factors that had kept me on the straight and narrow through high school, I found that I had far less discipline than I had given myself credit for. Without my support group to check up on me, or parents to know where I was spending the night, or even a longtime reputation and Christian witness to uphold, I had only my will to rely on for the first time in my life. As you might imagine, my will wasn't up to snuff after so little use, and I quickly found myself doing things I knew were not God's will for me.

That kind of moral crisis, of course, had a tremendous effect on the intellectual issues I was facing at the same time. It is a lot easier to find fault with a faith you are no longer living out, and it is a lot harder to believe in a God you are no longer obeying. College students often make the mistake of thinking that they can separate what they do from what they think and believe, but that sort of mind/body dichotomy is an intellectual myth. Physical sin affects what you think, and mental sin affects how you feel because the two sides of our lives are inexorably tied up together. It is no accident that when people begin to do what they know is wrong, they often begin to be unsure of what they know. That is what happened to me, I'm afraid, and that is why working at Glenn Welch's church saved me. Getting involved in ministry again forced me to clean up my act.

Having conceded that attending a secular college can be a great risk for a committed Christian, let me make one thing perfectly clear: It was a lot safer for me than attending a Christian college.

I was still a fairly new believer when, as a senior in high school, you sent me to visit schools. The thing I most remember was my amazement at how taken for granted Christianity was on those Christian college campuses. Here I was, filled to over-flowing with dreams and plans and questions and stories amidst hundreds of kids who had seen it all and heard it all a million times before. It wasn't just that most of them were intellectually uninspired or shallow—beyond that, they were bored with what mattered more than anything in the world to me.

The guys had the same girlie posters hanging in their rooms as at the secular schools, but they bothered me more. People slept through chapel, and it seemed to me it would have been better not to have required chapel at all. The dormitory Bible studies I sat in on were dead. The kids' spiritual lives seemed dead. The whole atmosphere was dead.

Now I was surely one hyperjudgmental high-school kid at the time, Dad, and I don't claim to have gotten the whole picture, but what I did see frightened me. In my secular high school I had taken a stand for Jesus and was in no danger of taking Him for granted. These Christian colleges, however, seemed to have the potential to do something even worse than attacking my faith—they could make it seem boring. No, I thought, I'll take my chances in the real world, where I can talk about my faith out in the open, to believers and nonbelievers alike, without the fear of boring somebody who has been jaded by overexposure to the joy of it all.

Besides, it also bothered me that those Christian colleges had what you call a Christian world-view. A world-view is some-thing that I believe an individual is supposed to develop in the context of his or her relationship with God, rather than simply accept from an institution. I wanted a school that would teach me how to read and write and think critically, not one that would impart to me a prepackaged set of ideas and interpretations. Maybe this isn't what Christian colleges do, but it certainly seemed that way to me. I know that most Christian schools may not consciously attempt to indoctrinate their students with a par-ticular system of thought, but all those institutional statements of faith worried me nevertheless. At a secular school I knew there would be a variety of perspectives, and I felt a whole lot safer in the middle of an argument than in the middle of what I perceived to be a conspiracy. I may have been grossly unfair—but I think I was also partly right.

My final consideration was purely elitist. I wanted to go to a top school with top professors and top students, and my perception was, and is, that to do that I had to go to a secular school. For whatever reasons, even the best Christian colleges do not carry with them the prestige or the traditions of academic excellence that the upper echelon of secular private colleges have. I was committed to developing my mind to its fullest potential, and no Christian school I visited seemed as singularly committed to intellectual achievement as the finest secular schools.

For all of the trials and tribulations of my college experience, I'm still convinced of this much: I did well to go the route of the secular college. I could have done better, of course, but God was gracious to me, and in the end I think I chose the better path for myself. I won't lie to you, Dad, and tell you that what was right for me is right for every kid. The truth is that every year I send high-school seniors to places like Eastern and Calvin and Seattle Pacific College because I recognize the advantages you outlined in your letter. We may disagree about my case specifically, but we are in full agreement on the most important thing about choosing a college. The ultimate criteria must always be whether a particular school is going to inspire the student to reach his or her fullest potential as a servant of the Kingdom of God.

Love,
Bart

P.S. I was hurt and very angry the night you asked me if I was a homosexual. I thought that you should have known better. I felt as though somehow I had been attacked. At the least, I felt unfairly challenged. But a few hours later I realized what you had been trying to do.

It is a painful thing to be gay in this world, especially if you are a Christian. There is little understanding and even less compassion. If I were gay, it would have been very hard for me to tell you and Mom about it and risk your rejection. I would have felt isolated, alone with my secret, but probably I would have kept it to myself for fear of losing your acceptance.

But just before you asked me about being a homosexual, both you and Mom let me know that regardless of how I answered, your love for me would not change. You wanted to know, not judge me, and only so you could understand what I was going through. You wanted to be sure that I was not left alone.

As it happens, I am not gay. But it always meant a lot to me to know that I could have been without losing you. God help the child who does not know that.

Seven

Flying Like an Eagle
When You Feel Like a Turkey

Dear Dad,

I think you're going to like this letter. At least I hope you do, because it's about the one thing that I think you were the very best at when I was growing up. I know that you don't consider yourself the perfect father, and as much as I would like to disagree with you, I'm afraid that you're probably right about that (which is why it's so difficult for me to understand how, in spite of yourself, you managed to produce a perfect son!). Whatever else you may have failed to do, Dad, you succeeded in making me believe without a doubt that I was the most essentially wonderful person you had ever laid your eyes on and that anyone who failed to recognize my inestimable value was simply oblivious to the obvious. You made me absolutely sure of myself. And that, more than anything else, has made all the difference in my life.

I know that some people think parenthood is all about instilling the proper principles, developing discipline, and setting a good example, but when everything is said and done, I think it has more to do with creating an indestructible sense of personal significance in a child who is going to need it for the rest of his life.

The more I become involved with ministry, the more I see that the world is a dangerous and hurtful place, filled with broken people who have been overcome and victimized because they lack an understanding of their own value. Regardless of background, everybody experiences failures and disappointments from time to time, and it is hard not to be discouraged or to despair. How people see themselves has a lot to do with how they approach those troubles and whether or not they are able to deal with them. How people see themselves has a lot to do with the other people around them, especially as they are growing up.

You are the first person who taught me that, back when I was a little kid sitting in on your sociology lectures at the University of Pennsylvania. I was only nine years old at the time, but I can still remember you explaining Charles Cooley's theory of the Looking Glass Self to the class and how proud I was that I could understand it. It's a pretty simple concept. The basic idea is that how a person sees himself is largely determined by how he thinks the most important people in his world see him. These people are what Cooley calls "significant others."

I didn't realize it then, but as I sat in that classroom, I was already looking at my most significant other. What I saw in your eyes was that I was unbelievably precious to you. A lot has happened between then and now, of course, but I have relied over and over again on that sense of personal significance which both you and Mom gave to me. I never needed it—or both of you—more than when I first moved to Minneapolis to be a youth pastor.

I have already said that the most crucial task for parents is making kids feel that they are infinitely valuable. We are beloved children of God. He sent His own son to redeem us. As Paul puts it, each of us was "bought at a price," and since that price was the life of Jesus Himself, we should have no doubt of our worth on any standard. That doesn't mean that we should have delusions of grandeur, though, or think that we are more than we are. "If a man thinks he is something when he is nothing, he deceives himself" (Gal. 6:3). The flip side to our infinite value is the recognition that we are people with serious limitations.

When I came out of college, I'm afraid I was a long way from that sort of recognition, perhaps because I hadn't yet come up against anything I wanted to do that I couldn't get done. I hate to say that I was arrogant, but I was at the very least a cocky guy who thought he had the world by the tail. I had an Ivy League education, a pretty girlfriend, an exciting new job at a prestigious inner-city church, and, I soon found out, a lot to learn.

It didn't take long for my lessons to begin. Almost from the moment I arrived at Park Avenue, I was in trouble. At first it seemed as though most of it came from things I couldn't control. The pastor in charge of the youth ministry had teamed me up with another guy on the staff, but just as we began to click as partners, the two of them became involved in a major disagreement that caused all sorts of division within the church and among the street kids we were working with. All of a sudden, my supervisor and my new buddy were completely at odds with one another. Before I knew what I was doing, I threw myself into the middle and began trying to mediate between the two. In my youthful arrogance, I was sure that I could solve everybody's problems in short order.

In fact, all I accomplished for my efforts was to undermine both my boss' and my coworker's confidence and trust in me— even though I wasn't part of the original disagreement. All my efforts failed to make things better, and some actually made things worse. In the end, my coworker left the church, but not before both he and my boss had been through a spiritual and emotional wringer. I don't think I really understood why Satan is called the author of confusion until I experienced the pain and futility of that struggle, which yielded nothing good at all.

Those problems left me feeling very much alone in a new city, where it seemed like everyone I knew was mad at me. I had tried to help, but I only made things worse for everyone—and I didn't even have a shoulder to cry on. I remember calling home to ask for advice and finding that I couldn't even explain what was happening to me because you and Mom didn't know the people involved. I must have sounded pretty paranoid, I suppose, because what you told me was to stop complaining and concentrate on the ministry instead.

Unfortunately, my ministry wasn't going any better. I had always excelled as a camp counselor and youth speaker, so I assumed that I would be a great youth pastor. The kids at Park

Avenue liked me, and I liked them. I figured I was home free. I quickly realized, however, that there is more to youth ministry than entertaining a bunch of high-school kids. The more aware I became of what I was supposed to be doing, the more I saw that I was failing. The kids in our neighborhood needed more than a Peter Pan-type of youth worker who could get them to think that being a Christian was cool—they needed someone who could patiently guide them beyond emotional conversions into solid relationships with God based on the example of Jesus Christ. They needed a pastor, and, to my dismay, I quickly learned that pastoring is not something I do very well.

I thank God that he provided two *real* youth pastors—John Hall and Brent Bromstrup—who were willing to guide, encourage, and teach me during our weekly lunches together. Without those faithful brothers, I don't think I would have accomplished anything at all. The rest of the staff at the church gave me a lot of support, too. Despite all their help, I felt like a hippopotamus trying to tap dance. Somehow God did His own thing in spite of my inadequacies. I saw kids come to know God, and I saw kids grow, but I never stopped feeling like I was a failure at my job, which was especially hard for me because I had never known anything but success until then. I went from being on top of the world to being alone and ineffective in a matter of months. To make matters worse, my girlfriend called to let me know she wasn't my girlfriend anymore. I had been dumped.

I don't know if it sounds as bad to you as it was for me, but for a long time I wondered how I could go on. Even God seemed far away then, and I felt I had completely lost my bearings and was lost at sea. Maybe it seems strange that a youth pastor who was joyously preaching salvation and the love of God was teetering on the edge of despair, but there I was. A light wind would have knocked me over. Then, you and Mom and Lisa showed up.

That family visit to Minneapolis was one of the best weeks of my life. I don't know if any of you knew the way I had begun to think about myself; you couldn't have done anything better if you had. You met everybody, of course, and you heard me out as we toured the city. It did me a world of good just to unburden myself with people who I knew cared about me, to know that my problems were your problems, too.

Even more importantly, you treated me as though I was the same successful person I had been when I left home, instead of like the complete failure I felt like just then. I remember your saying, "We are proud of you," more often than usual, and assuring me that if I couldn't make a go of it there, I could come home and work for you, Dad, because you always needed a person like me.

Lisa, ever the lawyer, took my side and made everybody else out to be a villain, even though my situation was nobody's fault but my own. "You're part of the natural aristocracy, kid, the elite," she told me, knowing I needed to hear it even if it wasn't true. "These people don't appreciate your unique greatness."

Most important of all was Mom, who thought it all through and, right before you left, gave me a pep talk that I'll never forget.

"Bart," she said, "you don't have to just stay here and feel helpless and defeated. You are a smart young man and a loving young man. But right now you have stopped looking at the people around you as people to be creatively loved, and you have started to see them only as part of a situation that is hurting you. You've become selfish. That isn't like you. You can certainly come home if you need to, but before you do, I think you need to see what God has brought you here to learn, and who He has brought you here to love and care for. Maybe you won't be a big star to everybody else, after all. But Dad and I believe in you, and we think you can make it here if you remember who you are."

That visit changed everything for me. The situations did not resolve themselves overnight, of course. When you left I faced the same problems with the same deficiencies I had before (and still have). My attitude, though, was transformed because I knew that even though I might fail sometimes, I still was infinitely valuable. Even though I couldn't solve everything, I had the ability to make a difference wherever I happened to be. Together, you reminded me of my indestructible sense of personal significance.

That was a turning point in my life. I grew up a lot at Park Avenue, and the people there were patient with me through it all. That pastor, Art Erickson, became a close and valued friend, and God worked mightily in the lives of young people even though I wasn't the most gifted youth worker in the world. Best of all, it was at Park Avenue that I met Marty Thorpe, who is now my altogether wonderful wife. In retrospect, none of that would have happened if I had not had the sense of personal significance that our family helped me to find again—I had it to begin with because you had given it to me. I know that I am infinitely precious because for as long as I can remember I have been infinitely precious to you.

You see, Dad, the things that mattered the most to me when I was a boy, and that still matter the most today, were those times when you let me know that I was your highest priority in the world. Over and over again, you said things and did things that made me sure that I was more important to you than your work, your money, your possessions, your adult friends, and even yourself. (I've thought about it, and the only ones I didn't feel more important than were Mom and Lisa. But Mom and you seemed like one entity, so that didn't really count, and you somehow made Lisa seem like someone you and I should love together, instead of like someone I was competing with.)

I doubt you even remember most of the episodes that made the biggest impressions on me, because they were not the "big events" of my childhood. Rather it was little offhanded comments and casual decisions that let me know who I was and where I stood. Like when we were driving to a church where you were going to preach before we went on to see an afternoon automobile race, and you told me that you would rather go with me than any of your grown-up friends because I was more fun to be with. You probably do not recall exactly what happened that Sunday. I do. It was the Langhorne 150, and Bobby Unser won in the Bardahl Special after Mario Andretti's STP Racer had a flat tire with twenty laps to go. I don't know very much about any of the countless other races we saw together when I was a kid, but that whole day was magical to me after you said that, and I remember every detail.

Later on, when I was seventeen and a new driver, I smashed up cars as though I were racing in the Langhorne 150 myself. Practically every time I drove, I managed to hit something. I had five accidents in three months before you realized that you had to take my license away because I was such a danger to myself and everyone else. Even so, you never said a word about the cars themselves except, "Cars can be replaced—you can't." I paid you back for the repairs as I remember, but that wasn't the point. The point was that I mattered to you more than those cars. The last accident was a bad one, so frightening to me that I barely spoke afterward. When I came home I was embarrassed and dazed. You took me out to shoot baskets that afternoon. I got the message. So what if I couldn't drive—I was still okay with you.

I know you probably remember the important milestones, like family vacations and my first date and both my graduations, but what I remember is that once you flew back from Chicago and drove straight to the field to be at one of my high-school soccer games and then flew right back again to finish your job in Chicago. You missed a night's sleep because you knew how much your being at that game mattered to me. I remember that stuff because it is what convinced me that, no matter what happened, I definitely counted for something.

Sometimes it's hard for a kid to believe that he counts, you know. A lot of bad things happen. Being beaten up at school can really destroy a kid's self-esteem and rob him of any sense of joy. I know that because when I was in sixth grade, I was beaten up on an almost daily basis. It was as much a part of my school day as lunch, and there was nothing I could do about it except wait until I either got bigger or we moved to another state. I was a little kid with a big mouth—a fatal combination in junior high. In elementary school the biggest kid in the class, Daniel Keough, had been my friend and protected me from harm, but Daniel ended up assigned to a different building altogether in junior high, and from then on I was a walking target. Even when the other guys got tired of pounding me, it didn't stop—the girls beat me up.

I can laugh about it now, but that was a terrible year for me. I hated going to school, and I walked the halls in fear of the numerous bullies who took turns making my life miserable. I know I told you about some of the beatings I took, Dad, but I couldn't tell you about all of them because I was so embarrassed. It was humiliating to be so vulnerable, and I especially did not want you to know about it because of the stories you had told me about your own childhood. You never got beat up unless there was more than one guy, and even then you made them pay for it. You were tough. I was scared and ashamed of it.

One day, my teacher called me out of class and sent me to the principal's office. I hadn't done anything wrong, but I was worried anyway—you *always* worry when they call you to the principal's office. When I got there, though, you were standing at the desk signing me out of school for a "family emergency." Some emergency—you took me out to eat lunch in a deli and then we went to an afternoon movie, which I liked so much that we sat through the second show. "School," you said, "is never as important as you are."

The reason those things made such a deep impression on me was because I knew you had chosen me over other things. Whenever you demonstrated your priorities, where things stood relative to one another in your life, I found that I was way up at the top. You had other things to worry about, of course, but none of them mattered more than I did. I have my own set of priorities now, and it's not the same as yours except right at the top. There, where the most important things in life are arranged, you and I are remarkably similar. If I ever have a son, I want him to have experiences like I did, where he cannot miss the realization that, at least to his father, he is infinitely more valuable than anything in the world.

There is something else that you gave me that I want to give to my son, so when the world defeats him he will not be destroyed. Along with the knowledge that he is infinitely valuable, I want him to realize that he can make a difference in his world, no matter what the situation may be.

In the end, it is undoubtedly the belief that our actions and decisions matter and can change things that gives our lives meaning and purpose. Armed with that belief, people can face the most overwhelming situation with hope, knowing that, win or lose, they have the potential to act instead of simply being acted upon. Without it, even people in the midst of great blessings cannot feel secure because they are always at the mercy of the people and circumstances that surround them. Unless we believe we can affect the world, we are bound to become its victims.

When I first met Marty, she was a counselor for chemically dependent women, most of whom were also poor. Every woman's story was different in some ways, but there was always one common feature: these women had all stopped believing that they controlled their own lives. People who give up that belief are bound to become somebody's victims. They can only react to the world and never act on it themselves.

I didn't start out believing I could make a difference, of course. No one does. We are born utterly dependent, unable to do anything at all for ourselves—except make a mess (which we do quite well). Gradually I became more independent, but as I grew up I experienced periodic reminders of my extensive limitations. Like getting lost in a shopping mall . . . running away from home when I was seven and realizing I had nowhere to go . . . getting punished . . . or finding out at the age of eighteen that you did not *have* to put me through college. You did not even have to feed me anymore. Indeed, growing up with someone as powerful as you for my father, it was easy for me to believe that, far from being capable of changing the world, I wasn't really able to do much of anything important. You, however, could do anything and everything. At least I always thought you could when I was a boy.

You and Mom both went to great lengths to show me that I was wrong, that I could make a difference, and that I could do things that you or Mom or anybody else in the world could never do, because God had made me.

When I was in the second grade, there was a new kid in my class named Larry. Larry was different from the other kids, and everybody disliked him from the moment he arrived. Looking back, I am sure he had a learning disability, but all I knew then was that he talked strangely, dressed badly, and wasn't very good at anything. Even Miss Hutchinson, our teacher, seemed to wish he would go away.

We were learning to read that year, using flash cards, and when it was Larry's turn he would miss the words so badly that we all thought he was doing it on purpose. Try as she might, nothing Miss Hutchinson did could make him understand. Day after day, I watched him miss as the class laughed at his efforts.

It was even worse for Larry on the playground. We excluded him from our games with the special cruelty of youth. Once in a while somebody picked a fight with him just so the rest of us could make fun of his wild lunges and strange noises. It bothered me to see him so mistreated, but because my own position among the other kids was fairly insecure, I held my tongue.

It went on like that until, one day, Miss Hutchinson lost her patience. As Larry missed yet another word, and the class dissolved into giggles, he tried to cover his embarrassment by joining in the laughter. Suddenly, Miss Hutchinson rushed up to him, grabbed him by the hair and pulled his head back so he was looking straight up, with his mouth wide open. "Stop it!" she hissed, as the classroom fell silent, "Stop it right now! Now you . . . sit down!" She released him, and he slouched into his seat. The class was back to normal before too long, but I wasn't.

By the time I got home, I was so upset, I blurted out the whole story to you and Mom the moment I came through the door. I don't know what I expected you to do, but it certainly wasn't what you did. You told me that you couldn't say anything to Miss Hutchinson because you had not been there, but that if I wanted to talk to her, you would come and be there with me.

Sure enough, the next morning we went to school early, and I went in to face her while you stood in the doorway, watching and making me brave. I told her how upset I was and how bad I felt about what she had done to Larry, and when I was done she took a deep breath. I was right, she said, and she was sorry for losing her temper. She promised me that she would apologize to Larry, and then we even talked about ways we could both try to be kinder to him. She even thanked me for caring enough to come and talk to her.

That was the first time I believed I could make a difference, and it gave me a strange sensation of power. Miss Hutchinson was kinder to Larry, and so was I. We became friends that year.

Although Larry was never the most popular boy in the second grade, he ceased to be an outcast, and he did have some happy moments. Later on, he came to my birthday party, and I think it was the only one he was invited to all year. Lisa always orchestrated my parties with great style, and that year she rigged it so Larry even won some of the games. There is a photograph of that party, and in it there is one little face smiling a strange, wild smile.

I wonder what became of Larry after that year. Miss Hutchinson became my favorite teacher of all time. After all, she was part of the most important lesson I ever learned: Bart Campolo was not only valuable, he also had the capability to be an effective force for good in the world.

Mom took me along to visit her elderly friends in order to teach me the same thing. I didn't like those visits at first, but she insisted that I go with her anyway and always told me how much my being there meant to the old women we visited. It was boring, usually, sitting around talking and being polite, but once I saw that she was right, that those visits were bright spots in those people's routinized lives, trying to charm them became the best kind of child's game for me. Once again, I felt powerful. There was something important I could do that simply would not be done if I did not do it, and I liked that. I still do.

Knowing I could make a difference for other people helped me to believe I could change my own circumstances, too. Years after my experience with Larry and Miss Hutchinson, I came up against a basketball coach from the old school of motivation-through-fear. You know, Dad, it seems unfair that I inherited your baldness, but missed out on your thick skin. Before long Coach Jackson's style had turned this sensitive little kid into an emotional wreck.

I did my best to take it like a man (whatever that means), but I always came home gloomy and depressed. I felt victimized by his constant threats and insults, but helpless to do anything about it. It is one thing to take a stand for someone else, but another thing completely to face up to your own tormentor. Finally, though, Coach Jackson went too far.

In the middle of a big game, he pulled me out for making a mental error. In front of the entire team, my mother, *and* my grandmother, he swore at me and told me that my head was in a location where, anatomically speaking, I knew it could not have been. I was utterly humiliated and by the time the game was over all I wanted was to quit the team and be done with it.

You, ever sensitive to my emotional discomfort, forbade it. I could only quit, you said, *after* I confronted Coach Jackson with my objections to his treatment of me. Since such a move was clearly suicidal, I figured that you had simply grown bored with fatherhood and were looking for a way out—and I noted that this time you didn't offer to go along with me. But I went anyway.

Coach Jackson wasn't quite as compassionate as Miss Hutchinson had been, but he understood enough of what I said to promise to lay off. "I was only trying to get you to play your best," he said, and I am sure that that was true. In any case, things got better.

Even if he hadn't listened to me, just saying what I did transformed the entire situation for me. I was no longer a helpless victim in my own mind. I learned that I could act. People do not always treat me the way I would like to be treated, but the things you taught me to believe about myself let me recognize that I do not deserve to be treated badly, and I do not have to accept it.

I see so many people here in the city, especially women, who are abused and victimized because they have forgotten or have never known their infinite value and their capability to make a difference in their own lives and in the lives of other people. They are susceptible to evil in whatever form it approaches them because they see themselves as people who deserve to be abused and who are unable to do anything to escape that abuse when it comes.

I once asked a friend of mine, a former prostitute, how she began, how she came to be exploited by strangers. What I found out was that she had been so sexually abused as a child that she had lost any sense of her own value. Made to believe she deserved to be hurt, she found herself in one bad relationship after another until finally a man approached her who told her she was pretty and that he loved her and wanted to take care of her. "I was so messed up, and he took me in. He was the first person who ever really loved me." She believed in that man, too, even though he was a pimp who sent her out to earn him money each night with her body. He told her that she was his girl, and she believed him because she didn't know any better.

There's one more thing to be said about the indestructible sense of personal significance that you gave to me: it made it a whole lot easier for me to become a Christian.

It's so hard for some people to believe that they were created to be part of the Kingdom of God because they feel worthless by worldly standards. Yet God did create them, and that fact alone endows them with the worth that comes from being the handiwork of the Almighty.

For others, it is unthinkable that someone would love them so much that He would sacrifice His own life to save theirs, because no one has ever placed them anywhere so high on a list of priorities. John 3:16 notwithstanding, they don't realize that Jesus' love for each of us is relentless and pure and that we're so precious to Him that He died to take away the sins that otherwise would have separated us from Him forever.

Even many who believe in the love of God find it unbelievable that they can make a decision to accept that love and become a new creation in the process. Yet that is exactly what God calls us to do; that is what His power working in our lives allows us to do if we let it. We not only become His children but also His servants, through whom He can change the lives of others and the world itself.

For me, though, all that stuff was easy. The Gospel was the natural extension of a love I had experienced all my life. It was the ultimate, infinite expression of realities that had been expressed to me for as long as I could remember: I had value—I was worth making sacrifices for—and I could make decisions that could change my life and the lives of other people.

Since I became a Christian, there have been all sorts of doubts and difficulties, and I have often found the peripheral issues of the faith hard to reconcile. At the center of it all, though, is the Good News of the love of God in the person of Jesus Christ, and the call to be transformed into a new creation. That was and is easy for me to understand and embrace. Thanks, Dad.

Love,
Bart

Dear Bart,

Your letter makes me think that I did something right in raising you. Making a kid believe in himself is be one of the most important things that a father can do for his son. This is especially true during those years when a boy's father is his "significant other." During those years what a boy thinks of himself is dependent upon what he thinks his father thinks of him.

Making you feel good about yourself was a more difficult task than you suspect. I wanted to build up your self-confidence without making you cocky—and with teenagers there is a very fine line between the two. Like most kids in their teens, you seemed to fluctuate between thinking too highly of yourself and being down on yourself. Let me remind you of a series of events that brilliantly illustrates what I mean.

You had it all going for you in your senior year in high school. You were a star soccer player, and, after taking your SAT tests, you were declared a National Merit Scholar. There was a special scholarship available at a very prestigious college for students who had this combination of abilities. You and I were both convinced that you were going to win that scholarship. There was only one thing standing between you and what would have amounted to a free $50,000 education, and that was an interview with the awards committee. Your ease with people and your gift of gab made both of us overconfident, and I believe your overconfidence was your downfall. It was hard for both of us when the committee passed over you. So far as I could figure, you lost out because the committee thought you were a little too sure of yourself and maybe even a bit arrogant.

When you got the news of being rejected, you went into a depression that was nothing less than horrible. Mom and I really got worried about you. You had lost something. The old Bart seemed to be gone, and the new one was shaky. Your depression was taking a spiritual toll on you, too. I had the sense that you felt that God was a million miles away from you.

For the next few months you seemed to be going nowhere fast. The early summer following your graduation from high school was particularly painful. You were joyless and seemed devoid of any kind of ambition. A good job was nowhere to be found, and being unemployed only added to your sense of woe. I knew that I had to do something to help restore you to that properly balanced kid who once had had it all together. It was time for me to consider some viable options.

Toward the end of June, I called some of my friends who had connections. I figured that if you had a good job and earned some decent money, you might be able to climb out of the doldrums. Partly through my efforts, you got a job at a warehouse for a camera company. Things, however, didn't get much better for you. Because of your careless driving and numerous accidents, we felt we could no longer maintain car insurance for you, and that meant you had a twenty-mile round trip to and from work each day on your bike. You really had a tough time of it and came home incredibly depressed, especially on rainy days.

I wasn't surprised that you had the kind of driving record that had gotten you into this mess. Sometimes when a person is down on himself, he will unconsciously self-destruct. There are enough psychological studies to verify this claim for anyone who doubts it. Someone in a deeply negative state of mind can even be subconsciously suicidal in ways that contribute to his being accident-prone.

When summer ended and you started in at Haverford College, I thought things would get better, but they didn't. You returned to school early to go out for the soccer team, but a reaction to a bee sting plus a sprained knee put you out of commission and kept your collegiate sports career from ever getting off the ground. You were severely affected—much more than I think you realize. Mom and I walked the floors at night wondering and talking about how we could get you out of it. Most of all, we prayed.

A breakthrough came when a pastor friend of mine, Glenn Welch, contacted me and told me that he needed someone to help him with the youth work at his church. I immediately thought of you. I not only knew that you could do the job, but I saw the position as an opportunity for you to regain your self-confidence.

At first, I thought that you might not accept the position. You hemmed and hawed when we discussed the matter. Your best excuse was that you didn't have a car, and a car would be needed if you were to work as a youth minister in a suburban church. I offered you my car. I was so desperate to see you take this position that I would have done anything in my power to make it attractive to you. In the end, I didn't have to do too much. You got together the money to buy an ancient Dodge, and you were on your way.

From the first week you worked at Christ United Methodist Church, things picked up. Kids who hadn't been attending youth meetings for months started turning out because you made church fun for them. Glenn told me that your enthusiasm was contagious, and in just a few weeks you had the youth program in high gear. Teenagers were coming to know Christ in a new and personal way. Parents were raving about the time and interest you spent on their kids. I was pleased with the reports, but what really thrilled me was the change in your attitude and demeanor. Success in youth work had gotten your juices going again, and your self-confidence was more than restored. You were on a roll again.

There is no doubt that getting you into a situation where you could do something you could be proud of and that others would praise had more to do with building you up than anything

I could have said or done for you directly. If you thank me for believing in you, I can only say that it was easy to believe in you. You had more abilities than I ever dreamed of having at your age. It was only a matter of getting you into a context where you could do your thing without being under pressure. Glenn Welch and that wonderful church of his gave you that chance, and Mom and I will always be grateful to them for that.

The fact that I was able to influence your sense of self-worth so heavily was due to your love for me. You had made me into what we sociologists would call your "significant other." In other words, you had made me into that person who was so important to you that what you thought of yourself was highly determined by what you thought I thought of you. You honored me and trusted me by doing that. I do not know for sure how I was able to get you to do this, or even if I was primarily responsible for engineering your feelings, but I was well aware that you looked up to me and that I could easily have created destructive disillusionment had I behaved in a way that disgraced you or hurt you. As a father, I tried to be guided by the words of an old, old hymn that I learned when I was a boy:

> I would be true, for there are those who trust me.
> I would be pure, for there are those who care
> I would be strong, for there is much to suffer.
> I would be brave, for there is much to dare.

Recently, a man I had once counseled told me that he was planning to walk out on his wife and children. I asked him if he had fully considered what his leaving would do to his boy, whom I knew idolized him. The man returned my question with a question of his own and asked, "You don't expect me to sacrifice my happiness for my wife and kids, do you?"

"Of course I do," I answered. "I really can't think of anyone more worthy of such a sacrifice."

He left his wife and children in spite of my probing question, and four years later his son was arrested in a drug bust. There is a great likelihood that the son's problems were related to his father's leaving the family to live with another woman. The one from whom that son had obtained his sense of worth had betrayed the boy's trust. Small wonder that the Scriptures say that the sins of the fathers shall be visited upon the children (Exod. 20:5–6).

I wonder if fathers who consider divorces have any idea of how what they plan to do affects their kids. Children often blame the breakup of their parents' marriage on themselves and feel that if they had been better children, their fathers wouldn't have left. I wonder if fathers have any idea what this kind of thinking can do to kids and how it can destroy their sense of worth and their self-confidence. No simple heart-to-heart talk with a child is likely to dissipate the consequences of desertion. A man had better be absolutely sure that there is no way he can stay with his family before he walks out on them. If his kids end up destroyed because dad has found a new romance, there will be a special judgment for that man. Jesus said:

But whoso shall offend one of these little ones which believe in me, it were better for him that a millstone were hanged about his neck, and that he were drowned in the depth of the sea.

Matt. 18:6

I must say that staying with Mom was *not* a sacrificial thing. She is the kind of wife who has always made me grateful to be married to her. Nonetheless, the realization that I could easily have messed up your life played no small part in keeping me from disastrous actions. I knew that I could easily destroy that positive image that you had of me and, in so doing, destroy the positive image you had of yourself. Such are the wages of sin.

All of this is to say that if you think of me as a good father, it is in part due to the fact that you were a good son. We helped to create each other.

Love,
Dad

159

Eight

What Are You Going to Do When You Grow Up?

Dear Bart,

One of my biggest concerns was what you would do about a choice of vocation. We always discussed what your future plans might be from the time you were a little boy. I remember you coming in from play when you were about six years old, tossing a ball back and forth from one hand to the other. "Remember when we talked about what I was going to be when I grew up?" you asked. "Well, I've decided! I'm going to be a juggler. And look! I already know how to do the bottom part!"

I often told you that I wanted you to choose a "Kingdom" vocation. By that I meant a vocation in which you would do all that you could, given your gifts and privileges, to change the world into the kind of world that God wants it to be. I wanted you to realize that becoming a Christian involves much more than just accepting certain biblical truths and living out a personal morality that is in harmony with the will of God. I wanted you to recognize that, in gratitude for what God in Christ did for us, all of life should be lived in grateful service to Him.

I beseech you therefore, brethren, by the mercies of God, that ye present your bodies a living sacrifice, holy, acceptable unto God, which is your reasonable service. And be not conformed to this world: but be ye transformed by the renewing of your mind, that ye may prove what is that good, and acceptable, and perfect will of God.

Rom. 12:1–2

This commitment requires that in choosing a vocation every person ought to ask, "If Jesus were in my place, with my talents and my opportunities, what would He do with His life?"

It is not so much that I question the choices that some young people make as it is that I question the reasons they make them. To become a lawyer is not a bad thing. It becomes a bad thing, however, when the primary reason for going into the profession is to make big money. There are too many lawyers who are willing to participate in suits against anyone for any reason as long as the price is right.

Ralph, one of the inner-city missionaries who works with our organization, the Evangelical Association for the Promotion of Education (EAPE), in Philadelphia, was driving some children to a Bible club. In attempting to change lanes on the expressway, he brushed the van against the rear fender of another vehicle. The man whose car he hit told Ralph that the accident was nothing to worry about and that they didn't have to call the police. He asked that Ralph sign a paper admitting guilt and told him that they could settle the matter later. The man said he didn't want to hold up all those kids on the way to their party. Ralph, who had come from a small town in Texas, was accustomed to trusting people. Unaware of the ways of big-city shysters, he signed the paper. An hour or so later, the man picked up some friends and drove to the hospital. All of them claimed to have been "grievously" injured in the accident. The following day each of them filed suit against our missionary organization, putting its future existence in jeopardy.

The lawyer handling the case was quite cynical about the whole thing and said that he figured that our insurance would cover it. Legal actions like this are carried out by all too many lawyers and have been responsible for driving out of existence many of the inner-city programs designed to help socially disadvantaged kids.

Thanks to the good work of the dedicated Christian lawyers on EAPE's Board of Directors, our organization will probably not be harmed by these unfair actions against us. So you see there is not only the potential for using the legal profession to do great harm but also the opportunity a Christian lawyer has to aid and protect Christian ministry.

I would like to see Christian lawyers join together and get the state bar associations to do something to police their profession and keep things like the suit against EAPE from happening. They need to commit themselves to changing the legal system for the better.

Most of all, I want to see young people become lawyers because they are committed to justice for the poor. There are plenty of lawyers who are willing to be "hired guns" for the rich, but very few are committed to working for the poor. Most poor people find it too expensive to take advantage of the American legal system. They simply cannot afford the high cost of justice in this country. It would be wonderful if there were large numbers of Christian young people willing to spend their lives standing up for those who have no voice.

From time to time, I meet lawyers who see their vocation in "Kingdom" terms and who, in the process, are willing to forego wealth. This kind of Christian service really turns me on. There is so much good that lawyers like that can do, and there is so much hope that they can bring to those people who feel trampled by the system.

Young people who want to be doctors also should see their calling as a Kingdom vocation. Joining the medical profession is certainly one way to identify with the Jesus who is also called the Great Physician. Unfortunately, not enough pre-med students see their vocation this way. I get more and more depressed as I read about studies that reveal that the most-often-cited reason for applying to medical school is because the applicants see the medical profession as a way to get rich.

Christian young people must be better than that. They should want to become doctors in order to serve hurting people in the name of their Lord. They ought to seek careers in medicine because they want to minister to the sick and the dying. There is a desperate need for Christian doctors who are willing to make a major commitment to the poor, both in the Third World and here in the United States. Our mission organization has clinics in

Haiti but no doctor to work in them. We have Christian community centers located in poor neighborhoods in Philadelphia, where we would very much like to provide medical services for neglected people, but we cannot find a doctor who is willing to sacrifice a lucrative income to do the job.

I don't want to paint too bleak a picture of the medical profession. I do know doctors who are taking their Christian discipleship seriously and are providing some wonderful models for young people. For instance, there is a group of doctors in Lancaster, Pennsylvania, who have come up with a unique plan that enables them to serve the people of the Third World. They have set up a clinic in a Central American country and they take turns each year serving there. The income from the medical practice they share in Lancaster is evenly divided among them so that the one in the field receives the same salary as those who keep the home office going.

Another group of Christian doctors and nurses I know in Pittsburgh also have come up with a Kingdom-like way of practicing medicine. They have turned their backs on the possibility for great wealth and set up a clinic in one of the poorest sections of their city. Half of their patients come from the poorest of the poor of the city, and these people are charged solely in accord with their ability to pay. The other half of the patients who come are well-off people who are encouraged to patronize the clinic by their pastors. The income from the paying patients is enough to keep the clinic going and provides the doctors and nurses with more than enough for their own needs.

I'm sure there are a lot of other opportunities for young people to go into medicine that would reflect the radical values of Christ and give evidence that they are committed to Kingdom vocations. I don't want to seem like I'm picking on doctors and lawyers alone, though. I worry about stockbrokers, businessmen, and blue-collar workers for the same reasons. Vocation should never be primarily determined by money or prestige. Vocation should be a means to Christian service.

I never thought that you would choose either the legal or medical profession or get into the nuts and bolts of business,

Bart. I always had the feeling that you would choose to do something that had to do with talking. I remember the time when, at the age of seven, you discovered that I got *paid* for preaching. Mom and I had taken you along to a fund-raising banquet for Young Life, where I had been the featured speaker. On the way home, you overheard us discussing what we were going to do with my honorarium. You broke in and asked incredulously, "Do you mean that they gave you money just for talking?" When I answered yes, I remember you saying, "What a deal! You get paid to talk! That's what I'm going to do when I grow up!" I don't know whether or not that discovery of yours qualifies as a divine calling, but there was no doubt in my mind that you had been smitten by the idea of being a public speaker. Fortunately, you had the talent to make your dream a reality.

You could have used your gifts in a number of ways, and I was genuinely touched when you decided to go into Christian ministry. The fact that you have committed yourself to using your speaking to promote and develop an inner-city mission program really pleases me. Your ability to articulate the hurts of inner-city kids and your skill in recruiting young people to volunteer to work with you are great assets in your efforts to revitalize inner-city churches. I like your idea of getting college kids to give their summers to run day camps and youth programs out of inner-city churches, which so often lack both human and financial resources. Your gifts seem ideally suited to turning collegians on to the possibilities for evangelism among urban youth. I am also confident that as you tell your story in the better-off suburban churches, you will be able to raise the necessary financial support to make these programs go. My prayers go with you. As far as Kingdom Builders Supply goes, I am behind you all the way.

I know that there are a number of people who see you as trying to "follow in your Dad's footsteps." No doubt, some of them wonder if I pressured you into your ministry since it is so much like mine. What you are doing is so much in line with what pleases me, some of my own friends are wondering whether or not I pushed you into this ministry for vicarious gratification.

Personally, I think that living vicariously through one's

children has gotten an undeserved bad name. In ancient days it was a primary motivation for having children. Perhaps you remember learning in Sunday school that the Sadducees of biblical times had no belief in the afterlife. Consequently, they thought that the only life possible after death was through one's children. While we Christians would not go along with that kind of thinking, I believe that kids should recognize that there is something very right about allowing their parents to gain some fulfillment from living vicariously through them. Needless to say, this should not be carried to extremes. We all know stories of parents who have ruined their children's lives by pressuring them into doing things that weren't particularly good for them. There are countless stories of kids who were made to be in kiddie beauty contests, to play sports, or to sing in the church choir solely to satisfy their parents' ego needs with little regard for the kids themselves. When oppressive conditions are eliminated, however, there are all kinds of wonderful, positive strokes that parents can get from having their kids do what they always wished *they* could have done.

My father was a poor, uneducated Italian immigrant who had little opportunity to do much more than earn a living for his family. When I was in college, he came to see me play in a basketball game in which I was a high scorer and won the game with a clutch basket. My father was not someone who showed his emotions very often, but after the game he hugged me and told me I had made him very happy. It was one of the few times that he ever hugged me, and when he stepped back, I noticed that he had tears in his eyes. I had always liked playing basketball, but I was doubly thrilled that night at having made my Dad feel so good. It seemed to me to have been one small way of paying him back for all he had done for me. A funny thing, Bart, is that once you did the same thing for me in a basketball game when you came off the bench for your high school and won the game with a nineteen-point effort. I got more of a thrill out of that game than I did out of any that I had *ever* played myself. I guess what goes around, comes around. If getting vicarious kicks through your kids' accomplishments is wrong, then judge me guilty.

I know that all of this puts some pressure on you, and I hope you don't find it difficult. When it came to your choice of a vocation, I got tremendous gratification when you decided to go into a Christian ministry that is something like my own. At the same time, I hope you made your decision because you believed it was the will of God for you and, therefore, the right thing for you to do with your life. Pleasing your old man might be a nice thing to do, but pleasing your Heavenly Father is what is ultimately important.

As you made your decision, I assume you did a lot of praying, but I don't think that God spoke to you in a loud, clear voice. He has seldom communicated with me in such a dramatic fashion. Unfortunately, there are always people waiting for some kind of crystal-clear message as confirmation from God about what they should do in life. Some of them, like your Grandpop Davidson, get that kind of calling, and their experiences can easily leave the rest of us feeling that we also should have had some kind of direct and unquestionable word from God. Grandpop can tell you exactly how and when the call to Christian ministry came to him. He can describe the church service in which he came to realize that God had called him into the gospel ministry. That wasn't the way it was for me, and as I ask around, I have found that it wasn't the way most people received the call to do whatever it is they are doing for God. Most of us move forward in life with fear and trembling, lacking the absolute certainty that everyone desires.

Some in Christian ministry have told me that they simply always knew what God created them to do. They have explained to me that being in ministry was something they grew up believing was right for them. Yet there are others I know who have prayed diligently for God's leading but still lack any kind of assurance about their calling and struggle over the question almost every day of their lives. Still others (like myself) have come to accept a sense of calling primarily through rational reflection on the question of how their lives might best be used to impact the world with the love and justice of God.

As I worked my way through college, I was constantly taking

stock of what it was that I was able to do (college is a good place to test one's self out on such matters) and trying to figure out what sorts of things gave me a sense of personal fulfillment. When it comes to choosing a vocation, I think that having a realistic view of one's abilities is of utmost importance. The problem is not that God can't impart new gifts to equip a person to do things hitherto unthinkable. As a matter of fact, there are many cases, both in the Bible and in everyday life, that validate the fact that if God calls somebody to do something, He will provide whatever is necessary to carry out that calling. The story of Moses is a case in point. Certainly Aaron, his brother, had better gifts for being a spokesman for Israel. Yet it was Moses whom God called, and it was Moses whom He used to tell old Pharaoh to let the children of Israel leave Egypt. Nevertheless, I think that in many cases God endows us by birth and upbringing with the gifts that are needed for us to carry out His will for our lives. In my case, it was after careful consideration of what I could and could not do that I decided to make preaching my vocation.

Personally, I think there are too many people who have taken up the preaching ministry, because of some misled sense of obligation without having given enough consideration to the question as to whether or not they had the ability to preach. Consequently, there are a lot of preachers in the pulpits of America who are not gifted enough to articulate the gospel with the excitement or artistry that it deserves. It is even worse when such preachers fail in the ministry and end up blaming either God or the church people for their own failures, often giving up the ministry, bitter and broken, and sometimes even turning from God.

In the choice of a vocation, I think a person ought to be as objective as possible in assessing what is possible for him or her to do. It is a good thing in this process to enlist the advice of close friends and parents. People who know you well and have had a chance to observe you over the years can provide good insights as to what your gifts and abilities are as well as your shortcomings. Talking to your pastor is a good thing, as is consulting with a professional counselor. These people should not, however, ultimately determine what is decided. Caution must be exercised in taking advice. I know of some good candidates for the ministry who were steered away from church vocations by well-meaning secular high-school counselors who found full-time Christian vocations beyond their comprehension or sphere of expertise. Studying the Minnesota Multiphasic Personality Test, which is given to most high-school students, can provide some help in assessing your interests and abilities, but such a test should not be considered the ultimate determiner of anyone's choice of vocation.

In your case, you had a particularly valuable forum to help you review your capabilities. You had your circle of close high-school buddies. Those guys you hung out with had come to know Christ about the same time you did, and together you formed a support group to keep each other faithful to his Christian commitment. I know you regularly prayed for them, asking God to give direction to their lives, and I suppose that they did the same for you. In many ways, they knew more about you than I did. I'm curious, Bart, did you get confirmation for your calling from them? Were they honest with you in helping you to evaluate your calling? The Bible says that the prayers of faithful friends accomplish a great deal of good.

There was something else I did as I was going through the struggle of trying to figure out what God wanted me to do with my life. I went on a retreat all by myself. I was nineteen years old and at the end of my sophomore year of college when I took a whole day and dedicated it completely to seeking God's will for my life. I drove to an old YMCA camp near Medford, New Jersey, and spent the day walking, sitting, thinking, and praying. I had often gone to that camp when I was in high school. I had gone there for numerous church retreats and Bible conferences. It was the scene of some happy teenage romances. That camp was capable of conjuring up an endless array of pleasant memories of friends and good times. It was also a place where I had experienced God in special ways. For me that camp was holy ground.

The campgrounds were empty that day in late May when I took my retreat there. I arrived early in the morning and did not leave until late in the afternoon. During those hours alone with God, I tried to let Him speak to me. I remained still for a long time and said nothing. I "centered down," as some of my Quaker friends would say. I waited in the stillness for that soft, still voice of God. I waited for some kind of stirring in the depths of my being. Nothing happened. There was no voice and there were no stirrings, but there was something else. A strange peace came over me, a very pleasant calm pervaded my being. I knew that God knew what I was thinking of doing with my life, and I came away from that day with the feeling that God felt that it was OK. I don't know why I don't do that sort of thing more often.

It occurs to me that Jesus took forty days in the wilderness to be alone with His Father before setting out to fulfill His calling. Perhaps if all of us took that kind of time to purify ourselves and seek His face, we, too, might sense the Holy Spirit falling upon us and a voice from heaven saying, "This is my beloved child in whom I am well pleased."

Perhaps the most important thing I can say to you about choosing a vocation is that God leads us one day at a time. Very often students of mine come to me and ask how to discover God's plan for their lives. I always respond by saying to them that they are asking for too much. I'm not sure that God promises anywhere in Scripture to reveal His entire plan for life to anyone. I tell my students that the real question is what God wants them to do right then—what decisions should be made that day.

When I was nineteen, I made a decision to be a pastor. That meant that I should plan to go through college and seminary and that's what I did. Then I pastored churches for a few years. By the time I was thirty, I had a sense that I ought to be doing something else with my life. No small part of that realization was the discovery that pastoring was no longer providing the excitement or fulfillment that it did during my earlier years.

To be honest about it, I wasn't too good at some aspects of being a pastor; I was not as patient or as willing to listen as I should have been. Pastoring is not easy, and I admire and respect those who are able to do it well more than I can tell you. Fortunately, I had been taking some graduate work on my days off and had accumulated enough credit to qualify as a college teacher. Both Eastern College and the University of Pennsylvania gave me invitations to teach. It wasn't long before I left the pastorate for the halls of academia.

When I first started teaching at Penn, my mother was really upset. She thought that I had abandoned my calling to serve God. In reality, the same God who had led me into the pastorate was now leading me into something new to do for Him. My years at Penn provided me with a unique opportunity to minister in a secular community, and I know I made a difference in my years there. My background as a pastor enabled me to provide counsel to a lot of troubled, mixed-up kids. My roots in the church made it possible for me to help a good number of collegians to find their way into Christian fellowship. At the same time, my sojourn at Penn forced me to take academic studies very seriously, and I learned things during those years that have helped me immeasurably in what I have been called to say and write for the Christian community.

You know that my decision to leave the University of Pennsylvania was a hard one. Yet after these many years at Eastern College, I know that that decision optimized what I could do for the Kingdom. Because Eastern is a Christian college, I have been encouraged in my endeavors to develop missionary programs. Without Eastern, I doubt if I could have started EAPE and all its outreach programs in urban America and in Third World countries. Eastern has given me office space for EAPE, and the students from the college provide countless hours of sacrificial service in our many missionary projects.

As I look back over the years, I see that each thing I did prepared me for the next. When I went into the pastorate, I did not know that I was being prepared for service in a secular university. Nor did I see that what happened to me at Penn was God's way of preparing me for my present ministry. In short, when I decided on that personal retreat that it was God's will for me to become a pastor, I did *not* come to grips with what God wanted me to do with my whole life—I only accepted what I was to do during the *next stage* of my life.

What I am trying to say to you is that life is never settled. Having made a decision to be in one particular ministry, be sure to be aware that God may have something new for you to do some day. Keep your eyes and mind open, listen to those who love you, take time to retreat to aloneness with God and always be ready for something new from Him. His will for you in the years to come may lead you into some presently unimaginable avenues of service. Be ever ready to go adventuring with God.

Love,
Dad

Dear Dad,

Your letter about choosing a vocation made me smile because it reminded me of a conversation we had on an airplane when I was in between colleges, somewhere around the age of twenty. I say "in between" because you and Mom never liked the term "dropped out," even though that was probably closer to the truth at the time. Anyway, I was waxing eloquent on the difficulties of choosing a career in the absence of a specific spiritual revelation from on high when you cut me off in mid-soliloquy.

"It's simple," you said bluntly. "You look at the needs of the world that you know about and decide which ones you can relate to or which ones hurt you the most. You figure out what gifts and abilities God has given you to work with and how you can best use them to meet the needs He has laid on your heart. Then you get the training you need and get to work."

Your letter shows that even though you may have become a little more sophisticated over the years, you haven't really changed much.

Of course, that approach only works if the person you are talking to already has the kind of strong sense of personal significance that I wrote to you about in an earlier letter, along with a commitment to serving the Kingdom of God. You did a good job of explaining how a person like that ought to go about finding his or her specific direction, but the real question in my mind is how can parents instill the heart of a servant in their child? In the midst of the most self-indulgent, self-gratifying, self-oriented culture in the history of the world, how do you raise a kid who is deeply committed to meeting the needs of other people sacrificially?

We live in a radically un-Christian society, with a value system that is practically the opposite of the one Jesus Christ set out in His Sermon on the Mount, but we seldom take that obvious fact into account when we think about the family in general. We make a big deal out of the things Jesus says about adultery and divorce, of course, and we teach our children to be honest and not to swear, but usually that's the extent of our practical applications.

As Americans, it violates our sense of patriotism to speak of not resisting evil or turning the other cheek, especially when we have a world to run. As responsible citizens who diligently save for a rainy day, it seems blasphemous to say, "do not store up for yourselves treasures on earth," and irresponsible to say, "do not worry about your life, what you will eat or drink, or your body, what you will wear." As Christian businessmen, we take issue with anyone who says, "you cannot serve both God and money."

The Beatitudes sound too passive, and we don't put much stock in persecution for the sake of righteousness because we are doing so well in this country. Besides, who would have the audacity to claim that anybody who says Jesus is Lord doesn't automatically go to Heaven, or that only a few people are ever going to find the road to eternal life? We know better than that sort of negative thinking in this country.

As a result, we have taken the commandments of Jesus and reworked them into a belief system that fits into our way of life instead of calling that way of life into question. Jesus said that the goal of life was to "Be perfect, therefore, as your Heavenly Father is perfect" (Matt. 5:48). In modern-day America, however, we have a different credo to guide our lives: "Be happy." Happiness has become our new ultimate concern.

Perhaps it began with that famous phrase from the Declaration of Independence that describes the most basic human rights as "Life, Liberty, and the Pursuit of Happiness." Somehow, though, happiness has become the acceptable justification for everything from choosing a college to filing for divorce. People lose weight to be happy, quit jobs to be happy, and have sex to be happy. Incredibly enough, people get married to be happy. They even have kids to be happy. Once they have those kids, they do anything they can to make them happy, too. Their reasoning is simple. How can your kids make you happy if they aren't happy themselves?

It wasn't always this way, of course. People used to get married and have children, not to make themselves happy but in order to survive. In the farming societies of bygone years the family was primarily an economic unit in which every member functioned as a valuable part of the labor force. Men and women had distinct roles and functions, and each needed the other to make things work. Furthermore, large families were normative because each successive child was an economic asset. People did not think in terms of *affording* their children—it was difficult to get along without them. Consequently, children of that era grew up with a genuine sense of value and purpose which grew directly out of their contributions to their families. If you asked a farmer near the turn of the century why he had kids, he probably would have matter-of-factly told you, "Because I need them."

Contrast that response with the reasons behind today's family, if you can find any. What exactly *is* the point of the family today? What is a family supposed to be? Why do people raise children in the first place?

I hesitate to ask those questions of you, Dad, because I'm afraid I might not like the answers. I know that you didn't need me in the way farmers needed kids years ago, but it is frightening for me to consider that I might have been conceived primarily for reasons of emotional gratification. Is a child's value and purpose in life really just to make his parents happy and to be happy himself? Is that really all there is to it?

The more I work with parents and kids the more I become convinced that happiness really is the primary motivation behind today's family. When I ask parents what they want their kids to do with their lives or what they want their kids to become, I inevitably get the same answer. "Oh, it doesn't matter to me what they do, as long as they're happy." In decisions about colleges, careers, friends, spouses, children, location—always the same criteria. "Whatever makes my daughter or son happy is all right with me." Families today are primarily based on the simple pursuit of happiness. Parents want their kids to be moral, healthy, well educated, hard working, and even Christian, but they want those things because they instinctively know that those things will ultimately lead to their kids' happiness, which is the parents' ultimate concern. That, I think, is the problem.

Happiness, you see, is a very elusive goal. Indeed, it seems like the more we try to make ourselves happy, the less happy we end up.

I remember going through a long period of depression one summer when I was seventeen years old. A girlfriend had broken off with me, I hated my summer job, and I had just had a car accident. All I did was mope around the house and watch television, and nothing anyone suggested to me sounded like the least bit of fun. I was sad, and I didn't know what to do about it. One day Mom came up to my room crying and sat down beside me. "Bart," she said, "I love you and it makes me so sad to see you this way. Just tell me what to do to make you happy, and I'll do it. All I want is for you to be happy again." A kind offer, to be sure, but her words only made me feel worse. I realized that my unhappiness was making her unhappy, and I felt pressured to find a way out of my depression—but I couldn't do it, Dad. Sometimes it is very hard thing to be happy.

Since then I think I've figured out why happiness is such an elusive goal. The reason is simple: you can only find happiness when you are looking for something else. Jesus said it this way: "Whoever finds his life will lose it, and whoever loses his life for my sake will find it" (Matt. 10:39). Our culture's preoccupation with happiness and personal fulfillment clearly has made us selfish people, but the worst part of it is that it *hasn't* made us happy. And it certainly hasn't produced a new generation of young people committed to serving the Kingdom of God.

In order to develop servant-hearted kids, parents must redefine their families, not as economic units, nor as happiness factories, but as missionary teams dedicated to Christian service. Perhaps that sounds radical, but stop and think about it for a moment.

If a modern family is an economic unit, dedicated to nothing more than achieving an ever-increasing level of wealth and material possessions, the kids in that family will see themselves as useless at best and very likely as liabilities as well. They do nothing to contribute to upward mobility, and actually slow their parents' progress toward a bigger and better house, car, wardrobe, and bank account. Marriage can be efficient, but children are bound to create problems for people on the fast track. Nobody with children actually looks at them that way, but in the absence of a clearly understood alternative goal, the kids are bound to figure out the obvious: the family is aimed at prosperity and they are just along for the ride. One of the most basic desires every person has is the desire to be important or necessary in some way. That isn't possible for kids in the family that is an economic unit. Those kids are bound to have some identity problems and are likely to become the kind of self-confident, compassionate young adults who will gravitate toward serving the Kingdom of God.

Exchanging economic prosperity for the more ambiguous goal of happiness doesn't help kids very much, either. As I've already said, happiness is a very elusive goal in the first place, and the pressure put on kids in whatever-makes-you-happy families makes things even worse. Furthermore, a family that puts happiness first simply cannot help but produce essentially selfish children. Happiness is a selfish goal. There must be a better way.

As far as I am concerned, that better way is to redefine the family as a missionary team. What that means is that parents who want their kids to become bona fide Christian disciples have to communicate by example and experience that following Jesus involves much more than personal salvation. I am not suggesting that kids don't need to learn the Good News of forgiveness and redemption through faith in Jesus Christ, but that is only the beginning. We must invite them to respond to the love and the grace of God.

We must introduce them to the vision of Phil. 2:1–5:

If you have any encouragement from being united with Christ, if any comfort from His love, if any fellowship with the Spirit, if any tenderness and compassion, then make my joy complete by being likeminded, having the same love, being one in spirit and purpose. Do nothing out of selfish ambition or vain conceit, but in humility consider others better than yourselves. Each of you should look not only to your own interests, but also to the interests of others. Your attitude should be the same as that of Christ Jesus.

What a tremendous passage for the Christian family! As followers of Christ we are called not only to salvation, but to live our lives for God and to use all of our resources to do the work of His Kingdom. For a family that must mean more than just going to church or saying prayers before meals; it must become the spirit and purpose behind every action and decision.

A Christian family must look not only to its own members' prosperity or happiness, but also to the interests of others. That is where the love and unity that Paul writes about come from; the shared sense of mission that grows out of the joy of being united with Christ.

Practically, I think, that means that every member of a Christian family needs to understand that the primary purpose of that family is not to achieve economic prosperity or even happiness, but to love and serve God and meet the needs of other people.

I know a family in Providence, Rhode Island, that is a perfect example of what I'm talking about: the Johns. I met them when I was a student at Brown, when I decided to volunteer as an assistant coach for an inner-city church basketball league. The head coach was Emil John, and every one of the players looked up to him as a father figure. He didn't just coach that team—he was personally involved with the life and family of every kid on it.

As I got to know Emil over the course of the year, I began to see that his ministry to our basketball team was only the beginning of his commitment to the church that sponsored it. Trinity United Methodist Church is located in a very rough part of Providence, surrounded by poverty, drugs, and crime. Emil has been there for more than twenty years, running everything from basketball leagues to an anti-drug club. But he is not the only one committed to ministry in that poor neighborhood. His wife runs a thrift shop there, and his daughter leads the Young Life Club for high-school kids. His sons coach the basketball teams along with Emil, and the whole family pitches in to help operate the community theater group that has grown up within the church. The Johns even run a soup kitchen on Sunday nights together with Emil's sister and her husband. Everywhere you look at Trinity, you see some of Emil's family working together to care for the needs of other people. His children are grown up, but their commitment to the Kingdom is tremendously strong, as is their commitment to their family. They are fun people to be with, too, full of the joy of the Lord and with a thousand stories to tell.

A kid growing up in a family like that has something only a common mission can provide; namely, the chance to participate as a full member. No longer are the parents the only ones who can make a contribution, for when the common purpose is to love and serve other people, even the youngest child can give something real. A little girl may not be able to earn a paycheck, but she becomes tremendously significant in an old folks home or at a hospital. Indeed, in that realm she may be more useful than her parents. A teenager may not be able to be happy on command, but he can serve food at the rescue mission and there develop a sense of meaning and importance.

Every family needs a "reason to be" outside of itself and its own well-being. Kids need to see in their parents' lives that life is a gift from God which He means for us to pass along. When a family begins to understand itself as a missionary team, it becomes a creative entity, with members always on the lookout for a lonely person in need of a home-cooked dinner with friends, or a neglected kid who would love to come along on an outing, or an old person who needs help cleaning the house. Kids develop a sense of compassion that offers their parents opportunities to help them discover how to express genuine love and understanding to people in need. Spiritual gifts and personal strengths assert themselves and can be encouraged and confirmed. Mutual love becomes mutual respect.

There is one more feature of the family that defines itself as a missionary unit that I think is especially important. It looks at wealth in the way Jesus looks at wealth: as a means of doing the work of the Kingdom rather than an end in itself. It amazes me to hear parents complain of their children's greed and ingratitude when I know that those parents have done nothing but encourage the notion that money is earned primarily to provide for personal needs and desires.

Materialism is a learned attitude, not part of our likeness to God. A family that claims its true purpose of serving God and raising Him new servants is able to teach its children something else. Instead of materialism, the Christian family that is a missionary team will learn an attitude of stewardship that always asks the fateful question: "What would Jesus do with our money if it belonged to Him?" This family knows the ultimate truth: their money *does* belong to Him.

I have seen families give up their own gifts at Christmastime so that they could have the thrill of giving them to needy children —and I assure you that they didn't miss out on the joyful spirit of the holiday. On the contrary, they multiplied their blessings by living it out.

I have known families that made a game out of shopping at garage sales and thrift stores so they could use their savings to help a kid in their church go to college. It was fun for them to see who could find the best bargains, and even more fun to know that they were making a difference in the life of a friend.

When I worked in a meat-packing plant, I had a supervisor whose family lived well below its means in a smaller house and supported a foreign missionary all by itself. "We have a ministry together with that guy in Africa," the man told me. "He needs us and we need him. I guess that means we are missionaries, too."

What great logic—and what a great way for a family to develop young people who understand that everything in life is a gift from God that is meant to be given away all over again.

Of course, you can't force your kids to care about other people any more than you can force them to care about God. Sadly, all the redefining in the world cannot guarantee that a family will turn out servants of the Kingdom. Then again, I don't think God expects or requires that from parents in the first place.

People are born free, and that freedom is a gift from God that doesn't come with a "Do Not Open Until Age 18" card on top of it. Parents can do everything right, and their kids can still go wrong—and God the Father of us all knows that better than anyone. We have all gone wrong before Him. Yet He loves us with a love so great that it overwhelms everything but itself. Again and again He invites us to come back to Him, to repent, to try again. He forgives us and He saves us, but He does even more than that. On top of everything else, God offers us the unbelievable privilege of participating in His ministry of reconciling the entire world to His love.

We have received the high calling of God in Christ Jesus, and that means that we not only have a new life, but a new purpose and meaning as well. We are not simply God's children —we are called to become His servants as well. There is work to be done. Being a full member of God's family requires a person to look beyond wealth or even happiness, to serving the Kingdom and meeting the needs of other people.

In a very real way, to be a full member of a Christian family requires the same thing. Individuals may eventually choose not to participate in a family that defines itself as a missionary unit, and at some point parents must allow that and understand that the freedom to do so is a gift of God. Yet in order for parents to communicate the full meaning of Christian discipleship to their children, they must understand the family as existing before God and be willing to say along with Joshua, "As for me and my house, we will serve the Lord" (Josh. 24:15).

I knew as a kid growing up that being part of our family meant standing for God and for the needs of poor people. I hope that one day my children will know the same thing, that it always means something to be a Campolo, the same way it means something to be part of the family of God. You gave me more than a happy childhood, Dad. You gave me a legacy. Like you, I may go through a lot of different stages, and God will probably change my direction a few times along the way. Nevertheless, I know what it means to be part of God's family, and that's the best place to start. I'll keep you posted.

Love,
Bart

Nine

Doing What's Right
When You Feel All Wrong

Dear Dad,

When I was in college, I saw a lot of kids who virtually ignored their parents except when they needed money. I often wondered how they could receive so much without feeling any obligation to the people who were giving it. As much as it bothered me, when my friends persistently avoided their parents' telephone calls and didn't bother to answer their letters, there was no way I could turn things around in my mind and blame those parents for failing to raise thoughtful kids. I couldn't do it because I knew that you and Mom had done a great job as parents, and yet I often failed and continue to fail to stay in touch with you and to let you in on my life the way that I should. I am just like the kids I knew in college. After all you've done for me, somehow I still tend to take you for granted.

I don't know exactly why it is that I don't call or write sometimes or why I don't come by when I know that there is some way I could help out around the house. It is fashionable these days for people to say that they are under a lot of pressure and that there simply isn't enough time, but I know better. It would be a lie to say that I'm too busy because no one is ever so busy that he can't make a five-minute phone call or send off a two-sentence postcard to say that things are all right or even that they're terrible, for that matter. My big sister Lisa (whom I am convinced has never failed in such matters) brought that point home to me once when I pleaded exam-week busy-ness after missing Mom's birthday. As you know, Lisa often isn't a very subtle person. She was angry and she let me know it.

"Did you watch any television last week—even for half an hour?" she demanded in a tone of voice that gave her away as a future lawyer. "Did you read the newspaper, or chat with your roommate, or play any basketball? Did you eat? Did you sleep?" She didn't wait for the answer. "Of course you did! So don't tell me there weren't five minutes you could have taken to send a measly birthday card to your own Mother. The truth is that it just wasn't important enough to you, Bart. You didn't think about it—or her. And that, my dear boy, simply is not acceptable."

She was right, of course. I knew it then, and I know it now. But somehow I managed to convince myself that you and Mom would understand. You would take my thoughtlessness in stride, I reasoned, because in spite of everything I had failed to do, you knew that I really loved you. You knew that because I knew it, and because it was true, I told myself.

Yet as I look back on that lost birthday and all the other episodes like it, I realize that I was only kidding myself. Oh, you understood, all right, and you forgave me. But what you understood was that although I probably did love you, it was not very much and it certainly was not enough. I didn't see then that love only becomes real between people as it is expressed in action. Jesus said it best: "Greater love has no one than this, that he lay down his life for his friends" (John 15:13).

Jesus did exactly that. His love for us was expressed in what He did for us—in coming to show us the truth about God's love, in dying for us so that we could enter into that love, and in rising from the dead so that we might do the same. To Jesus, love is not a collection of warm feelings toward the beloved, but a series of sacrificial actions on behalf of that person. That is why He is able to command us to love our enemies, because even though we cannot always control our emotions, we can in fact determine our actions because we are free.

Making sacrifices for other people is a free choice. The irony is that only when we do the actions that love requires will we really experience the feelings that love inspires. I didn't understand that love must express itself in sacrificial action, but I should have. I had you and Mom for parents.

Many of the young people to whom I speak fully expect their parents to provide not only the necessities of life but the luxuries as well. In the ghetto, of course, the situation is very different. Needy kids want the same things, but they don't expect to receive them. Rich or poor, however, I know a lot of parents who feel terribly guilty if they can't keep up with their kids' constant demands for new clothes, stereos, compact discs, skateboards, and whatever else happens to be in style at any particular moment.

We live in a tremendously materialistic culture, and kids growing up in the middle of it can't miss being affected. Everywhere they turn, there are messages telling them they have to have the right things or else they won't be acceptable or attractive to other people. Today when sixteen year olds say, "I need those jeans," they believe what they are saying. America has somehow convinced itself to measure people by what they look like and what they have, and that is bound to lead to greed.

Of course, sometimes the parents who complain loudest about their kids' greed are unhappy primarily because they themselves are already working overtime to finance their own desires for bigger and better cars, houses, boats, and furniture. I wonder how they can miss the obvious irony, and I don't enjoy being the one to point it out to them. Parents ought to expect no more from their kids than they do from themselves, in materialism as well as everything else.

It shocks me to see how much kids demand and expect from their folks—until I reflect on the way I always approached you when I was a kid. I never really thought about how whatever I was asking for translated into work or time for you. I perceived nearly all of it to be my birthright as your child. Even something as monumental as going away to college, I took for granted. I knew that everyone's parents couldn't afford such a thing, but I also knew that you and Mom could. And what you could do for me, I felt, you must do. Consequently, I never thought very much about the fact that you might have done otherwise, or about the sacrifices you were making, or about how indebted I was for all you provided. I had it coming.

I applied the what-you-can-do-for-me-you-must-do-for-me maxim to a lot more than just material things, of course. I came to expect you and Mom to see to it that my life went smoothly, no matter what I did or didn't do. When I decided to play Little League baseball, I didn't stop to consider how I would get there. Mom would drive or you would if you were home. When I came home late in the evening, I didn't wonder if I would get dinner. I just ate it. If I was sick, I stayed in bed until I felt better. I'm sure I saw Mom bringing in food and medicine, changing the sheets, and taking my temperature, but it never occurred to me that nursing me back to health was a labor of love, the same way those other things were. For years both of you bent over backwards in a million ways to make my life good, yet, for the most part, I figured that you had nothing better to do.

I'm sure that I thanked you once in a while, but that probably had more to do with wanting to keep a good thing going than with actual gratitude. Once again, I didn't perceive you as doing anything that wasn't your duty to me as my parents. It never occurred to me then that those sacrificial actions were the substance of your love for me.

Looking back, though, I cannot separate your love from the things you did because they are the same thing. That doesn't mean you bought me everything I wanted. I thank God that you didn't. That doesn't mean that every action was perfectly understood. Sometimes even the most sacrificial actions get misunderstood—like the time I hated my summer job, and you endured my endless complaints and whining without allowing me to quit. It would have been easier, I'm sure, just to give in and have been done with it, but you didn't, and I thought you were horrible for it at the time.

The fact that you did so much for me didn't mean that you didn't also have to say "I love you" or "You are special to me" over and over again. In matters of the heart, words are tremendously important. In the end, though, your love and Mom's love became real to me through what you did, consistently, day in and day out, as I was growing up. At the risk of being taken for granted, you made one thing crystal clear: I could count on you.

As I speak more and more to young people around the country, I am learning that most of them don't know anything at all about that kind of consistent love or about parents they can count on. These kids don't worry about taking their parents for granted because they have never had that chance. Instead, their parents are the focus of their lives precisely because their parents can *never* be counted on.

It is difficult for me to write about the kids who have suffered at the hands of their own parents. I worry that some of the people who read these letters are going to be deeply hurt by some of the things we describe or suggest because their families are so different from ours. I want those people to know that you and I care very deeply about their lives. There is nothing in the world that is more devastating than a destructive family, and if someone is in that situation, I pray that they will not despair as they read this letter, but will instead turn to someone trustworthy for help. Unfortunately, many people who have been hurt or are being hurt by their families don't realize that they need help, or even that such help is available to them.

Sally was fifteen years old when she confided in me that her father had forced her to have sexual relations with him from the time she was ten until she was fourteen. I would never have guessed her problem by looking at her happy-go-lucky appearance. On the inside, Sally was full of pain, anger, embarrassment, confusion, and guilt. Like so many victims of sexual abuse, she was certain that she had done something wrong to deserve her horrible fate. She hated what had happened to her, but she felt completely alone and helpless. After she heard me talk about sexual abuse in a sermon she found the courage to pull me aside and ask for help.

I am not a trained counselor, but I was able to listen to her, support her, and pray for her as she told me her story. Later on I was able to put her in touch with a friend of mine who works with victims of sexual abuse. My friend is not only a well-trained professional, she is also a survivor herself and living proof that restoration can happen. For the first time since her ordeal began, Sally could see some hope for healing in her life. I did my best to help her establish a relationship with Jesus Christ because I knew that she would need the love of God and the strength of the Holy Spirit as she struggled to piece her broken life back together. I left Sally with the best things I had to offer, but as I got on the plane to fly home after talking with her, I still felt helpless and upset. I wanted to find the man who had hurt her and beat him up, both to punish him and to keep him from hurting anyone else that way. How could he have betrayed his own daughter that way? How could anyone abuse his own child?

Sexual abuse is not so uncommon as we would like to think, Dad. One out of every three girls and one out of every eight boys in this country are sexually abused before they reach the age of eighteen, and most of that abuse comes from family members. Beatings and physical abuse are also common occurrences for many more kids than we know of, and that doesn't begin to touch on the millions of people who are not sexually abused or beaten but are still denied the consistent love of a parent they can count on. It is difficult to know which is more prevalent—abuse or neglect. These are serious subjects, Dad, and I don't pretend to be an expert on how to deal with them. What I do know is that when someone is in a destructive family situation, it must be stopped and dealt with. If anyone reading these letters is in trouble themselves, or knows someone who is, I hope that he or she will get professional help and turn to a trustworthy Christian supporter so that God can be a part of the healing as well.*

I was fortunate in that I never had to worry about being abused, and that's a big part of the reason I can reflect on my childhood so easily. But that is not enough. To be able to count on your parents means more than not having to worry about being hurt, and more even than not having to worry about their love for you. It means not having to worry about whether or not your parents will stay together.

---

* They can contact a Child Abuse/Parents Hotline 1–800–352–0386, or the National Center for Missing and Exploited Children 1–800–843–5678.

I guess there was a time when divorce was a big deal in this country, but it must have been before I was around. By the time I was graduated from high school, fully half of my classmates' families had broken up. As kids we didn't talk about it very much among ourselves, but we always knew when someone's parents were divorcing. We didn't talk, I think, because there was nothing we could say that would change anything. Divorce was—and is—a fact of life.

I know a lot more about marriage and divorce now that I am grown up and have a wife myself, but when I meet a kid whose parents are splitting up, I still don't always know what to say. In a way I feel like I have no right to say anything. You and Mom never gave me any reason to think about divorces except as they related to other people. Whatever else might happen, I always knew that you would stay together, the same way I knew that school would always open in September and that Lisa would always be smarter than I was. You don't think about things like that—they just are.

So what can I say to someone who is wondering all the time what is going to happen to her family? That I'm sorry? Of course, I'm sorry. That never seems like enough. I don't want to belabor this because I am writing to you, and you never let it be an issue, but I will say this: if parents get divorced because they want to be happy or free or fulfilled or any of that when they could have tried harder to make things work, they are selfish people and their kids will surely suffer. When people have affairs, they are shafting their kids for their own pleasure. When wives and husbands let their marriages become battlefields because they are unwilling to make sacrifices, they don't love their kids, no matter what they say, because love is made of sacrificial actions.

I know you love Mom, Dad, and I know she loves you, too, but I'm old enough now to know that there were times when one or both of you felt like walking out. I know you had opportunities for affairs with other women because I traveled with you. I know there were struggles. You and Mom worked hard to make things look good to me. It was your sacrifice to make sure I never had to worry, that I could always count on both of you—

together. You handled my need for security the same way you did all those other things. You were consistent with your love. I depended on you without ever really thinking about it, and you didn't let me down. You were by no means perfect parents, but your love was always there, in the million sacrificial actions that were the foundation of my childhood.

All of that is why the fact that I have often failed to be sacrificial where you and Mom are concerned bothers me. Of course, the sacrifices I owe you are different from the ones you made for me because you don't have to depend on me the way I had to depend on you. As I sit here trying to figure out just what those sacrifices are, I can't help but compare my relationship with you and Mom to my relationship with my Father in heaven. These are similar relationships in a lot of ways, although less so as I grow older because, although I am no longer primarily dependent on you, I am still completely a child before Him. The love He wants from me now is the same as the love you wanted from me when I was a kid: obedience—"If you love me, you will obey what I command," Jesus says to his disciples (John 14:15), and I hear echoes of your voice in my ears.

You have always commented with pride that I was a pretty easy kid to raise as far as obedience went, but I must finally admit that the biggest reason for that had nothing to do with being afraid of what you would do to me if I challenged your authority. Honestly, fear was seldom a significant factor. I just never have liked conflict. Usually, following even your most ridiculous commands was preferable to the arguments and lectures that came along with disobedience. Eventually I came to realize that in obeying you I was giving you the one thing you most wanted from me—I was loving you, really—and I began to get a kick out of making you happy that way. Of course, making you happy tended to work in my favor, too, but that's the way it usually works in matters of love. What you are giving and what you are getting become blurred in the joy of it all.

When I tell kids that obedience is the key to dealing with their parents, they usually think I am being naive. "It's not that simple," they tell me, and yet so often when we take the problems those kids are having with their parents and break them down into their basic elements, it *is* just that simple.

A child's obedience to his parents must gradually and inevitably give way to another kind of love. In the end, God is the only authority, and we all stand equal before Him alone. In the words of a wise man, "The ground is level at the Cross." Consequently, the sacrificial things I can do for you as a Christian adult must be different from those I did for you as a child. I am my own person now. I can't keep following your commands. Happily, there is something else I can do for you, Dad.

As I think about the things I have done and even more about the things that I have failed to do—I see clearly that inasmuch as I have loved you effectively, my actions have moved from obedience to involvement. As far as I can figure it out, that is what you want most from me now. I don't know when the shift began—I suspect it was before I even got to junior high—but somewhere along the line I realized that, from your perspective, loving you meant letting you in on my life. Like most parents, you didn't want to be left in the dark.

I am a big part of your life, and it matters to you that we stay connected and that you are a big part of my life, too. That's what Lisa was trying to tell me when she yelled at me about missing Mom's birthday. That is why it hurts you when I don't send a postcard or make a phone call. You want to be involved. This is the place where I have failed so often and where I sense I have hurt you the most. The worst of it is that I know what I should do. I tell kids about it all the time.

"Ask your parents for advice when you can," I say, "because they love to be a part of your thinking as you figure things out. You don't have to follow it always, but just asking them lets them know what's going on in your life. Invite your Mom out to dinner some night, just the two of you, and ask her about herself the way you would a real date. Or your Dad, maybe. Or set aside half an hour each week when you turn off everything else and pick a topic like friendship or travel or music to talk about with either one of them. They'll love it."

I think I have the most advice for college students because

that is where I failed so much. I tell them to send their Mom the school newspaper once in a while, a graded paper (so long as it's a decent grade), or a copy of their class schedule. I tell them to call, even for five minutes, at the same time every week so their folks can look forward to it all week long. I tell them to stamp and address twenty postcards all at once and send two a week, because it's the biggest return they will ever get on fifteen cents. "It takes a minute and a half for you, but it makes your folks' entire week," I tell them. I say all the right stuff . . . and then I forget to do it myself.

To some people, those may seem like little things. Those little things, however, let your parents in on your thoughts and decisions and everyday life, and they are the sacrificial actions of love. When love is communicated, when it is expressed in action, it becomes real in a wonderful way.

This is the risk you and Mom run: being taken for granted. You've been as reliable as a good wrist watch, and as a result I've had the privilege of concentrating on other things, secure in the knowledge that I am loved.

If that has meant that I have failed to love you back the way I should have, it is my own fault for not learning the lessons of love better. Believe me, Dad, I don't want it to be that way. I love you. I want you to know that, the same way that I know you love me. I want you to be able to count on me, too.

Maybe there's something I'm leaving out, though, something you really want from me that I don't even know about. I know you pretty well, but I can't read minds and I have no idea what it is like to be where you are in life. No kid ever knows that kind of thing. In fact, I would consider it a great favor if you would tell me straight out what it is that you want from me, especially as you get older, so I can know that I'm loving you the best way I can. Sometimes people just don't know what to do for each other without being told. I can't promise you I will be able to manage everything you want all the time, but I will try my best to love you—the real way—for as long as we are both alive.

Love,
Bart

Dear Bart,

If you have learned that love is something you do, you have learned the most important of all lessons. The Bible makes this truth abundantly clear, but all too few grasp its message. All the way though the Scriptures, love is seen as action that lies within the prerogatives of the will. Love is not something we effortlessly feel, as is so commonly assumed in our romanticized culture. Instead, it is that which we are commanded to do. The Bible says to love the Lord your God, to love your neighbor, to love your wife, and even to love your enemies. Now on that last one, people who instinctively feel positive emotions for those who hurt or humiliate them are strange. People who treat others as Jesus would want them treated, even when they don't feel like doing so, are lovers in the biblical sense.

Love is really impossible to define, although the Apostle Paul does as good a job as can be done in his brilliant thirteenth chapter of 1 Corinthians. My own working definition is simply this: love is a decision to do for the other person what Jesus would do for that person if He were in your place. I do not want to suggest that feelings are not involved in biblically prescribed love—in reality, there are deep and gratifying feelings connected with it. These fulfilling feelings, however, come as a *result* of doing. You cannot count on your feelings to make you do the right thing, but those who choose to do what love requires

eventually come to know a sense of inner joy and spiritual gratification that is what life at its best is all about. You said much the
same thing in your letter to me.

Love doesn't always give us the kinds of peak experiences
that romantic turnons provide—but then the pleasure of romance is only fleeting, while love is everlasting. What love at its
best really does is to lift us up to a higher plateau of living. A
wonderful old hymn refers to this as "higher ground." Love creates a new kind of humanity and lifts people up to a new kind of
ongoing existence. Romance can never be trusted, but love is
always there when you need it.

I have long been impatient with married men who claim to
love their wives but treat them like dirt. In one particular case, a
guy who had constantly been unfaithful to his wife sat with her
in my office and tried to tell me that, in spite of everything, he
really loved her. This guy had not even been kind to her when he
was with her. He had ridiculed her in front of other people. He
never did anything to make her life easier or better. Yet there he
was, sitting across from me, saying in cavalier fashion that he
really loved her. I figured that he wanted me to smile benevo-
lently and say, "Poor Harry. He really is a loving guy. He just has
some bad manners and personality weaknesses."

If old Harry was expecting something like that, he must
have been shocked when I shot back at him, "You don't love her
at all. Maybe she turns you on every now and then. Maybe you
enjoy the acceptance she provides when you don't deserve it.
Maybe you're afraid to face life without her mothering influence, but don't tell me you love her. Love is doing what Jesus
would want done for her. Love is responding to her needs and
providing whatever would help her to experience the life that
Jesus wants for her. I don't see any of that in you. Tell me that
you need her to exploit for your own ego purposes. Tell me
that you have some kind of sickness that drives you to hurt a
person who is loyal to you, but don't tell me that you love her
and then go on doing what you've been doing."

This turned out to be one of my more successful counseling cases. That man came to the realization that he had to stop

playing games and face the reality of the true nature of love. In the end, love meant that he had to make a decision to change—and he did. The marriage was saved.

In your relationship with Mom and me, you loved us enough to change. It took a while, but you got the message about what love required, and you began to do the things that express love and that generate those gratifying feelings that give life luster. You *do* make those caring telephone calls these days. You often remember your special people with notes. Yes, you still occasionally forget birthdays, but your overall pattern is one of concern, and you are doing better with every passing day. Love involves being willing to change, and in many ways you have heeded that call. Mom and I are proud of you. You have worked hard on something that did not come easy to you.

Love is being willing to listen, and you have always seemed to love Mom and me enough to listen to us. If there were something important or difficult to tell you, we could always be sure that you would pay serious attention to what we had to say. If there were suggestions we wanted to make about how you could improve as a person, you could be counted on to listen. If we saw you moving in directions that we felt could be hurtful to others or harmful to yourself, you were willing to think about what we had to say. You didn't always yield to our directions, but you made us feel that you would give careful consideration to our viewpoints and proposals. Mom and I always felt that you heard us when we had something important to say to you. That is love.

I want you to know that we have not taken this for granted.

Love,
Dad

Ten

Figuring Out
What Really Matters

Dear Bart,

Balancing was one of my most difficult struggles. How to reconcile the time demands of my career, on the one hand, with the need to spend time with you and Lisa, on the other, had me constantly straining for answers. How to give the best possible effort to my work and, at the same time, be a good father and husband kept me constantly perplexed. I think that many middle-class types like me have the same problem, and the way in which we handle it is one of life's most important ethical concerns.

I talked recently with a young married couple. The husband is a really great Christian guy, but he is not handling this problem of balancing well at all. He is very involved in missionary service and is the driving force behind an incredible work for God. His ministry has him on the road constantly. He is not paying much attention to his wife or his two sons. His wife loves him and thinks that what he is doing is wonderful, but she, nevertheless, feels neglected. She has silently and sadly resigned herself to a kind of married life that has left her lonely and disappointed. She has figured out how to make the best of her lot, and she is doing quite well, considering the overall situation. This young woman has learned to live with the hurt that goes with the awareness that her husband's work is his primary concern and that she must settle for whatever time is left over.

Something inside her is dying, and I hope that this guy doesn't wake up too late to what he is doing to her.

I did my best to tell him how I saw his situation, but I had the feeling that he didn't intend to be the one doing any adjusting.

This particular man has also neglected his two boys, who are seven and fourteen. Like their mother, the boys think that their dad is the neatest thing that ever came down the pike. But also like their mom, they sense that they are not very important in the grand scheme of things as far as their father is concerned.

This man knows better, but he can come up with a thousand justifications as to why he doesn't have more time for his family. Because his work is so noble, his wife and kids are made to feel guilty if they ever suggest that he do less of it and give more time to them. He's not balancing well at all.

I feel a particular pain as I listen to this good guy who is doing such a wrong and stupid thing. The reason I am so pained by his lifestyle is that I know that I may have been guilty of the same thing during your growing-up years. Did I balance things right? Did I divide my time in a way that left you, Mom, and Lisa knowing that you were always the most important persons in my life? I can't help but wonder . . .

In retrospect, I know I failed to take the biblical concept of the Sabbath seriously. The Bible teaches that one day each week should be set aside from all labor and should be spent with the family in spiritual renewal. Every family, according to the teachings of Scripture, should have a day each week to nurture relationships with one another and with the Lord. If Sunday is a workday, which it always has been for me, then another day should be set aside for this purpose. The particular day of the week that is observed as the Sabbath is not what is important; what is important is that we recognize that our observing such a day is a commandment of God.

If I had it to do over again, I would make one day a week a family day and have us all spend it together doing something fun and special. Doing that would have enabled me to balance life better and to be a better father.

The problem of balancing is as old as the church itself. The

Apostle Paul, way back in the first century, recognized that this was a primary problem for married Christians. He saw that there was an inevitable conflict between the time and energy required to do the work of building God's kingdom and the time and energy required to be a good spouse and parent. He wrote of that dilemma in 1 Corinthians without ever resolving for us how it should be resolved.

He that is unmarried careth for the things that belong to the Lord, how he may please the Lord: But he that is married careth for the things that are of the world, how he may please his wife.

1 Cor. 7:32–33

In that same chapter, however, Paul urges Christians who are married to pay proper attention to one another lest they become ready bait for extramarital messing around.

Defraud ye not one the other, except it be with consent for a time, that ye may give yourselves to fasting and prayer; and come together again, that Satan tempt you not for your incontinency. But I speak this by permission, and not of commandment.

1 Cor. 7:5–6

Paul says in verse 7 that concessions must be made when people are married in order to nurture relationships and, therefore, that it is impossible to be totally committed to do the work of one's Christian vocation and be married at the same time. On the one hand, it surely can be argued that being a father and husband makes a Christian in ministry more understanding of the situations that are normative in most people's lives. On the other hand, there is no doubt that for most ministers there is an unbearable tension between the call to faithfulness to the work of the church and the call to fulfill the obligations that go with being a good spouse and parent. This balancing act is difficult, and most of us drop the ball somewhere along the line.

I have often heard the problems of balancing time allotments discussed at ministerial get togethers. Regularly I have heard ministers and missionaries say with regret that they wished they had spent more time with their families and less time on their ministries. *Never once have I heard a minister say that he wished that he had spent less time with his family and more time on the work of the church.* That should tell us all a thing or two.

This problem of balancing may be even more of a problem for those in so-called secular vocations. People who work in offices or factories can find themselves torn apart in even more painful ways than those in religious work. Besides the conflict that exists between the time demands of work and family, these people are likely to find themselves condemned from the pulpit if they do not get involved in the programs of their local church. It's bad enough for a young husband to have to try to figure out what he should be doing about balancing the time demands of his career over against the time demands of his family, but then, on top of all that, he finds the preacher stepping in and laying a guilt trip on him if he isn't giving "sufficient" time to all the things that the church has for him to do. Preachers can be very unsympathetic to the man who puts his family time before the Thursday night men's fellowship meeting or the Tuesday evening door-to-door evangelism program.

If family life is as important to the Christian church as its leaders say it is, there should be more care exercised in what those leaders ask of people, lest they exhaust the time that families need for togetherness. Perhaps churches need to plan more intergenerational programs or projects in which a family could participate as a group. Certainly, the church should not be making it more difficult for men to be decent fathers and husbands.

Finding time for you always required that I be extremely creative. For instance, when my teaching load and graduate studies tied up my afternoons and evenings, I tried to compensate by spending time with you in the very early morning. Remember when we would get up at 6:00 A.M. and go out to the soccer field to kick the ball around for an hour or so? I still remember your standing at my bedside, all dressed in your soccer outfit, holding the ball in your hands and saying in your soft, eight-year-old voice, "Dad. It's time."

We would go out to the soccer field with only our dog, Lady, to watch. We would run up and down the field, yelling and screaming as we kicked the ball. Lady would follow, jumping and barking as she played with us. I never pass by that soccer field without remembering the good times we had there.

Another way that I made time to be with you was by including you in what I was doing. When you were just seven years old, I started taking you with me on weekend speaking engagements. Those were quality times. We had long one-on-one discussions about almost everything. Those trips meant so much to me that I've encouraged friends of mine, whose work also requires a lot of travel, to take their children along with them. You and I had especially good times on trips that required airplane flights, when we had nobody to talk to but each other. We explored cities together. We discussed the ways of the world and the customs of other kinds of people. We learned a lot about each other on those weekend trips. I was filled with sadness when our traveling days came to an end. When you got into your teens, you had your own life to live with ball practice and school activities. Like Puff the Magic Dragon, I suffered a bit when my little Jackie Paper wasn't around to play with me. I often wish I could relive those special times that we had together. I don't know why everybody whose work requires travel doesn't try to do what we did. It helped me do my balancing act.

Breakfast was always an important time with our family. Because my work often kept me from being home for supper, we made breakfast a time of special sharing. Mom went out of her way to cook up great food to start off each day, and all of us enjoyed the give and take in conversation as we sat around the table. Not only did I enjoy this time with my family, but my sociological studies at the university provided me with ample evidence that having meaningful discussions while eating together can be an essential component of the healthy socialization of children. Around the table, values can be communicated and meal times allow parents time for helping kids to evaluate life in the light of the Scriptures. Table talk is more likely to be remembered than any lectures parents may give to kids.

I believe that table talk should be planned to include significant topics. It was often during our breakfast hours that I tried to tell you about Christ's bias toward the poor and oppressed. It was around the table that we discussed the pros and cons of the arms race. I did my best to make our talks at breakfast important times of sharing as well as educational. Even as I write this, I especially recall an in-depth discussion we had one morning on interracial marriage.

A couple of students at Eastern College (whom you especially liked) were planning to get married, and there was some deplorable gossip going around the campus because he was Black and she was White. As we talked about this upcoming marriage, I made sure that you clearly understood that there was nothing unbiblical about interracial marriage. Furthermore, in that conversation, I also had the chance to teach you that while the Bible does not prohibit interracial marriage, it does have some very specific teachings against Christians marrying non-Christians. I think the message stuck. You ended up marrying a wonderful committed Christian.

One of the most important ways to maintain balance in the midst of the topsy-turvy world in which most young fathers have to live is through family rituals. Rituals are prescribed ways of doing certain things, like putting kids to bed, eating, or celebrating special days like birthdays and holidays. Tevye, in the musical, *Fiddler on the Roof,* referred to them as "traditions." Since the great Emile Durkheim, sociologists have called them "collective rituals."

Rituals have a variety of important functions. They build family solidarity and intensify the loyalty of family members to one another. They give children a sense of order about life, and this in turn contributes greatly to their emotional stability. Rituals are excellent ways for teaching children the vital things about life and helping them remember what must never be forgotten.

Family rituals were important around the Campolo home. Special days were always celebrated with great fanfare. On birthdays, we *always* made a fuss with birthday cakes and parties. Holidays like Christmas and Thanksgiving were *always* planned to follow an established pattern.

Mom was particularly good at rituals. She would put you to bed with an array of them that must have instilled in you a happy attitude of expectation about life. Every night, she would tell you special stories she made up about an incredible boy named Billy Anthony. Of course, we all knew that Billy Anthony was a thinly veiled, blown-up portrayal of you.

In Mom's stories, Billy Anthony was a wonder boy who could drive any kind of vehicle and was willing to perform all kinds of heroic feats to rescue people who were in trouble. I wonder if you've reflected much upon how important Mom's stories were in your character formation. I am convinced that the ritualistic day-in and day-out telling of those stories helped to build into your psyche the expectation that your life should be spent in service to others. I also believe that those stories taught you that, when difficulties arose in the course of helping others, you could prevail by facing them with self-confidence and assurance.

I often wonder why most parents don't recognize how important it is to give their kids a sense of well-ordered stability through rituals. As far as I'm concerned, life has become far too spontaneous for children in today's world. Most of them suffer emotionally because they don't know what to expect in their daily round of activities. Rituals, those expected routines in our lives, are essential to being civilized. Too many kids are denied them.

For fathers who are involved in careers that have them coming and going, rituals are of utmost importance. Family rituals can be what make such fathers put the demands of family life above the demands of their jobs. Too often, professionals live their own lives and expect their families to adapt to their schedules of activities. Rituals can correct this tendency and force fathers to realize that there are important events and ceremonies connected with their families for which business schedules must be sacrificed. Rituals can help fathers organize their lives around celebrations and observances that belong to the family, and this can keep them from becoming unbalanced workers, swallowed up by the time demands of their work.

Balancing is not only a matter of time, it is also a matter of values. Judgments and decisions have to be made in the course of every life and, in making these day-by-day judgments and decisions, people reveal what really matters to them.

One particular decision, more than any other, forced me to weigh what was good for my career over against what was good for you. When the weighing task was over, it was clear that if I did what was best for my career, the price would be too high in terms of your well-being.

As you were entering your junior year of high school, I had a chance to become the president of a small Christian college in New England. I really wanted that position, and I think I could have done some good for the Kingdom had I taken it. Mom and I talked it over and recognized that the consequences of uprooting you would be unpredictable. You were happy in your school, you were having a good time at church, and you had a great network of Christian friends. Even though you told me that you were willing to make the move, we felt that we owed it to you to let you enjoy having roots. Too often, as far as I'm concerned, parents allow the demands of their vocations to take precedence over the well-being of their kids and make moves that cause their children upset and pain. Mom and I were fortunate in being able to choose, and we chose not to take the risk. I knew that there would be other chances for me to live out my vocational dreams and visions, but I had only one chance to raise my son.

Your time to make hard decisions is at hand, Bart. You are a married man with a wife who deserves time. You are also starting out in a career of Christian service that demands time. Here's hoping you do well in the most important balancing act of your life.

Love,
Dad

Dear Dad,

I don't know how to say this except just to come out and say it: I wish we had spent more time together when I was growing up. I don't want you to feel guilty or bad, because it wasn't all your fault. You were trying to balance your family with your career and your service for God. I was intent on my friends, my sports, occasionally my studies, and, when I got old enough, girls. Somehow we both got busy, and the time got away from us. Not always, but too often.

You worked too much. I didn't invite you to be part of what I was doing often enough. It wasn't until I dropped out of college that we realized we were down to our last chance to really be together. We made the most of that year, and to me it was the best year we ever had. That was when we got close and finally figured out who each other really was. It was great having enough time to do it.

I feel sorry for that man that you counseled who was so busy trying to save the world that he had no time for his kids. The world will always be there, but his kids won't. There really is such a thing as too late. It makes me feel even worse to know that he's sacrificing his relationships with his wife and kids in the name of Christian ministry, because I know the kind of frustration that will cause for them.

It's one thing to resent your dad's business or his hobbies

or his adult friends, but how do you resent his working for Jesus without feeling bad and selfish? How do you compete with God? How can a Little League game or an afternoon walk or a few hours together baking cookies stand up against what your Dad says is his opportunity and obligation to do something important for the Kingdom? Those kids may even grow to hate God for stealing their father from them, the way they might hate another woman or alcohol, but they'll have a hard time admitting that, even to themselves, because they probably know it isn't right to hate God. Their father has probably taught them that much.

God isn't really stea ng their father, of course; ambition or workaholism or a mixed-up set of priorities are, but those kids may not understand that for a long time. You are probably wondering if that's how I felt. Sometimes. But not often, Dad, because you did take me with you. You let me be a part of your life away from home. I must admit that when I see your schedule now, I'm glad you weren't such a big shot back when I was a kid.

Why do I wish we had spent more time together? You managed well enough to keep me from resenting your career. You entertained at my birthday parties. You came to my games. You and Mom created rituals that gave me a sense of security and belonging. Why do I think you should have been around more if I didn't miss you back then? It's simple, Dad. Because I miss you now.

I'm twenty-six years old. I have a wife, a career, and a life of my own. My childhood is gone now, and I can't do a thing about it. A few years ago they tore down my elementary school to put up an office building. The other night, I ran into Robin Roach, who was the first girl I ever kissed, back when we were in seventh grade, and I felt so old when she told me she was a senior analyst for a major corporation. There's a parking lot now in the field where my friends and I used to camp out. I'm losing my hair. Everything that was a part of my childhood is slipping away into time, and all that is left of it for me to hold onto is a bunch of old photographs and my memories.

Who I am is all caught up with those special things that happened when I was a kid, and I think about them a lot these days. It wasn't very hard for me to come up with the stories in these letters, Dad. They are the stories I tell all the time when I'm trying to explain who I am or what I think or how I feel about something.

Some of the stories are sad, and some of the memories are painful, but most of them are a joy to recall. Over the years, though, all of those images of growing up have sorted themselves out inside me, according to their relative importance. A million hours of television are forgotten, but the twenty minutes I watched the great Karl Wallenda walk the tightrope over Veteran's Stadium are as fresh in my mind now as if they were yesterday and not fifteen years ago. I spent a lot of my childhood with my buddy, John Baxter, and we can sit for hours and talk about every model airplane and every argument we ever had. Not much about school, mind you, just the things that mattered to us as boys. I played in a lot of soccer games, but the state championship game is the only one that I still know by heart, the only one that means something to me even now. I cherish that game like a treasure because, even in defeat, my team and I played with all our hearts and we were proud. I dream sometimes about blocking the shot that beat us, but it doesn't bother me anymore that we lost. It was enough to have had the experience.

The times that I remember best, though, are the times I spent with you. I love those memories best of all, Dad, and they're a big part of who I am. That's the whole point of these letters for me. My childhood is gone, and I will never be able to be with you the way I was with you as a little boy. I will never be that small, and you will never seem that big again. But I have my stories, and they comfort me when I am overwhelmed by the world, when I am too old all of a sudden, when I lose my sense of wonder. They are all I have of my boyhood, and the reason I wish we had spent more time together is that I wish I had more of them now. It isn't that you didn't do enough, you see, for I would always want more. You were the king of the world back then, the imp of fun, the man with all the answers, the one who could always fix what was broken. You made life seem magical to me.

When you die, Dad, I will surely go to pieces for a while, because I still count on you more than anyone knows, but in the end I will be all right. I will have my stories, and in them I will always have part of you, the part that tells me who I am and where I came from. I only wish there was more because what there is means all the world to me.

Love,
Bart

Afterword

This is a very personal book. There are a lot of ideas and suggestions in it that I hope will be of some help to people, but essentially it is a story—our story. That is not what my father and I intended for it to be when we began, but that is what it became. To be honest, I am a bit uncomfortable putting our relationship out in front of people, but I am also hopeful that good will come of it.

The problem with any story, though, is that while it may be true, it is never altogether factual. Our perceptions of things are always conditioned by who we are. When a person says, "this is what happened," what we should hear is, "this is what *I* saw," or "this is what *I* experienced." Only God knows what really happened.

Our family understands that better than most because we love stories more than practically anything else. We tell them all the time, in sermons and around the kitchen table. Sometimes, at the end of a really good story, one of us will ask, "Did it really happen that way?" to which the standard family answer is always, "Well, if it didn't, it should have."

Maybe that is why I am a bit uncomfortable with putting my upbringing at center stage, because I don't want it to seem like my father and I are bragging about ourselves or one another or that our relationship is nothing less than a series of perfect illustrations. The stories in this book really happened. I know—I was there. Inasmuch as they are true, they are also our memories, and sometimes we wrote what we heard instead of what somebody else really said. I love movies where people say just the right thing at just the right time, but I know better than to expect real life to work that way. In real life you don't get to rehearse your lines.

If it looks as though my parents are the most absolutely wonderful people in the world, well, that's just the way it is as far as I am concerned. If it seems as though our lives are something out of a storybook, remember that that is exactly what you have here.

Bart Campolo

The Book of the Grail
by Josephus

The Book of the Grail
by Josephus

The Forgotten Early Account
of the Arthurian Legend

Transcribed and Edited by
E. C. Coleman

AMBERLEY

First published 2016

Amberley Publishing
The Hill, Stroud
Gloucestershire, GL5 4EP

www.amberley-books.com

British Library Cataloguing in Publication Data.
A catalogue record for this book is available from the British Library.

ISBN 978 1 4456 5658 8 (print)
ISBN 978 1 4456 5659 5 (ebook)

Map design by Thomas Bohm, User design.
Typesetting and Origination by Amberley Publishing.
Printed in the UK.

Contents

For the Lord of Neele made the Lord of Cambrein this book to be written, that never tofore was treated in Romance but one single time beside this; and the book that was made tofore this is so ancient that only with great pains may one make out the letter. And let Messire Johan de Neele well understand that he ought to hold this story dear, nor ought he tell nought thereof to ill-understanding folk, for a good thing that is squandered upon bad folk is never remembered by them for good.

Josephus c. 1205

Introduction to this Edition

It is not known when *The Book of the Graal* (known also as *Perlesvaus*) was first written, or by whom. There may have been a 'good clerk' named Josephus who was told to write it down upon the instructions of an angel, but more detail would be a greater incentive to acceptance of his authorship.

Nor can the date of its writing be pinned down with any great accuracy. If the 'Lord of Cambrein', who also ordered the book to be written, is the Bishop of Cambrai, subsequent datings suggest that he had to be one of two succeeding bishops who held the position between 1200 and 1237. The 'Lord of Neele' or 'Johan de Neele', for whom the Lord of Cambrein had the book written, is probably John de Nesle who is mentioned as living in 1214 and 1225. Written in medieval French, *The Book of the Grail* was translated into Welsh prior to 1368, and records in its translated title that it was originally written about the year 1200.

The Welsh translation, a sixteenth-century French version and a few surviving pages of a thirteenth-century copy were used in 1866 to transcribe the book into medieval French once again. This, in turn, was translated into Middle English under the title of *The High History of the Holy Grail* by Sebastian Evans in 1898. Since that time, apart from one modern language version, it has remained available only in the form presented by Evans, an academic curiosity ignored by much of the Arthurian world who preferred the later works of Mallory and Tennyson. It is the Evans edition that has been used as the basis of this edition.

No claim is made for the accuracy of the language used for this transcription. The main purpose has been to give a feel of antiquity and yet remain readable. Words such as 'aby' (to redeem by penalty), 'brachet' (a spoilt child), 'sithence' (subsequently, or since), 'guige' (a strap attached to a shield enabling the wearer to carry the shield on his back), 'Confiteor' (a prayer of general confession), 'gramercy' (an expression of surprise, or 'thank you'), and 'wot' (knowledge) have been replaced by more understandable equivalents. A few unresolved matters have been tidied up for the sake of narrative fluency, but no changes have been made to the order of events. Consequently, the following from Sebastian Evans' Introduction to his 1898 translation still applies:

> I commend the 'Book of the Graal' to all who love to read of King Arthur and his knights of the Table Round. They will find here .... what I take to be in all good faith the original story of Perceval and the Holy Graal, whole and incorrupt as it left the hands of its first author.

Percival and his quest for the Holy Grail first appear in Chrétien de Troyes' poem *Perceval, le Conte du Graal*, written somewhere around 1185. The poem breaks off after some 9,000 lines, possibly on the death of Chrétien. The work was then completed in a series of four 'continuations', each by a different writer. *The Book of the Graal*, however, is presumed to be by a single author who, nevertheless, also takes up the story where Chrétien breaks off. Consequently, the reader is assumed to know that Percival had already seen the Holy Grail, but had failed to achieve it by not asking the required question:

Whom doth the Grail serve?

Chrétien's Grail is, however, different to the one in *The Book of the Graal*. To Chrétien, it was simply a dish or paten which held a wafer for consumption at the Mass. It was the wafer which would help cure the Fisher King – the wounded king whose realm turns to wasteland around him. In his *Joseph d'Arimathie*, written at the end of the twelfth century, Robert de Boron first tells the story of the cup, or chalice, which was used to collect the blood of Christ as he hung on the Cross. Brought to England by Joseph of Arimathea, the chalice had now become the Holy Grail – the same object for which the Grail Knights of *The Book of the Graal* set out in quest. De Boron also introduced the 'sword in the stone' to the Arthurian myth, but *The Book of the Graal* had both a sword and an arrow which had to be drawn from stone columns. The annual beheading, which became the basis for *Gawain and the Green Knight*, makes its first appearance, and Camelot is the castle of the Widow Lady, the mother of Percival, although a comment, which has all the appearance of a later insertion, points out that this Camelot is not the same one as that belonging to King Arthur, Kay is not the good knight of other versions, Excalibur does not exist, Merlin is but briefly mentioned, and Queen Guinevere suffers a tragedy rather than the exposure of her love for Lancelot.

It may be of interest to note that no claim of historical accuracy can be made for King Arthur passing laws which demanded that, from the time the Holy Grail was achieved, all communion services in England should use a chalice styled after the Holy Grail – or that bells should be hung in churches. Nevertheless, the earliest communion chalices in England of the Grail type are from the thirteenth century – shortly after the publication of *The Book of the Graal.*

Clearly, although no date is indicated in *The Book of the Graal*, the story was set firmly in early thirteenth-century England. King John was on the throne and the aristocracy spent much of their time in jousting, hunting, and making courtly love. Their main theme in life was chivalry. The weak and the innocent – which was bound to include women – were to be protected. Honour and reputation is everything. There were strict rules of courtesy and loyalty, mercy had to be shown where possible and the truth always told. On the other hand, Jerusalem was in the hands of Islam and the Fourth Crusade has just been completed with the sack of Constantinople – guilty of being in the hands of the wrong sort of Christians. Already there was talk of a Fifth Crusade; therefore, there could be no compromise on the question of religion. *The Book of the Graal* was quite content that those heroes within its pages were undeviatingly Christian; to be otherwise was to place your head at very great risk. In this, *The Book of the Graal* did not shirk its responsibilities and, consequently, could be described as a handbook for the twelfth and thirteenth-century Military Orders such as the Knights Templar, the Knights of St John and the Teutonic Knights.

Here, then, is the frequently dark tale of a time that was already legendary by the beginning of the thirteenth century; a time when good, fearless men went out in search of adventures in which they could defend the weak, defeat wickedness and right wrongs. But only the very best of them can seek the Holy Grail and restore order where there is chaos, light where there is darkness, and good where there is evil. However, this is no place for weak, simpering damsels in distress. Time and again, the women encountered by the knights show courage, initiative and enterprise. Where they are treated badly by men, either with physical cruelty or mere disdain, they lose no time in appealing to the knights for help. Together they form a society where there is little moral shading, where the individual is either good or wicked, and glories in or suffers the consequences accordingly.

E. C. Coleman, 2016

The Original Introduction

This is the history of that most sacred vessel that is named by men the Holy Grail, wherein the precious blood of Our Saviour was received on the day that He was crucified that He might redeem His followers from the pains of Hell. This history was written by the good clerk Josephus by command of the Lord God who spoke to him through an angel. Thus may the truth be made known to good knights, worthy men, and all those willing to suffer pain and to work for the spread of the rule of Jesus Christ made new by His death upon the Cross.

This High Book of the Grail beginneth in the name of the Father, and of the Son, and of the Holy Ghost. All three being of one substance, which is God. And it was God's command to write this High Book. All those that read it should dwell upon its meaning, and forget the wickedness they bear in their hearts, for great goodness shall it bring them that hear it in their heart.

This Holy history was written for the sake of those worthy men and good knights whose deeds shall be remembered, and for the great and good knight whose family came of the soldier Joseph. Good knight he was without fail, for he was chaste in mind and body, hardy of heart, and of great strength. Boasting was unknown to him, and he hid his great courage beneath a mantle of kindliness. All these virtues were his for his lack of wickedness. But it needs be told, that Greater Britain fell beneath great misfortune, and sorrow covered the lands and islands when the good knight failed to utter but small words. Nonetheless, by his deeds of knighthood, he alone brought back gladness throughout the lands.

The good knight was of the family of Joseph of Arimathea, the uncle of his mother. This same Joseph had been a soldier in the service of the Governor Pilate for seven years. Such was the service done by this Joseph that when Pilate offered him wealth and land or any other reward of his choosing, Joseph requested only the body of Our Saviour when he was taken down from the Cross. For Pilate, such a reward was as of naught. He granted Joseph's wish under the belief that the soldier would treat the body of Christ in the manner of the meanest thief. But Joseph treated our Lord's body with all due reverence and laid Him in the Holy Sepulchre and placed alongside Him the spear that had pierced His side, and the most Holy vessel that had gathered the Holy blood from the wound.

The mother of the good knight was named Yglais. She was the sister of the grievously maimed Fisher King, of King Pelles, and of the King of Castle Mortal whose evil was matched only by the twin goodness of his brothers. Yglais was a good and loyal mother to the good knight, and to his sister, Dindrane. His father, whose family descended from Nichodemus, was Alain le Gros, son of Gais le Gros who dwelt by the Hermit's Cross. This Alain had eleven brothers, each of whom died young in the service of our Lord bearing their arms in defence of the Saviour's cause. Alain was the eldest; Gorgalians was next; Bruns Brandalis was the third; Bertholez le Chauz the fourth; Brandalus of Wales was the fifth; Elinant of Escavalon was the sixth; Calobrutus was the seventh; Meralais of the Palace Meadow was the eighth; Fortunus of the Red Land was ninth; Melaamaus of Abanie was the tenth, Galians of the White Tower the eleventh; Alibans of the Waste City was the twelfth. All smote the enemies of the Lord with the uttermost of their power, all died in the defence of His name. Of such family was the good knight whose history is written by Josephus the good clerk, and who shall tell you of his name and manner presently.

Part the Ist

The authority of the scriptures tells us that since the death of our Lord upon the Cross, no earthly King has taken up the cause of Jesus Christ more boldly than King Arthur of Britain. To him alone, and in company with the good knights that attended his court, fell many great adventures thanks to his high belief in God. Many true knights, the best the world hath seen, attended to the King and sat at his Round Table. Such was the noble manner of his Kingship that all the princes and barons strove to follow his example, yet none was praised as much as he.

But after some years had passed, a weariness fell upon King Arthur and the pleasures of charity and gallant deeds left him. Christmas, Easter and Pentecost passed without remembrance and many of his knights departed in sorrow at the change. His Queen, Guinevere, a lady of great beauty, became downcast and knew not what to do of her husband's malady. Even the Lord God did not send her comfort. It is from this time that this history beginneth.

On one Ascension Day, when the King was at his Castle Cardoil, he walked through the Great Hall and saw his Queen seated at a window. Sitting beside her, the King saw that her eyes shone with tears.

'What ails you, my Lady?' said the King, 'Why do you weep?'

'I weep, Sire,' the Queen replied, 'for neither you nor I have any cause to be joyous.'

'It is true, Madam, that I have little of which to feel joy.'

'Right, indeed you are,' said the Queen. 'On a high day such as this, the court would be thronged with knights, more than could be numbered. Now I am ashamed that so few are your knights, and adventures are but memories. I fear that God has truly made you forget your honour.'

The King replied with great sadness, 'Again it is true, my Lady. I have no will to work charity, nor can I face anything that may turn to honour. I have a great feebleness of heart that loses me my knights and the love of my friends.'

With great tenderness, the Queen said unto the King, 'My Lord, I know of a way to restore the courage of your heart. In the White Forest is the chapel of Saint Augustine which can be reached only by the bravest of knights. Should you repair to the chapel and ask God for His counsel He will listen unto you for He will know you have a good heart. Upon your return, with the Lord's assistance, you will again find your desire to do good.'

'Madam,' replied the King, 'your words have pierced my soul and I can no longer gaze upon your downcast form. I have oft heard of this chapel, and I believe it to be a worthy site to restore my spirit.'

'But remember, Sire, that the chapel is girdled with perils and adventure. Once it is gained, however, you will find a most wonderful hermit who lives by the building. He lives now only to glory God, and will aid you in your prayers.'

'Then,' sayeth the King, 'I shall proceed thither, armed and alone.'

'No, my Lord,' sayeth the Queen. 'Pray take with you a knight and a squire for the perils are great.'

'I will not, my Lady, for the adventures faced alone are greater than those faced in company. If it is the Lord's will that I succeed, then succeed I shall whether alone, or with others.'

'Please God, my Master, take at least a squire to aid you,' cried the Queen.

Knowing that her heart would be injured by refusal, the King replied, 'To please you, my Lady, I shall take a squire, but I cannot deny the notion that evil will come of it.'

As the King spoke these words, a tall, strongly-made young man entered the Great Hall. He was Chaus, the son of Yvain le Aoutres.

The King turned to his Queen and sayeth, 'Think you that I should take this one?'

'Indeed, I do, Sire, for I have heard much of his valour.'

At this, the King called out to the squire who came and knelt before him. Raising him up, the King said, 'Chaus, tonight you shall sleep in the Great Hall and, on the morn, you shall prepare my horse and my arms. We both shall leave at break of day without other company.'

That night, as the King and Queen left the Great Hall, the squire remained behind. Fearful of his duties, Chaus removed not his clothing nor his shoes with the intent of remaining awake throughout the night. But sleep enveloped him and he dreamed that the King had left the castle, alone and unarmed. Waking in fright, the squire put on his spurs and his sword, mounted his horse and rode with great fury after the King he imagined to be already near the White Forest.

And before long, the squire came upon a great forest. Entering the darkness, he found a track which, to his mind, had been made by the King. Then a clearing in the trees appeared before him and, upon casting around, he saw a chapel surrounded by a burial-ground in which were many graves. Alighting from his horse, Chaus entered the chapel which was empty save for the body of a knight which lay before the altar covered in a rich silken cloth. Around the knight were four gold candlesticks with candles lit. The wonder of the sight struck the squire for he knew not how the knight had been so arrayed, nor by whom the candles were lit. He knew not either where the King was, nor where to search for him. At this, Chaus removed one of the candles and hid the gold candlestick about his clothing and left the chapel to regain his horse and continue in his search for the King.

The squire had not continued long before he came across a fearful sight. In his path, lit only by a low moon, stood a foul-featured man dressed in black. So tall was the stranger that his head was above the squire even though the young man was on his horse. The light of the moon showed that the man held a two-edged knife in his hand. Pushing aside his fear, the squire demanded of the stranger, 'Have you met King Arthur in this forest?'

'I have not,' returned the man. 'But I am pleased to have met you, for you have left the chapel as a thief. You have carried off a candlestick of gold that was placed in honour of the knight that lay dead in that chapel. I demand that you yield it up to me that I may return it. Should you choose not so to do, I shall obtain it at a cost most dear to you.'

'By my faith,' replied the squire, 'I shall never yield it to you for I intend to present it to King Arthur.'

At this, Chaus gave spur to his horse but, as he rode past the stranger, the man thrust the knife deep into the squire's left side and he gave a loud cry of 'Dear God! I am a dead man!' So loud was his shout that it woke him from the dream he was suffering. The cry also brought the King and the Queen to his side as he lay in the Great Hall.

'What ails you,' sayeth the King.

As he lay on the floor of the Great Hall, the squire recounted his dream to the King and Queen.

'Then it was just a dream,' sayeth the Queen.

'Aye, my Lady,' replied the squire. 'But a dream like none other.'

Having spoken thus, Chaus lifted up his left arm and the King and Queen saw the handle of a great knife, its two-edged blade deep inside the squire's body. The squire then withdrew a gold candlestick from his clothing and gave it to the King with the words 'For this candlestick that I present to you, am I wounded to death!' He then continued by saying, 'Draw not forth the knife of my body, Sire, until I have made my confession.'

A priest was sent for and did take the squire's confession. Then the King withdrew the knife and the squire's spirit departed forthwith. In concord with the squire's father, the King sent the gold candlestick to the newly founded church of Saint Paul's in London with the command that the squire's adventure should be everywhere known and that prayers should be made for the soul of the squire who was slain on account of the gold candlestick.

That morning, King Arthur armed himself to go to the chapel of Saint Augustine. On his preparing to leave, the Queen said unto him, 'Whom will you take with you?'

'Madam,' replied the King, 'I seek no other company than God, for He has shown that I must travel alone.'

'Then so be it, Sire,' answered the Queen. 'May God guard you and grant your safe return. I know you have the will to do well and to see your praise raised up once again.'

Sayeth the King, 'May God remember it.'

The King took to his horse on the mounting-stage and received the shield and spear of Yvain Le Aoutres in honour of that man's noble son. At his side hung his sword and the King appeared in every aspect a brave warrior. His spurs caused his horse to leap forward as he rode toward his destiny in the White Forest. At this, the Queen asked of the assembled knights, 'Is he not a good man?'

'Yea,' they replied as one, 'yet the loss to the world of his charity, courtesy and noble character is felt beyond all horizons. May he return to his good beginnings with God's early blessing.'

King Arthur rode fearlessly into the forest and continued on until the time of evensong. At that time he came across a clearing wherein lay a chapel and a small house that seemed to be a hermitage. Alighting before the house, he opened the door and entered, taking his horse with him for fear of what may remain outside. Within its walls, the King laid down his spear and shield, unbuckled his sword and raised his helmet visor. Before him he saw food such as for horses and so removed his horse's bridle and allowed him to eat thereof.

A noise then assaulted his ears as if of strife in the chapel. It was as if the voices of angels were met by the sound of the fiends of Hell. Marvelling at this, the King went to the chapel and opened the door. At this the sounds ceased and nought could be seen inside but the images of our Lord and his Lady mother and the crucifixes. Entering further, the King saw an open coffin before the altar wherein lay the hermit who was named Calixtus, his long beard down to the girdle of his vestments. And he was on the point of death. But though night had fully come, the light as if of many candles remained around the hermit. The King, knowing him to be in the presence of a good man, decide to remain at his side until the spirit departed but, as he did so, a loud and fearful voice fell upon his ear telling him to leave forthwith, for the spirit could not be departed whilst he remained.

Much saddened by this, the King returned to the house and heard the chapel strife continuing. And his sadness deepened when he heard the angel voices weakening as the fiends grew louder and more clamorous. Then the angel voices were stilled and the King looked to the ground in despair. But then he heard the sweetest voice of a Lady. So sweet and clear did she speak that the sound of her voice would have lightened the heaviest grieving. The Lady spoke to the devils and sayeth, 'Begone from this place, for you have no right over the soul of this good man. Whatever he has done, he has made ample amends in the service of my Son and in mine own. The penance he hath done in this hermitage has washed away his sins.'

But the devils replied, 'True, my Lady. But longer hath he served us than he hath served you and your Son. For forty years or more he hath been a murderer and robber in this forest, and he hath but served you for five years. And now you wish to steal him from us.'

'I do not. No wish have I to take him by theft, for had his life ended in your service as it ended in mine, yours he would have been by right.'

At this the devils groaned with a terrifying sound as the sweet Mother of our Lord God took the departing spirit into her arms and gave it to the angels to deliver to Her dear Son in Paradise. And the angels sang the praises of the Lord God as the Holy Lady led them to the Realms of Light.

The next morn broke clear and fair and the King returned to the chapel expecting to find the hermit remaining within his coffin. But there was neither coffin nor hermit, but a new and gloriously carved tomb-stone in the floor marked by a red cross. And incense lay upon the air as the King made his prayer before departing.

Armed again, the King rode through the forest until he came across an open land most fair. At its entrance a spear barred the way whereby stood a damsel of great beauty. The King turned to her and saluted her by raising his helmet visor. 'Damsel,' he said, 'May God give you joy and good fortune.'

'Sire,' sayeth the woman, 'So may he unto you.'

'Damsel,' returned the King, 'Where is there hospitality in this land?'

'Sire,' replied the damsel, 'there is none save a holy chapel with a hermit beside.'

Astonished, the King asked, 'Is this then Saint Augustine's chapel?' For, but a night before he had believed himself to be at that chapel.

'It is, Sire, but the lands about and the forest are so perilous that no worthy knight hath yet returned but he be dead or deeply wounded. Yet the place of the chapel is of such worthiness that none go there without finding refreshment of the spirit. May God guard you for you appear a most noble knight and I pray you are not harmed. Indeed, Sire, I shall remain here until I see you again.'

'May it please God then, that I shall return to greet you.'

'May it please God indeed, for I then may ask you of tidings of him that I seek.'

At this, the King advanced to the spear that barred his path, and it fell away to let him pass.

Ere long, the King found himself in a fair wooded valley where he chanced upon the chapel of Saint Augustine and a hermit's house close by. Reining his horse to the bough of a nearby tree, the King sought to enter the chapel but found he could not so do though the door be open and no one barred his way. Again he tried to enter, and again he could not as if he was held back invisibly. Falling to his knees he implored Our Saviour to admit him. As he did so, the King heard the opening prayers of the Mass and saw the hermit approach the altar with his right hand holding that of the fairest child he had ever seen. The boy was dressed in a white linen robe and wore upon his head a golden crown in which jewels shone with great brightness. From the other side of the chapel there then appeared a Lady of great beauty and serenity. As the hermit sayeth his prayers, the Lady crossed to the altar, took up the child, and sat upon a rich throne, and kissed the child on her lap saying, 'Sire, you are my Father and my Son and my Lord, and guardian of me and of all the world.'

At this, the King marvelled and his wonderment grew as a flame of light came through a window behind the altar. A light brighter than any from sun, from moon or from star and brighter than any light from all the world. Then there were the voices of angels as they responded to the hermit's prayers. The Lady then offered the child to the hermit who took him and placed him on the altar as he began his sacrament. At this the King bowed his head. Upon looking up, and to his great astonishment and consternation, he saw that the child had vanished and been replaced by the body of a man bleeding from his side, from his hands, and from his feet. The man's brow was crowned with thorns. The sight moved the King's heart to tears and he felt wretched that he could do nothing to aid the wounded figure. But, as he wiped tears from his eyes, he saw that the dying man was gone and the child had returned to his mother.

At the final singing of the Mass, the voice of an angel sayeth, 'It is finished.' And the Lady took the child into her arms and the great flame of light flared to dazzle the eyes only to vanish leaving none within the chapel save the hermit knelt before the altar. Rising, the hermit turned from the altar and spoke to the King. 'Sire, now you might enter herein for you have known the presence of our Lord and His Holy Mother.'

The King entered the chapel as the hermit sayeth unto him, 'Sire, I know you well, as I also knew your father, Uther Pendragon. Your sins prevented you from entering the chapel whilst the Mass was being sung. Nor will you ever enter again until you shall have first made amends for your misdeeds towards God and towards the Saint of this chapel. Though you be the richest King in the World and your adventures, charity, and honour be set as examples to all men, of late your example is one of idle indolence. Nothing short of the greatest misfortune can become you if you do not return to that high point which once you obtained. Your court was the sovereign court of all the world, but now it is the least worthy. Sorry is the man who goes from honour to shame, but never shall a man be reproached who comes from shame to honour, for the honour wherein he is found rescues him to God. But never shall be rescued the man who hath renounced honour for shame, for the shame and wickedness wherein he is found shall declare him guilty.'

'Sire,' sayeth King Arthur, 'I have come here to make amends and to be better instructed than I have been. Well do I see that this place is most holy and I pray that you ask God that he show me how to amend my endeavours hereafter.'

Sayeth the hermit, 'God grant that you may amend your ways that you may help to fight evil by means of the grace given by our Lord on his crucifixion. For we have great sorrow in the land through a young knight that abideth in the castle of the Fisher King. God caused the Holy Grail and the Spear of the point which runneth with the Holy Blood to appear unto him, but he did not ask whom the Grail served or from whence it came. Accordingly, foul war is abroad in the land, famine and disease are everywhere, and the people starve. When knight meets knight they meet not in fellowship, but in combat. Of this you shall see when you return to your castle.'

'Sire,' sayeth King Arthur, 'May God defend me from wickedness and an evil death. From henceforth my ways shall be amended, thus may He bring me safely home.'

'Amen sayeth I. May God hear your plea.'

At this the hermit departed, commending the King to God.

King Arthur took again to his horse and began his return with great pace. As he met with the forest he was surprised upon by a tall knight on a black horse and carrying a black shield. The black knight also bore a lance that burned with bright flame from its point to the knight's gauntlet. Already at great pace, the knight closed fiercely with the King and would have struck him from his horse had not the King swerved before contact.

'What, Knight,' cried the King, 'have I done that you should so act towards me?'

'I have good reason not to have love for you,' replied the knight.

'But why, Sire, why?'

'For you have my brother's gold candlestick that was foully stolen from him.'

'You know then, who I am?'

'Yea,' sayeth the black knight. 'You are King Arthur that once was good and true, but are now evil. I shall do nought but defy you as my mortal enemy.'

This said, the knight ran again at the King as the King gave his horse spur and pointed his lance at the knight. They clashed most fiercely that both moved in their saddles and lost their stirrups. The shock of combat caused blood to flow from the King's mouth and nose and he marvelled that the burning lance of his enemy had not shattered to ashes. Again they rushed at each other with mighty pace. The King aimed his lance and hit the black knight on the shield with such force that the knight bent backwards in his saddle, but such was the knight's resolution that he reached forward and struck the King's shield such a blow that his lance pieced the shield and the King's armour and the King felt the iron of the lance in his arm. To the King's marvelling and the knight's consternation, the flame of the knight's lance was thereupon extinguished.

With the flame went the knight's courage, and he pleaded with the King to let him live. But King Arthur knew the world to be a better place without the black knight and charged at him, thrusting his lance through the knight's body and bringing him to the ground. There he left the knight's body as he turned his horse towards the forest entrance.

The King had not travelled far when he heard the noise of a great company of knights reach the place of his combat and saw them cast their eyes upon the dead knight. Sore afraid that the knights numbered many beyond challenge from him, the King applied his spurs to his horse when he saw the damsel he had left by the barrier spear come near.

'Sire,' sayeth she, 'for pity's sake, return and fetch me the head of the knight that lieth there dead.'

The King looked back and saw the multitude of armed knights and the great peril thereof. 'What, damsel,' sayeth he, 'would you have them slay me?'

'No, Sire, I would not. But I must have the head of that knight. No knight has yet refused me any request. Please, Sire, do not be the first so to do.'

'But, damsel, I am sore wounded in the arm and cannot bear my shield.'

'I know that well, Sire,' she replied, 'but I know further that your arm will never heal until you bring me the head.'

King Arthur turned his horse again and stiffened his body. 'So shall it be, damsel, whatever may befall me.'

The King rode towards the massed knights and was astonished to see that they had cut the dead knight's body asunder and each was carrying off an arm or leg or other part. He then saw a knight who had the black knight's head at the point of his lance. Riding up to the knight, the King cried out, 'Abide, Knight and speak with me.'

The knight stopped his horse and sayeth, 'What, Sire, is your pleasure?'

'Knight, I beseech you to give me the head that you carry at your lance point.'

'Indeed, I will, Sire, on but one condition.'

'What is your condition?' sayeth the King.

'That you tell me who slew the knight whose head I carry.'

'Otherwise I may not have it?'

'No, Sire, you may not.'

'Then I will tell you,' sayeth the King. 'In truth before God, it was King Arthur who slew him.'

'And where is King Arthur?' sayeth the knight.

'Sire,' replied the King, 'I have attended to your condition. You must seek King Arthur yourself. Render me the head as by our agreement.'

'Willingly,' sayeth the knight and lowered his lance for the King to take the head which he did.

As the King rode away, the knight took from around his neck a great horn which he blew. The loud blast caused all the other knights to return and close with the knight. On their return, the knights asked him why he had blown his horn.

'For this,' he replied. 'The knight you see riding away told me that King Arthur slew the black knight. I summoned you that you may know and wish to follow him.'

'We will not so follow,' the knights sayeth, 'for it is King Arthur himself that carries off the head and we have no power to do him evil since he has passed the spear barrier. But you shall suffer the penalty of letting him escape.'

With that, the knights killed the knight and cut his body asunder as they had done with the black knight.

Beyond the spear barrier, the King found the damsel and presented her with the black knight's head.

'Sire,' sayeth she, 'I thank you for your gift and the courage that brought it.'

''Tis of nought,' replied the King, 'for with gladness I was able to meet your request.'

'Sire,' sayeth the damsel, 'you may alight from your horse, for there is no danger to you this side of the spear barrier.' And the King obliged.

'Sire,' she continued, 'take off your coat of mail that I might bind up your wound, for none save me can make you whole again.'

The King took off his coat of mail and the damsel took the blood, which ran still warm from the head and washed the King's wound. After which the King put on his coat of mail.

'Sire,' sayeth the damsel, 'under God's dominion you would never have healed the wound save by the blood of the black knight. It was for this that the knights carried off the body in pieces, for they knew that you would have need to return to be healed by the blood. For myself, I had to have the head. By it, shall a castle be yielded up to me that was taken from me by knavery. I now needs must seek for the knight through whom it shall be rendered to me.'

'Damsel,' sayeth the King, 'and who is the knight?'

'Sire,' sayeth she, 'he is the son of Alain le Gros of the Valley of Camelot, and is named Perceval.'

'Why Perceval?'

'When he was born, Sire, his father was asked what name he should have for the baptism. He replied that the boy would have the name Perceval which would remind him throughout his life that the Lord of the Moors had stolen from his family much of the Valley of Camelot. With God's aid, Perceval might one day become a knight. Indeed, the boy was fair of image and gentle and, ere long, went to the forest to learn how to hunt deer with a spear. One day his parents, who much loved him, took him to a small chapel close by their house. Mounted on four pillars of marble and roofed with timber, the chapel had therein a small altar with, before it, a costly coffin engraved with the figure of a man. The boy asked his father and mother who lay within the coffin. His father told him that he knew not and knew little else though the coffin had been there since the time of his father's fathers. All that may be said is that letters carved upon the coffin told the reader that, when the best knight in the world shall come to that place, the coffin will open and the joints fall asunder. Then will be seen he that lieth therein.'

Sayeth the King, 'Damsel, have many knights passed thereby since the coffin was set there?'

'Knights beyond number, Sire, yet none have caused the coffin to open. When the boy was told the story he asked his father and mother how was a knight made? His mother made reply by saying that he had eleven uncles who had been made knights, yet none had survived beyond twelve years of their knighthoods. The boy replied that his question still remained. His father then replied that knights were good and worthy men of great valour who were clad in coats of mail to protect their bodies and with helmets upon their heads, and with shields, and lances, and swords to defend their bodies. On the morrow, the boy Perceval took one of his father's horses and, with his spear, entered the forest to hunt deer. Ere long, he came into a clearing and saw two knights engaged in combat. One knight had a red shield, the other a blue. In time he saw that the Knight of the Red Shield was about to vanquish the Knight of the Blue Shield. At this he threw his spear at the Knight of the Red Shield piercing the knight's heart, whereupon the knight fell dead. He had not known that a spear might pierce a knight's armour. As the Knight of the Blue Shield left the field in great joy, the boy took the dead knight's horse home to his father and told him the story and his parents did grieve that their son had taken the life of a knight. Sometime after, the boy left his home to attend the court of King Arthur as a squire. So well did he impress the King with his prowess and courage that the King made him a knight. Perceval then departed the court in search of adventure becoming of a knight and travelled throughout many kingdoms bringing help to the weak and sustenance to the poor. Now he is the best knight in the world and I must seek him. If you see him, Sire, you shall know him by his shield which is of green and beareth a white hart. Pray tell him that his father is dead and that his mother is at war with the Lord of the Moors who is strengthened by the brother of the Knight of the Red Shield whom he slew.'

'May God grant me such a meeting,' sayeth the King, 'for well will I send forth your message.'

'Now, Sire,' sayeth the damsel, 'I have told you of him that I seek but I have yet to discover your name. Pray tell me, Sire, what is it?'

The King replied, 'I am known as Arthur.'

The damsel stepped back as if in dread and sayeth, 'Arthur? Have you indeed such a name?'

'In truth I have.'

'So help me God, for I am indeed sorry for you. You have the name of the worst King in the world. Never again will he move from his Castle Cardoil, such dread hath the Queen lest anyone should take him from her. So it is said, for I have never seen either or any of them. I had hoped to go to his court but many knights I met who told me that the court of King Arthur is the most vile in all the world, and that all the knights of the Round Table have denounced it for the evil therein.'

'Damsel,' sayeth the King, 'I heard that at his beginning he did well beyond measure.'

'Well begun may be half ended. But what care anyone for his beginning when the end is bad?' sayeth the damsel. 'I am sorry beyond measure that such a seemly knight and worshipful man as you are should bear the name of so evil a King.'

'Damsel,' sayeth the King, 'a man is not good by his name, but by his heart.'

'It is true, Sire, but your name marks you in my heart with the same image of evil as the King. Whence go you now, Sire?'

'I go to Castle Cardoil where I shall find King Arthur.'

'Go then, and quickly. For I have no better hope of you since you go hence.'

'Damsel,' sayeth the King, 'you must say as you please, but it is to Castle Cardoil I go. God be with you.'

'And may God never guide you to such a place, the court of King Arthur.'

With that the King departed and entered into the deep forest where he heard a loud and terrifying voice saying, 'King Arthur of Greater Britain. You should be right glad at heart that God hath sent me hither unto you. He bids you to hold court at the earliest that you may, for the world that is made worse by you shall be greatly amended by your coming honour.'

In the silence left by the great voice, the King's heart grew large with joy for God had forgiven his many failings and now suffered him to restore the glory and honour as before.

At his arrival at the mounting stage at Castle Cardoil the Queen and the loyal knights made great joy of his coming. And he repaired to his chamber and dressed in a great robe of crimson silk with ermine. And the Queen sayeth unto him, 'Sire, such pain and suffering have you had.'

'Lady,' the King replied, 'good men must suffer to find honour, for none shall be found without suffering.' He then told the queen of his adventures and the manner of the wound in his arm, and of the damsel that had taken against him because of his name.

'Sire, sayeth the Queen, 'well you now know how right it is that a man of great wealth and power should have great shame of himself when he becometh sinful.'

'Indeed, it is so. Much did the damsel do for me by her speech, but nought can compare to the great voice in the forest telling me that God commanded that I hold court presently, and that I shall see an adventure that can right the world of the wrongs I have done. It shall be the fairest adventure that ever hath been known.'

'Sire,' sayeth she, 'your joy should be unbounded that your Saviour hath remembered you. Therefore, fulfil His commandment.'

'That I shall do, Madam, no one has more desire to do good, find honour, and give charity than I at this time.'

'Then, Sire, God be praised.'

Part the IInd

From Castle Cardoil, King Arthur sent forth messages under his seal for the barons and knights to assemble at Castle Pannenoisance on the feast of Saint John. Carried throughout all the lands and islands, his words caused wonder to those that read the King's summons. Whereas before, the well-doing of the King had waxed so feeble that none believed it could ever be restored, now a new desire was abroad. The King, under God's command, was well intent to make amends for his evil idleness.

With great joy the Knights of the Round Table that were scattered well abroad learned of this new desire and returned to the court with great celebration. Only Lancelot and Gawain came not thither on Saint John's day. By number there were one hundred and five knights in the great hall when the King and his Queen sat at the table. Kay and Yvain, the son of King Urien stood as stewards and saw that all had meat and drink. The Butler, Lucan, served the King with the great golden cup that was his alone by reason of his past glories. The sun shone through the windows upon the flowers and herbs that lay upon the floor and gave the great hall the scent of balm.

Upon the first meat having been eaten, the King and the knights looked in wonder as three damsels entered the hall. The first was riding a white horse which beareth a golden bridle and a saddle of ivory over a silken cloth of crimson and gold. This damsel was fine and seemly of body but not so fair of face. The damsel was richly clothed in a robe of green silk laced with gold. Her right arm was rested on the richest pillow decorated with tassels of gold and her hand bore a silver box bearing a golden crown wherein lay the head of a King. Her arm, the pillow, the box all held close to her by a cloth of gold around her neck. On her head, the damsel wore a close hat that covered all but her face. The hat flamed with the brightest of jewels as if it burned.

The second damsel rode a much broken down horse less white and appeared as a squire. On her back she bore a bag in which was carried a hound. She bore also a white shield bearing a red cross. In her left hand she carried a box made of lead bearing a copper crown. In the box was the head of a Queen. This damsel was of fairer face than the first.

The third damsel had no horse and appeared on foot with her gown tucked up for ease of running. This damsel bore a whip with which she prompted the animals forward. Of all the damsels she was the most fair.

As the first damsel approached the King at his table she sayeth, 'Sire, may our Lord grant you honour, and joy, and good adventure, and may the Queen and all the knights in this hall love you as their wise sovereign. Pray, Sire, do not hold it to be churlish of me not to alight from my animal, for I may not alight where knights are present until such time as the Grail shall be achieved.'

'Damsel,' replied the King, 'gladly I do not take it as churlish and would easily have you remain for your comfort.'

'Thank you, Sire. May I now tell you of the errand that I am about?'

'Pray do so, damsel, tell us at your pleasure.'

'Sire,' she sayeth, 'the shield born by this damsel belonged to Joseph, the good soldier who took down the body of our Lord from the Cross. This shield shall you take from me and hang on the great column of this hall. None shall touch it until it be a knight come hither for the shield. You shall know him to be the Knight of the Shield for he shall put in its place a shield that will be of red bearing a white hart. With the shield he shall bear away shall he achieve the Grail. Furthermore, Sire, you will tend the hound which, although now of sad countenance, will be alive with joy when the good knight comes.'

'Damsel,' sayeth the King, 'we shall full and properly keep the shield and the hound safely, and we thank you for bringing them to this place.'

'Sire, I have more to tell you. The best King that lives in the world, the most loyal and the most righteous, sendeth you greeting. But he is saddened to the depths of his soul that he has fallen into great troubles.'

'Damsel,' sayeth the King, 'full saddened am I to hear of such a thing. Pray, tell me, who is this King?'

'He is, Sire, the Fisher King upon whom great grief has fallen upon. Know you why, my Lord?'

'I do not, but would know for I might come to his aid.'

'His grief, Sire, came upon him from the want of a deed of a guest knight at his castle. To this knight appeared the most Holy Grail, but he failed to ask whom the Grail served, and the lands were turned to strife and pestilence thereof. Thereafter, knights fought with knights, men fought with men, and the land suffered. You, Sire, know well of this, for your goodwill did ebb away likewise and you have received much blame. For you, Sire, were the example to the world in well-doing but now you are the mirror of all that is calamitous. Even I, though at first bearing a good heart, have suffered and I will show you thus.'

At this, the damsel took off her hat where under grew not a single hair. 'Sire,' sayeth she, 'before the knight came to the Fisher King's castle, I had tresses of golden hair. But he did not ask the question of the Holy Grail. Nor will my hair return until such time as a knight goes thither to the castle of the Fisher King and asks the question. When that happens, the land will turn to plenty, knights and men will live in fellowship, and I will know my golden hair again. But, good Sire, and good knights, the adventure will be difficult as may be seen at the door of this hall. There you will find a great carriage drawn by three white harts. The traces are of silk, the axles of gold, and the carriage is made of ebony. All is covered with black silk in which is woven a golden cross. Beneath this cover are the heads of a hundred and fifty knights, some in boxes of gold, some of silver, and some of lead. The damsel bearing the shield holds the head of a Queen who betrayed the King whose head I hold, and the knights within the carriage. I pray you, Sire, send to see the costliness and manner of the carriage.'

33

King Arthur sent Kay to see the carriage. The knight looked and saw that it was indeed a remarkable carriage but thought himself to bring a jest to the King saying, 'Never beheld I a carriage so rich, nor have I seen three such white harts that draw it. They, my Lord, would serve us well for our table for they are full fat and tall.'

But the King grew hot with wrath at the words of Kay. 'No, Sire, I will not have such notions, not even for another kingdom.'

The damsel then sayeth, 'Sire, I know that Kay speaks in jest. Let him speak so, for I know well that you will pay him no heed. Sire, we must leave you now for we have stayed too long. Pray have the shield and hound secured as by our request.'

At the King's command, Yvain took the shield and hung it on the great column, and the Queen's maids took the hound to her apartments where it lay quiet and sad.

As the damsels departed, the King and Queen and the knights looked out of the castle windows and all said that they had never seen a damsel without hair, and felt full sorrow for the damsel with no horse who followed the others on foot.

As they came close by a great forest, the damsels saw a knight on a tall and bony horse. The armour of the knight was full rusty and his shield had been pierced in so many places that the colours thereon could not be seen, and he carried a strong and thick lance. Raising his helmet visor, the knight sayeth, 'Fair welcome, damsel, to you and to your companions.'

'Sire,' sayeth she, 'may God grant you both joy and good adventure.'

'Damsel. Whence come you?'

'From the court of King Arthur who is at Castle Pannenoisance. Is that where you are bound?'

'No,' sayeth the knight, 'I have oft seen the King, but glad I am that he has amended his taking up of good works.'

'Where then do you go, Sire?'

'To the land of the Fisher King, God willing.'

'What, Sire, is your name?'

'I am called Gawain, the nephew of King Arthur.'

'That name, Sire, is such as my heart would have chosen for you. Pray, Gawain, abide with us as our protector for we must soon pass a castle whereof there is some peril.'

'That I shall do willingly,' sayeth the knight.

As they passed through the empty forest, the damsel told Gawain the story of the shield and hound she had left at King Arthur's court and of the knight who had not asked the question.

Though eager to hear, Gawain could not stir his mind from the damsel on foot. 'Pray tell me, why may the damsel on foot not ride upon the carriage?'

'She may not, Sire, for as I have no hair upon my head, she may not go otherwise than on foot. This has come about for the lack of the knight who did not ask the question. Thus are the lands and islands in sorrow and strife. Only when the question is asked by a valorous knight may she ride.'

'Then let us pray that God will grant me the courage and the will to carry out your wish, whereof I may win the notice of God and the praise of the world.'

And thus they went through the green forest until all around began to change. The trees had no leaves and the wood was blackened as though by fire and no birds sang. The ground was also black and split asunder with great cracks from which came forth a stench truly great. And Gawain looked upon the damsels that were distressed by their fortune and grew angered that he could not amend their ills.

They then chanced upon a great valley wherein lay a great black castle surrounded by a tall and black wall. The place seemed to Gawain to be an abode of evil. Upon closing with the castle it was seen to be misshapen and suffered a black stream that issued from a mountain to pass through it with a noise of thunder. From the gateway he heard cries of lamentation from within saying, 'Oh God! What hath become of the good knight, and when will he come?'

'Damsel,' sayeth Gawain, 'what is this foul and hideous castle wherein so many suffer and cry for the coming of the good knight?'

'Sire,' she replied, 'it is the Castle of the Black Hermit. I beseech you not to intrude here for they cannot help me and your death will be at hand. Against them you have no might or power.'

When within a bow-shot of the castle gate they beheld the terrible sight of a hundred and fifty knights pour forth. The knights came to the carriage, lifted up the cover and took the heads thereunder and those of the King and Queen for the heads were their own and the rest their sovereign's. Then, as if in great joy, the knights returned to the castle.

Gawain had remained still to see this and felt great shame that he had allowed such a thing in sight of the damsels but they said unto him, 'Now knoweth you the strength of them and how little your might would have availed you.'

'Damsel,' sayeth Gawain, 'this is an evil castle from where people are robbed in such a manner.'

'Sire,' sayeth she, 'this evil will never be amended, nor this outrage be done away, nor the evil-doer therein be stricken down, nor shall the prisoners therein be set free until such time as the good knight shall come.'

And Gawain replied, 'And glad that knight shall be when by his valour and his boldness he shall destroy so much evil.'

'Therefore, Sire, shall he be the best knight in the world,' sayeth the damsel. 'I despair though that I know him not for I have better reason to see him than anyone alive.'

Gawain sayeth, 'I also wish to see him, for I wish also to turn and continue my journey to the castle of the Fisher King.'

'Then,' sayeth she, 'stay with me until we are beyond the black castle. Then shall I show you the way.'

At this they reached the end of the castle wall and saw a knight issue forth on a great horse. The knight held a strong lance and bore a shield of red whereon was a golden eagle. He spoke to Gawain with the words, 'Knight, I pray you bide a while.'

'What do you want of me?' sayeth Gawain.

'You must fight with me and take from me this shield, or I shall conquer you. This shield is greatly precious and you should try to take it from me for it belonged to the best knight in the world in his time, faithful, wise, and powerful.'

'Who was this knight?'

'Judas Machabeus, he who drove the Syrians from the Temple at Jerusalem and restored and purified it thereafter.'

'You speak truly,' sayeth Gawain, 'for he was a great and good knight.'

'Then you must try and take the shield, for your own is the poorest and most battered that any knight bore. Hardly may a man know the colour thereon.'

Then spoke the damsel. 'Thereby you may well see that his own shield hath not been idle, nor has his horse been as well stabled as yours.'

But the knight replied, 'I will have no long pleading. He must fight with me for I intend to defy him.'

At this the horses drew back and came together at a great pace. The knight smote Gawain on his shield and his lance passed through but breaking against Gawain's armour. Gawain's lance entered the knight's breastplate and drove through his body till he lay on the ground. Pulling his lance free he saw the knight leap to his feet and return to his horse to place his foot in the stirrup and thereby remount.

The damsel then cried out, 'Gawain! Do not permit him to mount his horse again for if he does his strength will increase mightily and you will not conquer him!'

The knight stayed his foot and sayeth, 'Is this then the good Gawain, the nephew of King Arthur?'

'It is,' sayeth the damsel. 'He it is without fail.'

'Sire, sayeth the knight, 'are you he?'

'I am Gawain.'

'Then, Sire,' sayeth the knight, 'I hold myself conquered. Had I known, I would not have been so bold to have challenged so noble a knight.'

The knight took then the red shield bearing an image of a golden eagle and gave it to Gawain. 'Take this shield that once belonged to the best and most faithful knight in the world in his time, for by none I know shall it be better employed than by you. Now, Sire, will you give me your shield as you have no use for it?'

Readily acceding to the knight's request, Gawain made to hand his shield to the knight when, to the surprise of all, the damsel on foot spoke for the first time to them. 'Hold, Gawain! If you deliver him your shield it will be born into the black castle such as only the shields of the defeated are born. The many knights inside will take it that you have been conquered and will come to claim you for the foul prison therein.'

Gawain then sayeth to the knight, 'Is it as the damsel sayeth?'

'It is, Sire,' replied the knight, 'and truly glad am I that I have been conquered for a second time. This second victory of yours has freed me from my sore troubles.'

'Of what troubles do you speak?'

'For I have for many a long time been engaged in jousts with many passing knights. Some have been cowardly, many have been brave, and much is the wounding I have suffered but none bore me to the ground with such force as did you. Since you now carry away the shield, never again shall knights dread to pass this castle, and never again shall I have to contend with them.'

'Then I am truly glad of my conquering of you, and I wish you well.'

'Sire,' sayeth the knight, 'I now must leave and return to the Castle of the Black Hermit, there to display my shame at my defeat.'

'God grant you do well,' sayeth Gawain.

Then spoke the damsel of the lost golden hair. 'Gawain, give me the shield that the knight would have carried off.'

'Willingly, damsel,' sayeth he and gave the shield to the damsel on foot who put it in the carriage. As she did so, a great alarming noise issued from the black castle that resoundeth through the blackened forest.

'It is the fate of the defeated knight. So great is his shame that he has been cast into the foul prison.'

With the black castle left behind them, Gawain sayeth, 'When it shall please you, I must return to my journey.'

And the damsel made reply, 'Truly it is so. May God guard you on your passage.'

Sayeth Gawain, 'Forget not, damsel, I am yours to command.'

'Thank you, Sire, and thank you for your company. Ahead thou shalt see a great Cross beyond which the forest returns well fair and you shall bid farewell to this foul blackness.'

Gawain turned to go, but the damsel on foot cried out to him, 'Sire! I had supposed you to be more heedful.'

'On what account, damsel?' sayeth Gawain in surprise.

'For this,' sayeth she, 'that you have never asked of my damsel why she carries her arm from a cloth of gold around her neck, nor of the precious pillow whereon her arm lieth. I believe that no greater heed will you take at the court of the Fisher King, nor will you ask the question needed.'

'My sweet friend,' sayeth the damsel on the white horse, 'blame not Gawain alone, but also King Arthur before him and all the knights that were at the court. For none of them was so heedful to ask me. Go on your way, Gawain, for it is now too late to ask for I will tell you not, nor shall you ever know it save only by the most cowardly knight in the world. That is mine own knight who goeth out to seek me but knoweth not where to find me.'

'Damsel,' sayeth Gawain, 'nor shall I ask you.'

With that the damsels departed and Gawain set himself forward again towards the great Cross and the fair forest beyond.

Part the IIIrd

Upon entering the green forest Gawain's mind was all turbulent, for the damsel on foot had sayeth he had failed to ask a question of the damsel that had lost her golden hair. Thereby, how might he ask the question of the Holy Grail? Thus troubled, he rode until evensong when he chanced across a small chapel and the house of a hermit in the forest. Before the chapel ran a clear stream beside which sat a damsel holding the reins of a mule. At the saddle-bow of the animal was hung the head of a knight.

'Damsel,' sayeth Gawain, 'may God be with you this evening.'

'Sire,' sayeth she, 'and with you also.'

'Dost thou wait for someone?'

'I do, Sire, I await the return of the hermit of this holy chapel for I would ask him if he knows of a certain knight.'

'Do you think he knows of such people?'

'I have been told so.'

At this the hermit came from the forest and gave greeting to the damsel and Gawain. He invited them into his house and gave their animals feed. He then made to take off the saddles when Gawain sayeth, 'Hold Sire! That is not work for you.'

The hermit replied, 'Though I be a hermit, I know well how to do such matters for I was a squire and a knight for forty years at the court of King Uther Pendragon before coming here twenty years since.'

'But,' sayeth Gawain, 'your features give you the appearance of a man of not yet forty years in this world.'

The hermit bowed his head.

After the saddles had been taken off, the hermit took the damsel and Gawain into the chapel, telling the knight to keep his sword by his side as the forest was perilous. And most fair was the chapel inside.

On return to the house the hermit gave them meat to eat and water from the stream. Then the damsel sayeth to the hermit, 'I am seeking a knight and am come to ask if you know of him.'

'Who is this knight?' sayeth the hermit.

'Sire, he is the pure knight of most holy lineage. He hath a heart of gold and steel, the courage of a lion, the body of a battle-horse, and is without wickedness in everything.'

'Damsel,' sayeth the hermit, 'of little can I tell you of him but that he stayed with me twice within the last twelvemonth.'

'Do you know of another who may know of him?'

'I do not, damsel.'

'And you, Sire,' sayeth she to Gawain, 'do you know of him?'

'I would tell you willingly damsel,' sayeth Gawain, 'but nothing I know of him nor of others that might.'

'And do you know the damsel without hair?'

'Yes, it is ere long since I left her.'

'Does she still carry her arm on a pillow from a cloth of gold round her neck?'

'She does.'

'Sire,' sayeth the hermit, 'what is your name?'

'I am called Gawain, King Arthur's nephew.'

'Then you have my highest esteem.'

'But, Sire,' cried the damsel, 'you are kindred to the worst King that is. Through King Arthur all the world is made worse. For hatred of him I hated a knight that found me nigh to Saint Augustine's chapel, and yet he was the finest knight I ever saw. He slew a knight within the barrier spear most bravely and put himself at much peril to gain for me the head that now hangs from my saddle-bow. But when he told me his name was Arthur the joy fell away for he had the name of that evil King.'

Sayeth Gawain, 'You must speak as you find, but I tell you that King Arthur hath just held the richest court that ever was held, and he has put away all evil and now seeks to bring more good and charity than was ever known before for as long as he shall live. And, damsel, I know of no other knight that beareth the name Arthur.'

'It is right that you come to his rescue for he is your uncle, but your words will mean nothing until he has proved his good intent.'

'Sire,' sayeth the hermit, 'the damsel must say as her heart commands. I say God defend King Arthur for his father made me a knight. Now am I a priest serving the Fisher King by the will of Our Lord and His commandments. All that do serve the Fisher King partake of His reward, for to serve a year seemeth like unto but a month. Such is the holiness of the place and of his castle where I have oftentimes done service in the chapel where the Holy Grail appeareth. Thus it seemeth that all who so serve remain youthful.'

Gawain then asked, 'Sire, by what path may a knight go to his castle?'

'None may show you the way, Sire. Only the will of God may lead you. Do you desire to go thither?'

'It is the greatest wish that I have.'

'If God wills it, may God give you the grace and courage to ask the question when the Grail appears. Be not like the others who failed to ask thereof and caused much evil to befall many people.'

On the morrow, Gawain rose to find his horse and the damsel's mule with saddle and bridle. Going to the chapel he found therein the hermit clothed for the Mass and the damsel praying before an image of Our Lady. There she prayed that God and the sweet Lady would help and guide her. And the tears washed down her face. On her rising, Gawain asked her, 'Why, damsel, are you so downcast?'

She sayeth, 'I am cloaked in desolation for I have been unable to find the pure knight. Now I must go to the castle of the black hermit and bear with me the head of the knight that hangs at my saddle-bow. That head shall be my payment for my safe passage beyond the castle lest otherwise I should be cast into the castle prison or be shamed. Then will I seek the damsel who lost her golden hair and go through the forest in her company.'

When Mass had been sung, Gawain parted company with the hermit and the damsel wishing them God's protection and they him also.

The next day, in search for the lands of the Fisher King, Gawain chanced upon a young squire standing by a horse. Cordially they exchanged salutes and Gawain sayeth, 'Wither go you, my friend?'

'I go, Sire, to seek the Lord of this forest.'

'To whom does the forest belong?'

'It belongeth, Sire, to the best knight in the world.'

'What,' sayeth Gawain, 'can you tell me of him?'

'He ought to bear a shield of white with a red cross upon it. I say that he is a good knight but little call have I to praise him for before he was a squire he slew my father in this forest with a spear. I shall never be at ease until such time as I have avenged my father who was the best of knights.'

'My friend,' sayeth Gawain, 'take heed of what I say. Since your enemy is such a good knight, so much more will be the evil of your actions.'

'Perhaps,' sayeth the squire, 'but on his encounter I shall run upon him as my mortal enemy.'

'As your heart commands, my friend. Meantime, where in this forest may I rest for the night?'

'I know not, Sire, for there are no lodgings for many leagues in all directions. Already it is noon and thou shouldst not tarry if you seek a safe house for tonight.'

Gawain bid the squire God's guidance and went at a great pace through the forest until the sun was like to set. At this, he saw beyond fair meadows a castle on a mountain. Great was the castle and enclosed in high walls with, in its midst, a great tower. When within a bow-shot a squire came from the castle gate and saluted Gawain with a welcome.

'God be with you this evening,' sayeth Gawain. 'What is this castle?'

'It is, Sire, the castle of the Widow Lady.'

'And the name thereof?'

'It is Camelot, Sire. The castle belonged to Alain Le Gros, a loyal and worshipful knight who has been dead for many years. His Lady remains but without comfort or guidance and thus the castle is attacked by those who would remove her by force. Chief amongst these are the Lord of the Moors and another knight. Already they have robbed her of seven castles. Her greatest desire is to see the return of her son for she has none but her daughter and five old knights to help her guard the castle. The gates are barricaded and the draw-bridge raised, Sire, but if you will tell me of your name I will return and tell my Lady of your coming that you may enter and lodge therein tonight.'

'I thank you, Sire,' sayeth Gawain, 'but my name shall already be known therein to your Lady.'

At this, the squire rode off at great pace to the castle and Gawain attended at a chapel near the castle mounted on four columns of marble and was a fair sepulchre. Inside he saw a coffin wherein it was not known who lieth there. And the coffin remained still and whole.

Meanwhile, the squire entered the great hall of the castle and sayeth to the Widow Lady and her daughter, 'Lady, beyond the walls cometh the finest knight I have ever seen. He is well armed and alone and requests to be lodged herein this night.'

An excitement beating within her breast, the Lady asked, 'What name hath he?'

'He told me, Lady, that you should well know his name.'

The Lady then wept with great joy as did her daughter. 'Dear Lord God,' sayeth she, 'it is my son returned. This is the greatest day of my life for now I shall not be robbed of mine honour, nor shall I lose my castle now I have a champion for my cause.'

Straightway the Lady and her daughter left the castle saying 'Haste! At the coffin shall we see whether it be he!' But they found Gawain at the chapel and the coffin not opened. At this, the Widow Lady fell down in a faint and returned only with great weeping.

The daughter of the Widow Lady sayeth to Gawain, 'You are welcome, Sire, but my mother took you to be her son arrived back and made great joy. Now, alas, it is plain that you are not her son for the coffin remains closed and whole, and still we know not who lies therein.'

Gawain raised the Widow Lady and sayeth she, 'Sire, what is your name?'

'Lady,' sayeth he, 'I am called Gawain, the nephew of King Arthur.'

'Then, Sire, you shall be welcome both for your own and for sake of my son.' The Widow Lady then biddeth a squire to take the horse and shield and lance of Gawain to the castle. She took the knight into the great hall and fetched him water to wash for his rusty armour had begrimed him mightily. She apparelled him in a robe of silk and gold and ermine and sat next to him with the question, 'Sire, can you tell me aught of my son whom I hath not seen for many a year and of whom I am in sore need?'

'Lady,' sayeth he, 'I can tell you nought of your son and mighty is my wish that I could for I also would wish to meet him. Pray tell me, how is he named?'

'His name is Percival which meaneth 'lost valleys' and he was the boldest of squires when he departed from this castle. Now I heareth that he is the best knight alive and the most strong and without taint of wickedness. But it is for his slaying of the knight with the red shield that I now much need his courage. For seven years he hath been gone from this castle and from his mother and his sister, Dindrane. Now the brother of the knight he slew and the Lord of the Moors do war upon me and would rob me of my castle. Of my brothers, King Pelles hath given up his land and become a hermit, and the evil King of Castle Mortal lays war against the Fisher King that he might have the most Holy Grail and the Spear of the eternally bleeding point. Pray God that they should never fall to him.'

'Lady,' sayeth Gawain, 'there was a knight at the court of the Fisher King before whom the Holy Grail appeared three times yet he failed to ask whereof it served nor whom it honoured.'

The daughter of the Widow Lady replied, 'Sire, it is truly as you speak and he was the best knight in the world, but though I love my brother and all brave knights it was by the failing of that knight that mine uncle the Fisher King hath fallen upon evil times.'

Sayeth the Widow Lady, 'Sire, it is the duty of all good knights to call upon the Fisher King. Will you therefore go?'

'Lady, I have no greater wish for long has that been my intent.'

'Then you are sure to see my son. Tell him of my evil plight and that of my brother the Fisher King. Moreover, Gawain, remember your duty should you be blessed with the sight of the most Holy Grail.'

'I shall do, Lady, as my God commands.'

As they spoke, five knights of the castle entered the great hall from the hunt and brought much good food. They knelt before the Widow Lady and sayeth, 'Lady, there is to be a great tournament in the valleys that aforetime belonged to you. Great tents are already put up and the brother of the Knight of the Red Shield and the Lord of the Moors are in attendance with many knights. It has been ordained at the tournament that the victor shall have garrison of your castle.'

And the Widow Lady weepeth, saying to Gawain, 'Sire, now you may see how I am to be treated. These knights say already that my home is theirs.'

'They may say as they wish,' sayeth Gawain, 'but it remaineth a great dishonour and sin among them.'

At this, the daughter of the Widow Lady fell at the feet of Gawain but he raiseth her up and sayeth, 'Damsel, be of brave heart.'

'For the sake of God, Sire, take pity on my mother and on me!'

'I have great pity for you both.'

'And therefore, Sire,' sayeth the daughter, 'these straits shall reveal you to be a good knight for by their goodness are great knights known unto God.'

That night Gawain slept with the other knights in the great hall but he slept most poorly for his mind troubled him greatly. On the morn he arose, took food and put on his armour and heard Mass in the castle chapel. Then asked he of the other knights whether they would go to the tournament. All sayeth, 'Yes, Sire, do you so go?'

'In faith, I do,' he replied.

Gawain and the knights took to their horses and bid farewell to the Widow Lady and her daughter who made great joy at Gawain attending to their cause.

After a great gallop, Gawain and the five knights came upon the fairest of lands with green forests and high rocks wherein sported many deer. 'Sire,' said the knights to Gawain, 'we are in the valleys of Camelot of which the Widow Lady and her daughter have been robbed by those that took also her seven castles.'

'That, brother knights, is a wrong and a sin to be avenged.' sayeth Gawain.

Soon they saw the pennants and the shields and the tents of the tournament where many knights were seen to be riding in gallop. The tents stretched from one hand to the other for many were the knights that rode there. One of the companions of Gawain showed him amongst the knights on the field of the tournament the Lord of the Moors and the brother of the Knight of the Red Shield who was named the Knight of the Red Chaos.

At this Gawain galloped into the affray laying low a knight who gave him challenge. The five knights followed and, though none had experience of battle, such was the example of Gawain that they sent their challengers from their horses. The Knight of the Red Chaos who knoweth not Gawain ran at him full tilt but was put aground with broken bones. Knight after knight fell to the lances of Gawain and his five companions. Upon seeing this, the Lord of the Moors rode up with a great band of knights. Gawain ran at him and they met with such ferocity that both their lances broke apart in splinters. The Lord of the Moors lost his stirrups and fell with such mighty force that his helmet gave a great dent to the ground. Gawain took the horse of the Lord of the Moors and gave it to one of the knights of the Widow Lady. Many a knight fell to Gawain and the five knights until the Lord of the Moors returned to the affray and ran at Gawain with the broken shaft of his lance. Again they met with great shock so that the lance-shafts were broken on shield and breast-plate. Crying to his knights not to enter the contest, the Lord of the Moors drew his sword, likewise Gawain. Many and heavy were the blows upon helmet and armour and the Lord of the Moors did bleed with much blood from the mouth and nose until his armour was all bloody. No more could he endure the assault of Gawain and he yielded himself up and his knights to Gawain and his five knights. Gawain took the horse of the Lord of the Moors and sayeth to one of his knights, 'Guard this horse for me.'

The many knights repaired to their tents and took counsel one of the other, all agreeing that the knight with the red shield bearing a golden eagle had done better than all of them. And they asked of the Lord of the Moors if he accorded with them. At this, he answered, 'Aye, it is so.'

To Gawain the Lord of the Moors sayeth, 'You, Sire, are the warden of the Castle Camelot.'

'Thank you, my Lord,' sayeth Gawain. And to the five knights he sayeth, 'Brothers, it is my will that the safe keeping of the Castle Camelot and the Widow Lady and her daughter be in your hands as witnessed by all the knights here present.' This they agreed right gladly.

To the Lord of the Moors, Gawain sayeth, 'You, my Lord, will go to Castle Camelot where you shall be the prisoner of the Widow Lady.'

But the Lord of the Moors sayeth, 'No, Sire. You defeated me in tournament, not in war, and you are not right to make me prisoner. Instead, ransom will I pay. What, Sire, is your name?'

'It is Gawain. I am the nephew of King Arthur.'

'Sire, although I have never met you, your name is oft spoken abroad. As the Castle Camelot is now in your keeping you have my promise that for a year and a day neither the castle nor the Lady need fear me or any other that I may prevent from molesting her or her daughter. This I pledge in the presence of these knights here present and I shall give you gold and silver in ransom.'

'Thank you, my Lord,' sayeth Gawain. 'I agree to those terms which you have said.'

At this, Gawain and the five knights returneth to Castle Camelot where Gawain gave the daughter of the Widow Lady the horse of the Lord of the Moors. Great was the joyous feast that night at which Gawain told the Widow Lady that she and her daughter were in the safe keeping of the five knights for a year and a day.

On the morn Gawain took leave after attending Mass, for such was his custom. He departed with commendation unto God from the Widow Lady and her daughter for he had left them in better keeping than when he found it.

It should be known by all that the Castle Camelot of the Widow Lady lies in the west whereas the Castle Camelot of King Arthur guardeth the entrance to England.

Part the IVth

Guided by God and adventure, Gawain went in search of the castle of the Fisher King praying that he might succeed in his holy errand. At evensong he came across a mighty house surrounded by large waters. Thinking this house to be the home of a worthy man, Gawain went to the gate of the house. As he drew night to a bridge leading to the gate he saw a dwarf who sayeth to him, 'Gawain. You are indeed welcome.'

'Dear friend,' sayeth Gawain, 'may God bless you for your kindness. Do you know me?'

'I know you well, Sire,' sayeth the dwarf, 'for I saw you at the tournament. You could not have chosen a better moment to have come hither, for my Lord is absent. But you will find my lady, the most fair and gentle and courteous in all the realm and she is not yet of twenty years.'

'My friend,' sayeth Gawain, 'what is the name of the lord of the house.'

'Sire, he is called Marin, lord of the Castle Gomeret.' Then sayeth the dwarf, 'I will go and tell my lady that the good knight Gawain is come and bid her to make great joy.'

On entering the chamber of the lady, the dwarf sayeth, 'Haste, Lady! Make great joy for Gawain is come to stay with you.'

Sayeth the Lady, 'Your news makes me both glad and sorry. Glad I am that the good knight will abide here tonight, yet sorry that he is the knight that my lord hateth most in the world. He has oft warned me against this knight saying that Gawain keeps not faith with any lady or damsel but would have his will of them, for what is bred in the bone will never be out of the flesh.'

'My Lady,' sayeth the dwarf, 'so I have heard it said, but it is not true.'

When Gawain entered the courtyard and dismounted he was greeted by the lady who took his hand and led him to the hall and made him to sit down upon a cushion. A squire led his horse to the stable and other squires helped him to remove his armour and brought him water to wash. And the dwarf brought him a scarlet and ermine robe to sit at the table with the lady. Many a time as they ate meat Gawain looked at the lady and thought her to be of great beauty. Had he been minded to trust his eyes and his heart he would have changed his purpose, but so strong was his heart that he quenched his desires so that he fell not in to wickedness and deceit for the sake of the high pilgrimage that he was on.

After meat, Gawain went to his bed chamber saying to the lady, 'May God be with you this night.' And the lady answereth the same.'

The dwarf sayeth to Gawain, 'Sire, I shall stay by the door of your bed chamber until you be asleep.'

Gawain replieth, 'Thank you, you shall be rewarded for your kindness.'

Seeing that Gawain had fallen in to sleep, the dwarf left the house and took a boat upstream of the river to a small island whereon was a small house. There slept Marin the Jealous, the master of his lady. The dwarf waketh him roughly, saying, 'Sire, how do you sleep so well when you cannot be sleeping with as much ease as does Gawain.'

The knight sayeth, 'How can you know such a thing?'

'I know, Sire, for I left your lady and Gawain abed together in warm embrace.'

'But,' sayeth Marin the Jealous, 'I forbade that she should ever allow Gawain to enter the house.'

'In truth, Sire,' sayeth the dwarf, 'he has brought her greater pleasure than I have ever heard or known of any man that ever brought pleasure to any lady. Pray haste yourself, Sire, for there is great danger that he may take her away from you.'

'No, I will not go,' sayeth the knight. 'But be assured that she shall pay dearly for this treachery even though she depart with him.'

Knowing nought of this, Gawain rose the next morn. There he met the lady who wept with distress for she knew the dwarf had gone to her master. 'Sire, for the sake of God have pity on me, for the dwarf hath betrayed me. You will depart for the forest and leave me to my lord who will cause me great hurt for that which I have not done. This will be a great sin for you to do.'

'Truly do you speak,' sayeth Gawain. At this he armed himself and left the house to watch from the forest. On his departing, Marin the Jealous returneth. 'Sire,' sayeth the lady. 'Welcome my lord.'

'You, lady,' he replieth, 'may you have nought but shame and evil fall upon you as the most disloyal woman that ever lived. I know that this night you took into my bed the very knight I have warned you against.'

'Sire, I gave him room in the house, but your bed hath never been shamed by me, nor never shall be.'

'You, lady, are a false woman and you lie.' At this he tore her clothing until nought but rags remained although she pleaded with him for mercy. Taking her long tresses he gave them to the hand of the dwarf and told him to drag her to the forest as he rode behind armed on his horse. At the forest they came across a pond of cold water and the knight threw her in as he cut rods from the nearby trees. Thus armed, he beat her until the water took the colour of her blood and her cries resounded through the trees.

On hearing the cries, Gawain galloped at great pace and arrived by the pond saying, 'Hold your hand, Sire! Why do you so treat the best and most loyal lady that I have ever known? Never have I found a lady that did me so much honour in her goodness, in her speech and in her bearing. You should have nought but praise for her. Pull her from the water, Sire, and I will swear on any holy relic that I never sought evil of her nor had I desire so to do.'

'Sire,' replieth Marin the Jealous, 'I will pull her from the pond on one condition. That you will joust at me and I at you. Should you defeat me then she shall be free of all blame, but if I conquer you she shall be held guilty. This shall be the judgement of the matter.'

'I ask for no more,' sayeth Gawain.

Bidding the dwarf to take the lady out of the pond, Marin the Jealous walked back his horse that he might fall upon Gawain in full strength. Both knights came at each other in a might rush, but as they were about to meet shield to shield, Marin the Jealous pulled his horse and rode at his weeping lady piercing her though with his lance. He then rode at great pace to his house with the dwarf running behind. Seeing the foul deed, Gawain raced thereafter and trampled the dwarf beneath his horse until he was slain, but the bridge was raised and the gate of the house was barred.

From the roof of the house, Marin the Jealous cried out, 'This, Sire, is your entire fault. It is you that hath brought shame and misadventure upon me. But you shall pay for it.'

At this, Gawain turned his horse and returned to the place where lay the lady that was slain. Taking her bleeding body upon his horse he found a chapel and lay her modestly inside praying that someone should care for her in death. He then departed with a heavy heart.

Deep in the green forest, still sore of heart, Gawain chanced across a sight he had not thought possible. Coming towards him was a knight of the strangest appearance. The knight was riding his horse whilst sat with his face towards the tail, his armour was hung loose around his neck and his shield and lance were borne with both with their tops at the bottom. As the knight came closer, Gawain heard him cry out, 'Gentle knight, for the sake of God do me no harm for I am the Knight Coward!'

'No, Sire,' returned Gawain, 'I shall not harm you. Indeed I know of no one who would.' Had it not been for his downcast thoughts, Gawain would have laughed to have seen such a sight. 'No, Knight, you shall have nothing to fear from me.'

On their drawing abreast, Gawain asked of the knight, 'Whose knight are you?'

'I am the knight of the lady who hath lost her golden tresses.'

'Then, Knight, you are most welcome, and be well assured that I mean you no harm.'

'May God be praised,' sayeth the knight, 'for I see from your shield of red with the golden eagle that you must be Gawain. In your presence I shall adjust my armour to its proper station and ride my horse as do other knights.' At this, Gawain helped the Knight Coward to arm himself properly.

Thereupon came another knight at a great gallop. He had a shield of black and white equal. 'Wait, Gawain,' he cried, 'I am here on behalf of Marin the Jealous whose wife you caused him to slay. I shall defy you ere you leave this ground.'

Replieth Gawain, 'I am heavy of heart for her death was undeserved.'

'That will avail you not for I hold you to answer for her death. If I conquer you the blame shall be yours, but if you defeat me my lord will still hold your life forfeit.'

'To this I will not agree for God knoweth well that no blame do I have.'

At this spoke the Knight Coward to Gawain, 'Fight him not, Gawain, for you may not depend upon me for help.'

'It is of nought,' replieth Gawain. 'I have long fought and had adventures without you, and with the help of God, I shall continue so to do.'

Seeing that the black and white knight was determined to bring him to combat, Gawain backed his horse before they met at a great gallop. Both their lances were shattered on the shields but Gawain overturned the knight and his horse. He then drew his sword and set to fall upon the other knight but the knight cried out, 'Hold, Gawain! Do you think to slay me? I am defeated and have no wish to die for another's folly. Pray, Sire, have mercy.'

Thereupon Gawain did think that the knight had done no more than follow his lord's bidding. Taking the hand of the knight in his, Gawain bid him fare well and the knight departed.

'Sire,' sayeth the Knight Coward, 'I cannot be as brave as you. As God may witness, had the knight defied me in such a manner I should have run away or fallen to my knees to beg his mercy.'

Gawain replieth, 'You wish for nought but peace, and a full noble wish that is. May God grant you as you desire.'

'In the name of God I thank you for your wish, for of war and battle comes nothing but evil. Nor have I the seams and scars that mark you in many places. Instead I ask God to defend me. And to God I commend you, Sire, for I am now to depart to find my lady without her tresses.'

'Before you depart, Sire, I have a question I must ask. Why does you lady have her arm slung from her neck resting upon a pillow?

'She holds her arm so, Sire, for that was the arm with which she held the Holy Grail up to the knight who would not ask of whom the Grail served. Since that day she will not use the arm again until she can return to the Fisher King's castle and a knight be found who hath the courage to ask the question. Sire, may I now go hither to find my lady?'

'Indeed you may, Knight, and may God go with you.'

'I thank you, Sire. But before I depart I wish to give you my lance. I have no use for it and yours is broken short.'

With that, the Knight Coward gave Gawain his lance and departed.

Gawain continued through the forest until the sun came close to set when he heard the sound of a great gallop. From the trees there came a wounded knight who cried out, 'What is your name, Knight?'

'My name is Gawain.'

'Then, Gawain, it was in your service that I was wounded thus!'

'How so?'

'This morn I went in to a chapel to pray and found the body of a lady you had borne there. I was minded to give her a burial and took her outside and beginneth to dig with my sword when the knight Marin the Jealous fell upon me and wounded me in many places. He seized the body of the lady and abandoned it to the wild beasts of the forest. Now I go to a chapel where I must confess to God, for well I know that I do not have long of this life. But I shall meet God more easily now that I have found you and told you of this story.'

'Sire,' sayeth Gawain, 'I grieve to find you thus and commend you most fully to God's care.'

They parted company and Gawain rode in to the night.

On the next day, Gawain came upon a castle that was both rich and fair. From the castle gates came an ancient knight with a hawk upon his hand. They both gave salute and Gawain asked the knight of whom belongeth the castle. And the knight replied that it was the Castle Orguelleux. The castle of the Proud Maiden that never asked a knight of his name.

The knight continued. 'And those of us who are her knights dare not ask the name of a knight on her behalf. But you will be well lodged within for she is both fair and courteous otherwise. She hath never had any lord nor will she so do until he be proved to be the best knight in the world. Come, Sire, let me escort you therein.'

From the mounting-stage before the hall the knight took Gawain within where squires removed his armour and he was given a robe of scarlet and fur. Then entered the damsel of the castle.

Gawain rose and sayeth, 'Damsel. I greet you well.'

'And, Sire, you also. Welcome indeed you are. Will you see my chapel?'

'At your pleasure, Damsel.'

The maiden took Gawain by the hand and led him to the chapel which was the finest and richest he had ever beheld. Inside were four tombs carved richly. On the right hand were three openings in the wall that were lined with gold and precious stones. Within each, lighted by a circlet of candles, lay a small chest of the finest work. The smell was of the sweetest balm.

'Sire,' sayeth she, 'see you these tombs?'

'I do, Damsel.'

'Three are made for the best knights in the world and the fourth for me. One tomb hath upon it the name Gawain, and the second hath the name Lancelot of the Lake. Each of them do I love for love's sake. The third hath the name Percival. Him do I love above the others. Within the three openings are hallowed chests wherein their heads may lie.'

At this, the maiden put her hand to the wall and took out a pin whereupon a broad blade of the sharpest steel fell and closed up the three openings.

'Thus shall I cut off their heads and place them in the chests therein. Afterwards their bodies shall be set in the three tombs which shall be shrouded both grand and rich. Thus I may never enjoy these knights in their life but they shall be mine until God calls me when I shall join them in company in the fourth tomb.'

Of his name, Gawain stayed silent and though given great honour by the maiden and her knights he wished well that the night may be over and he could leave the place. He heard also that the maiden sent knights in to the forest where they might meet the knights she sought and promised them great riches if one was brought in.

The next morn, after Mass and armed, Gawain said his fare well to the maiden and departed with no desire to remain longer within Castle Orguelleux.

As he rode at great pace through the forest he came upon two knights who mounted their horses at his coming and came to him with their shields up and their lances beneath their arms. 'Hold, Knight!' they cried, 'Tell us your name without falsehood.'

'I have no need of falsehood. I am called Gawain, the nephew of King Arthur.'

'Then, Sire, you are truly welcome. We have one request of you. Will you come with us to see the lady who most in the world wishes to see you and will make much joy at Castle Orguelleux where she waits.'

Gawain replieth, 'I have no leisure for such matters for I am bound elsewhere.'

'Sire,' they sayeth, 'we are commanded by the lady to take you thither whether by your will or not.'

'I have said plainly that I will not go with you.'

With that, the knights took his bridle and began to lead him towards the castle. But Gawain drew his sword and wounded one knight at which they both rode for the castle.

On receiving the knights, the maiden asked, 'Who hath done this to you?'

'It was, Damsel, Gawain. We found him in the forest but he would not come with us. We offered him force but he wounded my fellow knight.'

At this the maiden demanded a great horn be sounded which brought the knights of the castle to her full armed. She commanded them to follow Gawain and promised great riches to the knight that brought him in. Just as they were to depart at her command, two forest keepers came in to the castle. Both were wounded about the body.

'Who hath done this?' Sayeth the knights and the maiden.

'Gawain,' they replieth, 'He would not come to the castle with us and did cause us much hurt.'

'Is he nearby?'

'No, Damsel,' the keepers sayeth. 'He is far distant for he goes at great pace.'

At this, the knights sayeth to the maiden, 'Damsel, it will avail us nothing but shame and hurt to go after him. It was you, Damsel, that lost him for we knew him to be Gawain by his red shield that bears a golden eagle. But you forbade us giving you his name.'

'Then, but by the grace of God, my life is finished for I did not ask his name,' sayeth the maiden. 'Never again shall brave knights abide in my castle. I have lost the first of the great knights and thus I have lost the other two. Myself have I condemned by my pride.' The maiden then bowed her head and wept.

At that time, Gawain was riding through the forest when he heard a hound howling. The dog came to him keeping its nose to the ground whereupon it found a trail of blood that led off the trail. Gawain followed the hound until it led him to a decayed manor within a marsh. Passing over a near ruined bridge he came to the Waste Manor which was much cracked and crumbled. The hound stayed at his heel as Gawain entered. Therein he found the body of a knight which had been stricken through the breast unto the heart. Thereupon, a weeping damsel entered the room with a shroud with which to wrap the dead knight.

'You are welcome, Sire,' sayeth she to Gawain, 'but little cheer have I to offer you for I am in the midst of despair.'

Sayeth Gawain, 'May God grant you comfort and ease from your suffering.'

The damsel spoke to the hound saying, 'This knight is not the one I sent you to bring. I must have the knight that brought death to this knight.'

'Doest thou know who hath slain him?' sayeth Gawain.

'I do, Sire. It was Lancelot of the Lake that slew him in the forest. May God grant me vengeance upon him and all at the court of King Arthur who have brought nothing but evil upon us. This knight shall be avenged for he has a bold son whom is my brother and many good friends besides.'

With that, Gawain left the damsel after commending her to God. He departed the Waste Manor praying to God that he might meet Lancelot.

Part the Vth

Gawain travelled until the sun began to set when he came upon a fair manor and chapel. An orchard surrounded by a high wooden fence lay in front of the chapel. Thereby stood a hermit who looked in to the orchard and gave great shouts as of encouragement. Upon seeing Gawain, the hermit sayeth, 'Welcome, Sire.'

'May God be upon you,' replieth Gawain. At this the hermit had Gawain's horse taken to the stable. Taking the knight by the hand, the hermit led Gawain to the orchard and bid him look inside the fence.

Gawain looked therewithin and saw two damsels and a squire and a child that was riding a lion.

'Sire,' sayeth the hermit, 'this was the cause of my joyous cries. Saw you ever a child so fair?'

'No, Sire, I have not.'

They entered the orchard and the damsel brought Gawain a robe of scarlet and ermine.

'Sire,' sayeth the hermit, 'none may command the lion or ride him save for the child alone and yet the boy is of no more than six years. He is of noble family although his father is the most cruel man known. His father is Marin the Jealous that slew his wife on account of Gawain. The boy will not bide with his father for he knoweth him to be wrong. I am the uncle of the boy and see that he is tended by the damsels and the squire. But much the boy desireth to meet Gawain which is good, for on the death of his father he ought to be that knight's man. If you know anything of Gawain such news would be greatly welcome.'

'By my faith, Sire, I can give you tidings on that account. See you the shield I bore? That is the shield of Gawain.'

'Are you he?' sayeth the hermit.

'Truly, Sire, I am Gawain. And the death of the lady caused me much anger but her slayer retreated to his castle.'

The hermit sayeth to the boy, 'Fair nephew. That which you most desire is come. Come and greet him.'

The boy alighteth from the lion and put it in its den and closed the door thereon. To Gawain he sayeth, 'Welcome, Sire.'

'May you grow in honour before God,' sayeth Gawain. And he picked the boy from the ground and held him dear.

'Sire,' sayeth the hermit, 'through you his mother came to her death. He will be your man but he needeth your guidance and help.'

At this, the child fell to his knees in front of the knight and raised his hands as if in prayer.

'Look, Sire,' sayeth the hermit, 'he offers you his homage. Does not your heart move?'

Gawain took the child's hands in his own and sayeth, 'It is with gladness that I receive your homage and the honour therewith. Always shall you have my help and guidance when you needeth it. What, pray, is your name?'

'I am called, Sire, Meliot of England.'

'Truly he speaks,' sayeth the hermit, 'for his mother was the daughter of a rich lord of the kingdom of England.'

That night Gawain was treated well fair by the hermit and the damsels and the squire. After Mass, the hermit enquired of him, 'Wither go you, Gawain?'

'To the land of the Fisher King, God willing.'

'May God guide and protect you better than the knight that was here before you. Through him the lands are all fallen in to sorrow and the good Fisher King doth languish thereof.'

'May God have me do as His will directs. And you, Sire, may God stand beside you in the care of the boy Meliot.'

Thereupon the knight taketh his leave and came upon meadows and a forest most fair. At this, Gawain met a squire with a most sorrowful countenance.

'Where have you come from, my friend?' sayeth Gawain.

'I come from the forest, Sire.'

'Whose man are you?'

'I belong to the worshipful man that owns the forest.'

'You seem much downcast,' sayeth Gawain.

'I cannot be otherwise, for there is no joy in losing a good lord.'

'Who is your knight?'

'The best in the world,' sayeth the squire.

'Is he slain?'

'No, Sire, but he has been sore troubled this long time past.'

'And what is his name?'

'Those with him know him as Parluifer.'

'Will you tell me where he is?'

'I cannot, Sire, beyond that he abides in the forest. To tell you more would be against my knight's will.'

Gawain then saw that tears brightened the eyes of the squire and sayeth, 'What ails thee?'

'Sire, may I never know peace until I have entered a hermitage to save my soul for I have wrought the greatest sin any man can. I have slain my mother, the Queen, for she telleth me that I shall not be King after my father's death. Instead, she sendeth me to be a monk or a clerk and putteth my young brother in sight of the kingdom. Upon my father learning I had slain my mother he withdrew to this forest to make a hermitage and renounce his kingdom. Nor have I now any will to be King from the great disloyalty that I have wrought. I am, therefore, resolved that it is better that I should be banished than my father.'

'And what is your name?'

'My name, Sire, is Joseus. I am of the lineage of Joseph of Arimathea and my father is King Pelles and mine uncles are the Fisher King and the King of Castle Mortal. The Widow Lady of Camelot is mine aunt. The good knight Parluifer also is of this kin.'

With that the squire Joseus departed and Gawain entered the forest. There he found a spring from which flowed a fair stream by which there led a path much used. Journeying along the trail he came across a fair house and chapel. Outside the chapel sat a man of most pleasing appearance dressed as a hermit. He had white hair and no beard upon his face. At his side a squire held a strong and tall war horse on which was buckled a shield bearing a golden sun. In front of the hermit lay mail armour.

On seeing Gawain the hermit appealed to him saying, 'Ride gently, Sire, and make no noise, for we have no need of worse than we have at present.'

Gawain reined his horse and the hermit continued, 'Do not take it as a discourtesy, Sire, for willingly would I have asked you to lodge with us but within the chapel lieth a knight that is said to be the best in the world. Though he be sorely sick should another knight approach I could not prevent him from rising and challenging the coming knight. And if the sick knight was slain it would be a great loss to the world.'

'What is the name of this knight?' sayeth Gawain.

'I have named him Parluifer, meaning dearness and love.'

'May I see him?'

'Not, Sire, until he be whole again and of good cheer.'

'Is there nothing that I can say that will allow me to see him?'

To the sorrow of Gawain, the hermit replieth, 'No, Sire, nothing can you say.'

'May I then ask the lineage of the knight?'

'He is of the lineage of Joseph of Arimathea, the good soldier.'

Then came a damsel to the door of the chapel and calleth very low to the hermit who rose up and took his leave of Gawain. The damsel and the hermit entered the chapel and closed the door and the squire led the horse to the house taking the armour. Gawain turned his horse and entered the forest with inner hurt for the shame he felt for not knowing if the knight within the chapel was the son of the Widow Lady.

For many a long time Gawain journeyed through lands and kingdoms before he found the fairest of lands with a rich castle therein. Going thither he saw the castle with walls of great height. At the gate of the castle lay a lion chained. On either side of the gate were two engines that shot forth quarrels from their cross-bows with great force that none dare approach. On the walls walked men dressed in white robes as if of priestly manner and knights dressed in a manner ancient. On the same walls were many crosses and holders of relics. Three tall crosses rising from a chapel could be seen within the castle, one taller than the others. At the top of each of the crosses was a golden eagle. The priests and knights all knelt towards this chapel and made joy as if they could see God in Heaven with His Holy Mother.

Gawain was mightily confused. He could not approach the castle for fear of the great cross-bows, nor was there any way to the right or to the left and he was loath to return. At this a priest came forth from the castle. 'Sire,' sayeth Gawain, 'you are most welcome.'

'Good fortune to you, Knight,' sayeth the priest, 'what is you pleasure?'

'May I ask, Sire, what is the name of this castle?'

'It is the entrance to the land of the Fisher King wherein they are beginning the service of the Most Holy Grail.'

'Then, Sire, I seek your permission to advance further for I have journey long and hard to reach the land of the Fisher King.'

'Such a thing I cannot do, Knight, for to enter and approach the Holy Grail you must bring with you the sword with which Saint John the Baptist was beheaded.'

'Then must I be poorly treated for that I do not have the sword?'

'You should understand, Knight, that should you obtain the sword great joy will be made of you within these walls and wherever the Fisher King ruleth. But mark well, Knight, the sword is held by the most foul and unbelieving King that lives.'

'Therefore I must return,' sayeth Gawain, 'though most sorrowful I feel.'

'Thou needest not feel sorrowful, Knight, for should you capture the sword then it will be well known that you are worthy to behold the Holy Grail. But you should take great heed to remember the knight who did not ask whom the Holy Grail served.'

At this, Gawain departed in great sorrow that he had come close to the Holy Grail yet could not approach it. And he remembered not to ask of the priest where the sword that was used to behead Saint John the Baptist lay. But he remindeth himself that if God intended that he should be successful He would guide him to the place.

One day, Gawain came upon a small hill whereon was built a chapel. By the chapel was a townsman that sitteth upon a mighty battle-horse. They saluted each the other.

'Sire,' sayeth the townsman, 'I am of sorrow that your ride upon a horse that is lean and spare of flesh. It seemeth to me that you should be better horsed.'

'Nothing can be done, Sire,' sayeth Gawain, 'only when it please God shall I have a better horse.'

'Wither go you, Sire?' sayeth the townsman.

'I go to seek the sword wherewith the head of Saint John the Baptist was cut off.'

'Then, Sire, you run a sore peril for the King that hath it believeth not in God and is most foul and cruel. His name is Gurgalain and many are the knights who have gone thither but have not returned. Nonetheless, if God grant you the victory and you win the sword will you give me your word to bring it to me so that I may see it, for which I will give you my horse for your own?'

'Sire, you are most courteous but you know me not.'

'I do not doubt that you are an honourable and sincere man and that you will hold to your covenant.'

'And to this do I pledge you my word,' sayeth Gawain, 'that if God allows me to win the sword, I will show it to you on my return.'

And they departed that place on each other's horse.

Gawain rode at great pace until the night cometh but could find no castle nor house therein to lodge. With the rising moon he came across a broad meadow wherein a fair stream flowed. There he found a large tent white of sides and with a covering of red silk. The cords of the tent were of red silk and the pegs that pierced the ground were of ivory. The tops of the poles were golden and each bore at its top a golden eagle. At the door of the tent Gawain alighteth and took off his horse's bridle letting him feed upon the grass. Against the side of the tent he placed his lance and shield. Gawain then entered the tent and wondered at what he saw. In the centre lay a broad couch of red silk on which was placed a bed of feathers. A coverlet of ermine lay atop and at the head of the bed lay two pillows such as the fairest ever seen. All around lay a sweet scent as if of balm. On the ground were spread silken cloths. A seat of ivory was placed at each side of the couch each bearing a rich cushion. At the foot of the couch were two golden candlesticks with tall wax tapers therein. In the tent also was a table of ivory banded with gold and set with precious jewels. On the table was a cloth spread and a silver bowl and a knife with an ivory handle and golden vessels.

Gawain laid himself down on the couch and wondered at the tent and that not a soul was to be seen. At this he thought to take off his armour.

Thereupon a dwarf entered the tent and saluted the knight. The dwarf then came to the couch and began to take of Gawain's armour. The knight remembereth the lady who was slain though a dwarf and sayeth, 'Stand back from me, my friend, for I am not minded to disarm myself.'

'Sire,' sayeth the dwarf, 'you may disarm without misgiving for until the morrow you shall have no cause for alarm. Never were you lodged more richly or more honourably than tonight.'

With that Gawain began to disarm with the help of the dwarf but he brought in his lance and shield and sword by the couch. The dwarf brought him a silver bowl of water that he may wash, after which the dwarf brought him a robe of cloth of gold with ermine trimmed.

'Sire,' sayeth the dwarf, 'be not troubled over your horse for I shall see that he is at ease and fed and return him to you.'

Thereupon, two squires entered the tent with meat and wines and set them upon the table. They bid Gawain to eat and placed great torches in a tall stand of gold. They then departed.

As Gawain ate, two damsels of great beauty entered the tent and saluted him most courteously which he returned in kind.

'Sire,' sayeth the damsels, 'may God tomorrow grant you the strength to destroy the evil custom of this tent.'

'Of which evil custom do you speak, damsel?'

'Of a right foul practice, which causes me much grief, but it seemeth to me that you are the knight who, by the help of God, will cause the defeat of it.' In truth, though they would not give the evil custom a name, it was an eternal struggle against the armoured purity of chastity and honour.

Thus, the two damsels took him by the hand and led him to the stream in the meadow. 'Sire,' sayeth the elder damsel, 'what is your name?'

'My name is Gawain.'

'Then, Sire, we love you all the more for well we know that the evil custom of the tent shall be defeated. But only on the condition that you choose tonight the one of we two that most pleaseth you.'

But Gawain was most minded to sleep for he was weary and made his way to the tent. There the damsels helped him lay down and sat upon the bed and lighted the candles and awaited his requests. But Gawain said only, 'Thank you, damsels,' and closed his eyes.

'By God's wounds,' sayeth one damsel to the other, 'if this were truly Gawain, the nephew of King Arthur, he would not speak thus, nor would he deny such sport. This must be a false Gawain and we have done him honour for no purpose. Tomorrow he shall truly pay his reckoning.'

Then in to the tent came the dwarf and the damsels sayeth unto him, 'Keep a good watch over this knight that he might not flee for he is a false knight that gains lodging by the pretence that he is Gawain. We know this for if he had been the true Gawain and had spent a night in our company he would have wished for many another.'

'He will not go, damsels,' sayeth the dwarf, 'for his horse is in my safe keeping.'

But Gawain sleepeth not and heard all that had been said.

On the morn, Gawain awoke to find his armour and arms ready for wear. Outside the tent he found his horse with saddle and bridle and the dwarf waiting to help him depart. Sayeth the dwarf, 'Sire, you have not served the damsels as they would have wished and they make sore complaint of you.'

'If I deserve their complaint,' sayeth Gawain, 'then I am truly sorry. But I am not aware of any ill that I have done them.'

'They say, Sire, that you are most churlish, which a pity is for so gallant a knight as you appear to be.'

'They must say as they see. For myself I do not know who to render thanks for the good lodging I had last night save God. It would be right and proper to thank them.'

At this, two knights well armed rode up to the tent and thinking that Gawain was want to leave without a fair departing sayeth, 'Sire, last night we left the tent for you and all that was therein, and now you depart without payment. Pay for your lodging, Sire!'

'What would you have me do?' sayeth Gawain.

'You should pay for your victuals and the use of the tent.'

Then appeared the two damsels who addressed Gawain, 'Knight, now shall we see whether you are the nephew of King Arthur.'

And the dwarf sayeth, 'By my faith, I doubt much that we shall lose the evil custom that keeps good knights from coming by this knight.'

So Gawain felt him great shame so to be mocked and knew that he might not depart without a contest.

One of the knights descendeth from his horse as the other backed his horse for a charge. Then he came on at Gawain who met him full on with great blow. Gawain's lance pierced the knight's shield and the lance entered the body of the knight and threw him and his horse to the ground.

'By my faith!' sayeth the elder damsel, 'Look at Gawain the False. He doth do better than he did last night!'

Gawain pulled his lance from the knight's body and did dismount taking his sword from its scabbard. At this, the wounded knight cried out for mercy and holdeth himself vanquished. Gawain delayed his action for thought of what to do. Then the elder of the damsels sayeth unto him, 'Knight, the evil practice that keeps good knights away cannot be done away with until you slay this knight.'

The wounded knight turned to her and sayeth, 'Hear the great disloyalty of this woman. She who pretendeth to love me more than any in the world, now pleads my death.'

'I tell you plain, Sire,' replieth the damsel, 'the evil custom will not leave until you be slain.'

Thereupon, Gawain thrust his sword through the knight's body and killed him.

Now the other knight mounted his horse and backed away to charge in full measure. So doth Gawain and the two met with such hurtle that their lances break short, their shields pierce, saddle-bows splinter and girths burst asunder sending both knights to the ground whereon blood came from the mouths of both knights.

Then the dwarf cried out, 'Damsel, your Gawain the False doth most well!'

'Truly you speak,' sayeth the damsel. 'He must remain with us.'

Gawain was minded to let the knight live and did not further attack him when he cried out for mercy. But the damsels cried to Gawain, 'If you slay him not, the evil custom will not be overthrown. You must smite him at his foot for he is of the lineage of Achilles and cannot die otherwise.'

'Damsel,' sayeth the knight, 'you shame me with your love that hath turned against me. May there never be more such as you.'

Gawain still had pity on the knight and took the saddle from the horse of the dead knight and put it on his own. At this, the dwarf helped the knight to mount his horse, whereon the knight fled towards the forest at great pace. And the damsels cried out, 'Knight, your pity will be our death this day! For the Knight without Pity has gone for help, and if he escape, we shall be dead and you also.'

Thereon, Gawain mounted his horse and took a lance that was by the tent and followed the knight and smote him to the ground saying, 'No further may you go!'

'Much grief that causes me,' sayeth the knight, 'for I should have avenged me on you and the damsels before fall of night.'

And Gawain drew his sword and thrust it in to the knight's foot and the knight stretched himself forth and died.

The damsels make great joy of Gawain and tell him that he hath saved them from the evil custom. They made to tend to his wounds but he telleth them to take no heed.

'Sire,' they sayeth, 'again we offer you our services, for well we know you to be a good knight. Take as your lady-love which of us as you please.'

'Thank you, damsels,' sayeth Gawain, 'your kindness I am want to honour, but I can do no more than commend you to God.'

'But why will you leave us? Far better would it be for you to stay with us in this tent and be at comfort.'

'No, damsels, I have not the leisure to bide here and must return to the trail.'

At this, the younger damsel sayeth, 'Let him go, for he cannot be a true knight.'

But the elder sayeth with downcast eyes, 'It sore greiveth me that he goes, for had he stayed it would have pleased me right well.'

And thus Gawain departed and entered the forest.

Part the VIth

Gawain rode through the forest until he came across a high wall that went beyond sight wither it led. There was but one gate in the wall. On entering, Gawain beheld a land most fair with many orchards and well-garnished gardens. In the centre of the land was a great high rock on which a sat a great long-necked heron that kept watch over the land. On seeing Gawain, the bird cried out so loud that the lord of the land who was the King of Wales heard it and sent two knights to enquire who had arrived.

As the knights came to Gawain they cried out, 'Hold, Knight, for the King of this land would speak with you. No knight passeth through this land without the King speak to him.'

'Willingly,' sayeth Gawain, 'for I knew not the custom.'

The knights led him thither to the great hall wherein was the King and Gawain alighteth from his horse and set his lance and shield against the mounting stage. The King made great joy of him and asked him wither he goeth?

'I go, Sire,' sayeth Gawain, 'into a country where before I have never set foot.'

'Well I know this,' sayeth the King, 'for you are passing through my land to reach the country of King Gurgalain to capture the sword whereby Saint John the Baptist was beheaded.'

'It is true what you say, Sire. May God grant that I take the sword.'

'That may indeed be the will of God, but it is my will that you shall remain in my land for a year before you may depart.'

'God's mercy!' crieth Gawain. 'Why should I be so constrained?'

'For well I know that you will take the sword but not return by my land.'

'Sire, I pledge you my word that with the help of God, should I obtain the sword, I will return by you.'

At this, the King relenteth and sayeth, 'Then I will allow you to depart from me as you will for there is nought that I more wish to see than the sword.'

Gawain departed the next morn and entered a dark and gloomy forest. At noon he came by a marble fountain. Rich pillars surrounded the fountain and all were banded in gold and set with precious jewels. On the main pillar was a golden dish held by a silver chain. In the midst of the fountain was an image carved so finely that it seemed to live. As Gawain approached the image went down below the water and was hidden. Thinking to take a drink with the golden dish, Gawain reached towards it when a voice cried out, 'You are not the good knight who is served herein and who thereby is made whole.'

Gawain looked and saw a young clerk clad in white come to the fountain. On his arm the clerk bore a white napkin and he carried a small square vessel of gold. Then three most fair damsels came dressed in white robes with white cloths upon their heads. One carried bread in a small gold vessel, another carried wine in an ivory vessel and the other carried meat in a vessel of silver. They came to the dish on the chain and put therein the vessels that they carried and made the sign of the cross. They then went back as before but to the marvelling of Gawain there seemed to be but one damsel returning. The clerk took the golden dish from the chain and replaced it with the one he carried and walked in to the forest.

Gawain went after the clerk and sayeth, 'Young, will you speak with me?'

'What is your pleasure?' sayeth the clerk.

'Whither carry you the golden dish and that which is therein?'

'To the hermits that live in the forest and to the good knight that lies sick in the house of his uncle King Hermit.'

'Is it far from hence?' sayeth Gawain.

'To you, Sire, but I shall be there much sooner than thou shall.'

'By God,' sayeth Gawain, 'I wish I were there now that I might see him and speak with him.'

'So may you wish, Sire, but you are not there now and he is not here.'

At this, Gawain departed and rode through the forest until he chanced upon a hermitage. 'Sire,' sayeth the hermit, 'whither goest thou?'

'To the land of King Gurgalain, Sire. Is this the way?'

It is, Sire, but many good knights have passed hereby that have never returned.'

'Is it far?' sayeth Gawain.

'The King and his land are close by, but the castle wherein is the sword is far off.'

Gawain bided at the hermitage and after Mass rode to the land of King Gurgalain. There he encountered many folk expressing great sorrow. On the trail he met a knight riding at great pace to a castle. 'Sire,' sayeth Gawain, 'why do the folk of this castle, the land about and the country express such sorrow? For on every side I hear them weep and hold their heads in their hands.'

'I will tell you, Sire,' sayeth the knight. 'King Gurgalain hath but one son and he hath been taken by a giant who hath done much other mischief and wasted much of the land. Now hath the King sent word abroad that whosoever shall kill the giant and bring back his son he will give the fairest sword in the world and as much treasure as can be carried. But the King hath not found a knight with the courage so to do and blames his own faith and thus invites Christian knights to bring their aid.'

Joyous of these tidings, Gawain rode on to the castle of King Gurgalain where the King greeted him greatly and asked his name and whereof he came.'

'Sire,' sayeth Gawain, 'my name is Gawain and I am of the land of King Arthur.'

'And a goodly land that truly is,' sayeth the King, 'but mine own hath no one with the courage to rescue my son. Should, howsoever, you have the necessary valour to act on my behalf and place yourself in danger for the sake of my son, I will give you the richest sword that ever was forged and which was used to cut off the head of Saint John the Baptist. Every day at noon the blade flows full bloody for at that hour the good man hath his head cut off.'

The King sent for the sword and showeth Gawain the scabbard that was heavy with precious stones and had mountings of silk and fastenings of gold. The hilt of the sword was of gold also and the pommel was set with a most holy sacred stone that Enax, a high Emperor of Rome, hath had set therein. The King then drew the blade from the scabbard and it came full bloody for it was noon. And the King held it before Gawain until the time had passed and the blade came as clear and as green as an emerald. It seemed as long as a full sword but when put in the scabbard it seemed but two hand spans in length. Gawain's desire for the sword grew at the sight he had seen.

'Knight,' sayeth the King, 'this sword will I give you, and I shall do another thing whereof you shall have joy.'

'And I, Sire, with the help of God and His Holy Mother will do as you need.'

And the King showeth Gawain the way to the lair of the giant and the good knight left with the prayers of the people after their own faith. He rode until he came to a land much wasted by the giant wherein was a great high mountain. Thereon lived the giant most cruel and horrible who feared no man in the world and no knight had the courage to seek him. The path to the giant's castle proved to be a pass so narrow that Gawain could not take his horse, nor his shield, nor his lance and had to press himself through the rocks armed with sword alone. Such the giant could with ease step over but not an earthly divide man.

As he cleared the pass, Gawain came to a level land wherein sat the giant with the son of the King before his castle. When the giant seeth Gawain he gave a fearful shout and took up a great axe and ran to the knight. The giant, thinking to strike Gawain on the head, swung the axe but Gawain stepped aside and with a leap cut off the giant's arm, axe and all. At this the giant went back to the King's son and took him in his good hand and crushed him to death. Then the giant returneth to Gawain and picked him up in his good hand to crush him also but falleth down from his great wound. As he fell Gawain thrust his sword into the giant's heart and slew him.

Gawain cut off the giant's head and with much sorrow took up the body of the King's son and returneth to his horse. He then rode to the castle of King Gurgalain and delivered up the body of the King's son which brought much sorrow throughout the land. But the King was an honourable man and heaped much praise upon Gawain for slaying the giant and gave him the sword for which the deed had been done. And the head of the giant was hanged at the gate of the castle.

The King did then cause a great fire to be lit and had the body of his son set in a great brass bowl wherein it was soon on boil and cooked and fed to the high men of the land.

The King sayeth to Gawain, 'There is yet more I would do for you.' And he sent for all his knight and people to attend upon him at the castle.

The King told his knights and people that from the example of Gawain it was his wish that he baptised a Christian. And a hermit was sent for and did baptise the King with the name Archis. The King did then tell the knights and people that if any were not willing to believe in God, he would command Gawain to cut off their heads.

Thus by the miracle of God and by Gawain was the King of Albanie baptised.

At this, Gawain departed and rode to fulfil his vow to the King of Wales to whom he showed the sword as he had given his word. The King ordered the sword to be placed in his treasury and Gawain cried 'This, Sire, is betrayal!'

And the King sayeth, 'I am of the lineage of the man who cut of Saint John the Baptist's head, therefore it is mine of better right than yours.'

But the knights of the King joined with Gawain and sayeth, 'Sire, Gawain hath been a true and loyal knight. You should yield to him that which he won fairly else the world think evil of you for your deed.'

The King wondereth at this and was loathe to give up the sword but sayeth, 'I will yield the sword only on the condition that the request of the first damsel Gawain meets and sayeth my name shall not be denied her request in full whatsoever that request might be.'

At this, Gawain readily agreed for he was much anxious to be gone from the place. With the sword he departed and went to the place whereat he had vowed to show the sword to the townsman who had exchanged his horse for his own. When the townsman arrived he took the sword and looked at it closely before smiting his horse with his spurs and galloping towards the nearby town.

Gawain set after him at great pace but the townsman had entered the town before he could catch him. There the knight seeth a great procession of priests and clerks and many crosses and relics and he saw the townsman entered the church before the procession. On entering the church Gawain sayeth loudly, 'My lords, yield up to me the sword the townsman hath plundered from me by treachery!'

But sayeth the priests, 'Sire, we know well that the sword is that which was used to cut off the head of Saint John the Baptist and the townsman hath brought it to this place to consecrate as a holy relic and to provide a holy sanctuary. He sayeth that it was given to him freely.'

'Not so, my lords,' sayeth Gawain. 'I showed it to him to fulfil my pledge and he hath taken it by treachery.'

Seeing him to be a good knight, the priests ordained the return of the sword and Gawain departed most joyfully.

Gawain had gone scarce far when he encountered a well armed knight that appeareth ready for combat. 'Sire,' he sayeth to Gawain, 'I have come to help you for it is known that you were treated evilly in the town, I am from the castle that gives help to all stranger knights that pass by whenever they have need thereof.'

'May God bless such a castle,' sayeth Gawain. 'But I complain not for right was done me by the town. What, Sire, is the name of the castle?'

'It is the Castle of the Ball. Since you have been delivered as of your right, will you come hither with me and lodge the night at the castle? My lord is a good man and will welcome you rightly.'

Thither they went to the castle which was fair and welcoming and were met at the mounting stage by the lord and his two fair daughters who played with a ball of gold. The lord greeted Gawain right well and bid his daughters take him in to the great hall. There he disarmed himself and was given a red robe. After dining on meat the two maidens sat with him and provided great cheer.

At this, a dwarf came rushing from a side door and began to beat the maidens about the face and head with a whip. 'You fools!' he cried. 'Know you not that you make cheer with him whom you should hate! For this is Gawain, King Arthur's nephew, who hath slain your uncle!'

The maidens left the hall in great shame and Gawain was greatly chastened. When the dwarf had left the hall the father of the maidens sayeth unto Gawain, 'Be not troubled by what he sayeth, for the dwarf is our master, he teacheth my daughters and he is with great anger that you have slain his brother the day that Marin the Jealous slew his wife on your account. Since that time there has been much sorrow in this castle.'

'I also am sorry,' sayeth Gawain, 'for blame of her death is neither mine nor hers as God knoweth.'

On the morn, Gawain rode many a day until he came again to the castle at the entrance to the land of the Fisher King. There he saw that the lion had gone from the gate and the cross-bow engines were not there. He saw a grand procession of priests and rulers from the castle coming to meet him. A squire, fully clothed in his rank, took the horse and armour of Gawain and the good knight went forward to meet the procession. There he displayed to them the sword at noon and the blade came all bloody and they bow down and sang hymns to the Lord. Great joy was made of Gawain and all prayed that God should lead him to the castle of the Fisher King and that the Holy Grail should appear unto him and he should ask the question. To which he answereth that he would do as God commanded.

The chief priest sayeth unto Gawain, 'You, Sire, have great need for rest for you have travelled long and hard.'

'It is true and I have seen many things of which I am ashamed. Tell me, Sire, what is this castle called?'

'It is the Castle of Inquest where there is nought that you may ask that may not be answered. This has been ordained by the Holy Ghost.'

'Then, Sire,' sayeth Gawain, 'pray tell me of the three damsels that were at the court of King Arthur. One held the head of a King, the other of a Queen. And they hath a carriage wherein was the heads of a hundred and fifty knights some in gold, some cased in silver and some in lead.'

'It was, Sire, a Queen that betrayed and hath slain the King and the knights and the heads were carried in remembrance of our first King Adam who was betrayed by his Queen Eve. And the people that were after him and the people yet to come remain in much sorrow for her treason. The heads of the knights sealed in gold signify God's new law, those sealed in silver, God's old law, and those sealed in lead signify the false law of the unbelievers. Of such is the world made.'

'Tell me also, Sire, of the Castle of the Black Hermit whereof the heads were all taken from the Damsel of the Carriage. That damsel sayeth to me that the Good Knight should cast them all out when he comes to the relief of the folk that are therein.'

'As you know well, Sire, when Eve gave Adam to eat of the apple, all mankind went to Hell, alike both the good and the evil. Thus God became man to save these good souls with His Grace and Might. Thus also the Castle of the Black Hermit doth signify Hell and that the Black Hermit doth signify the Devil and the Good Knight shall cast them out those within. By such allusion and example doth unlearned hermits come to know God's will.'

'What of the marvel of the damsel without tresses who sayeth that she should never again have hair until the Good Knight achieveth the Holy Grail?'

'The damsel is without hair from the time that the knight did fail to ask the question of the Holy Grail. This doth signify the good soldier Joseph who was without hair on his head until Our Lord redeemed our people by His blood and His death. On this his hair grew again. The carriage she leads doth signify the wheel of fortune for though the carriage goeth on wheels she lays the burdens of the world on the two damsels that follow her. The fairest follows on foot and the other on a horse much broken down and both are but poorly clad. The shield of the red cross that was left at the court of King Arthur doth signify the Cross on which our Lord died and may not be taken up by anyone except with the command of God.'

Of this Gawain knew well for he had oft heard of the shield that hung in the great hall of King Arthur waiting for the Good Knight that should come to take it. Sayeth he to the chief priest, 'Much now do I understand, but I am in great sorrow for a lady that her husband did slay on my account though no blame was in her or in me.'

'Truly there was great significance in the death of the lady. When on the Cross Our Lord was smitten in the side by the spear thus was the old law destroyed. The lady doth signify the old law.'

'Sire,' sayeth Gawain, 'I met a knight in the forest who rode his horse backwards and carried his shield and lance upside down and hath his armour hanging from him. But when he hath seen me he set himself to right and rode as any other knight.'

'The old law had turned to the worst before Our Lord's death upon the Cross. As soon as He was dead God's new law began and all was restored.'

'Also, Sire, a knight with a shield of black and white challenged me to joust within him on behalf of Marin the Jealous who had slain his wife. He I vanquished and he did pay me homage.'

'When the old law was destroyed all mankind that remaineth are subject to the new law and shall be forever more.'

'Sire, I marvelled greatly at a child who rode a most savage lion in a hermitage. None dare to come near the lion save only the child and he was not above six years. The child was the son of the blameless lady that was killed on my account.'

'The child doth signify the Saviour of the world who was born under the old law. The lion doth signify the people of the world and the beasts and the birds that none may be governed save by virtue of Him alone.'

'That, Sire, bringeth me great joy at heart. One day I found the fairest of fountains in the forest wherein was an image that hid beneath the water when it seeth me. A clerk brought a golden vessel as three damsels filled another golden vessel hanging from the main pillar. The three damsels then departed seeming to me to be just one. Thereon the clerk took the golden vessel from the pillar and set the one he carried in its place before departing.'

'This, Sire, cannot be told to you beyond that you already know. For it is a secret of the Saviour and must remain within his bosom.'

'Then, Sire,' sayeth Gawain, 'may I ask you of a King to whom I returned the body of his son whereon he had his son cooked and made to be eaten by the high folk of his land.'

'By your example the King hath turned to Christ, and by Christ's example made sacrifice of his flesh and blood through his son that the people of the land might follow him in his new devotion. And therefore was all evil belief uprooted from the land so that none remain therein.'

Sayeth Gawain, 'Blessed be the hour that God did send me there!'

'Blessed indeed,' sayeth the priest.

On the morrow, when he had heard Mass, Gawain departed and rode in to the fairest land he had ever beheld. The meadows were many coloured with flowers, the rivers flowed clear and full with wholesome fishes, and the forest aboundeth with wild deer and hermitages. One night he came upon a hermitage wherein the good man had not gone forth for forty years When he seeth Gawain the hermit looked forth from the window and sayeth, 'A good welcome to you, Sire.'

'And may God give you joy,' sayeth Gawain. 'Will you give me lodging this night?'

'I cannot, Sire, for none hath entered herein for forty years but myself and I have sworn to allow none other in but God. But, Sire, if you continue but a little further you will see a castle wherein all good knights are lodged.'

'What is the name of the castle?'

'It is the castle of the good Fisher King and is surrounded by plentiful waters and is of the fairest setting under God. But they will only lodge good knights.'

'May God grant that I may be amongst that company. Before I go thither good hermit, will you hear my confession for I must be cleansed of all sin?'

'Gladly,' sayeth the hermit and heard him of Gawain's true repenting.

The hermit then continued to say, 'Sire, if God is willing, do not forget to ask that which the other knight forgot. Be not afraid at what you see at the entrance to the chapel and ride on without fear. Worship at the holy chapel within the castle for there is where the flame of the Holy Spirit comes down each day for the most Holy Grail and the point of the lance that is presented there.'

'As God guides,' sayeth Gawain as he departeth.

It was not above long before Gawain came upon a right fair castle. In his approach he saw a chapel and went in to pray on his knees for the aid of God. He then rode on until he came upon a rich tomb that was enclosed all around. As he rode passed, a loud voice cried out, 'Touch not the sepulchre, for you are not the good knight through whom it shall be known who lieth therein!'

Coming to the castle gate, Gawain saw that it was reached by three great and horrible bridges whereunder flowed most savage waters. And the first bridge was a drawbridge of length a bow-shot but not above the length of a man's foot in width. Narrow seemed the bridge and the waters swift and deep below. And Gawain knew not what to do.

At this, a knight came forth from the castle and crieth above the waters, 'Knight, pass quickly over the Eel Bridge for night approaches and they of the castle are even now awaiting us.'

'But, Sire,' sayeth Gawain, 'how may I pass over the bridge?'

'All I know, Knight, is that this is the only entrance to the castle. If you desire to come in you must come over without hesitation.'

Gawain was ashamed at his delaying and that he had not harkened too well to the hermit who had told him that of no mortal thing need he be troubled at the entrance to the castle. Knowing him to be confessed and so less in dread of death he crossed his breast and commended his soul to God and gave spur to his horse. To his marvelling the part of the bridge on which he rode grew to a width of easy passage and thus he completed his passing without harm. Then, as if by a hidden engine, the drawbridge raised itself full upright.

The next bridge seemed as long as the other and with fearful water beneath. When Gawain came to the bridge it appeared to be made of thin ice. Again he commended his soul to God and ran at the bridge whereon it turned to solid stone and bore him and his horse with ease. Again the bridge was drawn up.

The third bridge was a great and rich bridge with marble column with tops of gold. And he crossed without hindrance but of the knight could nothing be seen.

The castle gate had set above it an image of Our Lord triumphant on the Cross. On one side was His Holy Mother and on the other

Saint John. All were of gold and with precious stones that flashed like fire. On his right hand he seeth a golden image of an angel that pointed towards the chapel wherein the Holy Grail might be seen. At the gate, Gawain seeth a great and fearsome lion that stood on its feet. But when Gawain passed the lion it fell down in to a retreating crouch.

Within the court of the castle Gawain dismounted and put his lance and shield against the wall before mounting a flight of marble steps. The great hall was a marvel to behold with painted images of gold and of red and of green. There also was a high couch next a table. As he looked in wonder, two knights entered the hall and sayeth to him, 'Welcome, Knight.'

On his returning their salute they made him sit upon the couch and take off his armour. They then brought him two golden basins of water to wash him. After that, came two damsels that brought him a rich robe of cloth of gold and who sayeth unto him, 'Knight, be of good cheer whilst you are here, for this is a lodging of good and loyal knights.'

'That shall I do,' he replieth, and thanked them courteously for their service.

Gawain then looked about him in wonder for he knew it to be night, yet the hall was lit with a light so bright it was as if the sun shone within, but there were no candles burning.

Then the knights said to him, 'Do you wish to see the lord of the Castle?'

And Gawain made reply, 'Gladly I would see him, for I wish to present him with a sword.'

They took him to the chamber wherein lay the Fisher King. The chamber was strewn and sprinkled with the sweetest of balm, green herbs and reeds. The Fisher King lay upon a bed held by silken cords from ivory columns. The coverlet was of sable fur. His cap was of sable fur covered with red silk on which was embroidered a cross of gold. Under his head was a pillow smelling of sweet balm and at the four corners of the pillow were four stones that gave off a bright light. By the bed was a silver eagle on a copper column. At its neck it bore a cross of gold holding a piece of the true Cross on which Our Lord was crucified. This the Fisher King much worshipped. At the four corners of the bed were four tall gold candlesticks in which were tall candles.

Gawain entered the chamber and saluted the King. And the King made him right welcome.

'Sire,' sayeth Gawain, 'I present you with the sword whereof Saint John the Baptist was beheaded.'

'Thank you,' sayeth the King. 'I knew full well that you would bring it for neither you nor any other knight would have come here without the sword. And if you had not been without great valour you would not have gained it.'

And in to the chamber came three damsels. Two sat at the foot of the bed, the other at the head. And the King took the sword and kissed it before giving it to the damsel at the head of the bed for safe keeping.

'What is your name?' sayeth the King.

'Sire, my name is Gawain.'

'Gawain, the brightness of light that shines here within comes from God for love of you. For every time a good knight comes thither to lodge at this castle it appeareth as brightly as it now does. For myself, I wish that I could welcome you more cheerily than I do but I have fallen in to a sickness from the moment the knight of whom you have heard lodged here. On account of but small words he delayed to speak did this sickness fall upon me. I pray therefore that in the name of God you remember to speak them for much joyous I should be if you restored to me my well-being. And here beside me is Dindrane the daughter of my sister that hath been plundered of her land and disinherited in such manner that never can she make regain save through her brother whom she seeks. We have been told he is the best knight in the world but tidings of him there is none.'

'Sire,' sayeth the damsel to her uncle the King, 'I thank Gawain for the honour he did to my lady-mother when he came to her castle. He brought peace to our land and gained the keeping of the castle for a year and a day and sent my lady-mother's five knights there with us to keep it. But the year hath now passed and war will be begun again and God helps us not. And I find not my brother whom we have long lost.'

'Damsel,' sayeth Gawain. 'I only helped you as I could and would so do again. More than any knight in the world I wish to see your brother. But no true tidings have I of him save that I was at a hermitage where was a King hermit and he bade me make no noise for the best knight in the world lay sick therein. And he told me that the knight's name was Parluifer. I saw his horse being led before the chapel by a squire and his shield bore a golden sun.'

'My brother's name is not Parluifer. He was baptised as Percival and it is said by them that hath seen him that no more handsome knight was ever known.'

And the King sayeth, 'And such was the knight that lodged herein. None better have I known to be a good knight but I had no good reward for sheltering him for I may not help myself or any other. In the name of God, Gawain, remember me this night for great confidence have I in your valour.'

'If, Sire, it pleaseth God I shall do nought to bring dishonour upon me.'

At this, Gawain was led in to the great hall where he met twelve ancient knights all of whom had lived for more than a hundred years but none seemed above forty years. They sat him at a rich ivory table and sat round about him. They then filled their drinking horns and drank in his honour saying, 'Remember the good King's prayers ere this night is passed.'

And Gawain replieth saying, 'May God help me in my remembrance.'

Then came dishes of venison and wild boar in gold and silver vessels. Golden candlesticks were placed on the table with tall lighted candles but their brightness was dimmed by the light all around the hall.

Thereupon, two damsels entered the hall from a side chapel. They moved upright in silence as if with no steps as mist across a meadow. The first maiden held in her hand the most Holy Grail. The second maiden held the Spear from the tip of which blood dripped in to the sacred vessel. Side by side the damsels came towards the table whereat the knights were sat and a sweet and holy smell fell upon them. Gawain looked at the Holy Grail and the Spear but it seemed to him to be two angels bearing golden candlesticks in which candles burned. The damsels departed in to another side chapel and Gawain's mind was filled with praise of God. The other knights were fearful of what they had seen and looked to Gawain for he had not asked the question.

Again the Damsels issued from the chapel bearing the Holy Grail and the Spear and came again before Gawain. But he saw only three angels of whom one bore a small child. The knights beckoned to Gawain but the knight looked only at the angels. And three drops of blood fell on the cloth before him and he was in such wonderment that he spoke no words. And the damsels left the hall.

Again the damsels entered the hall and the knights were all in dread and looked at one another. Gawain had not taken his gaze from the three drops of blood. He went to kiss them but they vanished away and he was sorrowful that he had not touched them. Then appeareth in front of him the two damsels bearing the most Holy Grail and the Spear. But he saw three angels of whom one carried an image of Our Lord upon the Cross with Crown of Thorns and a deep wound in his side. And Gawain was moved to great pity. And the knights sayeth to him that he shouldst say the words, for if he delay never again would he have the moment. But Gawain heareth them not and looketh upon the image of Our Lord. And the damsels left the hall.

At this, the ancient knights rose and left the hall leaving Gawain alone. Then he seeth the doors to the great hall had been made fast that no one might pass through. Thereon he slept on the couch until the morn was announced by the sound of a loud horn.

Gawain rose and put on his armour and buckleth his sword to his side. It was his wish to take leave of the Fisher King but all the doors remained fast against him. But he could hear the fairest singing from the chapel and was sorrowful that he could not take Mass as was his custom. Then a damsel came in to the hall and sayeth, 'Sire, you may hear the service that celebrates the bringing of the sword that you presented to the good King and great joy would have been made had you been there. But you are not permitted to enter the chapel for you did not ask the question. So holy is that place that no man nor priest may enter from Saturday noon until after the Monday Mass. You alone, Sire, may have entered had you said but a few words.' As Gawain bowed his head in shame, the damsel sayeth, 'May God be you guardian, Sire, for I believe it not to be by your fault that you did not speak the words whereof this castle would have had great joy.' With that she departed.

And Gawain heard again the sound of a great horn and a loud voice heard he saying, 'He that is from without, let him go hence! The gate is open and the lion is in his den and the bridges are lowered. Thereafter the bridges shall be lifted against the King of the Castle Mortal that warreth against this castle, and therein shall be his death.'

Thereupon Gawain left the hall and found his horse all made ready at the mounting stage with his lance and shield. Beyond the gate he found the bridges wide and long and rode until he came to a great river and he passed by its side. He then entered a forest where there came upon him a storm most fierce and the rain compelled him to put his shield over his head. In such manner he continued until, to his marvelling, he saw a knight riding with a bird on his arm on the far side of the river. Behind the knight rode a fair lady dressed in bright silks for no rain did fall on them and the sun did shine brightly. Then he saw a squire on the other side of the river also idling beneath the sun. And he calleth across to the squire and sayeth, 'Squire, how is it that the rain falleth on me on this side of the river, but on the other side it raineth not at all?'

'Sire,' replieth the squire, 'then you must have deserved it, for such is the custom of the forest.'

'Will this tempest that is with me last for ever?'

'No, Sire. At the first bridge you come to it will cease.'

It was as the squire telleth. The storm continued most fierce until he came to a bridge and crossed. The clouds vanished and he saw before him a great castle where many knights and ladies and damsels were at joy in the fields before the gate. Gawain rode there and alighted but could find no one to take his reins. They continue merry around him but all avoid him. At this, he remounted and left seeing nothing but ill-will towards him. As he departed he came across a knight and asked of him, 'Sire, what castle is this?'

'See you not, Sire, it is a castle of joy?'

'As God is my witness, they are not over-courteous for none came to take my reins nor would any speak with me.'

'They have courtesy in plenty, Sire, but this is no more than you deserve. They take you to be as slow in deed as you have proved to be in word for they saw by your armour and your horse that you come from the Forest Perilous whereby pass all the knights of discomfort.'

Gawain rode on in sorrow and shame until he came to a land much parched and barren. There he findeth a poor castle wherein he entered. All around was poor and wasted. And a poorly clad knight came to him and sayeth, 'Sire, you are welcome.'

The knight took Gawain by the hand and led him to the hall that was in condition most poor. Two damsels entered the hall. Both were poorly clad but were fair of feature and made great welcome to Gawain. Thereon he sought to take off his armour when a knight entered the hall with the tip of a lance through his body. And he knoweth Gawain. Sayeth the knight, 'Haste you, Sire! Take not off your armour! It is with great joy I meet you for I have left Lancelot in combat with four knights who think that he is you. They are kindred to the knights you slew at the tent where you defeated the evil practice. I tried to help Lancelot but was smitten by one of the knights as you see.'

At once Gawain left the hall in haste and full armoured and mounted his horse. As he departed the knight of the castle sayeth, 'Sire, I wish to go with you but I may not depart from the castle until it be restored with people and the land be mine again through the valour of the Good Knight.'

Gawain did not make reply but spurred on his horse and entered the forest and followed the trail of blood made by the wounded knight. Afore long he heard the sound of sword and axe upon armour and shield and came in to a clearing where Lancelot was sore beset by three knights and a fourth lay dead upon the ground. Then another knight retired from the combat as he was much wounded by the knight who had brought the message to Gawain. As he left his horse he fell dead upon the ground. But the two knights that remained were full in force and pressed Lancelot greatly. Gawain rode at one of the knights and sent him and his horse rolling to the ground where he lay slain. The other departeth at great speed and Lancelot cheered the arrival of Gawain.

As Gawain gathered up the horses of the slain knights he telleth Lancelot of the poverty of his host at the castle and how ill-clad the fair damsels hath been. 'Shall we give him what we can provide of these knights?' sayeth Gawain.

'Indeed, good friend,' sayeth Lancelot. 'But it grieves me that one escaped and we cannot grant him more.'

'I assure you, my friend, that the poor knight will welcome even what little we can supply.'

They then rode to the castle and gave the poor knight the three horses and armour of the slain knights and he made great joy and thought himself a rich man. And the two damsels helped the two knights take off their armour. At this, the poor knight sayeth, 'Sires, I should provide you with a robe but none I have except my own jerkin.' The knights asked that he hath no concern in the matter but the two damsels took off their torn gowns and their ragged short coats and gave them to the knights who accepted them with grace for to have refused would have been bad grace against the damsels. At this, the damsels had great joy that the knights had accepted their poor clothing.

'Sires,' sayeth the poor knight, 'the knight that brought the tidings of the combat, he that was stricken though by the lance, is slain and now lays in the castle chapel. He confessed himself to a hermit and asked to be remembered of you. He asked also that you should be at his burial for no better knights are there, so he told me.'

'That we will,' sayeth Lancelot, 'for he was a good knight. Sad it is to me that we do not know his name nor of what country he is from.'

The two knights bided at the castle and were lodge by the poor knight as well as he may. In the morn they went to the chapel to hear Mass and to be at the burial of the knight. Thereupon they departed and took their leave of the poor knight and the two damsels.

As they rode, Lancelot sayeth to Gawain, 'They know not at King Arthur's court what has become of you and many believe you to be slain.'

'Then, brother knight, I shall repair there straight way for long have I toiled in my search. There I shall rest until I gain once more the will to seek adventure.'

Gawain then recounteth to Lancelot how he had been in the presence of the Holy Grail at the castle of the Fisher King, 'And even as it was before me, I could not ask the question whom it served. But I am both sorry and glad. Glad for the great holiness that I witnessed, and sorry that I could not answer the prayer of the Fisher King. Much shame did I feel at the castle and my only comfort comes from knowing that the best knight that ever was also failed before me.'

'Truly, brother, there is much ill that you have brought about by your failure to ask the question. But now God tells me where I must go. I shall go to the castle of the Fisher King and to make amends for what has been done.'

At this, the two knights parted without a word but with their hearts joined in goodwill for each other.

Part the VIIth

Riding at great pace through the forest, Lancelot saw a knight come to him well-armed. 'Sire,' sayeth the knight, 'from whence come you?'

'I come, Sire, from the court of King Arthur.'

'Do you have tidings of a knight that bears a shield of green such as I? If so, he is my brother.'

'What is the name of your brother?'

'It is Gladoens. He is a good and brave knight and he rides a strong and swift white horse.'

'Sire,' sayeth Lancelot, 'are there other knights of your land that bear a shield of green as do you and he?'

'For certain, Sire, there are none.'

'Why do you ask of him?'

'For a certain man hath stolen one of his castles for he was not there. And I know that he will return to restore it to him.'

'Is he a good knight?'

'He is the best of the Isles of the Moors.'

Sayeth Lancelot, 'Sire, if you please, raise your helmet visor.'

The knight raised the visor of his helmet and showed Lancelot his face.

'Knight,' sayeth Lancelot, 'truly you much resemble him.'

'Then, Sire, do you have any tidings of him?'

'I do, Knight,' sayeth Lancelot, 'I can tell you all, for long he rode beside me. Never have I seen one look like another as you do to him.'

'This should it be for we were born of the same mother on the same day. My brother saw light before me and is, therefore, the better and more sharp of mind than I. And though my armour be near me, my skin is nearer still, and my brother is closer even than my skin. As well there is a damsel of the Isles of the Moors that loveth him beyond measure who hath not seen him above a year and even now searches in the forests of the world for him. Pray, Sire, tell me where I may find him.'

'I will tell you, Sire, though it causes me great pain.'

'Hath he done you some misdeed?'

'No, Sire. So much hath he done for me that I owe you my service.'

'Please, Sire, tell me what you mean?'

'Knight, this forenoon did I bid his body farewell and help to bury him.'

'Truly, Sire? Is my brother slain?'

'He is, Sire. And much to my grief for he was slain whilst aiding me. Sad am I to tell you this for no knight have I had so much regard in so short a time as I for your brother. He saved me from death, and so I am bound to you in honour of him.'

'This is great grief to me, for I have lost all by his slaying.' And the knight wept in his sorrow.

At this, Lancelot sayeth, 'Gentle Knight, pray put aside your grief for he will not return by it. Instead, I shall ride at your side and together we shall restore your honour.'

'Truly, I have great need of your help and I shall owe you much if so God guides us.'

'It shall be,' sayeth Lancelot, 'as God commands.'

With that, they went their way together the knight taking much comfort from the words of Lancelot. And they rode until they reached the land of the Moors where they saw a castle on a high rock above lands of meadows.

'This,' sayeth the Knight of the Green Shield to Lancelot, 'was the castle of my brother and is now mine through misfortune. And yet it was stolen from him by a knight of such skill at arms that he feareth no other knight that lives.'

At this, a squire rode from the forest with a slain wild boar across his saddle. And the Knight of the Green Shield asked him whose man he was. And he answereth, 'I am the man of the Knight of the Rock that once belonged to Gladoens. And he cometh behind well armed for he is seeking the brother of Gladoens for whom he hath much disregard.'

Then from the forest came the Knight of the Rock and Lancelot saw him and smote his horse with his spurs. The proud and hardy Knight of the Rock did likewise and the two came at each other most swift. So much did they hurtle that their lances broke upon their shields and Lancelot brought down the Knight of the Rock and his horse also. Lancelot drew his sword and came above him and the Knight of the Rock pleadeth for mercy saying, 'What is this to you, Knight? Am I not challenged by the brother?'

'Indeed, you are, Sire, for I am now his brother as by honour bound.' With that, Lancelot cut off the head of the Knight of the Rock and gave it to the Knight of the Green Shield saying, 'Tell me, Sire, now that he is slain doth the castle belong to you of entirety?'

'It does, Sire, for by his death all claim by his family is vanquished.'

Lancelot lodged that night at the Castle of the Rock and in the morning departed, leaving the knight with his lands and people as before. Before he gave spur to his horse, Lancelot sayeth to the knight, 'Sire, you have my most faithful pledge that should you ever be in peril or in any jeopardy whereof I may help you, and I am free and in place so to do, you shall have my help for ever more. For your brother gave his life to help me.'

Again Lancelot rode through the forest until he espied a knight in a sorrowful situation. Bent forward over his saddle-bow the knight groaned with pain. Sayeth the knight to Lancelot, 'Sire, for the sake of God and His angels, turn back for you are going to the most cruel pass in the world where in I was much wounded through the body. I beseech you, Sire, turn back!'

'Of which pass do you speak, Knight?'

'It is the Pass of the Beards. It is named thus for when entered a knight must leave his beard or be challenged. I took the challenge and I believe me wounded unto death.'

'It was gallantly done, Sire, but I shall not take the way of the coward and turn back. I would rather be smitten through the body with honour than lose with shame a single hair of my beard.'

'Then, Sire,' sayeth the knight, 'may God guard you for the castle thereby is more cruel than you think. And may God protect the knight that destroys the evil therein for shameful is the way they treat knights that pass thereby.'

After bringing what comfort he could to the knight, Lancelot rode on until he crossed a great bridge leading to a castle. There he saw two knights holding the reins of their horses and with their lances and shields leaning against a wall. Behind them lay the gate of the castle all covered with beards and the heads of many knights hung therefrom. As he came close the two knights mounted their horses and came before him saying, 'Hold, Sire, and pay your toll!'

'What, Sire? Do you demand a knight pays a toll?'

'All those that have beards. Those without beards have no such obligation. But you, Sire, have a beard most fine and we are sore in need of it.'

'Why do you need my beard?'

'For the forest hermits that make hair-shirts.'

'Then, Sire,' sayeth Lancelot, 'they must do without mine for I shall not give it up!'

'There is no difference, Sire, in your beard to any other. You shall give it up or you shall pay dearly.'

Seeing that they were determined to shame him, Lancelot lowered his lance and raised his shield and ran hard at the first knight. His lance pierced the other's breast and threw him dead from his horse. At this, the other knight ran at Lancelot and breaketh his lance upon his shield whereon Lancelot bore him to the ground with such force that he was right wounded. Thereon the Lady of the castle came forth from inside with two damsels and saw Lancelot stand over the wounded knight with his sword drawn.

'Sire!' the Lady crieth. 'Stand back from him and harm him further not. Come and speak with me without harm.'

'My Lady,' sayeth one of the damsels. 'I know this knight well for he is Lancelot of the Lake, the most courteous knight at the court of King Arthur.'

94

Lancelot came before the Lady and sayeth, 'Lady, what is your pleasure?'

'I desire,' sayeth she, 'that you lodge in my castle and that you make me amends for the shame that you have done me.'

'Lady, no shame have I done you but it was a shameful business your knights were on. They were minded to take the beards of stranger knights by force.'

'Very well,' sayeth she, 'I will forego any ill-will I may have if you will lodge in the castle tonight.'

Then sayeth Lancelot, 'Lady I have no desire for your ill-will, therefore will I lodge in the castle tonight.'

Lancelot entered the castle and his horse was brought in to the courtyard after him. And the Lady had the dead knight brought to the chapel and buried. The other she had disarmed and commanded that his wounds be mended. Then Lancelot was disarmed and given a rich robe and the Lady telleth him that she knows full well who he is. He replieth, 'Well it is for me that you know who I am.'

Thereupon they sat at table to eat. The first course of foods was brought in by knights in chains that had their noses cut off. The second course was brought in by knights led by squires. The knights were in chains and had their eyes put out. The third course was brought in by knights who had but one hand. The fourth course was brought in by knights that had but one foot. The fifth course was brought in by knights that were tall and fair of feature. When they had delivered their course of food they gave the Lady their swords and kneeled down whereon she cut off their heads.

The Lady then took the hand of Lancelot and led him to her chamber and sayeth, 'Lancelot, you have seen the manner in which I rule my castle. All the knights you have seen were defeated at the gate of my castle.'

'And, Lady,' sayeth he, 'they have been treated most foully by the chance that hath befallen them.'

'Such a mischance would have befallen you but for your being a good knight. And greatly have I desired for such as you to pass by this way for I will make you Lord of this castle and of me also.'

'Lady,' sayeth Lancelot, 'I am willing at be at your service and I have no wish to refuse the Lordship you offer. I thus hold you to this Lordship of the castle and of you.'

'Then, Sire, you will abide with me in this castle for I love you more than any other knight that ever lived.'

'I cannot,' sayeth Lancelot, 'for I may abide not in any castle above one night until I have been to where I must go.'

'Where are you bound?'

'To the castle of the Fisher King.'

'Full well I know this place. The Fisher King doth languish on account of two knights who lodged at his castle but did not ask the question. Is that where you wish to go?'

'Yes, my Lady,' sayeth Lancelot.

'Then pledge me by your faith that you will return to me to tell me that you have seen the most holy Grail and that you have asked of whom doth it serve.'

'This I promise,' sayeth Lancelot, 'even if you were beyond the sea.'

But then a damsel entered the chamber and sayeth, 'Sire, your promise is of nothing worth, for the Holy Grail will not appear to one of such wanton behaviour as you. You, Sire, love the Queen Guinevere, the wife of your Lord, King Arthur. While such an unworthy love remains in your heart, you will never behold the Holy Grail.'

At this did Lancelot feel his face much burn.

'Lancelot,' sayeth the Lady, 'do you love other than me?'

But Lancelot would only reply that the damsel must speak as she was minded.

That night he lodged at the castle and was greatly angered by the damsel who sayeth that his love for the Queen was as if disloyal to his King. After hearing the Mass he took his leave of the Lady of the castle whereon she constantly besought him to keep his covenant. And he replieth that he would so do without fail.

After riding all day, Lancelot found the trail goeth through a burial ground surrounded by a hedge of thorns. Therein were many tombs and sepulchres and a chapel wherein candles were lighted. There he set himself and passed a dwarf digging a grave and did not speak with him. 'Lancelot,' sayeth the dwarf, 'you are right not to salute me for of all the men in the world you are the one I most hate. May God give me vengeance of your body, and soon for you will be stricken down now that you are come here.'

Lancelot looketh hard at the dwarf but did not make reply. He entered the chapel putting his lance and shield without. Within he found a damsel wrapping the body of a knight in a winding sheet. But as she did so the wounds on the body opened up and began again to bleed. At this, the damsel sayeth to Lancelot, 'Now I see that it was you that slayeth this knight that I prepare for his tomb.'

Thereon two knights entered the chapel each bearing the body of a dead knight which they set down in the chapel. And the dwarf cried out unto them saying, 'Now shall we see you avenge yourself on the enemy of your friends.' For one of the knights was the knight who had fled from Lancelot and Gawain and had gone to the place for the bodies of his companion knights. And he sayeth to Lancelot, 'You are our mortal enemy for by you were these three knights slain.'

'And well they deserveth it,' sayeth Lancelot. 'But whilst within this chapel I am in no peril of you. And I stay here until the dawn for I know not the forest hereabouts.'

When the day broke the two knights were outside. And Lancelot did take up his lance and shield and did mount his horse. At this, the dwarf cried out to the two knights saying, 'What ails you? Will you let your mortal enemy depart thus?'

Thereupon the two knights mounted their horses and rode one each to the two entrances to the burial ground. Lancelot rode in slow manner to the unknown knight and faced him at the entrance he had chosen. The knight delayed in response and Lancelot thrust his lance through the knight's body and he fell from his horse dead. On seeing this, the other knight who had fled from the first combat turned and fled to the forest in great fear.

Lancelot took the horse of the knight he hath slain and rode into the forest until he came to a hermitage with a hospitable hermit where he heard Mass and did sleep. On the morrow as he mounted his horse a knight with a squire rode up to him and sayeth, 'Sire, to where do you travel?'

'I go, Knight as God commands. And you, Sire, where do you go?'

'I go, Sire, to see my brother and two sisters who I hear have fallen on such misfortune that he is known as the Poor Knight for which I have much sorrow.'

'I know of him, Sire, and poor he is, more is the pity. Sire, will him you take a message from me?'

'Willingly, Sire,' sayeth the knight.

'Then, Sire, present him with this horse and tell him that it is from Lancelot that lodged with him.'

'Gladly I will, Sire, and blessed may you be for it for he that doth a kindness to a worshipful man will not lose by it.'

'Salute the damsels for me,' sayeth Lancelot.

'As you command, Sire,' sayeth the knight and gave the horse to his squire as they departed from the hermitage.

Lancelot also departeth from the hermitage and entered a waste land where lived no beast nor bird nor anything to eat. Before him he saw a city of much great size and he entered and seeth that the walls were broken down and the gates ruined. Inside the Waste City there were no folk of any sort and he wondered at the sight of palaces in much decay and graveyards unkempt. Churches were fallen down and markets abandoned. He came to an ancient palace and stood outside whereupon he heard much sorrow coming from within. Voices of knights and ladies sayeth in much grief, 'May God have pity on you that you must die in such a manner and that your death may not be stayed. How we hath hatred for him that giveth you such a death.' But nothing could Lancelot see.

Then looked he in to the great hall and seeth a young knight come in to the hall clad in a red jerkin. About his waist was a great band of gold and a rich clasp at his neck flashed with many precious stones. On his head he wore a great cap of gold and in his hand he held a mighty axe. And the knight sayeth to Lancelot, 'Alight from your horse, Sire!'

'As you wish, Sire,' sayeth Lancelot, and he alighted and tied his horse to a silver ring by the mounting stage and he put aside also his lance and shield. 'What is your pleasure?'

'Sire,' replieth the knight, 'you must take this axe and cut off my head for so it hath been ordained. Should you not so do, I will cut off your head.'

'But why?' sayeth Lancelot, 'For you have harmed me not and I do not wish the blame of your death.'

'For, Sire, you will not leave until you have done that which I demand.'

'But, young Sire, you appear gentle and of good form. Why do you take you death so graciously? You know full well that in combat I shall slay you before you slay me.'

'It is as true as you say but there will be no combat. I wish you to promise me before I die that you will return to this city within a year and you will set your head at the same peril without challenge as I now do.'

'Sire,' sayeth Lancelot, 'betwixt dying here now and living for another day I choose to live as would any man. But tell me, Sire, why are you so dressed so grandly to meet your death?'

'Ere long, Sire, I shall be before the Saviour of the World and I should dress as richly as I may. I am purged of all wickedness and misdeeds by confession and I repent me truly thereof.'

At this, the knight gave the axe to Lancelot and the knight saw that it was of good sharpness.

'Sire,' sayeth the young knight, 'pray hold your hand towards yonder church as a sign of fidelity.' And Lancelot did as he was bidden. 'Thus, then, will you swear upon the holy relics within that church that on this day at this hour and within a year you will come to this place and put your head in the same peril as I have placed mine, without neglect?'

'This I swear and give you my most solemn pledge.'

With that, the knight did kneel and Lancelot took up that axe and sayeth, 'May God have mercy upon you.'

And he did let fall the axe and cutteth off the young knight's head with such force that it did fly far from the body. Lancelot cast aside the axe and left the hall and mounteth his horse and taketh up his lance and shield. He looked back in to the hall and saw that the body and head of the knight had disappeared and there was the sound of much sorrow from unseen knights and ladies. They cried of vengeance within a year. And Lancelot departed from the Waste City.

Part the VIIIth

Though Gawain had failed to ask the question of the Holy Grail at the castle of the Fisher King, there had been another good knight who had done likewise. And much to his sadness and sorrow for his failing, great misfortune had fallen upon the knight. In time, wearied of much soreness and down at heart, he came to the hermitage of his uncle, King Pelles, and retired for long within to restore his faith and courage. King Pelles gave him the name of Parluifer and told passing knights that his nephew was in poor times and could not meet them. But one day as King Pelles had gone in to the forest the knight took himself to be quit of his illness and felt himself to be sound and lusty. At this, he raised up and armoured himself and mounted his horse taking his lance and his shield with the golden sun thereon. Now he heard the birds sing and saw the green of the forest and right joyful was he. And he prayeth unto God to find him an adventure wherein he might be tested for he did not know where his courage lay.

And the knight came to a clearing in the forest and rested beneath a shading tree. There he heard the sound of a horse and prayeth that it might be a knight against whom he might be tested. He sayeth unto God, 'Grant that there be a brave knight on that horse that I may prove whether there be any valour of knighthood within me. For I know not what strength I have nor whether my heart is sound. And it is only by trial against a good and brave knight that I might find my courage. Dear Saviour, bring such a knight before me and grant that he slay me not nor I him.'

And from the forest came a knight well armed and bearing a white shield whereon was a golden cross and he came at a swift pace with his lance low. And in great joy the knight from the hermitage put his lance low and smiteth his horse with his spurs shouting, 'Knight! Raise your shield as I do mine for I defy you on this side of death. May you prove to be a good knight who shall try me hard. I am not as I once was and better I shall learn of a good knight than of a bad.'

With that he struck the knight full hard on his shield and making him lose his stirrups. And the knight sayeth, 'Sire, what misdeed have I done you?'

But the knight from the hermitage sayeth nothing for he had no joy that the other knight had not been set low. Again they hurtle together that their lances splintered and their shields full battered and their faces ran with blood. And they drew their swords whereon the Knight of the Cross of Gold calleth out, 'Gladly I would know who you are and why you hate me for you have wounded me sorely and I have found you to be of great strength.' But no answer came and they fell on each other with their swords and the forest rang with the sound of their swords on armour as though neither bore any wounds.

At this, the hermit King Pelles came from the woods with a damsel and rode between the two knights crying to the Knight of the Golden Cross, 'Hold, Sire! Great shame be on you for you have much wounded a knight who hath long lain sick in this forest.'

But the knight replieth, 'No more than he hath wounded me, Sire. Never would I have run at him had he not challenged me. Nor will he tell me who he is or why he challenged me thus.'

Then asked the hermit, 'And you, Sire, who are you?'

And the knight replieth, 'I am Lancelot of the Lake, son of King Ban of Benoic. And who is this knight?'

'This, Sire, is your cousin, Percival, the son of the Widow Lady.'

The hermit King then made each knight take off his helmet and embrace as kin.

And the damsel washed their wounds right tenderly and speaketh of Lancelot to the hermit King, 'Sire, this knight must rest awhile for his wounds places him in peril.'

'And Percival?'

'He, Sire, will soon be healed.'

All returned to the hermitage where the damsel tended their wounds to make them whole. There within lay the true shield of Percival with a white hart on a field of green. This shield was well known to Lancelot and he would not have accepted the challenge had that shield been borne. Now he lay in much discomfort as his wounds were tended.

Part the IXth

And a squire came before King Arthur and kneeled saying, 'Sire, I am the son of the Knight of the Red Shield of the Forest of Shadows who was slain by the son of the Widow Lady. His shield hangs upon the column. Do you, sire, have tidings of this knight?'

'Gladly I would have tidings of him,' sayeth King Arthur, 'for I wish no evil to come to him. Of all the knights in the world he is the one I most desire to see.'

'Yet, Sire, it is an honour for me to hate him for he slew my father. He that should bear that shield was a squire when he did that foul deed and I am much in sorrow that I did not find him when he remained a squire. Now must I be a knight to challenge him and I pray, Sire, that you make me a knight as you have done others.'

'How are you named?' sayeth the King.

'I am called Clamados of the Forest of Shadows.'

Then stepped forward Gawain who was in the great hall. Sayeth he unto the King, 'Sire, if this squire be the mortal enemy of the good knight who should bear that shield, it will not be well for us if you advance this squire to be a knight and thus to be the equal enemy of the good knight. For the bearer of that shield is the most chaste and best knight in the world and of holy lineage. Long have you waited, Sire, for his coming. I say this not to hinder the advancement of the squire but nought should you do that will give the good knight cause for complaint against you.'

At this, Queen Guinevere spoke saying, 'Gawain, well do I know you guard the honour of the King, but much blame will come upon him if he does not make him a knight for he hath never refused any who are with knightly grace. Nor will the good knight bring complaint for he knoweth well that those who are so advanced take on the knightly virtue of slowness in taking offence and are sober in their deeds. I tell you, Sire, that he will listen to reason and I commend the King to make him a knight and thus avoid the blame of false delay.'

'Lady,' sayeth Gawain, 'if this be your wish, then let it be so.'

The King then maketh Clamados to be a knight. Robed as such, all the court declared him to be the fairest knight they had seen in memory. Clamados did then wait and was on constant watch for the good knight that should come for the shield, but the hour and the place were not yet upon them.

At length Clamados wearied of his wait and determined upon an adventure to prove his knighthood. He rode long and hard in to the forest bearing a red shield as had done his father before him. And he came upon two mountains whereof a narrow pass went between. At the entrance to the pass he espied three damsels one of whom had been shorn of her tresses and beside them stood a carriage drawn by three fair harts. And he knoweth of their story from the court and sayeth unto them, 'Damsels, do you have tidings of the knight who should bear the white shield with the Cross of Red?'

'He is the one we seek,' sayeth the Damsel of the Carriage, 'and we pray God that we shall soon find him.'

'Amen to that,' sayeth Clamados. Then sayeth he, 'Why wait you here?'

'We wait, Sire,' sayeth the damsel, 'for a knight who will guard us through this narrow pass. For within is a lion of most ferocious and horrible nature that none dare enter therein unguarded. The lion abideth with a good knight who hath control of him, but oft the knight is on adventure and then the lion doth bestir himself most savagely.'

'Damsels,' sayeth Clamados, 'as you are in quest of the same knight as I, I will gladly guard you through the pass.'

And they entered the pass most narrow until they came to a castle with a fence and a lion sat at the gate. And the lion saw them and put up his ears. He then rose to his height and ran full speed at Clamados with his jaws agape and with a roar that shaketh the forest trees. At this the damsels crieth to Clamados not to meet the lion whilst on his horse for the lion would destroy the horse. And Clamados alighteth and braced himself with his lance whereupon the lion did run and was pierced right through. Clamados drew back his lance and thinketh to strike again but the lion raised him up on his hinder legs and put his fore feet on the shoulders of the knight and hugged him towards him as one man does another. And the armour of the knight was torn asunder and his flesh torn most grievously. At this, Clamados doubled his valour and heaved the lion over and drew his sword and thrust it in to the heart of the lion whereon the lion gave a great roar that shook the mountains and he fell slain.

Clamados cut off the head of the lion and hung it by the gate. And he mounted his horse all bloody and the damsels cried, 'Knight, you are sore wounded!'

'Pray God,' sayeth he, 'that it is as of but small hurt.'

Thereupon a squire came forth of the castle and came to them full pace. 'Hold, Knight,' sayeth he, 'for you have done a foul deed. You have slain the lion of the most courteous and valiant knight that was ever known. And you have done great outrage by hanging the head at his gate!'

'My friend,' sayeth Clamados, 'well may it be that the knight is most courteous, but the lion was most wretched and foul and would have slain me and others that passed by. If your lord loved this lion he should have had him chained. For better I thinketh that I slay him than he slay me.'

'But, Knight,' sayeth the squire, 'this is a land forbidden to travellers for there are those who would plunder the lands and castle of my lord. It was against the coming of his enemies that he allowed the lion to be unchained.'

'What is the name of your lord?'

'It is, Sire, Meliot of England, who even now has gone in quest of Gawain of whom he holds this land and is most dear to him.'

'But Gawain abides at the court of King Arthur. Tell your lord to depart thence and there he shall find him.'

'If only my lord knoweth that you hath slain his lion, then, Sire it would be hard on you should you meet him or Gawain.'

'If he be as courteous as you say, my friend, no offence would he hold against me for defending myself and others. May God forbid that I should meet any that would do me evil for so doing.'

Thereupon Clamados and the damsels departed and went safely through the narrow pass. Ere long they came upon a rich castle set amongst meadows, high forest, and great waters, but of people there were none. Nonetheless, they intended there to go when they met a squire who told them that better it would be if they continued to where there were people in plenty. Thus they went on and came beyond a forest where they saw a great abundance of bright tents surrounded by a long wall of white linen. Within they heard the sound of great joy. They entered and saw ladies and damsels in great numbers and all of great beauty. The damsel of the shorn hair and her companions were greeted with much cheer and two damsels led Clamados to a tent where they took off his armour and washed his wounds. They brought him a rich robe and led him before the Lady of the Tents who made great joy of him.

'Lady,' sayeth she of the shorn tresses, 'this knight hath saved my life for he hath slain the lion which barred many from coming. Pray make great joy of him.'

'Damsel,' sayeth the Lady, 'none can make greater joy than I or the damsels herein, for we wait the coming of the good knight and there is none in the world that we would more desire to see.'

'Lady,' sayeth Clamados, 'who is this good knight?'

'The son of the Widow Lady of the Valley and Castles of Camelot.'

'Tell me, Lady, do you say that he will come hither presently?'

'I believe this so to be.'

'Then, Lady, also shall I have great joy thereof. May God lead him here soon.'

'Knight,' sayeth the Lady, 'what is your name?'

'It is Clamados, my Lady. I am the son of the lord of the Forest of Shadows.'

At this, the Lady threw her arms around the neck of Clamados and kissed him. 'This is joy indeed. For you are the son of my brother and I have no one close in family as you are. You, dear nephew, should be the lord of all my land and of me as is right.'

When they heard this the damsels of the tents make great joy of him. And he bided there until his wounds were whole. And the damsels wondereth much why the good knight did not come, for in their midst was the damsel who hath tended his wounds from his conflict with Lancelot. For she telleth them that he was healed but Lancelot lay still within the hermitage.

Bound of a promise to Lancelot that he would return as soon as God willed, Percival rode in to the forest and came upon a castle wherein he would seek lodgings for the night. He was met by a tall knight with face much scarred. Other than his household no others lodged in the castle. Upon making his salutation, Percival heard the knight say to him, 'Now shall you have the reward you so richly deserve. Never shall you leave this castle for you are my mortal enemy and you have thrown yourself in to my keeping. For I am Chaos the Red, brother of the Knight of the Red Shield whom you slew. I now war against your mother and this castle have I taken from her. Now I shall wring the life out of you.'

'Sire,' sayeth Percival, 'you are bound as a brother knight to afford me safe lodging for the night. In the morning let us see what the break of day should bring.'

'No!' crieth Chaos the Red. 'Only as a dead man will you lodge here!' And he thereupon ran in to the hall and taketh up his sword and ran at Percival who cast aside his lance and ran at Chaos the Red. And Percival was in great anger that the other did war against his mother and had taken this castle. So fierce did Percival strike the other that his sword cut through his armour and deep in to his flesh. But Chaos the Red brought his sword against the helmet of Percival such that sparks flew therefrom and his shield was cut through. Bewildered by the might of his opponent, Percival brought his sword down and cleaved through the sword arm of Chaos the Red. Bereft of his arm and sword, Chaos the Red ran at Percival who struck him on the helmet with such force that he fell dead.

At this, a cry went up from the castle household who had witnessed the combat from the hall balcony. 'Sire! You have slain the strongest and most redoubtable knight in England. We knoweth that this castle is by right your mother's and will offer no challenge.

Kind Sire, may we take up the body of our lord and take it to the chapel for the sake of his knighthood?'

Percival assented and they took the body away and wrapped it in a shroud and gave it seemly burial. After which they came to Percival and sayeth, 'Sire, here are the keys of the castle which you have won for your mother. All the doors are barred and none within but we servants and two damsels.'

Percival sayeth, 'What is the name of this castle?'

'It is known, Sire, as the Key to Wales.'

'Thus I command you to go to my mother, the Widow Lady, and tell her of what has passed. Salute her for me and tell her that I am sound and whole and that she shall see me as soon as God commands.'

On the morn, Percival departed and came to the bright tents behind the wall of linen. But there was no sound of joy as when Clamados arrived with the shorn lady. There was the sound of much sorrowing. On alighting amidst the tents a damsel from the castle came unto him saying, 'For shame, Sire, have you come to this place.' She then crieth out to the Lady of the Tents saying, 'Lady! Behold here he who hath slain the best knight of your family.' Then she crieth out to Clamados who was within the tent saying, 'You, Clamados, here is the knight that slew your father and uncle! Now shall we see what you shall do!'

At this, the Damsel of the Carriage appeared saying, 'Sire, you are indeed welcome. Let others sorrow, but I make great joy of your coming!' She took him into her tent and made him lie on a rich couch as her companion damsels removed his armour. She then took him to the tent of the Lady of the Tents who was in much sorrow and sayeth, 'Hold your sorrow, for here is the good knight on whose account these tents are pitched and on whose account you have been making great joy until this day.'

Sayeth the Lady, 'Is this then the son of the Widow Lady?'

'It is.'

'But he hath slain my family's greatest knight and the one who protected me from mine enemies.'

'Lady,' sayeth the damsel, 'this is the best knight in the world and will be able better to protect and defend us.'

The Lady took the hand of Percival and made him sit next to her. 'Sire,' she sayeth, 'whatever the road you have taken here, my heart bids you welcome.'

'Thank you, my Lady. Truly Chaos the Red would have slain me within his castle and caused me to defend myself with all my power.'

And the Lady looked in to his face and felt a passion within her that grew strong and fervent. 'Sire,' sayeth she, 'if you will grant me your love, I shall pardon you of the death of Chaos the Red.'

'Willingly your love would I have, as you have mine.'

Then sayeth the Lady, 'How shall I know your love?'

'For there shall be no knight in the world that shall desire to do you a wrong, but I shall be at your side to defend you.'

'But such a love is no more than a knight ought to bear to a lady. You would surely do as much for another.'

'That may well be, Lady,' sayeth Percival, 'but a knight may do more to help one than another.'

The Lady desired greatly to hear from Percival of his inward love but he would say no more. She looked upon him deeply with her heart unrestrained but he would not give a greater pledge of his love for her despite her great beauty. She could not move her eyes from him nor diminish her desire and the damsels looked upon her with wonder that she had so soon forgotten her mourning.

Then entereth Clamados in to the tent and beheld the knight who, when only a squire, had slain his father and had now slain his uncle. And he saw that the Lady looked upon him with great sweetness.

'Lady,' sayeth he, 'this is a great shame that you do bring upon yourself. For seated at your side is your and mine mortal enemy. Never again shall anyone trust in you.'

'Clamados,' she replieth, 'this knight hath just arrived and I shall do him no evil but give him lodging and harbour him safely. Nor has he done ought that might be adjudged as murder.'

'Lady, he slew my father in the Lonely Forest without challenge and smote him through with a spear. Therefore I pray you that you give me my right of avenge, not for being one of your kin for that I no longer give regard, but as a stranger who gives this appeal.'

Percival looked at Clamados and saw him to be an upright knight that stood with dignity. 'Sire,' sayeth he, 'you should not hold me guilty of evil towards your father for I had no mind towards evil. May God defend me from such a shame and grant me the strength to defend myself from such blame.'

But Clamados stepped forward as if to issue a challenge to Percival. 'Hold, Sire!' sayeth the Lady. 'There shall be no challenge in this tent. We shall wait until the morrow and take counsel that right shall be done to each.'

Clamados went his way saying that no man should put his trust in woman. But he understood not the great love that the Lady bore for Percival. Meantimes, the Lady was in much sorrow for Percival did not show her any measure of love beyond that already said.

On the morrow Mass was sung when in to the chapel came a knight all armed and bearing a white shield whereon was a golden lion. He came before the Lady and sayeth, 'Lady, I am in search of a knight that hath slain my lion. If you shield him from me, I shall do you as much or more harm as I would have done to him for I must have my vengeance on him. Therefore, I pray you, for the love of Gawain whose man I am, that you do me right.'

Sayeth the Lady, 'What is the name of this knight that you seek so vengefully?'

'He is called Clamados of the Forest of the Shadows.'

'And what, Sire, is your name?'

'It is Meliot of England.'

At this the Lady crieth, 'Clamados! Do you hear what this knight sayeth?'

And Clamados sayeth, 'I do, Lady. But again I pray that you do right by me in the matter of the knight who slew my father and my uncle.'

To which Meliot sayeth, 'Lady, I know not of this other knight. I am here to right the foul deed done to me and to my lion and I wish it to be done straightway for I must depart. If you do not give me the right, it is you I shall challenge.'

'Clamados,' sayeth the Lady, 'do you again hear what this knight sayeth?'

'I do, Lady. Truly I did slay his lion, but not until he had come upon me and given me the wounds of which I am barely healed.

Percival hath done me much more wrong and I pray that you will let me take vengeance of him first.'

'But you see that he is armed in full and wishes to depart forthwith. Meet him first, Sire, then we will talk of the other.'

'Thank you, my Lady,' sayeth Meliot, 'for Gawain will think well of this. This knight hath slain my lion that defended me from all my enemies, but worse, he insulted me greatly by hanging the head of the lion at my gate.'

And the Lady sayeth to Meliot, 'You have no true quarrel with him in the matter of the lion for he was defending himself. But the insult he did you can be seen at this court and if you desire to deliver battle, no blame shall befall you.'

Clamados then went and armed himself and mounted his horse. A tilting ground was made in the midst of the tents and the ladies and damsels gathered there all around.

Sayeth the Lady to Percival, 'I wish that you should be Marshall of the field.'

He replieth, 'As my Lady commands.'

Meliot and Clamados charged at each other at great pace and met in such collision that their shields and armour were both pierced and much blood both gave. Again they came at each other and both horses fell to the ground. Now they drew their swords and fell to pounding each other most fiercely.

The Lady sayeth to Percival, 'Go you and part these two knights that they may not slay one another for they are both sore wounded.'

And Percival sayeth to the knights, 'Withdraw yourself back, you have done enough!'

The Lady came to Clamados and sayeth, 'Fair nephew, are you wounded badly?'

'I am,' he replied.

'I never saw braver knight and all for a misunderstanding. A man need not always stand upon his rights but allow for natural justice.'

The Lady had Clamados placed on his shield and taken to a tent where his wounds were searched and found to be sore perilous.

And Clamados sayeth to the Lady, 'Do not let the knight that slew my father depart unless it be with a good hostage that he may come back when I am healed.'

'I shall do as you request, nephew.'

The Lady then went to Meliot and had his wounds searched and they were less than Clamados. She commanded the damsels to tend upon him with much kindness. To Percival she sayeth, 'You should abide here until such time as my nephew be healed for you know he has complaint against you. Nor would I wish that you depart with no being cleared of the blame.'

'Lady,' sayeth Percival, 'I have no wish to depart without your leave. But I shall clear my name whensoever and wheresoever God shall decide. I do not wish to abide here for I must be elsewhere. This, then, I pledge to you, that I shall return hither within a term of fifteen days from the time Clamados shall be made whole.'

Then up spoke the Damsel of the Carriage and sayeth, 'Sire, I shall remain here in hostage for you.'

But the Lady then sayeth, 'No! You must pray that he remaineth here with us.'

And Percival sayeth, 'Lady, I may not stay. For I left Lancelot sore wounded in the hermitage of my uncle.'

'Sire,' sayeth the Lady, 'I had prayed that remaining here might have pleased you as well as it would have pleased me.'

'Lady,' sayeth he, 'remaining with you would please everyone, but I have given my word that I would tend to Lancelot and I have to keep my bond as a worthy knight.'

'Then you will promise as a worthy knight that you will return the soonest you may? That you will return within the term appointed by you after you have learned that Clamados is healed, to defend yourself against his accusations?'

'And what if he should die?'

'Then, Sire, it is my fervent wish that you would return for love of me. For right well should I love your coming.'

'Lady, be assured that if I am in place so to do, I shall never fail you or your need.'

At that he departed with the Damsel of the Carriage commending him to God. He came full pace to the hermitage of his uncle thinking to find Lancelot therein. But his uncle telleth him that Lancelot had healed of his wounds and was all sound. And he had departed.

Part the Xth

Lancelot had ridden through the forest a long way when he chanced upon a castle. On approach to the gate he saw an old knight and two damsels who greeted him right well and bid him alight and go in to the hall. The joy of the damsels was exceeding great as they took off his armour and bid him rest.

Then sayeth the old knight, 'Sire, I beg your pity upon these damsels, my daughters. On the morrow comes a knight to rob them of this castle and they have no defender other than me. And I am too old and feeble. We have no kin to aid us nor have I found a knight willing to take up his arms on our part. You, Sire, seem of such great valour that we pray you will defend us on the morrow.'

Sayeth Lancelot, 'What is this you say, Sire? I have barely come beneath your roof and yet you wish me to engage in battle?'

'Sire,' sayeth the old knight, 'hereby you may prove your valour to be as great in deed as it appears in display. Thus may you defend my daughters in their right of claim and win the love of God and the praise of the world.'

At this, the knight and his daughters pleaded with Lancelot to take up their cause, and he raiseth them up for he had great pity.

'Sire, damsels,' he sayeth, 'I will aid you to the uttermost of my power. But I would wish not to remain here overlong.'

Sayeth the damsels, 'Sire, the knight that would rob us of our claim comes on the morrow and without a brave knight to defend us we shall be lost. Our father is old and our family is fallen and decayed.'

'Why doth this knight come to rob you of your castle?'

'On account of Gawain, whom we gave harbour here.'

Lancelot lay within the castle that night. On the morn he went to Mass and armed himself and looked from the castle windows at the gate barred and shut. Then he heard the loud blast of a horn three times beyond the gate.

'The knight is come,' sayeth the father of the damsels, 'and he thinketh there is no defence.'

'May it please God,' sayeth Lancelot, 'that there is.'

And there was another loud blast from the horn. And the old knight sayeth, 'Sire, the knight without thinketh that no one will come forth to accept his challenge.'

At this, Lancelot did mount his horse and with the damsels at each stirrup went to the gate. The damsels then prayed of him that he save the honour of the castle without which they must flee as beggars.

There was another blast of the horn and Lancelot rode from the gate with shield up and lance lowered. There he saw the other knight and rode at him with full pace. The knight seeing him come cried out, 'Knight! What is this? Are you here to do me evil?'

'Yes,' replieth Lancelot, 'for that evil you would do I defy you in the name of the knight and the daughters therein.'

Both delivered lance to shield with great might but none were unhorsed. Lancelot drew his sword and thrust it at the knight and pierced his arm and side whereon the knight's horse tumbled and fell to the ground. Lancelot alighteth right quickly and ran to the fallen knight with sword in hand.

'Hold, Knight!' sayeth the fallen knight. 'Pray withdraw from me and slay me not. What, Sire, is your name?'

'My name is for those on whom I choose to bestow it.'

'I would gladly know your name for a good knight you seem to be as I am taught by this encounter.'

'I am called Lancelot of the Lake. And what is your name?'

'I, Sire, am Marin of the Castle Gomeret, the father of Meliot of England. Again, Sire, I pray you do not slay me.'

'So shall I do unless you withdraw you enmity towards this castle.'

'By my faith,' sayeth Marin, 'do I withdraw it for ever. Never again shall they be troubled by me.'

And Lancelot sayeth, 'I cannot accept your pledge unless you enter the castle to repeat it.'

'Alas, Sire, I cannot mount my horse for my wound.'

Lancelot helpeth Marin to mount his horse and led him in to the castle where the knight gave his sword to the old knight and his daughters. He yielded up his shield and lance and made vow upon the holy relics that never again would he make war on them. He then returned to Castle Gomeret as the old knight and the damsels made great joy.

And Lancelot departed with the damsels and the old knight commending him to God and rode many a long time until he came to a city in a wide plain. Over the city there rose much smoke and from its gates came forth a multitude making great joy with much music. And when they saw Lancelot their joy redoubled. Many approached him, with the lords and provosts of the people, and sayeth, 'This joy is because of you, this sound of gladness is for your coming.'

'But why?' sayeth Lancelot.

'For, Sire, this city began to burn on the death of our King, nor might the fire be quenched until we have a new King crowned in the midst of the fire. And we know of you, Sire, and would grant you the crown for we know you to be a good knight.'

'Thank you, Sire,' sayeth Lancelot, 'but I have no need of a kingdom. Indeed, I pray to God that he defend me from such a want.'

'But, Sire,' sayeth they, 'would you see this great city burned away by the refusal of a single knight? To be King here carries much in riches and you would save the city and the people and thereof you shall have great praise.'

And the people led his horse in to the city and the ladies and damsels looked from the high windows upon him saying, 'Look at the new King they are leading in. Now will the fire be quenched.'

But many sayeth, 'What a great pity it is that so fine a knight shall end thus.'

Yet others sayeth, 'Be quiet! It is better that there should be great joy that the city be saved by his death. For ever prayers will be made throughout the kingdom for his soul.'

Lancelot was taken to the palace which was a fair and rich place hung with curtains of silk and the people came to do him homage in their finest clothing. But he refused to be their King or their lord. Thereupon a dwarf leading a horse which beareth a most beautiful lady entered the city. And they tell him of Lancelot and his refusal to be King and the story of the fire.

At this, the dwarf entered the palace and called the provosts and lords about him saying, 'My lords, since this knight is not willing to be King, give me the crown and I will govern this city as you wish.'

And they replieth, 'In faith, since the knight refuseth the honour and you desire it we will grant it to you and permit the good knight to leave.'

Therewith they set the crown on the dwarf's head and Lancelot maketh great joy thereof. Commended unto God by the people of the city who saw him leave, they sayeth that he did not wish to be King for he did not want soon to die.

As the sun fell beyond the trees of the forest, Lancelot came upon a hermitage and chapel all builded new. The hermit young and without beard came out and sayeth, 'Sire, you are welcome here.'

And the knight sayeth, 'And may God be with you. But I have never seen a hermit so young.'

The hermit replieth, 'My only regret, Sire, is that I dallied for so long.'

With the horse of Lancelot stabled, the hermit led the knight in to the hermitage where he was disarmed by the squire and set at ease. The hermit then sayeth, 'Sire, have you any tidings of a knight that lay sick for a long time in the house of a hermit?'

'It is not long, Sire, since I saw him in the house of the good King Hermit, who hath tended me and healed me of wounds that the knight gave me.'

'And is the knight healed?'

'He is, God be thanked. Why do you ask?'

'For my father,' sayeth the hermit, 'is King Pelles, and the mother of the knight is my father's sister.'

'Then all the more do I love you, for I have never found any man who hath done me as much kindness as King Pelles. Tell me, Sire, what is your name?'

'My name is Joseus, and, Sire, what is your name?'

'I am Lancelot of the Lake.'

'Then, Sire, we are close in kin.'

'And right glad am I so to be.'

At this, Lancelot looked in to the chamber and saw shield, lance, and armour. 'Sire,' sayeth he, 'why do you have these arms?'

And the hermit, Joseus, sayeth, 'This is a lonely part of the forest and none but my squire and I do live here. So, when robbers come, we defend ourselves.'

'But hermits neither assault, nor wound, nor slay.'

'Sire,' sayeth the hermit, 'God forbid that I should wound or slay.'

'How then, do you defend yourselves?'

'When robbers come, we arm ourselves and if any come to me I catch hold of him and my squire slaith him or wound him in such manner that he will not return.'

'In God's name, were you not a hermit you would be a truly valiant knight.'

And the squire sayeth, 'Truly do you speak, Sire, for I know of none more strong or hardy throughout the Kingdom of England.'

That night as they slept, four robbers came to the hermitage for they knew that a knight abideth therein. They were seen by the hermit as he gave prayers in his chapel and he woke his squire and bid him arm himself and bring arms for the hermit. 'Shall I awaken the knight?' sayeth the squire.

'No, for he is our guest,' sayeth the hermit.

Taking a coil of rope, the hermit and his squire went to the stable where the robbers were intent on taking the horse of Lancelot. With a great shout the hermit beareth one robber to the ground and bound him tightly. At this, the other robbers thought to rescue their fellow and Lancelot awoke and went to the stable sword in hand. There he found the hermit and squire had all four robbers bound tightly.

The hermit sayeth to Lancelot, 'Sire, it grieves me to find you awakened.'

'But no, Sire, I am grieved that you did not wake me sooner.'

'Such assaults happen oftentimes and are not worthy of your disturbance.'

The robbers asked for mercy but Lancelot sayeth that God would not permit thieves to flourish. With the light of day, the robbers were taken deep in to the forest by Lancelot and the squire and hanged in a place wasted by fire.

On his return, Lancelot telleth the hermit that the world had lost a good knight on account of his becoming a hermit. But the young hermit sayeth that many men were now alive that he hath so done and that was a good thing.

Lancelot mounted his horse and received the hermit's commendation to God. And the hermit did bid him to salute his father and cousin for him and also Gawain. And Lancelot departed.

He rode for many days until he came to a land of broad meadows wherein ran a wide river. And Lancelot seeth a man rowing a boat on the river. In the boat were four knights. Two were sitting and one lay with his head in the lap of a damsel. He was covered with a rich covering of ermine and another damsel sat at his feet. The fourth knight was fishing with a golden rod and put his fish in a small cockle-boat that came behind. Lancelot came to the river and saluted the knights and damsels and they returned his salutation with great courtesy.

'My lords,' sayeth Lancelot, 'is there a castle nigh, or other lodgings?'

'Yes, Sire,' they replied, 'beyond the mountain there is a fair and rich castle and this river floweth all about it.'

'Whose castle is it?'

'It is the castle of the Fisher King, and the good knights lodge there when he is in this country. But he has found much fault in the knights that have lodged there of late.'

And Lancelot rode to the foot of the mountain and espied a hermit in his chapel. Thinking to rid himself of sin before entering the castle wherein the Holy Grail appears Lancelot confessed him to the hermit saying that he repenteth of all sin save only one. And the hermit asked him what it was that he would not repent.

'Sire,' sayeth Lancelot, 'I can admit the sin of my arm and of my lips but never of my heart. For my love for the Queen is deeper than any in the world and yet she is the wife of a good and honourable King. My love for her is such that I cannot withhold it for it is rooted deep within my heart and it seemeth to me not to be a sin but the highest and finest of duties. All I do in my knighthood I do only as an obligation to her.'

'Alas!' sayeth the hermit, 'You tell me of a mortal sin and you tell me that your deeds of knighthood are done in the shadow of such a sin. You, Sire, are a traitor towards your earthly lord and you have turned against Our Saviour. Of all the seven deadly sins, you have committed the one whereof the delights are the most false. Dearly shall you be punished unless you straightway repent.'

'No, Sire. For she hath in her such beauty and worth and wisdom and nobility that no one who ever loved her can take it to be a sin.'

'But, Sire, you talk of a blessed and anointed Queen that hath taken her vows before God. Yet now she is given over to the Devil for her love of you and your love of her. Knight, my fair friend, abandon this cruel folly and repent of this sin. Do this and I will take the penance upon myself and pray to the Saviour every day that as He pardoned him who pierced His side with the spear, so may He pardon you of this sin.'

'Thank you, Sire, but no. I have no wish to renounce it as a sin. Happily will I do penance but I will serve my Lady the Queen for as long as it is her pleasure, and long may I have her goodwill. So dearly do I love her that I have no desire for repentance. I know that God is merciful, and may He have pity upon us for no treason have I done to her, nor she toward me.'

Then sayeth the hermit, 'Plain it is, Knight, that I cannot avail against you whatsoever I say. Therefore, may God grant the Queen and you the desire to able to do the will of Our Saviour. Until then I tell you that however long you remain in the castle of the Fisher King you will never see the Holy Grail for the mortal sin that remaineth in your heart.'

And Lancelot departeth from the hermit and came unto the castle of the Fisher King. There he saw the bridges that Gawain had seen but they were broad and long and he crossed them at ease. There also did he see the likeness of Our Lord upon the Cross above the gate and two lions that guardeth the entrance. The lions were unchained but he passed between them without heed and entered the courtyard and alighteth before the great hall. He was greeted by two knights and taken in to the hall where he was disarmed by servants and given a rich robe by two damsels. About him he saw the hall clothed in silken curtains and adorned with images of the saints.

The knights led Lancelot to the chamber of the Fisher King where he lay upon the richest bed known in the world. At his head sat a damsel and another at his foot. The chamber was lit as though by sunlight even though it be night and no candles could Lancelot see. Lancelot saluteth the King most nobly and the King replied as though to a worthy knight.

'Sire,' sayeth the Fisher King, 'have you tidings of my sister's son, that was the son of Alain le Gros of the Valleys of Camelot, whom they call Percival?'

'I have, Sire,' sayeth Lancelot. 'It is not long passed since I saw him in the house of the King Hermit, his uncle.'

'Then tell me, Sire, is he a good and worthy knight?'

'He, Sire, is the best knight in all the world. I know this well for I felt his valour and knighthood cause me much wounding before we knew of each other.'

'And what is your name?' sayeth the King.

'I, Sire, am called Lancelot of the Lake, son of King Ban of Benoic.'

'Then, Lancelot, you ought to be a good and worthy knight as I have heard witness. Close by is the chapel wherein abides the most Holy Grail. The sacred vessel hath appeared to two knights that have been herewithin. I know not the name of the first knight, but never saw I any so gentle and quiet, nor any that had better likelihood to be a knight. Yet it was through him that I have fallen in to decay. The second knight was Gawain.'

'Sire,' sayeth Lancelot, 'I know the name of the first knight.'

'Then,' sayeth the King, 'pray tell me for I would dearly wish to know.'

'It was, Sire, your nephew, Percival.'

The King started as if burned by a cinder. 'Have a care, Sire, of what you say!'

'I speak truly, Sire, for I know him well.'

'Then why did I not know him? Through him I have fallen in to this decay. Had I known then I should be whole of my limbs and my body. Pray, Sire, when you see him again tell him to come to me or I shall die. And he will wish to aid his mother whose men have all been slain and whose land has been robbed and cannot be regained but by his aid alone. Even now, his sister searches for him throughout all kingdoms.'

'Gladly will I do so, Sire, should I encounter him. But it is difficult for he oft changes his shield and conceals his name from all that are with him.'

And they honoured Lancelot right richly and gave him meats on a table shining with gold and silver vessels. But the Holy Grail did not appear, for though Lancelot was one of the three most valiant knights of renown he bore in his heart the sin concerning the Queen. And two damsels took him to his bed and remained with him until he was asleep.

He rose on the morrow with the light of day and went to hear Mass before taking his leave of the Fisher King and departing by the lions at the gate. In his heart he thought of nothing but the Queen for great was his desire to see her again. Great also was his desire to see Percival but no tidings came of him except that he was far distant.

Lancelot rode in to the forest in great mind to find Percival. Therein he came upon a knight and a damsel clothed in rich robes of silk and gold of such splendour as he had never seen before.

The damsel wept constantly pleading with the knight to have mercy upon her. But the knight stayed silent and spoke not.

Upon the approach of Lancelot the damsel sayeth to him, 'Sire, I beg you, please speak to this knight on my behalf.'

'On what account do you wish I should speak with him?'

'Sire,' sayeth she, 'for a year he hath urged his love upon me and hath made a covenant that I would be his wife, and thus I am dressed to be. But my father will not allow the marriage for he is more rich than this knight. Yet I have come to him for I love none other, nor can I. But now he will not honour his covenant for he loves another better than me. This hath brought me great shame.'

And Lancelot looked upon this fairest of damsels with great pity and sayeth to the knight, 'Sire, this you shall not do. You shall not shame so fair a damsel with whom you have made covenant. For there be not a knight in all of England or in Wales that would not be well pleased to have so fair a damsel for wife. I pray, Sire, that you honour your covenant with her. This would be of such rightness that I would hold it a favour to me and my honour.'

But the knight sayeth, 'No, Sire, I will not for I have no desire so to do.'

'Then, Sire,' sayeth Lancelot, 'I have never seen so base or lowly knight and no lady nor damsel ought again to put trust in you for the disgrace you intend upon this damsel.'

'Sire,' sayeth the knight, 'I have a greater and more worthy love than this damsel. And no more shall I have to do with her.'

'But what do you intend to do with her?'

'I shall take her to my house and give her in charge of a dwarf who dwells therein. Then I will marry her to a knight or some other man. Hungry dogs will eat dirty meat.'

'As God doth witness,' sayeth Lancelot, 'this is the most foul manner I have ever beheld. Had you been armed as I am you would already feel my wrath.'

At this the damsel sayeth, 'No, Sire, harm him not I pray you for I truly love him. Just make him honour his covenant to me.'

Lancelot looked upon the knight and sayeth, 'Knight, will you honour your covenant with this damsel?'

'No, Sire, I shall not. Nor shall I under duress.'

'By my God, Sire, you shall so do or bring death upon yourself. For I say this not for the damsel alone but for the honour of all knights who would honour their word. This, Sire, is my covenant to you, if you do not honour her as should a true knight I shall slay you so your manner remaineth not as a reproach to other knights.'

At this, Lancelot drew his sword but the knight sayeth, 'No, Sire, slay me not. What would you have me do?'

'You must take this damsel in true and honourable marriage.'

'Then if the choice is death or marriage, Sire, I will take her for my wife.'

Then Lancelot sayeth to the damsel, 'Is this your wish?'

'It is my sweetest wish, Sire, but yet further may I pray you to stay with us until we are married?'

'As you wish, damsel.'

Together they rode through the forest until they came to a chapel by a hermitage and the hermit wedded them with much joy. Upon the end of the Mass Lancelot wished to depart but the damsel asked that he should go with them to her father to witness to him that she was rightfully wed. 'Sire,' sayeth she, 'the castle of my father is close by.' And Lancelot agreed.

And soon they came upon the castle of the old knight who Lancelot had defended against Marin the Jealous Knight and the old knight was in great despond for he knew not of his daughter. But Lancelot told him of her wedding and great was the joy of the old knight. At this, Lancelot bade farewell and departed again to the forest.

Thereupon he saw a damsel and a dwarf riding at great pace and they came to him and the damsel sayeth, 'Sire, from whence come you?'

'I come, damsel,' sayeth he, 'from the castle of the old knight that is in this forest.'

Sayeth she, 'Did you meet a knight and a damsel on your way?'

'I did,' sayeth Lancelot, 'and he hath wedded her.'

'Is this true?'

'It is true. But had I not been there he would not have married her.'

'Then shame and misadventure upon you,' sayeth the damsel, 'for you have robbed me of the one thing in the world that I love the most. You should know, Sire, that she shall never have joy of him, and that had he been armed as you are he would never have bowed to your will. Yet again, Sire, you have harmed me. You and Gawain have slain my uncle and two cousins in the forest. Those whom you had me put in to their graves in the chapel where you watched, the chapel where you saw my dwarf was making the graves in the burial ground.'

Sayeth Lancelot, 'Damsel, it is true that I was there but I departed from the grave-yard with my honour safe.'

And the dwarf sayeth, 'But only for the knights were craven and failed.'

'My friend,' sayeth Lancelot, 'I would rather they would be cowards than knights of courage.'

And the damsel sayeth, 'Sire, you have done much outrage for you slew the Knight of the Waste Manor whence the hound led Gawain. Had he there been known he would not have departed so soon for he was loved no better than you. May God grant that you meet a knight that may avenge the evil in your heart and that of Gawain. That, Sire, would bring great rejoicing for many a good knight have you slain. Be assured, Sire, any trouble I may bring you I shall so do as quickly as I may. And, Sire, may you always have the wind in your face.'

But Lancelot would not answer the reviling so the damsel and the dwarf departed henceforth.

And Lancelot rode through the forest until he arrived at the house of the good King Hermit who made great joy of him. And the King Hermit asked if he hath come upon Percival but he hath not. And the King Hermit asked him if he hath seen the most Holy Grail but he hath not.

Thereupon the King Hermit sayeth, 'Well do I know why this was so. Had you the same desire to see the Holy Grail as you had to see the Queen then the Holy Grail would have been revealed unto you.'

'Sire,' sayeth Lancelot, 'my desire to see the Queen is for no other reason than her wisdom, her courtesy, her grace and her precious worth. This every knight is bound so to do for in her lives every honourable virtue that a Lady may have.'

'Then may God grant you safe passage through life, and may you do nought that will deserve His wrath on the Day of Judgement.'

On the morrow, Lancelot departed after hearing Mass and journeyed straightway to the court of King Arthur where the King and Queen sat with many knights and barons.

Part the XIth

As Lancelot returned to the court of King Arthur, Percival rode at great pace through the forests of England to the land of the Queen of the Tents. Therein had he left the Damsel of the Carriage as hostage for his return to accept the challenge of Clamados whose father and uncle he had slain.

But as he came night to the land of the Queen of the Tents he came upon the Damsel of the Carriage who greeted him with great joy. The Damsel sayeth to Percival that Clamados hath died of the wounds given him by Meliot of England and that Meliot was all healed.

'Sire,' sayeth she, 'the tents and the linen wall are all come down and the Queen has taken herself and her maidens to her castle. By my joyous meeting with you, you may know that you are no longer bound by your bond. Also, Sire, you should know that your sister, Dindrane, goes in search of you for your mother hath much need of you. Never again shall your sister know joy until she hath found you. Even now she searches for you in all the kingdoms of the world in great sorrow for none hath she found who can give her tidings of you.'

Bidding the damsel the protection of God, Percival rode to Wales until he came upon the Castle of Tallages which is seated high over the sea on a great rock. Thereon a knight rode from the castle gate and Percival asked to whom the castle belonged and the knight telleth him that it belongeth to the Queen of the Maidens.

He entered the castle and alighted at the mounting stage and rested his shield and lance. Before him rose the steps to the great hall and on each step were many knights and ladies but none greeted him. All were silent. At this, Percival saluted them all and ascended the steps to the door of the great hall which was shut. Taking the ring that hung thereon he struck the door and made a great sound that echoed within the hall. The door was opened and a knight stood at the door and sayeth, 'Knight, you are welcome.'

'Thank you, Sire,' sayeth Percival, 'and may God look well upon you.'

At this, Percival took off his helmet and the knight leadeth him to the chamber of the Queen. She rose to meet him and made great joy of him and made him sit next to her all armed.

With that a damsel entered the chamber and sayeth, 'My Lady, this is the knight who saw first the Holy Grail. He did I see at the court of the Queen of the Tents, where he was accused of treason and murder.'

The Queen turneth to her knight and sayeth, 'Haste now, and let sound the ivory horn.' And the knight hastened away to do her bidding.

When the sound of the ivory horn was heard throughout the castle the knights and ladies on the steps to the great hall rose upon their feet and made great joy and sayeth that their penance is now done. Thereupon they entered the hall and did meet the Queen who came from her chamber leading Percival by the hand.

And the Queen sayeth, 'Look upon the knight through whom you have the pain and trouble and by whom you are now released.'

And the knights and ladies cried out, 'And welcome may he be!'

'Welcome he is,' sayeth the Queen, 'for no other knight in the world had I more desire to see.'

At this, the Queen had Percival disarmed and had him brought a rich robe of silk and gold for his comfort. Then sayeth she, 'Sire, four knights and three ladies have been upon the steps of the hall since the time you were at the castle of the Fisher King and you did not ask the question of whom the Grail served. Since that time they have had no other place to be, nor to eat, nor to drink. And they have had no joy since that time. Therefore you need not marvel at their great joy at your coming. Nonetheless, Sire, we have another great need of your coming. For a foul knight wars upon us yet he is the brother of the good Fisher King. He is known as the King of Castle Mortal.'

'My Lady,' sayeth Percival, 'the knight of whom you speak is my uncle, as is the good Fisher King and the good King Hermit. But truly, Lady, there is none more foul and cruel than the King of Castle Mortal. Nothing deserves he of love or good fortune for he wars also against my uncle the Fisher King and means to take the Castle of the Holy Grail and the Spear.'

'Sire,' sayeth he Queen, 'it is for the aid I have given the Fisher King that the King of Castle Mortal doth challenge me for my castle. Oftentimes he comes to an island by this castle and he hath slain many of my knights and damsels. May God grant us vengeance upon him.'

At this, the Queen took Percival by the hand and leadeth him to the windows of the great hall and sayeth, 'Sire, there you may see the island where goeth your uncle to lay his plans for his assaults upon this castle. And see below the ships I hold for our defence.'

In the days that followed, the Queen gave great honour to Percival and made great joy of him. But though she loved him the Queen knew that never may she have her desire of him, nor should any lady nor damsel thereabouts for he was a good and chaste knight.

Ere long it came about that Percival heard that his uncle had arrived at the island and was intent on challenging the Queen for its possession. And the Queen would send many knights against the King of Castle Mortal but Percival prayed her not so to do for he would stand alone. With this, Percival had him rowed in a barge to the island full armed. And the King of Castle Mortal marvelled at this for no knight had before come from the castle to meet him in challenge.

And when the barge took the ground of the island Percival issued forth. Above him watched the Queen, the knights, ladies and damsels from the castle hall and seeth the approach of the nephew and the uncle.

The King of Castle Mortal was tall and strong and hardy and he knoweth not the knight who came upon him body to body, sword to sword. But Percival knew his uncle and came at him with sword drawn and shield raised and dealt him a great blow upon his helmet that maketh his body bend. And the King replied with many blows that caused the knight's helmet to bend and crack. And the King searcheth Percival with his sword with many blows that nought but the armour of the knight saved him from great wounds. And the Queen and all those at the windows marvelled that Percival could receive such blows yet yield not. Then Percival layeth another great blow against the King but his sword fell upon the shield of the King and near split it asunder.

And the King took him back and looked upon the shield that Percival carried and sayeth, 'Knight, from whence did you obtain this shield? On behalf of whom do you bear it?'

'I bear it,' sayeth Percival, 'on behalf of my father.'

'Was your father Alain of the valleys of Camelot? A knight who bore a shield of red whereon was a white hart?'

'He was indeed my father, a man without blame for he was a good and loyal knight.'

'Then you are my nephew for his wife was Yglais, who is my sister.'

Sayeth Percival, 'And therein I find no worth nor honour for none of my kindred lack loyalty as you do. I know that on reaching this island I should meet you and that you make war upon the good Fisher King and on the good Queen of this Castle. And may it please God that the Queen shall have no further need to guard her castle against you, nor shall the good Fisher King defend the sacred vessel and spear that God hath placed in his keeping. For God loves only those who regard highly loyalty and honour. You know nothing of either, therefore I do the work of God in defying you and holding you my enemy.'

The King now knoweth well that his nephew stood against him and Percival came to him with sword raised and in great rage as a lion. At this, the King ran full fast to his ship and leaped therein and pushed from the shore. Percival followed him to the beach and cried, 'Tell me evil King that I am not of your family! No knight of my mother's family did ever flee from another knight! You should know that this island is conquered and never will you here be seen again!'

And the King sailed from the island with no mind to return.

Percival returned from the island in his barge and went in to the castle of the Queen where he was met with great joy. And the Queen asked him if he was harmed.

'Lady,' sayeth he, 'no wound have I thank God.'

At this, she disarmed him and gave him great honour commanding all there to obey his wishes. For now the evil King had so meanly departed they know he will not return for dread of his nephew.

Part the XIIth

At the castle of King Arthur there was great joy at the arrival of Lancelot and Gawain. And the King asketh of them if they have seen his son Lohot but they say they have seen nought of him in the forests or islands.

The King sayeth, 'Much I marvel for I know not where he is nor have I tidings beyond those brought by Kay who slew Logrin the giant and brought me his head. For this I did most willingly increase the lands of Kay. And I love him greatly for he hath avenged me of the evil done by the giant.'

But had the King known truly of Kay and his deeds he would not have so highly honoured his chivalry and courage.

One day the King sat with the Queen and meat when a damsel of great beauty alighteth before the castle. She was Dindrane, the sister of Percival. And she came up the steps of the hall where sat the King and sayeth, 'Sire, I come before you as the most dismayed damsel ever you have known. I come, Sire, to ask the help of your brave and noble heart.'

'Damsel,' sayeth the king, 'I shall do as much for you as God permits for I cannot allow the plea of such a damsel as you to go unheeded.'

At this, the damsel looked at the shield that hung in the midst of the great hall and sayeth, 'Sire, it is my wish beyond all other that you allow me the aid of the knight that comes to take this shield.'

'Damsel,' sayeth the King, 'insofar as it be the wish of the knight I shall be most pleased to grant your request.'

'Sire, if he is as good a knight as his fame brings before him he will not refuse your request nor mine should I be here when he cometh. For had I found my brother whom I have long sought then no aid should I need. But I have sought him in many lands and could find nothing of him. To my sorrow I have had to ride through many lands at great danger to my body but God did ride beside me and I lived.'

'Damsel, I shall refuse you nothing for a right cause troubleth me not.'

'Sire,' sayeth she, 'may God be thanked for your great worth.'

And they sat her down at meat and gave her much honour. On the tables being cleared the Queen took the damsel to her chamber where she and her maidens make great joy of her. And the hound that was come with the shield lay on straw in the chamber and he would not stand for the Queen nor the knights but when he seeth the damsel he came to her and made great joy of her and the others did marvel at this for none before had he done this.

And the Queen asked the damsel if she knew the hound and she sayeth, 'No, Lady, for as I understand, I knoweth him not.' But the hound now staith with her and will leave her not.

Every day the damsel entered the chapel and wept before the image of the Saviour and prayed to His Mother for she was sore afraid of losing her castle. And the Queen sayeth to her, 'Damsel, who is your brother?'

'My Lady,' sayeth she, 'I have heard throughout the lands that he is one of the best knights in the entire world. But he departed from my father and mother a young squire. Now my father is dead and my lady mother is without help or counsel and a foul knight intends to rob her of her castle and slay her men. The castle would have long been taken were it not for Gawain that made her safe for a year and a day but the term is now nigh to its end and my mother lives in dread for she has nought but her castle. Thus hath she sent me to search for my brother whom she hath heard to be a good knight. But I cannot find him and so I am here to ask the King for the help of the Knight of the Shield if he hath pity upon me.'

And the Queen sayeth, 'Damsel, my wish is that you hath found your brother for it would bring great joy to me that your mother hath found his aid. May God grant that the Knight of the Shield come quickly and give him the courage and wisdom to help your mother.'

'May God so grant Lady, for never was there a good knight that hath not pity.' And the damsel told the Queen of her father and mother and how a great sadness did hang about her.

One night as the King lay with the Queen he awoke and could not return to sleep. He arose and looked out upon the dark sea that was quiet and without wind. Far off the King saw a light as if of a candle and much marvelled at what it might be. And the light came closer until the King saw that it was a ship that came towards the castle. He saw that it came near the shore and went to see it. At the helm was an old man who allowed the King to come thereon. When the King entered the ship he found a knight that lay full armed upon a bed of ivory. Candles in golden candlesticks were lighted at the head of the knight and his feet and when the King drew nigh he saw that the knight was of great comeliness.

And the old man sayeth to the King, 'Sire, pray draw back and let the knight rest for he hath had much to endure these many days.'

'Sire,' sayeth the King, 'who is the knight?'

But the old man sayeth, 'Only he can tell you that, Sire.'

At this, the King departed and returned to his Queen who he told of the strange knight. And the Queen rose and dressed in silk and ermine and went to the great hall with the King.

And the door of the great hall opened and there entered the old man from the ship bearing a tall candle in a golden candlestick. He was followed by the knight all armed and with his sword in his hand. And the queen sayeth, 'Knight, you are indeed welcome.'

'Lady,' sayeth the knight, 'I thank you and may God witness your kindness.'

And the Queen sayeth, 'Knight, have we aught to fear of you?'

'No, Lady, you have nought to fear of me.'

The King then seeth that the knight bore a shield of red whereon was a white hart and the hound that heareth the voice of the knight came in to the hall and made great joy around the legs of the knight.

And the knight went to the main column of the hall and took down the shield of white with the red cross and hung in its place the shield of red with the white hart. He then went to the door of the hall as if to depart.

The King sayeth unto him, 'Knight, pray do not leave so hastily.'

But the knight sayeth, 'Sire, no time have I to linger, but you shall see me again.' And he entered his ship with the hound and left the shore.

As the sun rose and hearing of the visit of the knight the Damsel Dindrane came to the King and sayeth, 'Sire, did you talk of me and my fears to the knight.'

'I did not,' sayeth the King, 'for to my sorrow he departed before I could.'

'Pray God that you are so good a King that you will not forget your covenant with a damsel so forlorn as I.' With that she left the court to continue her search for her brother and the King was most sorrowful that he hath not remembered the damsel when the knight came.

At this, Gawain and Lancelot entered the hall and when they heard the tidings of the knight and the shield they were both much grieved to have not seen him.

Gawain sayeth, 'This is ill-chance that I have not seen him.'

And Lancelot sayeth, 'I have seen him at close quarters and none have I faced body to body that hath wounded me so. And I him, and we lay together at the house of the King Hermit until I was healed.'

'Lancelot,' sayeth Gawain, 'I would gladly suffer wounds to have known him for as long as you.'

The King sayeth, 'It is our duty to seek this knight for a damsel needs his aid and such tidings must quickly reach him.'

The Queen sayeth, 'Sire, this will be a great service to the damsel for she is the daughter of Alain le Gros of the Valleys of Camelot. Her mother is named Yglais and her own name is Dindrane.'

'Lady,' sayeth Gawain, 'she is the sister of the knight that hath borne away the shield. I know her from the time I lodged at her mother's castle.'

'That,' sayeth the Queen, 'gives account of why the hound loveth them both.'

And Gawain sayeth, 'I shall go in quest of this knight, Lady, for I have great desire to see him.'

'And I also,' sayeth Lancelot, 'for I would gladly see him.'

The King sayeth, 'Pray do not forget, Sires, the damsel who hath great need of tidings of her brother and to whom I am bound in covenant so to find.'

'Sire,' sayeth Lancelot, 'we shall tell him that his sister hath been at your court and that she seeks him most urgently.'

The two knights left the court and rode together through the forest until they came to a high Holy Cross where all the roads did meet. Gawain sayeth, 'Lancelot, choose which road you will that we may go our way alone. Thus we may sooner hear tidings of the Good Knight. Let us meet here at this Cross one year hence to tell each other how we have fared. For, may it please God, let one path lead to him.'

And Lancelot taketh the way to the sunset, and Gawain to the sunrise. And they departed commending each other to God.

Part the XIIIth

Gawain rode until the decline of day and lodged well in the house of a hermit. And the hermit sayeth unto Gawain, 'Sire, whom do you seek?'

'I, Sire, am in quest of a knight that I would find with great gladness.'

But sayeth the hermit, 'Sire, there are no knights that dwell in this land.'

'No knights, Sire? Why not I pray you?'

'At one time there were many. But now all are gone save for one knight who lives alone in a castle and another who lives alone upon the sea. It is he who hath slain all the others.'

'And who, Sire, is the Knight of the Sea?'

'I know not, Sire,' sayeth he hermit, 'all that is known unto me is that his ship goes by the sea to an island that is beneath the walls of the castle of the Queen of the Maidens. From that island he chased an uncle that made war upon the castle. Any knight that came to the aid of his uncle was slain until none remained and the castle was safe.'

Sayeth Gawain, 'Sire, since when did he begin his life upon the sea?'

'Scarce twelve months, Sire.'

'And how far is the sea from us?'

'It is close by, Sire, and easily reached. Often have I walked there and seen his ship pass by. I have seen him also, full armed, of great comeliness and as noble as a lion. Never, Sire, has any knight been more dreaded. Had it not been for him the Queen of the Maidens would have been robbed of her castle. But he goeth not there but searcheth the islands and seas for the boastful and the arrogant to bring them down. The Queen is in great sorrow that he goeth not to the castle for she hath great love of him and would willingly make him a prisoner of her desire.'

'Sire,' sayeth Gawain, 'do you know the shield that this knight beareth?'

'I know nought of such things, Sire. I know nought beyond the dismay throughout this land caused by this knight.'

After Mass, Gawain departed and found the sea. Nothing could he see of the ship and he rode along the shore until he came upon the Castle of the Queen of the Maidens. The Queen made great joy of him and showed him the island that Percival had taken from his uncle. She sayeth, 'Sire, this knight doth cause me much pain in my heart for he will not enter the castle. He has not come within its walls since he made his uncle flee but stays upon the island or upon the sea.'

'And where is he now?' sayeth Gawain.

'As God may witness,' sayeth the Queen, 'I know not nor may any other for he comes and goes as he wish.'

And Gawain felt deep despond at not knowing of the whereabouts of the knight. After Mass he departed to continue his search and rode along the shore but of the ship there was nought. He then came upon a great forest in which he entered and saw a knight riding at a great gallop as though to flee from someone who would slay him.

'Hold, Sire,' sayeth Gawain, 'why do you ride so fast?'

'I flee, Sire, from the knight that hath slain all the others.'

'And who is this knight?'

'I know not who he is, Sire, but should you go towards him you will soon discover him.'

'It seems to me, Sire,' sayeth Gawain, 'that we have met before.'

'We have, Sire, for I am the Knight Coward whom you met when you defeated the Knight of the Black and White shield. I, Sire, am the man of the Damsel of the Carriage. I pray you therefore, Sire, that you do me no hurt for the knight from whom I flee looks so fierce that I thought I would die when I saw him.'

'You need not fear me, Sire, for I know your damsel well.'

'If only other knights would say as you do, Sire, for no fear have I save for myself alone.'

With this, both departed from the other and Gawain turned to seek the knight from whom the Knight Coward had fled. And he came upon a sand hill by the shore and saw a knight all armed and on a fine horse and he beareth a shield of gold with a green cross. And Gawain sayeth, 'God grant that this knight may give me tidings of him that I seek.'

And he came upon the knight and made salute and sayeth, 'Sire, have you tidings of a knight that beareth a shield of white whereon is a red cross?'

'I have, Sire,' sayeth the knight, 'for he shall be at the assembly of the knights within forty days.'

'Where will the assembly be held?'

'In the Red Land. Many knights shall be there and he will be found without fail.'

And Gawain thanked the knight and felt great joy at such tidings. He then departed for the Red Land and saw not the knight of the gold shield and the green cross return to the shore and enter in his ship and put to sea.

Gawain rode until he came upon a fair castle. Close by he saw a damsel following two knights who bore the body of a dead knight on a litter. And Gawain saluted the damsel and sayeth, 'Who is the dead knight?'

And she replieth, 'Sire, he was a knight who hath been slain in great outrage.'

'And where do you take him?'

'I take him, Sire, to the Red Land.'

'Why there, damsel?'

'For whomsoever is best at the assembly of the knights shall avenge the death of this knight.'

With this, the damsel departed and Gawain went to the castle close by and found none therein save an old and feeble knight and a squire who waited upon him. The old knight lodged him well and made the castle door be made fast shut. On the morrow,

Gawain was want to depart but the old knight sayeth to him, 'Sire, I granted you lodging last night and hope that you may reward me by defending me against a knight who would slay me for granting lodging to the King of Castle Mortal, he that wars against the Queen of the Maidens.'

'What shield doth he bear?' sayeth Gawain.

'He bears a shield of gold with a cross of green. And he is a hardy and true knight.'

'Have you tidings of another knight whom I seek? He is called Percival and hath carried away from the court of King Arthur a shield of white that beareth a red cross.'

At this, the old knight looked from his window and saw a knight near the castle bearing a shield of gold with a green cross. Gawain did arm himself and mounted his horse and issued forth from the castle with lance lowered and shield raised. But the knight moved not nor did he prepare for battle and Gawain marvelled at this. But the knight had no ill intent towards the old knight and had come thither to meet knights that sought adventure. And Gawain looked behind him and saw that the castle door was closed and the drawbridge raised. To the knight he sayeth, 'Sire, do you intend to do harm here?'

'No, Sire, I do not,' replieth the knight.

At this, the damsel of the dead knight came riding at a great pace and came to the two knights saying, 'In the name of God, shall I ever find a knight to take my vengeance to the evil knight that lives in the castle?'

'Is he evil? sayeth Gawain.

'He is the most evil you ever saw,' crieth the damsel. 'He gave lodging to my brother and made him swear he would defend the old knight against a knight that would appear before the castle. When the knight appeared my brother set out to keep his covenant. They met in combat so fierce that their lances thrust through their shields and pierced their hearts and both were slain. With this, the old knight issued forth from the castle and took away their armour and horses leaving their bodies to the beasts and the birds. But for my coming with two knights just such would have come about.'

'Then,' sayeth Gawain, 'the Lord God must surely be thanked for protecting this knight and me from such harm.'

And the knight sayeth, 'It seemeth to me that the old knight would have knights slay each other. How can this be?'

'For, Sire,' sayeth the damsel, 'he covets their armour and horses.'

'Damsel,' sayeth Gawain, 'whither go you?'

'To join my dead knight that lieth upon a litter.' With that, she departed at great pace.

And the knight sayeth his farewell to Gawain. And Gawain sayeth to him, 'Sire, forgive me my churlishness for I have not asked your name.'

But the knight sayeth, 'Pray, Sire, do not ask my name until I ask you of yours.' He then rode to the forest and Gawain continued on his way. As he rode he met many knights and damsels and asked them of the Knight of the White Shield with the red cross and all told him that the knight would be found at the assembly in the Red Land.

One night he lodged with a hermit who asked whence he had come. 'Sire, I have come from the land of the Queen of the Maidens.'

And the hermit sayeth, 'Have you seen Percival the Good Knight that took the shield from the court of King Arthur?'

'To my great sorrow,' sayeth Gawain, 'I have not. But a knight that bore a shield of gold with a green cross told me that he would be found at the assembly at the Red Land.'

'Then, Sire,' sayeth the hermit, 'the knight of which you speak was none other than the knight for whom you search. Indeed, he hath lodged here and has left me his hound that I might care for it.'

'But,' sayeth Gawain, 'the shield he bore was not the shield by which he may be known.'

'This he doth,' sayeth the hermit, 'so he may not be known. The shield from the court of King Arthur awaits him at the hermitage of Joseus the son of the King Hermit. It is the very hermitage where Lancelot lodged and did hang the four thieves who tried to rob the hermit.'

And Gawain sayeth, 'Such great misfortune have I found for should I have known his name I would have laid before him the message I bear from King Arthur. Even now, Lancelot searches throughout England for him. Twice I have seen him and spoken to him only to lose him.'

'Sire,' sayeth the hermit, 'he is a knight that keeps close to himself and is wary of others for he will not waste a word, nor will he be untruthful, nor will he speak a word that he would not want to be heard. Nor will he do shame of his body for he is chaste and will not commit outrage upon anyone.'

'This I know well,' sayeth Gawain, 'that all the valour and purity that should be in a knight is abundant in him. Therefore, I am of great sorrow that I am not amongst those he knows for to know such a knight brings great worthiness upon others.'

Gawain departed the next morn after Mass not knowing that the hermit with whom he had lodged was Josuias, the brother of the wife of the King Hermit and the uncle of the hermit Joseus and, as was his nephew, a brave and noble knight who had renounced all his power and possessions for the love of God.

And Gawain rode until he came to the Red Land where he seeth the assembly of the knights with many tents and pennants. All had their shields outside their tents but nowhere could Gawain see the shield for which he made search. He did not know, that the knight had changed his shield to blue barred with gold that none may know him. There did Gawain find the damsel that waiteth for the knight who shall have mastery of the tournament.

As Gawain watched he saw a knight that bore a blue and gold barred shield that sendeth to the ground all knights he challenged. Desirous of taking part in the combat until he should find the knight whom he sought Gawain rode on to the field and came before the Knight of the Blue and Gold Shield. They met with such force that both were all but felled from their saddles. Again they met and their lances broke apart at the hurtle and the handles of their shields came apart from their fastenings. Once more they came at each other with the fury of lions and many marvelled that their bodies were not pierced or broken. But God would not allow good knights to slay each other but to know instead the worthiness of each other. Even their armour did not protect them but only the love of God in whom they had faith and to whom they prayed for their salvation. But the knights then fell upon each other with their swords and dealt one the other with mighty blows until the many knights did part them for they had fought as had no other.

And the damsel that brought thither the slain knight sayeth to them all, 'Sires, declare for me the knight who hath done the best that I might seek vengeance and thus bury this noble knight.' And they sayeth that the Knight of the Shield of blue barred with gold and the Knight of the Red Shield that bore a golden eagle hath done better than all of them. But the Knight of the Blue and Gold Shield had fought longer than the other and thus he was judged best.

The damsel then sought the Knight of the Blue and Gold Shield but could find him not for he had departed. She then sayeth to Gawain, 'Sire, as I cannot find the Knight of the Blue and Gold Shield I now come to you to avenge the knight that lieth slain upon the litter.'

But Gawain sayeth, 'Damsel, it would bring great shame to me to do such a thing for only the best knight at the assembly can do it with honour. The Knight of the Shield of blue and gold has been chosen and it is he who must avenge your wrong. I know him to be the best and cannot bring shame upon me by pretending his place.'

'But, Sire,' sayeth the damsel, 'he hath already entered the forest and I have lost the aid of the best knight in the world.'

'How know you him to be the best knight in all the word?'

'Well I know it,' sayeth she, 'for it was to him that the most Holy Grail did appear in the Castle of the Fisher King for he only was of the goodness of mind and body. But he forgot to ask whom the Grail served and thus sore harm hath befallen the land. He it was that came to the court of King Arthur to take the shield which he alone can bear. To this time I have known him but now he hath changed the colours of his shield and I know him not.'

'Damsel,' sayeth Gawain, 'the tidings you bring me cause me much pain for I also seek him. But he will not tell me his name and he changeth his shield often. It seems I shall only know him from the blows he lays upon me for never in arms have I known a knight of such strength and valour. But such would I gladly suffer that I might be known unto him.'

'Pray, Sire,' sayeth the damsel, 'will you give me your name?'

'I am called Gawain.' And with that he commended the damsel unto God and did depart from her. As he rode he prayed to God that the Saviour might lead him to such a place where he might find Percival that he might be his brother knight.

Part the XIVth

The good knight Lancelot rode to the hermitage where he hanged the four thieves and was greeted with great joy by the hermit, Joseus. But the hermit knew not of the son of the Widow Lady. The knight had been to the hermitage once since he left the court of King Arthur but the hermit knew not whither he had gone.

Lancelot entered the chapel and saw the shield of white with the cross of red and sayeth, 'Sire, but this is his shield, do you hide him from me?'

'I do not,' sayeth the hermit, 'for he hath taken another shield of gold with a green cross.'

Nor had the hermit seen Gawain but sayeth to Lancelot, 'Sire, you have earned the enmity of the kin of the four robbers you hanged and they search for you in this forest. I pray you greatly that you be on your guard against them.'

'As it pleases God,' sayeth Lancelot.

After lodging in the hermitage for the night, Lancelot departed after Mass and rode through the dark forest until he saw a strong and well-made castle whence came a knight with a hawk upon his wrist. The knight came to Lancelot and sayeth, 'Welcome, Sire, may God attend you.'

'And you also,' sayeth Lancelot. 'Pray tell me, Sire, what castle is this?'

'It, Sire, is the Castle of the Golden Circlet. I am come today for it is the day ordained for the adoration of the Gold Circlet.'

'What, Sire, is the Golden Circlet?' sayeth Lancelot.

'It is the Crown of Thorns that Our Saviour wore upon His brow when He was put upon the Cross. The Queen of this castle hath set it in gold and precious stones and once a year allows the knight and ladies of the kingdom to see it. But it is said that the first knight to achieve the most Holy Grail shall come to take it. Thus it is that no stranger knight shall be allowed in to the castle. But, Sire, if you will allow it, you may lodge with me at my dwelling nearby.'

'Thank you, no, Sire,' sayeth Lancelot, 'for I must go forward whilst the light of day remains.' At this, he departed from the knight and rode past the castle and thought to himself, 'What honour should come to a knight who by his valour should take the Golden Circlet from a place so strong.'

At this, he came upon a damsel escorting the body of a knight upon a litter. 'Damsel,' sayeth he, 'may God be with you.'

'And with you also,' sayeth she.

'What, damsel, do you do with this body of a knight?'

'I, Sire, am made to keep this body of the knight with me by the hatred I bear for the knight that hath killed him. Also I have no liking for the knight who should avenge him for him I cannot find.'

'Who hath slain this knight?'

'The Knight of the Dragon.'

'And who say you should avenge the slain knight?'

'The knight who was held to be the best at the assembly in the Red Land. The same that fought with Gawain and was judged best for he had fought the longer.'

'Surely,' sayeth Lancelot, 'he must have been a knight of exceeding great valour to have bettered Gawain. What shield did he bear?'

Sayeth the damsel, 'At the assembly he had a shield of blue and gold but before he hath carried a shield of green and a shield of gold with a green cross.'

'And Gawain did not know him?'

'No, Sire, and he is much sorrowful for not knowing that he hath fought the son of the Widow Lady, Percival.'

'Do you know, damsel, whither they have gone?'

'No, Sire, neither one nor the other.'

With this, Lancelot commended the damsel unto God and departed from her. It was the time of the setting sun and the rocks and forest grew dark and Lancelot was much alert to the dangers and cast his eyes to both sides of the trail but he saw not the dwarf who spied upon him from the trees. The dwarf then went at great pace to a house wherein lived a damsel of great beauty but who had a heart of evil for she had grown amidst robbers and was nurtured by wrongdoing. Full many knights had she drawn to their slaying by her beauty and her evil ways.

And the dwarf sayeth unto her, 'Damsel, here cometh through the woods the knight that did hang your uncle and three cousins.'

'This day have I long waited,' sayeth she, 'for I intend to have the better of him both for my share in his wealth and for the slaying of my kin. Look now to your arming for I may need your aid.'

'And you shall have it, damsel, for he shall not pass by without being slain for his misdeeds.'

And the damsel went right quick to put herself on the track by which Lancelot was to pass. And she stood there of great beauty and with her dress parted and not held in a seemly manner.

Thereupon, Lancelot came and saw the damsel who saluted him and sayeth, 'Sire, the night is dark and I have a house which my forefathers built for the lodging of knights that pass through this forest. And you should know that there is no other lodging nearby.'

'Damsel,' sayeth Lancelot, 'I thank you heartily of this kindness for I seek lodging and would willingly accept such an offer from so fair a maiden.'

On their coming to the house there were none there save the dwarf who stabled the horse of Lancelot and did wait upon him.

When they entered the hall Lancelot did feel a darkness about the place that did not settle his mind. At this, the damsel sayeth, 'Sire, disarm yourself and be at ease for you have full assurance of safety.'

But Lancelot sayeth, 'Pray do not concern yourself for no trouble do I have with my armour.'

And the damsel sayeth, 'But, Sire, no knight hath ever been armed within here. Are you fearful of something for you are quite safe? Do you have enemies hereabouts?'

'No knight is loved by everyone,' sayeth Lancelot, 'and many do cover their hatred with disguising flattery.'

At this, the table was set and Lancelot sat at meat with the damsel. She then took him to a rich couch where he lay but had brought to him his helmet, shield and lance. But on the soft couch his eyes closed and he did fall asleep. With this, the dwarf mounted the horse of Lancelot and rode to the dwelling of the five robbers who raged to slay the knight that had hanged their kin.

And the dwarf sayeth in great excitement, 'Up, Sires! Avenge your kin! He is with the damsel and I bring his horse as a token of this truth.' And the robbers are in great joy and arm themselves and set forth to the house of the damsel.

As Lancelot slept the damsel did creep upon him and silently draw his sword from its scabbard. Holding it aloft she circled the knight to mark the place she might strike him for to slay the knight would bring her great worship amongst her robber kin. But as she held the sword high the door to the hall opened and there came therein the five robbers and the dwarf.

With this, Lancelot did jump up and the damsel ran to the robbers. The chief of them came at Lancelot and he took up his lance and thrust it through the body of the robber. He then ran at the four remaining robbers thinking to slay one but the damsel came at him with his own sword. Letting his armour take the blow he held the sword and pulled it from the hand of the damsel. Now with sword in hand he ran to the nearest robber and brought the blade down right heavy, but the damsel ran beneath and the sword struck her on the head and she fell slain. Lancelot was sore grieved by this for a knight does not kill damsel nor lady but he reckoned it to be the work of God against the evil in the damsel.

Then the robbers pressed their attack and he dealt two of them wound for wound until they withdrew to the door of the hall. At this the dwarf did cry loudly, 'You cannot retreat from a single knight! Stand, I say, and avenge your kin!' And Lancelot felled him with a single stroke of his sword and he lay slain. The knight then advanced to the door where stood the robbers but they went outside as though to wait in ambush. But Lancelot closed the door and barred it so that none may enter. And he took the bodies of the slain, even that of the damsel, and threw them out of the window so that they lay by the robbers that waited outside. This done, he rested his wounds as the robbers made plan to keep him inside until he starve or has need for water. But the hall had plenty of meats and drinks. Only the need for a horse held Lancelot within for he knew not what the dwarf had done with his horse for a knight must be mounted to defend him against other knights and brigands.

As the sun did rise and the birds began their song Lancelot placed himself in the hands of God and prepared to meet whatever the day may bring.

Part the XVth

Gawain was heavy with sorrow that he had thrice met Percival but had known him not. He went to the High Cross to meet Lancelot but of him could find him no sign. To return to the court of King Arthur without success could not be done. Gawain, therefore, returned to the search for Lancelot or Percival. And he came upon the hermitage of Joseus who gave him great welcome. And Gawain asked him of tidings of Percival but the hermit answered saying that he had not seen the good knight since before the assembly in the Red Land. Nor did he know where Percival may be found. As they spoke thus, a knight bearing a blue shield rode to the hermitage. After a good welcome by the hermit Gawain asked of him if he had seen a knight with a blue and gold barred shield in the forest.

'I have, Sire,' sayeth the knight, 'I spoke with him this day. He asked me if I have seen a knight that bore a shield of red with a golden eagle and I could but tell him I have not. When I asked why he sought for this knight he telleth me that such a knight had shown great valour at the assembly in the Red Land and he wished to make acquaintance with him for he was a good knight.'

Sayeth Gawain, 'His desire cannot be more than that of the knight that he seeketh for there is none in this world that he would more gladly meet than the Knight of the Blue and Gold Shield.'

And the knight seeth the shield of Gawain and sayeth, 'You, Sire, seemeth to be that knight whom he seeks.'

'Truly do you speak, Sire. Pray, can you tell me where I can find him?'

At this Joseus the hermit sayeth, 'He will not have gone forth from this forest for this hermitage is his safe refuge and he hath brought here the shield he took from the court of King Arthur.'

And Gawain made great joy at the sight of the shield. And the knight sayeth unto him, 'Sire, are you Gawain?'

'I am, Sire.'

Then, Sire, long have I sought for you. I bear a message from your man, Meliot of England, whose mother was slain on your account. Now his father hath been slain by Nabigant of the Rock on your account and who challenges for the land of Meliot. He prayeth that you go to his aid as a lord is bound so to do.'

But Gawain was sore troubled by these tidings. He was a good knight and a good lord to those in his service and under his protection. But nought could he do but say to the knight, 'Pray, Sire, tell Meliot that I will hasten to his aid as soon as I may but I am bound by the enterprise I am now on and I cannot leave it with honour until it is achieved.'

And the knight departed on the morrow after Mass. Gawain put on his armour ready to mount his horse when he saw a knight riding a tall horse and bearing a shield of gold with a green cross come forth out of the forest. And he sayeth to the hermit, 'Sire, know you this knight?'

And the hermit replieth, 'Truly I know him well, Sire, for he is Percival, the knight whom you seek.'

'May God be praised,' sayeth Gawain. And he set off on foot with the hermit to greet the knight. And Percival dismounted as Gawain sayeth, 'Right welcome are you, Sire.'

And Percival replieth, 'And may God smile upon you, Sire.'

The hermit sayeth to Percival, 'This, Sire, is Gawain, nephew of King Arthur.'

'Then right glad am I to see him for all who speak of him do so with honour and joy.' To Gawain he sayeth, 'Sire, can you tell me of a knight that was at the assembly in the Red Land?'

'What shield did he bear, Sire?'

'A shield of red with a golden eagle. He was the most sturdy knight I have met save only for Lancelot.'

'Sire,' sayeth Gawain, 'that was the shield I bore when I fought against the Knight of the Blue and Gold Shield, a knight who held within him all that knighthood shall mean amongst the valiant.'

And Percival sayeth, 'All that I may have done that day was shown in equal measure by you, Sire.' And he came to Gawain and they clasped each other by the hand in manly brotherhood.

In the hermitage, Gawain sayeth to Percival, 'Sire, when you took the shield from the hall at the court of King Arthur your sister, Dindrane, also was there. She hath prayed most fervently that she should have the aid of the knight that bore the shield away. But the King failed to tell you and your sister is greatly troubled thereof. At this, the King was want to search for you to tell you of the woes of your sister but Lancelot and I did undertake to search for you. This, Sire, is the fourth time I have encountered you and now make great joy at giving you the message for your mother gave me the fairest of lodgings at Camelot. Now she hath been robbed of all her castles save Camelot and has but few knights to defend her. Your father, Sire, is dead and your widowed mother looks to you for aid and comfort. Pray, Sire, honour your mother and go to her defence.'

And Percival sayeth, 'I thank you, sire, for your tidings. I shall do as you say for none other do I bear thanks as I do my mother, now a widow.'

'And you shall have much deserved praise,' sayeth Gawain, 'for God knows that which is right throughout all worlds.'

And the hermit sayeth, 'And so speaketh God through the scriptures for he that honoureth not his father and mother neither believeth in God nor loveth Him.'

With this, Percival sayeth, 'What tidings are known of Lancelot?'

'He but lately lodged herein,' sayeth the hermit, 'but before then he lodged here when we were set upon by robbers and he hanged four of them in the forest. Whereof he is much hated by their kinfolk who have taken oath to make him suffer for their loss. And they abound in this forest. I told him of this but he made much light of it and sayeth that he will do to them as he hath to their kin.'

Then Percival sayeth, 'This, Sire, I shall not allow for even the best knight may not prevail against much greater force. I shall not leave this forest until the well-being of Lancelot is assured.'

And Gawain sayeth, 'And I shall be at your side, Sire, for as he would not turn aside a plea for aid, nor shall I abandon him when he needs my sword.'

Percival and Gawain departed from the hermitage. And Percival bore the shield of white with the cross of red. As they rode through the forest they came upon a knight riding at great pace as if in much fear of what followed him. And Percival sayeth, 'Hold, Sire. Why do you ride as if in much dread?'

And the knight sayeth, 'Sire, I have come from the forest of the robbers. They have chased me to slay me but they are now gone to the house wherein they hold a knight who they say hath done them great harm. This knight hath hanged four of their kin, slain another and a dwarf in their service and did also slay a damsel who deserved to be slain for her part in the deaths of many good knights who came to her for lodging.'

'And know you the knight?' sayeth Percival.

'No, Sire, I do not. But he hath been wounded and lives only on what remains of food in the hall where he is entrapped. Nor hath he a horse on which to fight or escape.'

'Thank you, Sire, for these tidings,' sayeth Gawain, 'but we must go fast to this place to aid Lancelot.'

And the knight sayeth, 'Sires, if you will permit me I would accompany you to the house to see the justice of God brought to these robbers. I am the cousin of the Poor Knight of the Waste Forest that hath two poor damsel sisters where Gawain did joust with Lancelot and the knight that brought you tidings thereof died in the night.'

'Indeed, Sire,' sayeth Gawain, 'well remember I that courteous knight and the courteous damsels. May the Lord God grant them much good.'

And the knight led Percival and Gawain towards the house where Lancelot lay trapped. But as they came night they heard the sound of sword on armour and they spurred their horses to a gallop. On sight of the house they saw Lancelot under great combat from three robbers. Another robber lay slain upon the ground for

Lancelot had issued sword in hand from the hall and fought the robber for his horse. Now the three remaining robbers pressed sore upon Lancelot.

At this, Percival and Gawain lowered their lances and ran at two of the robbers and knocked them from their horses such that they were slain. The third robber tried to flee but the knight who was cousin to the Poor Knight took courage from the actions of Percival and Gawain and pierced him through with his lance until he be slain also.

With this, there was great joy at the meeting of Lancelot with Percival and Gawain. And they held council and decided that the horses of the robbers should go to the Poor Knight and the houses of the robbers and all the treasures therein should be given to the sisters of the Poor Knight. And right gladly did the cousin knight depart to bear this message to those in receipt.

Then sayeth Percival, 'Brethren, I must now depart in search of my sister and go to the aid of my widowed mother. Pray salute the King and Queen for me and give them word that I shall attend the court as soon as God permits.' And Percival went in to the forest as Lancelot and Gawain turned towards the court of King Arthur.

Percival then entered a forest that was unknown to him. It was a waste forest with no people and only wild beasts could be seen. And he came upon a hermitage in a valley by a mountain and alighted without the chapel. When he looked in he saw the hermit singing a requiem Mass over the body that lay before the altar covered with a shroud. He would not enter the chapel for he was armed and listened at the door with great reverence. Thereon the hermit did come to him and Percival sayeth, 'Sire, for whom have you done this service?'

And the hermit sayeth, 'I have done it, Sire, for Lohot, the son of King Arthur.'

'Who hath slain him?' sayeth Percival.

'I will tell you, Sire,' sayeth the hermit. This forest is part of the realm of England and hereabouts lived a horrible and cruel giant named Logrin who hath wasted this forest and the land hereabouts. And it pleased God to send Lohot in search of adventure. The son of the King did not retreat from the giant but fought him long and hard with much courage until Logrin was defeated and fell slain. At this, Lohot, in great weariness from the combat, fell in to a deep sleep by the slain giant. Thereupon came Kay, a knight from the court of King Arthur, who came silently upon Lohot and struck off his head. The traitor then struck off the head of the giant and tied it to his saddle-bow. Kay then repaired to the court of King Arthur and presented the king with the head of the giant. And the King is right joyous at this and gave Kay much honour and new land. Then came a damsel to my hermitage and led me to the body of Lohot. She asked me for the head of the knight in reward and I this granted. She then set the head of the knight in a casket of gold and precious stones wherein were many sweet scented herbs. She then departed I know not where.'

Percival sayeth, 'A great sore pity is this for I have often heard that Lohot was growing well in chivalry. The King should know of this for Kay begs a fate that is right and just for his evil actions.'

Percival departed on the morrow after Mass and rode in search of tidings of his mother. At noon he heard the sound of a damsel in great distress crying to herself. He looked and saw in a clearing the Damsel Dindrane kneeling with her arms stretched out in prayer. And she sayeth, 'Sweet Saviour of the World and your precious Mother pray hear my plea. I have searched through all the land of Greater Britain yet I can find no tidings of my brother whom it is aid is the best knight in all the world. But what avail him of his knighthood if we cannot have his aid and comfort? His most gentle and loyal mother hath great need of him for if she loses her castle we must be wanderers and beggars in a strange land. Her brother the good Fisher King languishes and her brother King Pelles serves Our Saviour as her other brother, the King of the Castle Mortal makes war on her with the Lord of the Moors and would rob her of her castle and land. All of the brothers of my father have died and can no longer give us aid.'

On hearing this, Percival rode from the trees and the damsel seeth him come and seeth also the white shield with the cross of red. And she clasped her hands to heaven and sayeth, 'Dear sweet Lady that did bear the Saviour of the World, you have not forgotten me for now here comes the knight who will bring aid and comfort to my mother and to me. Lord God, grant him the strength to do thy will. Give him the might and courage to protect us.'

At this, Percival came upon her and she took his stirrup to kiss his foot but he sayeth, 'No, damsel! I am a knight of the Round Table and will act as God doth command. No need have I for such from any damsel.'

And the Damsel Dindrane sayeth, 'Sire, have pity on my mother and on me as the Holy Mother had pity on Our Saviour as He hung upon the Cross. There is none other to whom we can fly for aid for I am told that you are the best knight in the world. I have been, Sire, to the court of King Arthur and throughout all manner of lands in search of my brother who is a knight also but I have not found him. Also King Arthur did forget to tell you of my troubles when you took the shield from where it did hang in the hall.'

And Percival who knoweth this to be his sister but sayeth nothing of it sayeth to the damsel, 'So much hath the King done for you, damsel, that he did send his two best knights in search of me that I might come to you. And be assured, damsel, that in the sight of God I shall do all that I may to aid you and your mother.'

With this, Percival helped the damsel to remount and they rode together through the forest. And the damsel sayeth to Percival, 'Sire, I must go on alone to the Perilous Graveyard.'

And he sayeth, 'Why do you go thither?'

And the damsel replieth, 'A holy hermit did tell me that my uncle the King of Castle Mortal that warreth upon us may not be overcome by any knight save I bring him some of the altar cloth from the chapel of the Perilous Graveyard. I have therefore vowed to the Holy Mother that I will obtain some of the cloth for it is the holiest cloth in Christendom being that which Our Lord was covered in the Holy Sepulchre. Yet none may enter the Perilous Graveyard except alone. Thus I go this night and may God protect me for the place is fearful and full of dread. Pray, Sire, you continue towards the Castle Camelot where awaits my mother, the Widow Lady. There you shall see how we need your aid and comfort.' Then she sayeth, 'Sire, this is the path I must take. You may see it is little frequented for no knight hath the courage to take it beyond here. May our lord have you in His keeping and may He remember me also this coming night.'

Percival knew full well that he could not forbid nor aid his sister in her trial for such she had to do alone. And he sayeth, 'Know you well, damsel, that I shall do all that I can under God to aid you and your mother. And may He be at your side this night.' And he departed knowing that save for the King of Castle Mortal none of his family would knowingly be disloyal nor fail in their word nor do any base deed.

The Damsel Dindrane went on alone in great dread until she came upon the gate to the Perilous Graveyard. As the sun set she saw a tall Cross whereat she knelt and kissed the image and prayed to the Saviour of the World that He would bring her forth from the burial-ground with honour.

The Perilous Graveyard was wide and ancient and contained many knights who had died in the forest but only those who had repented of their sins could be buried therein. And Dindrane entered the dark burial-ground and saw that it was full of tombs and coffins and fear settled upon her as a dark cloak. But no evil spirit could abide in the graveyard, for it had been blessed by Saint Andrew, yet no hermit could remain therein after the sun had set for it was soon beset by the shades of knights that had died in the forest but did not lay in the blessed burial ground.

And soon the Damsel Dindrane heard the sound of the shadow knights and then seeth them as they ran back and forth roaring beyond the graveyard wall. Such spectral knights there were in multitudes and they fought one with the other with lances and swords of fire until the forest resounded thereof. Yet none could enter the burial ground. And the damsel did almost swoon in fear. But she made the sign of the Cross and commended her spirit to the Saviour and His Holy Mother. Then she saw a chapel small and ancient and alighteth and entered wherein she found a great brightness of light. Within stood an image of Our Lady to whom the damsel prayed that she might survive the night. On the altar she saw the Holy Cloth and could smell the sweet scent that came from it as of no other scent in the world. As she came unto the cloth it rose from the altar and went so high that she could not reach it. And she wept and crieth, 'Dear God! Is it my sins that cause the cloth to be raised beyond me?'

Then the damsel fell to her knees and sayeth, 'Holy Father, I pray you, never did I evil to anyone, nor did I shame to myself, nor have I knowingly done against your will, but rather I serve you and your Holy Mother with love and fear. All the trials I have suffered I have done so in your holy name, nor have I set myself against ought that should please you. I pray you, Dear Lord, that you should release my mother and me from the great grief which is set upon us for she is a Widow Lady without comfort. You, Lord, who hath the world at Your command, grant me tidings of my brother and let him be alive that he might come to our aid in Your holy name. Grant also Lord, Your blessing on the knight that is gone to aid my mother. Remember, Lord, Your pity and compassion on that dear Lady's woes. Pray, Dear God, remember also that I am of the family of Joseph of Arimathea who spurned gold to take the body of Our Saviour from the Cross and did lay him in the Holy Sepulchre. Let it be Your pleasure, Lord, that You help a Lady of virtue and her forlorn daughter.'

At this there was the sound of rending as the cloth above her head parted, the greater part going upon the altar and the lesser part into her beseeching arms. Thus it was since the death of Our Lord that the Damsel Dindrane was the only one ever to touch the sacred cloth or did God grant a piece thereof. And she kissed the cloth full reverently and put it next to her heart.

Still yet the noise of combat was sounded without the graveyard and flames lighted the dark sky from the clashing of their swords and the damsel was sore afraid. Then spoke a voice from above to the spirits of the dead knights at rest in the burial ground. And the voice sayeth, 'Prepare for lamentation for sore loss hath befallen you. The good Fisher King who made Our service every day in the chapel of the Holy Grail is dead. And his castle is taken by his brother the King of Castle Mortal. No more shall the Mother of God enter the chapel on the Lord's Day and no more shall the most Holy Grail appear. Gone are the Guardian Knights, gone are the priests, gone are the damsels that attended the Holy Grail and the Holy Spear.' Then the voice spoke to the Damsel Dindrane and sayeth, 'And you, damsel, may depend no more upon stranger knights for none save your brother can bring you aid.'

And a great wailing went up from the graveyard and amongst those that fought beyond the walls. Such was the sound that it was as if the world itself did tremble.

And the damsel near did swoon and sayeth, 'Dear God, we have lost the good Fisher King and I can no longer turn to the good knight for aid and comfort.' She then stayed in prayer in the chapel until the light of dawn did bring quiet upon the lands thereabouts.

The damsel then rode to the Valley of Camelot where she came upon Percival looking upon the castle that he had not seen since he departed as a squire long years before. And she sayeth, 'Sire, I have tidings of the worst kind for my uncle the good Fisher King is dead and my uncle, the King of Castle Mortal, hath taken the castle wherein is sheltered the Holy Grail.'

And Percival sayeth, 'Can this be true? Is he dead?'

And she replieth, 'So help me God, it is true.'

'This then is evil tidings indeed for I had hoped to see him again and bring an end to his troubles.'

'Alas, Sire,' sayeth the damsel, 'for you I also bring yet more bad tidings for I also know now that none may help my mother nor I but my brother for whom I have sought these many years. The castle will soon be lost, for soon the Lord of the Moors will begin warring upon us again and we will have to abandon it and go to my uncle the hermit King Pelles.' Thus weeping in great sorrow that her long search for her brother had been in vain she rode beside Percival through the valleys, mountains and castles that were all robbed of her mother by the Lord of the Moors.

As they drew night the castle the Widow Lady therein looked out and saw her daughter with a knight. 'Fairest God,' she sayeth, 'grant that this knight may be my son without whose aid I shall lose this castle and his inheritance.'

And Percival remembered the chapel built on four columns of marble that lay between the castle and the forest and where his father did teach him of the story of knights and how there be none of greater worth than a good knight. Also remembered he of the coffin therein that would not open for any save the best knight in the world. And Percival made to ride past the chapel but the damsel sayeth, 'Sire, no knight should pass the chapel but should enter to see the coffin.'

At this, he alighted and lay down his sword and lance and entered the chapel. Therein he came to the rich coffin and lay his hand upon it. The coffin did then open to show him that was inside. And the damsel fell at his feet for pure joy. With this, the Widow Lady entered in to the chapel with her five ancient knights. She seeth that the coffin was opened and her daughter was full of great joy and she knoweth that this knight was her son and ran to him to kiss and embrace him. 'Know I now well,' sayeth she, 'that our Lord God hath not forgotten me but hath brought me my son.' And then sayeth she, 'My beloved son, none may doubt that you are the best knight in the world. Only for you hath the coffin opened.' All therein then prayed as the Widow Lady sent for her chaplain who came and did read letters from within the coffin, and he sayeth that the body inside was that of one of the good men who took our Lord down from the Cross. This was true for within the coffin were iron pincers all bloody with the sacred blood that had pulled the nails from the Cross. And they saluteth the Lord with full reverence before leaving the chapel whereon the coffin did close up again.

And the Widow Lady did take Percival to her castle and telleth him of the shame that hath befallen her and of how Gawain did gain her the grace of one year and a day from the warring of the Lord of the Moors, which was soon to end. But she sayeth, 'Now I know that I shall be guarded well by you against him that coverts this castle. He is a knight most horrible and without due cause hath robbed me of my valleys and castles. Now I claim none of this land save only enough for my tomb. The land is yours and you may avenge yourself and your family as you may and as God may permit. Remember, Son, you do no wrong if you hurt an enemy of your family but remember also that the scriptures sayeth that none should do evil to their enemies, but pray to God that He amend their ways. Now you are come I have no anger against my enemies but wish them to return to righteous ways. As the scriptures sayeth, "To curse a sinner is to curse yourself." My son, before I go to face the Guardians of Heaven's gates it is the greatest wish of my heart that you amend for the shame that you have earned by not asking the question of the Holy Grail. Since you did not ask the question the Fisher King fell into great ailment from which no respite could he find. But such could have only been at the command of God and we must all yield to His will and pleasure.'

On hearing this, Percival felt courage flow through him and he determined upon a path of honour for the sake of his family and his name before God.

On the morrow, one of the ancient knights of the Widow Lady was in the forest hunting when he came upon the Lord of the Moors, an evil knight who had robbed the Widow Lady of much of her land and now waited for the time but a few days distant that would end the year and a day promised to Gawain before he would fall yet again upon the Widow Lady. And the Lord of the Moors asketh the knight why he hunted in his forest. And the knight replieth that the forest did not belong to the Lord of the Moors but to the Widow Lady, and her son, Percival, was come to obtain the return of the land. At this, the Lord of the Moors knew much anger and did slay the knight with his sword.

When the body of the slain knight was returned to the castle the Widow Lady sayeth to her son, 'This is the manner of gift I receive from the Lord of the Moors. He taketh my land and put my knights to the sword. Since before you were born he hath robbed me of my land and you were baptised with the name "Percival" to remind you of the valleys that he hath taken.'

At this, Percival took two of the ancient knights and rode in to the forest until they came upon a castle from whence issued five knights all full armed. And Percival sayeth, 'Whose men are you?'

And they sayeth, 'We are men of the Lord of the Moors and we go to seek the son of the Widow Lady. If we shall find him we shall have great reward from our lord.'

'Then, Sires,' sayeth Percival, 'look no further for I am he.' With this his spurred his horse and rode at the first knight and thrust his lance though him that he fall to the ground slain. The ancient knights did also ride forward and knocked two knights from their horse wounding them grievously. The two knights remaining tried to flee but Percival faced them and they did lay down their weapons. Thereupon did Percival take them prisoner and took them with the wounded knights to the castle of his mother. There he sayeth to her, 'Lady, here are four prisoner knights in exchange for the knight you did lose. Also is there another knight who lies slain upon the ground as did your knight in giving message to the Lord of the Moors.'

And the Widow Lady sayeth, 'Thank you, my son, but rather would I have peace than another slain knight and prisoners.'

'Lady,' he sayeth, 'I can only act as God provides. Where he sendeth warriors I can only fight them as a warrior. When he sendeth peaceable knights I shall be at peace with them.'

When the Lord of the Moors heard that Percival had slain one of his knights and taken four others his wrath grew greatly and he gave command that he would grant a castle to any knight that would take the son of the Widow Lady. And thus came eight knights all armed and did chase the deer in the forest near the castle of the Widow Lady that they might be seen from its walls.

After Mass, the Damsel Dindrane did say to Percival, 'Sire, by the grace of God I have a piece of cloth from the most Holy Shroud without which this castle and the land may not be reconquered. Pray hold it full reverently for it is as a shield of God.'

And Percival did hold the cloth with much reverence and kissed it and put it to his forehead before placing it next to his heart.

Percival did then arm himself fully as did the four ancient knights. They then mounted their horses and issued from the castle like lions unchained. And they came to the eight knights and asked of them whose men they were and they answered that they were men of the Lord of the Moors and were come to take the son of the Widow Lady. And Percival sayeth, 'Not unless God wills it!' At this, Percival and his knights ran at the others and knocked five from their horses. The remaining knights did run upon Percival but were brought down in a great tumble.

And the noise of combat did sound through the forest and did fall upon the ears of the Lord of the Moors who hunteth nearby and he came at full gallop.

As the prisoners were taken to the castle one of the ancient knights did say to Percival, 'Look, Sire! Here cometh the Lord of the Moors, the knight who hath robbed your mother of many castles and much land and hath slain many of her knights.' And Percival turned and looked upon the Lord of the Moors as he came at full gallop at him.

The good knight made the sign of the Cross upon his breast and commended his spirit unto God and run full hard at the Lord of the Moors. They did hurtle with much violence and the lance of Percival did splinter as he brought down the knight and his horse together. As the Lord of the Moors lay upon the ground Percival alighted and drew his sword whereupon the Lord of the Moors sayeth, 'Hold, Sire! Would you slay me?'

'No, Sire, not yet, for there is more for you to do before I send you to the pit of Hell where you belong.'

And the Lord of the Moors then jumped up with his sword and sayeth, 'I go nowhere at your command or that of your mother who this day shall find shelter only with the beggars.' With this, he ran upon Percival and struck him hard upon the helmet. But Percival stood beneath the blow and did strike back wounding the Lord of the Moors so that he was disarmed.

The Lord of the Moors was taken in to the castle where Percival did say to his mother, 'Here, Lady, is the Lord of the Moors that would take this castle from you for this he intended to do today as the year and a day grace obtain by Gawain is now ended.'

And the Widow Lady sayeth, 'God be praised!'

Then the Lord of the Moors sayeth, 'Lady, though your castle should be mine by conquest, your son hath taken me and my knights. I therefore yield to you this castle on condition that you let my knights and myself go free.'

But before the Widow Lady could answer, Percival sayeth, 'No, this will not be! For it sayeth in the scriptures, even in the Old and New Laws of God, that murderers and oppressors shall suffer His justice. You have done my mother great shame and slain her knights. No pity did you show her or her daughter. And I will not disobey the command of God but shall do His work and bring you His justice.' With this, Percival had brought forth all the prisoner knights and had their heads struck off and their blood poured in to a large cauldron. And he then drowned the Lord of the Moors in the blood saying, 'You wanted the satisfaction of the blood of the knights of my mother, now know the satisfaction of the blood of your own knights.'

The heads and bodies of the knights and the Lord of the Moors were taken to a bone pit and cast therein and the blood was taken and poured in to a stream which did turn red.

And when tidings of this spread throughout the land, many knights did return to the Widow Lady and many brought keys to the castles that had been robbed of her so that now she hath much contentment save for the loss of her brother the good Fisher King.

One day as the Widow Lady sat at meat with Percival and the Damsel Dindrane, the Damsel of the Carriage and her two companions came in to the hall and saluteth them with honour. And they sayeth to Percival, 'Sire, God be praised that right speedily did you bring comfort to your mother. Now, Sire, may you bring equal haste to your destiny and go to the castle of the Fisher King for there the law of God is denied. The King of Castle Mortal doth rule there and sayeth that he shall give aid to those who deny the law of God but will destroy those who keep their faith.'

And the Widow Lady sayeth, 'Fairest son, great sorrow am I in that this evil man is of my family.'

And Percival sayeth, 'Lady, no longer is he your brother or my uncle since he hath denied God. For this we should hate him more than any infidel.'

'My son,' sayeth the Widow Lady, 'I pray that you never will forget or neglect the laws of Our Saviour for no better Lord can you serve, nor one that will give you reward as will He. Remember, son, that none can be good knights who do not serve and love the Lord. Always be swift in His service and delay not His work. Be forever at His command whether it be eventide or morning so that you shall honour your family. May He grant you the courage to go on to the end even as you have begun.'

And the Widow Lady and her daughter did rise and go to the chapel there to pray for Percival that he might receive long life for he was known throughout the world for his wisdom and his courtesy as well as for his valour.

Part the XVIth

King Arthur and Queen Guinevere were sat at meat with Lancelot and Gawain at Castle Cardoil when two knights entered the great hall. They carried before them the bodies of two knights that were full armed even though the knights were slain. And the knights sayeth to King Arthur, 'Sire, the loss of these two knights has come about through your most fearful enemy. This shame will further lose you many knights unless God shall show you great mercy.'

And the King sayeth, 'What hath brought this evil about?'

'Sire,' sayeth they, 'the Knight of the Dragon has entered your realm and destroys your knights and castles. None may contend with him for he is of greater height than any that live and carries a sword that is three times longer than any sword carried by other knights. His lance is more heavy than a knight may carry and two knights may shelter under his shield. On that shield is the image of the head of a dragon which sends forth flames at his adversaries. None may stand against him for he destroys all that so do.'

Sayeth the King, 'from whence doth such a knight come?'

'He comes from the Land of the Giants and is sore displeased for the death of the giant Logrin, the head of whom was brought to you by Kay. He is come, Sire, to take vengeance on your body or on the knight that you love best.'

'Then we must look to God for our protection,' sayeth the King. But he was sore afraid inside and asked Lancelot and Gawain for their counsel. And Lancelot sayeth that he and Gawain should depart and meet this fearful enemy and bring him down. But the King sayeth, 'No. Not for a King's ransom would I allow you to go. For methinks that this is not a knight but a fiend from Hell. Truly, any knight that conquers him will win great renown, but you are my best knights and I will not place you in peril. You shall stay by my side and come the day we shall face him together.'

But there was great dismay in the court that no one would go forth against the Knight of the Dragon.

Part the XVIIth

Percival departed from his mother and sister and entered the forest and came upon a wide clearing wherein stood a tall red Cross. On one side of the clearing was a young knight dressed in white robes and bearing a golden dish. On the other was a fair young damsel in white also bearing a golden dish. As Percival did look a strange and beauteous beast, the like of which he had never before seen, ran from the woods crying piteously. The beast, all white and with eyes as green as emeralds, ran to the young knight as if for aid but comfort there was none. The beast then ran to the damsel but again could find no comfort. It then ran to Percival who reached from his saddle as if to pick the beast up and give it comfort but, at this, the young knight cried out saying, 'No, Sire! Do not hold him for he must endure his fate.'

The beast then ran to the Cross and within its shade twelve small dogs came through its mouth from the inside of the beast where they had been biting and clawing. The beast then tried by showing signs of submission to crawl to the Cross but the dogs did leap on it and tear it apart and then ran howling into the forest. With this, the young knight and the damsel came to the Cross and picked up the parts of the beast and put them on the golden dishes with the blood thereon. They then kissed the ground and the Cross full reverently before entering the forest.

Percival came to the Cross in wonderment at the mystery he had seen and in like manner kissed the Cross in adoration. At this, a voice called to him in great agitation saying, 'Stand back from that Cross, Sire! You have no right to be near it!' He looked and saw two priests coming from the forest and the first priest fell to his knees at the foot of the Cross and began to adore it in a most worshipful manner. But the second priest did push the first one to the side and began to beat the Cross with a large rod whilst weeping loudly.

Percival looked on in anger and sayeth sharply, 'What sort of priest are you, that you behave in such a manner?'

And the priest sayeth, 'Who we are, Sire, or what we do is no concern of yours!'

And Percival was much angered but would not cause harm to a priest. Therefore he did ride into the forest where he came upon a knight full armed who rode towards him saying, 'For God's sake, Sire, look to your safety!'

'Who are you?' sayeth Percival.

'I am the Knight Coward, Sire, and I am a man of the damsel of the shorn hair.'

'But, Sire, if you are a coward, why are you dressed as if for combat.'

'For I hope to delay any knight that would come at me, Sire, and thus escape being slain.'

'Are you truly a coward, Sire?'

'I am, Sire, and much more.'

'By the wounds of Christ, Sire, no knight should have a name like yours. Come with me, Sire, and I shall have it changed for you are a knight of brave appearance.'

'Dear God, no!' sayeth the Knight Coward. 'Do you wish to see me slain? I have no wish to change my courage nor my name for no good knight will do me harm when he knoweth me to be a coward.'

'Then, Sire, you will be slain for not all knights are good. Now ride ahead of me so that I may see you and that you may not retreat.' And the Knight Coward did so with much grudging.

Not far had they ridden when they heard the cry of two damsels bewailing loudly and they did seek out the sound and saw a tall man full armed driving two damsels before him with a large rod and they had blood on their faces. And Percival came up to them and sayeth, 'Hold, Sire. Why do you treat these damsels thus?'

And he sayeth. 'These damsels have taken mine inheritance which was given to them by Gawain.'

And the damsels sayeth, 'In God's name, Sire, come to our aid for this is a robber who lives in the forest and is the last of his family. The others were slain by Gawain, Lancelot, and another knight and the victor knights gave our father the robber's horses and to us they gave the robber's house and treasures. Now he is come to slay us. Pray, Sires, help us in the name of all that is Holy.'

Percival sayeth, 'This is true what they say, for I was there when they were given the house and the treasures.'

'Then,' sayeth the robber, 'you it was that did slay my kindred. Now I shall have my vengeance.'

And the Knight Coward sayeth to Percival, 'Take no heed of what he sayeth, Sire. Let us withdraw and leave this place unharmed.'

'No, Sire,' sayeth Percival, 'we cannot leave these damsels thus with honour.'

'Indeed, Sire,' sayeth the Knight Coward, 'I can.'

And Percival sayeth to the robber, 'I have here mine own champion who will defend the damsels on my behalf.' And he took his horse back to leave the Knight Coward facing the robber. The Knight Coward looked all ways to flee but could not with Percival behind him.

With this the robber did run hard at the Knight Coward and broke his lance against the knight's shield, but the Knight Coward sat all straight and did not fall from the saddle. And Percival cried out, 'Knight! This is my honour you defend and the honour of the damsels.' But the knight remained unmoved still seeking flight.

The robber then drew his sword and ran hard at the Knight Coward and struck him hard upon his helmet but the knight moved not. Thereon the robber did strike him many times about the helmet and body until blood ran from the Knight Coward's mouth. With this, the Knight Coward sayeth, 'Sire, I am now wounded and it seemeth to me that you intend to slay me. Such is truly the act of a coward that he would harm another who doth not harm him.' And the Knight Coward drew his sword and ran full hard at the robber and knocked him from his horse. He then alighted and struck the head off the robber and gave it to Percival saying, 'This, Sire, is the trophy from my first combat.'

And Percival sayeth, 'I thank you, Sire. Remember now that you are a knight and fall not back in to the ways of the coward for it is too great a shame to be born by a knight.'

The knight replieth, 'Nor will I, Sire, and greatly do I wish I had done this long back for never would I have been treated with contempt when I should have earned honour.'

And Percival sayeth, 'Knight, I commend these two damsels to your care. Take them back to the house from which they have been removed by the robber and see them safely therein. Also, Sire, from this time forth you shall be known as the Knight Hardy for it is a more honourable and true name than that you did come here with.'

The damsels thanked Percival and rode off with the knight they now did name Knight Hardy.

Percival crossed mountains and forests until he reached the land about Cardoil, the castle of King Arthur. And the land was spoiled and laid waste and Percival asked the people why this was so and they say unto him that a knight did war upon the King and the knight was such that no other knight could endure against him. Percival rode to the castle and alighted before the great hall. There he was met by Lancelot and Gawain who made great joy of him as likewise did King Arthur and his Queen. All the court that know of him were in great joy and those who knew him not gazed upon him in wonderment for his valour went before him.

As the court sat to meat the door of the hall opened and four knights came in each bearing the body of a slain knight. All the slain were as if struck by lightning. And the knights sayeth to the King, 'Sire, again great shame is put upon this land by the Knight of the Dragon. He comes and destroys as is his want and sayeth that none in this court dare face him.' And Lancelot and Gawain are much troubled that the King will not allow them to meet the Knight of the Dragon. And the many knights in the hall did murmur that there was none amongst them who could meet such a knight.

At this, the damsel who bore the body of the knight on the litter entered the hall and sayeth to the King, 'Sire, I beseech you that you give me your aid. For there beside you sits Gawain and the Knight of the Blue and Gold Shield that did contend at the assembly in the Red Land. And both were known to be brave knights but the Knight of the Blue and Gold Shield endured the longer. But he did leave the field and I have not found him to ask that he should fulfil the wish of my heart.

Percival then sayeth to Gawain, 'Sire, it seemeth to me that you were the best knight at the assembly.'

But Gawain sayeth, 'I thank you, Sire, but it is your courtesy that speaks. The knights assembled all gave you the prize, and rightly so.'

And the damsel sayeth, 'Nor should he deny me that which I ask for the knight whose body I bear is the son of his uncle, Elinant of Escavalon.'

With this, the countenance of Percival did change and he sayeth, 'Make sure you say the truth, damsel, for well I know that Elinant of Escavalon was the brother of my father, but of a son I know nothing.'

'He, Sire,' sayeth the damsel, 'was Alein of Escavalon and well deserve he for his deeds to be known for he was of much valour and, had he lived, would have been among the best knights in the world. The Damsel of the Circlet of Gold did love him greatly and sayeth that upon whoever doth avenge him shall she bestow the Circlet of Gold although she hold it great regard for it is most Holy. There can be, Sire, no greater reward for any knight.'

'Damsel,' sayeth Percival, 'know you where the Knight of the Dragon now is?'

'I do, Sire. He is on the Isles of the Orchards where he hath committed great outrage on a land that was once among the fairest. Even now he is close by the Castle of the Damsel of the Golden Circlet and it grieves her heart to see her knights taken by him and slain.'

And Percival thinketh to himself that God has put this adventure upon him and thus it was the command of God that he should seek out the Knight of the Dragon and put an end to his outrages. And so he departed from the castle in company with Gawain and Lancelot as the King gave his command that all the hermits around Castle Cardoil should pray to God for his safe protection for no knight had ever faced such danger as he. And he was followed by the damsel who brought the slain knight.

They came upon an open land before the forest and saw there a great castle surrounded by running waters and girdled with high walls. And the castle did turn as doth a potter's wheel. It turned faster than the wind and the knights marvelled much for such a castle they had not seen and the damsel sayeth that it was the Castle of Great Endeavour. At the gate were many chained lions and bears all roaring and the sound of great copper horns made the ground shake. On the walls were seen many bowmen with arrows of copper that no armour could withstand. And the damsel sayeth that Lancelot and Gawain should not go near for they would fall to the bowmen. She sayeth to Percival that she should take his shield and lance and go to the castle walls to announce him, for none save the knight who go to battle with the Knight of the Dragon and seek out the Golden Circlet and the Holy Grail may be received into the castle. And Gawain and Lancelot were sore grieved that they may not give their fellowship to Percival who took his leave of them with great sorrowfulness saying, 'I commend you to the Saviour of the World.'

And they replied, 'May he that died upon the Cross defend your body, your spirit, and your life.'

With that he rode after the damsel who showed his shield to the castle. He rode over three bridges that raised behind him and showed such courage that the lions and bears did hide from him and the castle stopped its turning as he entered.

When Gawain and Lancelot saw the castle had stopped its turning they rode close as if to enter in aid of their brother knight, Lancelot. At this, a knight came to the castle wall and cried, 'Hold, Sires! If you come closer the bowmen will let loose upon you, the castle will turn again and the bridges be lowered.' They did stop and heard from the castle the sound of much joy and the people saying that the knight had come who would save them from the knight who bore the spirit of the Devil. And the two knights turned away in great sorrow and rode into the forest.

Ere long had passed, Gawain and Lancelot came unto the land wherein lay the Waste City. And Lancelot sayeth to Gawain, 'Now, Sire, it seemeth that God hath ordained that I am to be slain.'

Gawain sayeth, 'No, Sire. This cannot be. Why should God so ordain?'

'For he hath directed me here.' And Lancelot told Gawain of the young knight whose head he had struck off at the knight's request, and how he should return to the Waste City within a year to meet the same fate.

'Then, Sire,' sayeth Gawain, 'I shall stand by your side and do all I can to end this foolishness for neither the world nor the King nor, Sire, even I, can allow the unworthy death of so good a knight.'

'But I know full well, Sire,' sayeth Lancelot, 'that you would follow your word with your honour had the eye of God fallen upon you, and thus must do I.' And Lancelot raised his hand in salute and turned to the city.

As he did so, a knight was seen issuing from the Waste City and, upon coming near it, was seen that he was none other but the Poor Knight of the Waste Forest, who sayeth to Lancelot, 'Sire, that you have done much good by me and by my sisters I have come to an accord with the people of the Waste City that you shall not be bound by your promise to return until forty days after the most Holy Grail shall be achieved. That, Sire, is all the further life I could obtain for you. Pray remember, Sire, this loyalty you have found in me.'

'I shall never forget it, Sire, and I thank you for putting off the day until after I shall rejoice at the achievement of the Sacred Chalice.'

And the Poor Knight returned to the Waste City and Lancelot and Gawain rode towards Castle Cardoil wherein was King Arthur.

Part the XVIIIth

And the people of the Turning Castle are in such joy as was unknown before. It had been prophesied that the castle would not cease its turning until a knight should come who was golden haired, who had the look of a lion, and a heart of steel. He had to pure and chaste, be without taint of wickedness, be of great valour, and firm in his belief in God. Also he had to bear the shield of Joseph of Arimathea who had taken Our Saviour down from the Cross. Such a knight was Percival and no other. Now released of their dread of the Knight of the Dragon they saved their souls by being baptised in the laws of God.

Percival was right glad when he saw the people turn to God. And the damsel sayeth unto him, 'Sire, now you must finish that which you are started on. And it must be finished soon for the Knight of the Dragon doth destroy much of the land and many knights are slain.'

After Mass on the morrow, Percival rode from the castle in company with the damsel who took the body of the knight Alein of Escavalon, the cousin of Percival. They rode until they came to the Isles of the Orchards wherein lay the Castle of the Golden Circlet. They entered the castle and did find the Queen of the Golden Circlet in great sorrow, and she took them to the castle wall and there did show them the Knight of the Dragon sat on his horse with four slain knights on the ground. The Queen sayeth, 'There, Sire, is the cause of great misery through the land for no knight shall conquer him.' But Percival looked upon him silently and sayeth nothing. And the Queen sayeth, 'Four of my best knights hath he slain this day. But you, Sire, who have no force nor aid from other knights, if you can defeat him I shall give you right willingly the sacred Golden Circlet for I can see from your shield that you are a Christian knight. Should you defeat him it will show that the true God was born of man and liveth in Heaven.

At this, Percival was right glad. He crossed himself and touched his forehead and left the castle followed by the damsel. As they reached the open ground beyond the castle gate, the damsel sayeth, 'I have carried the body of this knight to the site where he was slain. Now, Sire, you may have your cousin for I have done all that was right in the sight of God.' With this, she returned to the castle to stand by the side of the Queen.

Percival looked to the Knight of the Dragon and seeth that the knight was of height greater than any he had known or heard of. He held before him a great black shield which bore the image of a dragon that turned its head and sent forth a stream of flame that carried a great stench.

And the Knight of the Dragon seeth Percival and was in great scorn for Percival came to the field alone. Thus the Knight of the Dragon took not up his lance but his sword that was long and burned with red heat.

Percival couched his lance and raised his shield and gave spur to his horse that he ran at full pace at the Knight of the Dragon thinking to smite him through the breast. But the knight raised his shield and the dragon thereon breathed a fire that burned the lance of Percival to the very gauntlet. At this, the knight brought his sword down upon the helmet of Percival but the good knight raised his shield and the blow fell upon the red cross made by Our Saviour's blood and harmed him not. And the Knight of the Dragon looked upon this in wonder for none he had faced had so survived such a great knock. He then rode to the body of the knight brought by the damsel and sayeth to Percival, 'Have you charge of the burial of this knight?'

'I have,' sayeth Percival.

And the Knight of the Dragon turned his shield against the body of the slain knight and burned it to ashes and sayeth, 'Now you have nothing but ashes to bury, how think you now?' And Percival was in great wroth at this discourtesy and ran hard at the knight and did bring his sword down upon the black shield and cleft it almost to the head of the dragon. But the Knight of the Dragon did hit Percival on the shoulder and cut him most deep. As they parted, Percival saw that his sword now burned red from the flame of the dragon. He ran again at the knight and thrust his burning sword down the throat of the dragon and the dragon did roar with a great loudness and turned its head away from Percival and sent a river of fire at its bearer. And the Knight of the Dragon was burned to ashes. The dragon now free from the shield went to the sky as if returning lightning and could not be seen.

And the Queen came to him and had him taken in to the castle and had his wounds cleaned and cared for, and the damsel took up a handful of the ash of the Knight of the Dragon and put it on the wounds of Percival that they heal the quicker. The Queen then sayeth that all her knights should be at the command of Percival and she returneth Percival his sword and sayeth that those who would not be baptised should die by it. She then placed the Circlet of Gold upon his head and he baptised her in the name of the Lord and she took the name of Elysa in His name. Many came to be baptised in the name of Our Saviour. And they knew Percival by the name of the Knight of the Golden Circlet and his name was spread through the land and when it came to King Arthur and Gawain and Lancelot at Castle Cardoil they knew not which knight it was that had destroyed the Knight of the Dragon.

When he was made whole, Percival departed from the Castle of the Golden Circlet leaving the sacred Circlet under the protection of the Queen, now known as Elysa. And he rode long in to the forest until he came upon a mighty castle known as the Castle of Copper. In the castle was a great copper bull that was worshipped most horribly by the people and it bellowed most mightily that it could be heard throughout all the land. At the gate of the castle were two giants made of copper who fought each other with great iron hammers, and no one could enter the castle for they would be crushed by the hammers or the feet of the copper giants.

And Percival did come close to the castle gate and saw the copper giants. As he did so a loud voice from above sayeth that he might go past the giants in safety and, believing in our Lord, he came to the gate and the giants did stop their fighting and allowed him to enter without harm. Inside he found many people who worshipped the bull and did not follow God and His laws, and none were armed for they believed that strangers could not enter the gates past the copper giants. And Percival seeth that they kneel down in adoration of the bull that bellowed loudly and he knew them to be wrong in their worship. The voice then told him to gather up the people in the great hall which he did. He then made them all pass through the gate to see which of them would believe in the true God. One thousand and five hundred put he through the gate but thirteen only did escape the iron hammers. And the copper bull did melt and the Devil therein fled. The thirteen believers were baptised and put the bodies of the unbelievers in to the waters known as the River of Hell which flowed to the sea as a great pestilence. They then departed for the forest where they built hermitages and did penance for the rest of their lives for the time they had spent worshipping the copper bull.

Percival then repaired to the house of the King Hermit who greeted him with great joy. In telling of his adventures the knight asked of the King Hermit if he knew the meaning of a strange sight he had seen in a clearing in the forest. And he told the King Hermit of the white beast which had disgorged twelve dogs. And the King Hermit sayeth unto him that the white beast signified our Lord Jesus Christ and the dogs were the twelve tribes of Israel who had not followed the laws of God and did set our Lord upon the Cross where His body was torn and rent. And the twelve dogs were scattered throughout the forest as the twelve tribes were scattered throughout the world, where they live without the protection of God until they give full reverence to our Lord. And the knight and the damsel signify the divinity of our Lord and they did collect the torn beast in their golden dishes, for as the scriptures say that he was raised to Heaven to join His Father.

'But what, Sire, of the two priests? One of whom did worship the Cross most reverently but the other beat it with a rod as he wept most piteously.'

And the King Hermit sayeth that the first priest, whose name was Jonas, worshipped the Cross for on it God had died for our sins and he was indeed much grateful for the sacrifice of our Lord. Alexis, the second priest, did believe the Cross to be the giver of great pain and suffering to our Lord and he had deep wroth that our Lord should suffer pain so.

Percival told also of the Knight of the Dragon and sayeth that he had never seen a knight so big and horrible. The King Hermit sayeth that only a most pure knight could have overcome such a devil and it was a good thing for now that devil hath returned to other devils who do nought but torment each other. The devil had burned the body of the slain knight but it had no power to burn his soul. And the Turning Castle was also the work of a devil and Percival had stopped it turning and converted the people therein by his goodness, for nothing can prevent the will of a pure and good knight.

And Percival sayeth that he had sore missed the fellowship of Gawain and Lancelot for they would have been full in his aid. But the King Hermit sayeth that they could not for though they be good and hardy knights who worshipped the true God, they were not pure and chaste.

And the King Hermit sayeth to Percival, 'Since you were made a knight you have done much good work in the name of Our Saviour. Had you not destroyed the copper bull and its believers they were have remained so until the end of the world. You have had much suffering but you must endure it willingly for no honour comes without pain. Now, Sire, you are ready to do the one thing for which God cries out. All of those that live in the land of the Fisher King no longer live in the laws of God for fear of the King of Castle Mortal who hath taken the Castle of the Holy Grail. Though he be your uncle and my brother, you are the only mortal who can claim the castle by right for the good Fisher King was your uncle and brother of your mother. Now it is in the hands of a man who is disloyal to God and a traitor to his family. You should know that the castle is strengthened by nine bridges each guarded by three strong knights. The knights and priests of the Fisher King are scattered and the chapel of the Holy Grail is empty. No other enterprise, Sire, should God so willingly see carried out in His name.'

'So you commend, Sire, so shall I bend my will. There is no reason why he should have the castle. Of better right is my mother that was next-born to the Fisher King of whose death I am most sorrowful.'

'As indeed you must be, fair nephew. For it was on your account that the good Fisher King fell into languishment when you failed to ask the question of the Holy Grail. Had you returned it is said that you could have ended his suffering but I believe that God chose the way you have taken. I have with me a white horse that I wish you to have. Let your banner fly above her when you come upon the castle and you shall be availed of the power of God, for you will face twenty-seven knights guarding the bridges. No single knight can overcome them save by His power. I pray that you always have God and His sweet Mother in your mind. If you do and you face great danger let fly your banner as a messenger of the power of God and your enemies will lose their valour, for nothing will confound a foe more than the virtue and might of God. It is well known that you are the best knight in the world but rest not alone upon your knighthood or your strength but stiffen them with the virtue of God. And you should know that there are two lions at the gate, one is red, the other white. Always put your trust in the white for he takes the side of God, and if your might should fail, look him in the eyes and he will look at you and you shall know the will of God. When you know His will, do as He directs for then may you overcome those who combine against you and you shall pass the nine bridges and the knights that guard them. And may God grant that you pass them safe in body and set right the laws of our Lord where they have been trampled by your uncle.'

Percival departed after Mass and rode towards the castle of the Holy Grail whereupon he came across a hermit riding full fast, but the hermit did join him when he saw his shield. And the hermit sayeth, 'I see from your shield, Sire, that you are a Christian. None other have I seen this many days for the King of Castle Mortal hath driven them from the land. No men who worship God and His sweet Mother dare stay.'

And Percival sayeth, 'But you shall stay, Sire, for the honour of God was not won in retreat. He shall lead you and I shall ride with you. Are there more hermits in the forest?'

'There are, Sire, twelve in number and they assemble by the Cross at the edge of the forest. We are minded to go to another part of England and there do penance for we must abandon our chapels for fear of the dread King that hath seized the land. This King doth demand that we live not under the laws of God.'

They rode to the Cross and found there the hermits amongst whom was Joseus, the son of the King Hermit, and Percival and Joseus did greet each other well and with great joy. Percival sayeth to the hermits, 'Sires, you are holy men and the bearers of God's message on Earth, to you the people from kings and knights to soldiers and ploughmen look for guidance in this life. God has now granted you a test of your holy valour wherein others may reflect their own courage on behalf of God. Shall you be seen to be wanting in holy hardiness? Will you allow the enemy of God to prevail? Will you stand with me in the service of God?'

And the hermit Joseus stepped forward and sayeth, 'I shall stand with you.'

And the other hermits stepped forward also and sayeth they will stand with him also.

Percival sayeth, 'God be praised that He hath such good men in His service. Follow me, Sires, and pray as never before that God's work may be done.'

And they went their way to the Castle of the Holy Grail and came upon a chapel like unto that before Camelot. Percival put his shield and lance at the door and entered, whereon a tomb before the altar did open of its own accord and the hermits were struck with wonderment for the tomb had never before opened. And inside lay the sweet smelling body of one of the good men who had taken the body of Christ from the Cross as at Camelot, and the company of hermits prayed with full reverence at the discovery and sayeth that God had sent them the best knight in all the world for their protection.

Their devotions completed, Percival led them to the castle where they beheld the nine bridges each guarded by three hardy knights. The knights had heard that the tomb had opened for Percival and were sore afraid but the King of Castle Mortal sayeth to them that Percival was but one knight and could fall from the blows of another single knight.

Percival crossed himself and commended his life unto God as the hermits knelt in prayer. He then lowered his lance and raised his shield and ran full tilt at the knights guarding the first bridge. The knights all fell upon him and broke their lances on his shield. One knight he knocked from the bridge with his sword and, though the others fought long and hard, they fell slain also in to the river below.

He then came to the second bridge and the three knights came at him with great hardiness. One he struck slain from his horse but the others gave many blows in reply to his. At this, the hermit Joseus asked of the other hermits if to go to the aid of Percival would be a sin. And they sayeth that God's work can never be a sin. He then threw back his grey cloak and showeth his armour beneath. He unsheathed his sword and rode across the first bridge and fell upon one of the knights and sent him to the ground slain. Percival then sent his enemy to the river below where he drowned. And Percival was greatly tired by the combat and knoweth that he had not the strength for the knights guarding the next bridge. But he looked up and saw the eyes of the white lion and he heard the voice of God saying to go back across the first bridge. Taking Joseus, he obeyed God's command and returned to the hermits. As he did so he looked back and saw the first bridge rise up that would have entrapped him but for the eyes of the lion. And the lion seeing the bridge raise up broke its chains and ran with a great roar across the bridges and did bring the first bridge down again that Percival may continue his way to the castle gate.

And Percival made to spur his horse on again but met the eyes of the lion and he then crieth to the hermit Joseus, 'Take up my banner and follow me!' And Joseus took up the banner with its field of white and the cross of red and rode beside Percival. And the knights of the third bridge were sore afraid at their coming. The first knight received the lance of Percival though his breast and fell slain. The others put their arms aloft and did plead for mercy which the hermit Joseus sayeth to Percival to be a good thing. And so their lives were spared. Thus it was with the knights of the fourth bridge and they promised to be good Christians from then on.

Percival did then think in him that the virtue and might of God was most powerful, but a good knight should do the work of God from his own valour. Surely God would be much pleased with a knight who suffered on His behalf as He had suffered for mankind. At this, Percival sent the hermit Joseus and the banner back across the bridges they had taken.

Percival rode at the knights guarding the fifth bridge and found them to be of much hardiness. None would be knocked from his horse nor would they bend before his lance. With this, the hermit Joseus took up the banner once again and rode to join Percival. Ere long all the knights at the fifth bridge were slain and Percival came to understand that trying to do the work of God without God's aid was for the foolish, not for the worthy.

The knights guarding the sixth and seventh bridges saw the work of God and threw down their arms and begged for mercy which, on the advice of the hermit Joseus, Percival did grant. At this, the red lion did burst from its chains and in great rage did fall upon the knights of the eighth bridge and slay them that they should not set like example to the knights of the final bridge. And the white lion did attack the red lion and tear it to pieces. The white lion did then raise it up to its hind legs and looked at Percival who understood that the banner should be retired with the hermit Joseus and that no mercy should be shown to the knights of the ninth bridge, for they were hard in their condemnation of God and were foremost in the service of their master.

The hermit Joseus returned to the other hermits and bade them mount their horses. He then stayed at their centre and raised the banner, but in accordance with the wishes of Percival did not go beyond the eighth bridge. At this, the knights guarding the ninth bridge think to them that they should plead for mercy but only in falsity for they may then slay Percival in treacherous manner. But Percival knoweth in his mind the guidance of the white lion and bore down upon them full armed. But they cast aside their weapons and did not flee and Percival was most confounded for it was not seemly for him to slay knights who had disarmed themselves. As he came to them his knightly virtue came firm upon him and he raised up his lance and reached not for his sword. The white lion saw this and understood and fell upon the knights and did slay them for the treachery they bore in their hearts.

Then they heard a great cry from the walls of the castle and they did look up to see the King of Castle Mortal. The King drew his sword and thrust it in to his own body and did fall from the walls to the deep and fast water beneath. And they did wonder at this for they knew not why a King should die thus rather than in courageous combat. And they wondered more that the King should be the brother of the good Fisher King, the King Hermit and the Widowed Lady who had all lived virtuous lives. For wickedness is hard and beguiling and harmful to the soul, whereas goodness is kindly and simple and humble before God. But it seemeth to all that God hath ordained that evil men shall meet evil ends and that good men shall have their reward at the right hand of God.

Percival and the hermits did enter the castle and found the chapel of the Holy Grail was empty whereon the hermits did fall to praying to God for the return of the sacred objects once there within.

And the good knights who had served the Fisher King and had fled before the King of Castle Mortal heard of the arrival of Percival and returned all joyous and Percival made much welcome of them. And soon it was known that the Saviour of the World was well pleased with Percival and his deeds for a bright light as if of many candles was seen in the chapel and when the door was opened the Holy Grail and the Sacred Spear were seen within by the hermits with the sword by which Saint John the Baptist was beheaded and many other relics and images all bright with precious stones. And the tomb of the Fisher King was covered with a cloth of silver and gold and no one knew who had done this save only that it was done by command of our Lord.

Part the XIXth

That Whitsuntide King Arthur sat with his Queen and his many knights in the great hall at Castle Cardoil. And the King seeth that the light doth come in the windows at both sides of the hall. He sendeth a knight without the hall to enquire why this should be and the knight came back and sayeth, 'Sire, the sky now shows two suns, one in the east and one in the west.'

And the King thinketh that such be not possible but a great voice came in to the hall and sayeth, 'All is possible to the Lord God for now he showeth His great joy that the good knight who took the shield from this hall hath conquered the land that truly belonged to the Fisher King. The King of Castle Mortal is defeated and slain and the Holy Grail is now returned to the chapel. And the Lord God now demandeth that you make pilgrimage to the Castle of the Holy Grail, for when you return your faith shall be doubled and the people of Greater Britain shall thus give high and noble service to the Lord.'

At this, a richly clothed damsel of great beauty entered the hall carrying a golden box brightened with many jewels. She saluted the King and Queen most courteously and sayeth, 'Sire, I have come to your court for it is the most high in all the lands and I bring you this golden box as a gift. It has inside the head of a knight, but none may open the box save him that did slay the knight. I therefore pray you, Sire, that you may attempt to open the box, and if you fail, that your knights shall do likewise until he who hath slain this knight is revealed. And further, Sire, that the revealed knight may be given grace of forty days after you have made your pilgrimage to the Holy Grail.'

'Damsel,' sayeth the King, 'and shall we know who the dead knight is?'

'Truly, Sire, for inside are letters declaring his name and the name of the knight that did slay him.'

And the King placed his hand upon the box as if to open it but he could not. Then Gawain and Lancelot and all the knights followed and all tried but none could open it. At this, Kay entered the hall all boastful and sayeth, 'What is this? I have slain many knights and struck off their heads. If this knight be of much hardiness then he must be one who hath fallen to me. If this hall were filled with knights heads that I had struck off you would see that I am the knight most able to open the golden box.'

And the King sayeth, 'Come, Kay, we need not to hear of your boldness. Prove yourself with the opening of the box.'

Kay did take up the box and as soon as it felt his hand the box did open and reveal the head inside. And Kay sayeth, 'So I have sayeth, none other could do it but me. Even those you prize most high did fail. Therefore, Sire, you should think the more high of me.'

The King sent for one of his chaplains and sayeth to him that he should read the letter within the box. And the chaplain did look upon the letter and gave a great sigh and sayeth, 'Sire, my Lady, these letters sayeth that the head therein is that of the knight named Lohot, the son of King Arthur and Queen Guinevere. He had slain the giant Logrin and, tired from his endeavours, did fall asleep. Then upon them came Kay and he struck off the head of the sleeping knight and of the giant and took the head of the giant to the King in false claim that he had slain the giant.'

At this, the Queen fell into a swoon and the King near fell down in horror for he had thought that his son had been the good knight whom had defeated the King of Castle Mortal and caused the return of the Holy Grail and the sacred relics. Kay fled and the court fell in to deep mourning. And all were in despair that the damsel had made covenant that he who had slain the knight might not meet God's justice until forty days after King Arthur made the pilgrimage to the Holy Grail.

When the King could be raised from his mourning, Lancelot sayeth to him, 'Sire, the time hath come when you should make a pilgrimage to the Castle of the Holy Grail for you have made a covenant with God so to do.' And the King was ready but the Queen could not be roused from her mourning for her son.

And the King sendeth the head of his son to the Chapel of Our Lady at Avalon where there was a hermit that was much loved of our Lord. Then the King departeth in company of Gawain and Lancelot and a squire to carry their arms.

Kay did leave England and went to Lesser Britain where he lodged with Briant of the Isles. And Kay did tell Briant of the woe that had befallen King Arthur and that the King was on pilgrimage to the Castle of the Holy Grail. Briant was a knight of much hardiness and many knight and castles and who had no love for King Arthur. Thus he began to war against King Arthur and his land and his castles.

Part the XXth

King Arthur in company with Gawain and Lancelot and a squire rode long in to the forest but could find neither house nor castle for their lodging that night. And they sent the squire up a tall tree to see if such lodging is in sight and he sayeth that he can see a ruined house where a fire burned therein. And they go there and pass over a wattle bridge into a courtyard and can see the fire burning hot in the house. They entered the house and sat by the fire all armed, and the squire did go in to a chamber and did prompt issue forth crying unto the Holy Mother. And they asked him what aileth him and he sayeth that the chamber is full of many dead men. Lancelot rose from the fire and entered the chamber and saw a great heap of dead men. But when he returneth Gawain sayeth that there is nought to be feared from dead men, and God would save them from the living.

At this, a damsel of great beauty entered the house lamenting and saying, 'Dearest God, how long must I suffer this penance, when will it come to an end?' The damsel wore clothes all torn and her feet were not shod and did bleed and she carried the body of a dead man and took it to the chamber with the others. When she seeth Lancelot she made great joy and sayeth, 'At last! My penance is finished.'

And Lancelot sayeth, 'Damsel, are you a creature of God?'

'I am, Sire, and nought should you fear. I am the Damsel of the Castle of Beards that did treat knights with great cruelty. You did away with the toll I demanded from the passing knights but made covenant with me that when you achieved the Holy Grail you would return to me, but you saw it not. Instead a penance was laid on me for the cruelty I did the knights, for never a knight came but I cut off his nose, took out his eyes or struck off his hands. Now I needs must to bring to this house all the knights that have been slain in the forest. Now, thanks to God and to you, I am relieved of this penance and may return with the daylight.'

And Lancelot sayeth, 'And glad I am, damsel, so to do, for I have never seen such a penance placed upon so beautiful a damsel as you.'

'Alas, Sire, there is yet more for which you must prepare yourself and may God shield you from it. Every night cometh a band of black knights from where no one knows and are right foul and hideous.

'The black knights then fight each other in long and arduous combat. But a knight who came passing as have you drew a circle around us with his sword and we sheltered therein in good remembrance of Our Saviour Lord and His Precious Mother. You, Sire, should do likewise for our protection.'

And Lancelot drew a circle around them with his sword and they waited inside and bore in mind the Saviour and His Mother.

Thereupon, a great band of black knights came through the forest at great pace and entered the house and fell upon each other. They also tried to fall upon the King and the two knights but the black knights could not enter the circle drawn by Lancelot. And Lancelot was sore raged that he might not go against them and drew his sword but the damsel sayeth that he should stay within the circle for safety. But Lancelot was not a knight to let a challenge go unheeded and he leapt from the circle and fell upon the black knights. As he did so, the King and Gawain joined him and they did cause much harm upon the black knights until they were all slain. And when the black knights fell to the ground they turned into ashes and the ashes became ravens and fled the house.

They then rested within the circle but ere long another band of black knights fell upon the house carrying the bodies of slain knights, and they demandeth that the damsel put the bodies within the chamber but she sayeth, 'No! I am finished with my penance. Never again shall I be at your command.'

And in great rage the black knights ran with their lances upon the damsel and her companions but they could not breech the circle. With this, the King and the two knights did leap from the circle and fell upon the knights but they were soon sore pressed, for the black knights were in great number and were of greater prowess than their earlier brethren. And the moment came when it seemed that the King and his knights would be defeated but the sound of a ringing bell was heard and the black knights fled with a great noise to the forest and all was silent. With this, the damsel sayeth, 'This is the sound I have heard every night and it hath saved my life for the black knights then flee to the forest. If it had not sounded yet more black knights would have come such as could not be defeated.'

And this is a great wonderment for at that time in Greater and Lesser Britain the bell was unknown and only the horn or clappers of steel or wood gave forth a great sound. And the King marvelled much for he thought the sound of the bell could only be that of God.

On the morrow they departed from the ruined house and the damsel went her way to her castle. The King and the two knights then met three hermits who sayeth that they were to bury the slain within the house and there place a hermit to restore the house and build a chapel for the needs of the faithful. And the King was right pleased at this and bid the hermits well. Also the King for the term of the pilgrimage did hear the sound of a bell every hour and it brought him great joy for he knew it to be of God.

And the King did say unto his knights that henceforth on the pilgrimage he was not to be declared their King but he wished to be concealed as a brother knight. And thus they followed his accord.

That evening they came upon a fair house in the forest and the lady therein came to greet them well and took them inside and they disarmed and were given fair robes to wear. Then she sayeth that she knew Lancelot and sayeth, 'Sire, once you saved me from great dishonour whereof I am now in much unhappiness. But it is better that I have unhappiness in honour, than find pleasure in dishonour and shame, for shame endures whilst sorrow is passing.'

At this, the knight of the house entered from hunting and seeth Lancelot and sayeth, 'By my beard, Sire! I know you. It was you that robbed me of my happiness by making me marry this lady. But she hath never had joy of me, nor shall she.'

'Then, Sire,' sayeth Lancelot, 'you do not your duty as a husband. Truly I did make you marry her but did so only that you would not bring disgrace upon her and her family.'

'That mattereth not, Sire, for I still love the one you made me give up and she hateth you and now hath great power in this forest.'

'I know, Sire,' sayeth Lancelot, 'for I have spoken with her and know of her feeling to me.'

At meat the King asked the Lady to sit by him but the knight sent her to sit with the squires and sayeth, 'Now you may see the way I treat her and so shall I continue so to do, for this I have promised the one I do truly love.'

And Lancelot seeth that the knight is not overburdened with courtesy and sayeth quietly to the King that if he should meet the knight in the forest he would use his sword to teach him to show less churlishness to the lady.

They departed the next morn and rode through a land that was quiet and without people until they came upon a small castle by a deep valley and they saw that much of the castle had fallen into the chasm. They came to the gate and saw an old priest and asked him the name of the castle. And he sayeth to them that it was Tintagel.

The King sayeth to him, 'How did much of the castle fall into the chasm?'

And the priest sayeth, 'It came about, Sire, when King Uther Pendragon held a court to which came the king of this castle whose name was Gorlois. And he took with him his wife, Ygerne, who was the fairest Lady in all the kingdom. And King Uther was mightily smitten with her. At this, King Gorlois departed and took his Queen with him for dread of the intentions of King Uther. Then King Uther laid siege to this castle until King Gorlois had to leave in search of aid. With this, King Uther demanded that his sorcerer Merlin give him the resemblance of King Gorlois which the sorcerer doth. And that night King Uther did lay with Ygerne who hath in mind that it was her husband. And that night the seed was planted that was to become King Arthur, for his mother was

Ygerne and his father was Uther. For that sin, the bedchamber and much of the castle fell in to the chasm.'

Of this King Arthur knew nought and was discomforted in front of Gawain and Lancelot but they were both his subject knights and, to the priest, he was but a brother knight. And both knights through loyalty and brotherhood made neither opinion nor question of his lineage but held him in honour and regard.

And the King sayeth, 'What became of King Gorlois?'

The priest sayeth that he was slain by King Uther who then married Ygerne. And so King Arthur was brought about through sin but is yet the best King in the world.

They then went to the castle chapel which was right rich and within lay a fair tomb which was the tomb of Merlin the sorcerer. But the priest sayeth that the body of Merlin was not therein for when the coffin was brought in to the chapel the body was taken, but whether by God or the Devil was not known.

That night they lay at the castle and departed on the morn. They passed through many strange lands and islands and in journeying Lancelot brought to his mind that the time was nigh when he must return to the Waste City and fulfil his covenant to set his head at risk. And he telleth the story of the knight he had struck the head off on the vow that he would return and place his own head in peril. And he sayeth, 'The time is come when I must go thither, for I must meet my covenant or else be considered unworthy. Should God allow me to live, I shall join you again on your pilgrimage.'

With this, they held his hand in parting and wished him God's speed and commended him to the Saviour of the World. And his heart was heavy, not for the challenge he must face but that he could not ask the King to salute the Queen on his behalf, for he would not that the King nor Gawain should know of his love for that Lady.

When he came to the Waste City he found it as before, in ruin and much disordered. And he heard the lamentations of many ladies and damsels who sayeth, 'We have been betrayed for the knight doth not come as he vowed. This day is the day when he should redeem his pledge. Never again should trust be placed in a knight. As the others before him he hath betrayed us with his fear of death yet he struck off the head of the young knight. Now he saves his own head.' And nowhere could Lancelot see the ladies and damsels who cry out in their lamentations.

Then he came to the palace where he slew the knight and alighteth and tied his horse to a ring near the mounting stone. At this, a knight appeared with the same axe that Lancelot had used to strike off the head of the young knight. And the knight did sharpen the axe with a stone. Lancelot sayeth, 'Are you to slay me?'

The knight sayeth unto him, 'You have vowed to set your head in jeopardy as did the young knight who was my brother. Him you slew without defence and now you must stretch out your neck so that I may strike off your head. Let there be no contention in this matter for it was your deed and your vow that hath brought you here.'

Lancelot sayeth, 'May I see a priest that I may confess?'

But the knight sayeth, 'There are none here that will help you. You shall die as you are.'

And Lancelot knelt down and crossed himself saying, 'Have mercy on me Lord and accept my soul to your service. I surrender myself to you not as a good knight but as one who hath tried to do your service in this world.' At this, he remembered the Queen and sayeth, 'Dear kind, gentle, lady, never again shall I see you. Death does not trouble me but never to see you again is the worst death a man should ever know. My love for you has never failed nor shall the love of my soul if God should allow. Thus permitted, you should know well, dear lady, that you are loved in the next world as is no other in this world.'

And Lancelot did come upright and bare his neck that he might receive the axe and the knight raised the axe and brought it down right forcefully. As he did so an Angel spoke to Lancelot and sayeth that God was with him. At this, Lancelot bowed his head in worship and the axe came past his head. And the knight was sore angered and sayeth that Lancelot should keep his head still and he raised the axe again. But as he did so, two damsels of great beauty came to a window and one of them crieth out, 'Sire, if you would have my love for ever more throw down the axe!'

And the knight cast aside the axe and sayeth to Lancelot, 'Sire, I beg your mercy, pray forgive me!'

Lancelot sayeth, 'But, Sire, it is for me to cry mercy from you that you slay me not.'

The knight then sayeth, 'Though you have slain my brother, I will not do this. Rather, Sire, that I will defend you to the utmost of my power for by your valour you have saved this city and the people.'

And the two damsels came to Lancelot and sayeth, 'You, Sire, are the knight we loved most in the world for we are the sister damsels to whom you, Gawain and another knight did give the houses and treasures of the forest robbers that you slew. Many knights, Sire, have come by here as you did and vowed to return to face the axe but none have done so as you have done. Should you have failed us, never again would the city rise and be returned of its people.'

And they took Lancelot to the great hall and disarmed him and set him at ease whereon came a great noise of joyfulness. The damsels took him to the window and showed him the many people who came from the forest to return to the city. Ere long priests arrived in procession and went to their abandoned churches and praised God for the knight who hath rescued them by his knightly virtues. And Lancelot received much honour.

Part the XXIst

King Arthur and Gawain rode through the forest until they came upon a knight riding at great pace. And Gawain asked him from whence came he. And the knight sayeth, 'I, Sire, am from the land of the Queen of the Golden Circlet where the Queen hath sore troubles. Her land and castles have been taken by Nabigant of the Rock and he now demands the Golden Circlet that was won by the son of the Widow Lady when he slew the Knight of the Dragon.'

'How doth he make such a demand?'

'A damsel is to take the Golden Circlet to the Meadow of the Tent of the Two Damsels where Gawain did away with the evil custom. There an assembly of knights is to be held and Nabigant of the Rock intends to win it by combat on the field.'

'Will you, Sire, be attending the assembly?' sayeth Gawain.

'I shall, Sire, but first I must inform all the knights I can find to tell them of this event.' With this, the knight took his leave and departed.

And Gawain took the King to the Meadow of the Tent of the Two Damsels for he knew the path from the time he had vanquished the evil custom.

The tent was as before richly decorated within and without. And Gawain took the King in and sat him on a couch with a quilted cushion and they washed in water brought by squires who also disarmed them. At the head of the couch was a noble chest wherein where many rich clothes and Gawain dressed the King and he in white silk laced with gold.

Thereupon, the two Damsels of the Tent entered and Gawain sayeth, 'Welcome, damsels.'

But the damsels sayeth, 'Sires, you are welcome, but it seemeth to us that you take from us that which is ours. Yet you, Gawain, would not do as we requested when we last met.'

And the elder damsel sayeth, 'There is not a knight in the kingdom who would not be joyous at my desire to love him. I prayed for your love, Sire, but you would not grant it, but you come to our tent and take that which is not yours as if we were lovers.'

And Gawain sayeth, 'I act only in accordance with the custom of the land and in expectation of the courtesy you should show. For you hath told me that when the evil custom was overthrown, all knights may come here for lodging and find they are honoured as guest knights should be.'

'This is indeed true, Sire, but you gave us churlishness and must expect churlishness in return.'

The elder damsel then sayeth, 'The three-day assembly of knights begins tomorrow and the prize will be the Golden Circlet. If nought else, you and your comrade will be able to boast that you have the most noble lodging in the land.'

And the younger damsel looked at King Arthur and sayeth, 'Sire, will you be as a stranger to us?'

'No damsel need be a stranger to me, for any damsel will be safe in my presence. Happy I am to honour you and obey your commands.'

'I thank you, Sire, and have but one request of you. Will you, Sire, be my knight in the assembly?'

'Even should I wish so to do, I cannot refuse such a request for no true knight shall refuse a damsel.'

'What, Sire, is your name?'

'My name is Arthur, and I am from Castle Cardoil.'

'Have you ought to do with King Arthur?'

'Damsel, I have oft been at his court, and if he were not the king to whom I am most loyal, I should not be in the company of loyal Gawain.'

And the King smiled upon the damsel who knew not who he was. But his showing was not as his heart for he loved his Queen and would not countenance dishonour upon her.

That night they lay in great comfort and the damsels would not depart until they were asleep.

On the morrow, knights came from across the land and set up their booths and tents in rich array. And the elder damsel came to Gawain and sayeth, 'Sire, for my hospitality I request that you carry a shield of red at the assembly and that you shall be known as the Red Knight.' And Gawain agreed right willingly.

And the younger damsel came to King Arthur and sayeth, 'Sire, it is my wish that you bear a shield of gold. For it will be better on you than any other knight. And I ask that you thinketh of me as I shall think of you this day.'

'Thank you, damsel,' sayeth the King, 'the knight doth not live who would not think of your worth and courtesy.'

And they heard that the damsel hath brought the Golden Circlet and Nabigant of the Rock had issued the laws of the assembly. And the younger damsel sayeth to the King, 'Know, Sire, that there is no other knight here today more worthy than you nor hath arms so noble. Take care you honour them and show you to be a good knight for my love.'

King Arthur replieth, 'May God grant it so.' And the King with Gawain mounted their horses and went to the assembly.

The younger damsel sayeth to the elder, 'What think you of my knight? Doth he not please you?'

The elder damsel sayeth, 'He doth, sister. But I have no liking for Gawain for he doth not do as I ask of him. And for this he shall suffer dearly.'

And the King and Gawain charged upon the field as two lions unchained. Two knights did they knock from their horses and sent the horses to the two damsels who received them with much joy. Gawain then saw Nabigant of the Rock and caused him and his horse to tumble. King Arthur sent many a knight to the ground until it was time for evensong when they left the field. That night all the knights in assembly agreed that the Red Knight and the Knight of the Golden Shield were the best among them.

King Arthur dined with the younger damsel by his side and Gawain sat with the elder damsel. Much wine did they have until they went to the couches to sleep full weary of the buffets they had received that day.

On the morn, the younger damsel came to King Arthur and saluteth him saying, 'Sire, it is my request that this day you shall bear a shield of blue, and since you can do no better than you did yesterday, you should do no worse.'

The King replieth, 'May God so will it.'

The elder damsel came to Gawain and sayeth, 'Sire, have you remembrance of a time when you won the sword that struck off the head of Saint John the Baptist?'

'I do,' sayeth Gawain.

'Remember you also the covenant you made with the king who tried to take the sword from you? A covenant that you would obey the request of the damsel who first gives you his name?'

Again, Gawain sayeth, 'I do.'

'Then, Sire,' sayeth she, 'be aware that I am that damsel and I tell you in truth that the king was the King of Wales. And my request is that you bear your own shield of red with the golden eagle and that on this day you prove to be the worst knight on the field.'

And Gawain was sorely troubled for never hath he broken a covenant and sayeth, 'Damsel, you know I can do no other than grant your request.' At this, he departed from her and rode on to the field.

King Arthur rode as before and sent two knights to the ground. Gawain came in the midst of the combat and the knights all sayeth, 'See, here comes Gawain, a brave knight who is the nephew of good King Arthur.' And Nabigant of the Rock seeth Gawain and came at him at full gallop but Gawain cast down his shield and did flee from the field. There being no knightly virtue in defeating a fleeing knight Nabigant of the Rock did not pursue him. Gawain came against other knights and did flee from them also and they sayeth, 'Never have we seen such cowardice of a knight!'

As other knights came to engage him, Gawain fled to the protection of King Arthur who was sore put to the effort of defending him and was much confounded by the cowardice shown by Gawain. And the many knights sayeth, 'Now can I take vengeance on this knight for what he hath done to my family or my brother knights.' And the King did keep them away for the long day. Both knight and King were pleased that the end came with evensong and they could leave the field without much buffeting.

At the tent a dwarf appeared and sayeth to the damsels, 'Your knights are worse than may be imagined! He of the blue arms did fare well enough, but Gawain is of such cowardice that even I may send him to flight.'

To the King he sayeth, 'And you, Sire, why do you keep him company? Had he not been there you would have been the best today, but he skulked by you to avoid the buffets. No good knight should stand by a coward even though before he did slay two knights by this tent.' And the elder damsel did smile at these words.

The knights that left the field at evensong could not agree to whom belonged the Golden Circlet for the Red Knight and the Knight of the Golden Shield had not appeared on the field that day.

When the damsels and the dwarf had left the tent Gawain told the King of his covenant and his duty to observe it. And the King sayeth, 'Sire, you have had much blame this day and I have had great shame put upon me for my defence of you. Never did I believe that you could have pretended cowardice for your valour is renowned throughout the land. Pray God that on the morrow you are not required to do the same for your name shall be cast down as never before.'

And Gawain sayeth, 'Sire, I am still bound by my covenant. May God grant me ease of my suffering.'

In the morning the elder damsel came to Gawain and sayeth, 'Sire, it is my wish that today you bear the gold shield first borne by your brother knight on the first day of the assembly. And furthermore that you prove yourself to be the best knight on the field but you shall not say your name other than it be the Knight of the Gold Shield.'

And Gawain sayeth, 'As it pleaseth you, damsel.'

The younger damsel came to the King and sayeth, 'Sire, pray grant me that you will bear the shield of red this day and that you will do as well as the first day or better.'

And the King replieth that he was right pleased with such a request.

They galloped to the field and fell upon the knights so that many are knocked to the ground. The King did lay low many knights but did not seek out combat as willingly as he would, for it was his wish that Gawain should win the Golden Circlet. But the King did seek out Nabigant of the Rock and tumbled him most severely from his horse. As the procession to evensong was passing, the damsel bearing the Golden Circlet came on to the field and the knights were called upon to name the best among them. And they said that the best knights were the Red Knight and the Knight of the Golden Shield but of the two the best knight must be the Knight of the Golden Shield, for he hath done best on the first day and on the last. But had the Red Knight done as well as he had done on the first day it was he who would have won. And the Golden Circlet was awarded to Gawain but none there save King Arthur knew whom he was.

They returned to the tent where the damsels made great joy of them. And the dwarf came and sayeth, 'Damsels, it is better that you lodge these knights than the coward Gawain for had you lodged him great shame would you have brought upon yourselves.' And the damsels laughed at him and made him begone.

And the damsels say unto Gawain, 'Sire, what will you do with the Golden Circlet?'

'I shall return it to the knight that won it first and thus lift the burden from the Queen of the Golden Circlet.'

That night the King and Gawain lay asleep in the tent when the younger damsel came to the King and sayeth, 'Sire, much have you done as my knight. Now I come to reward you.'

But the King, whose heart was full of his Queen Guinevere, sayeth, 'Damsel, honour I love above all else and nought I put above your honour. May our Lord God help you to preserve that honour.'

The younger damsel then sayeth to the elder that such knights gave them neither comfort nor solace and may God preserve them from such guests. And the elder damsel sayeth that, but for the Golden Circlet, neither knight should leave the land but she hath loyalty to her Lady, the Queen of the Golden Circlet. And the damsels departed.

As the King and Gawain departed on the morrow, Meliot of England came upon the knights who had been to the assembly and sayeth to them that he is in search of Gawain whose man he was that the knight could aid him to take back his castle and land robbed of him by Nabigant of the Rock. And the Knights telleth him that Gawain had proved a coward and his aid would be of no avail and Meliot turned away in his sadness.

The King and Gawain rode until one night they came to the Waste Manor where Gawain had been led by the hound and where he found the body of the knight slain by Lancelot. They lodged the night there and were known by the knights therein. And the Lady of the Waste Manor sent for knights to come to her aid for she held King Arthur and his nephew Gawain that were both brother knights of Lancelot. Many knights came and she chose seven that were to lay in wait outside for when the King and Gawain did depart and find themselves on the points of their lances.

Meantime, Lancelot had left the Waste City where he was much honoured and came upon Meliot. And Meliot told Lancelot that Gawain who had once been full of much valour had now turned coward. But sayeth Meliot that he would still search for Gawain for he did not believe what he had heard of him. And Lancelot sayeth unto him that he would join him in his search.

Together they rode until they chanced upon the Waste Manor where the King and Gawain were lodged. And the King and Gawain sayeth to one another that they should face the knights that waited outside although there be seven of them. They came fully armed to the gate and rushed out to fall upon the knights, and the sound of swords upon steel fell upon the ears of Lancelot and Meliot. These knights then came to the gate and came upon the waiting knights as hawks among sparrows. The knights of the Lady were fallen or scattered with great swiftness and the King and Gawain gave great greetings to Lancelot and Meliot.

And the Lady of the Waste Manor did come to the gate holding the hand of a young squire and seeth Lancelot and sayeth to him, 'Sire, you did slay the brother of this squire and one day he or another shall come to slay you.' But Lancelot did not make reply.

The King and his knight departed and Meliot told them of Nabigant of the Rock who hath taken his land and will not return it except by combat with Gawain. And Gawain asked leave of the King to go with Meliot to gain return of his lands and the King doth grant it willingly. At this, the King and Lancelot rode on towards the Castle of the Holy Grail.

Gawain and Meliot repaired without delay to the castle robbed by Nabigant of the Rock and came before the gate. And Nabigant rode out with no other knights for he knew Gawain to be a coward and therefore aid needed he none. Nabigant sayeth no words to Gawain but came at him full furious with lance lowered. Gawain did hurtle at him and strike him through the breast even to the heart and he fell slain. The knights of the castle that serveth Nabigant then issued from the castle but were soon sent in flight from the field by Gawain and Meliot. More knights came from the castle but they brought the keys and paid homage to Meliot as their lord.

Now Gawain departed in pursuit of the King and Lancelot and came upon a damsel riding at a fast pace through the forest. And he sayeth, 'Damsel, God's greeting be upon you. Why do you ride so fast?'

The damsel sayeth, 'Sire, I am going to the great assembly of knights that is to be held at Palace Meadows where I shall search for the knight that won the Golden Circlet at the Meadow of the Tent.'

'Why so?' sayeth Gawain.

'I am sent by the Queen of the Golden Circlet to beseech the knight to come to her aid. For Nabigant of the Rock hath robbed her of her castle and there can be none better in the world to defend her than the knight who hath won the Golden Circlet.'

'Then, damsel,' sayeth Gawain, 'both you and the Queen may rest in ease for the knight who won the Golden Circlet hath already slain Nabigant.'

'Sire,' sayeth the damsel in joy, 'Can this be true?'

'Indeed, for I know the knight well and I saw him slay Nabigant. Furthermore, damsel, I have here the very Golden Circlet which I bear on behalf of the knight to the Castle of the Holy Grail.' And he showed the damsel the Golden Circlet in its ivory and jewelled box. He then sayeth, 'Thus it is that your Queen shall no longer bear the guardianship of the Golden Circlet and may be at ease.'

And so the damsel departed to tell her Queen of the joyous news. Gawain turned towards the assembly at Palace Meadows for he knew if the tidings of the event had reached the King and Lancelot there they would repair straightway. As he rode he came upon a squire full weary from a long journey and asked him from whence he came. And the squire answereth, 'Sire, I am from the land of King Arthur where there is a great war, for none know the whereabouts of the King. Many say that he is slain for none have heard of him since he left Castle Cardoil with Gawain and Lancelot. Now the Knights Briant of the Isles and Kay burn all the land and carry plunder from the houses. The knights of the Round Table number no more than five and thirty and of them ten are sore wounded and they are all that remain to defend Castle Cardoil.'

And Gawain took the squire and rode hard to the assembly where he found the King and Lancelot already in combat. They had heard that the prize of the assembly was to be the golden crown of a queen and her white horse and whosoever was the victor would have the duty of defending her country for she was now dead. And Gawain rode hard in to the fight and like Lancelot sent many knights to the ground. But none fought as did King Arthur who seemed like a lion against stags and scattered all before him. With the end of the contest, the knights sayeth that none fought as well as the Knight of the Red Shield, for so King Arthur had armed himself.

And a knight brought forth the golden crown and the white horse and put them before the King who sayeth, 'To whom doth the crown and horse belong?'

The knight sayeth, 'Sire, they belonged to Queen Guinevere, the wife of King Arthur whom many believe slain. As her knights may not leave Castle Cardoil, where they defend the land of the Queen, I was sent to attend assemblies that I may hear of tidings of the King or of Gawain and Lancelot and much sorrowed am I that nothing can I find of them for the land is in great despair.'

Of the sorrow of the King no words can be known for he loved his Queen beyond all measure, and his knights took him to one side where he fell to his knees and wept. At his side knelt Lancelot that loved the Queen but in his heart alone and he wept also for that all his deeds of knighthood were now as nought, for no longer had he a bright soul to be championed. By them knelt Gawain in full sorrow for the loss of his Sovereign Lady and the good wife of his King.

And Lancelot sayeth to the King, 'Sire, allow me to return to Castle Cardoil that I might defend your land. Thus may you and Gawain continue to the Holy Grail and obtain the help of God to give you strength in your loss and victory over those that despoil your realm.'

Gawain sayeth, 'Truly, Sire, it should be as Lancelot has asked. No better knight could you send and no better cause can you now have than finding the help of the Holy Grail.'

And the King sayeth to Lancelot, 'Go, Sire, and be the guardian of my land. Look to its proper rule and hold it for me until God allows me to return. For now I have no heart to return and see the ground where she walked and live in halls that no longer hear her laughter.'

And Lancelot did leave for Castle Cardoil full of sorrow and sadness.

Part the XXIInd

King Arthur and Gawain rode to the Castle of the Holy Grail. And the King took with him the white horse of the Queen and held her gold crown close to him. Percival greeteth them with great joy but fell to weeping when he heard of the death of the Queen. He took them to the Chapel of the Holy Grail and they saw the sepulchre of the good Fisher King where the rich covering was changed anew every day by the hands of angels only. They saw also the sword that had struck off the head of Saint John the Baptist, which had been brought thither by Gawain. Now Gawain gave to the Chapel the Golden Circlet that was the Crown of Thorns worn by Our Saviour and the King gave the golden crown of the Queen.

And the King saw that the castle was of great strength and beauty and was known by names other than the Castle of the Holy Grail, these being the Castle of Eden, the Castle of Joy, and the Castle of Souls. By the castle ran a river which was said to rise in Eden. It encircled the castle and flowed to the hermitage of a holy hermit and there did go beneath the ground and was not seen again. It was said that all good men that stayed there had souls that went straight to Paradise when their life in this world.

And the King was looking from the castle windows with Gawain when he espied a long procession led by a man dressed in white. This man carried a large Cross and all the others carried smaller Crosses and candles, save for the man at the rear who bore around his neck a golden ornament the like of which had not before been seen. And they asked Percival who these folk were and he sayeth that they were hermits that gathered three times a week to pray at the Chapel of the Holy Grail, but the man behind with the golden ornament he knew not.

The King did meet the hermits and the knights bowed their heads in reverence at the Crosses and saw the words in stone above the chapel door which sayeth:

All who entereth herein
Shalt be as silent as the rose
For God is herewithin
And any tumult shall be his
And those who carry out his works
And them alone.
Thou shalt speak only if God looketh
Upon thee.

As they came together in the Chapel the golden ornament was taken from the last man and placed upon the altar where it was raised and issued forth a sound that the King knew full well for it was the same sound he had heard every hour. And the hermits then prayed full reverently and sang sweet psalms and the King and the knights knelt before the altar. Then the golden ornament was raised again and the sound came forth three times whereupon there did appear the Holy Grail in five manners, the first four of which it is not permitted to say, but in the last appeared as a chalice the like of which there were none in England. And the chalice was borne by an angel bathed in pure light and the angel looked upon Percival. And the knight raised himself from his kneeling and, knowing full well that God looketh down upon him, placed his hand on his heart and sayeth, 'Whom doth the Grail serve?'

At his question, the nine orders of Angels filled the height of the chapel singing 'Holy, holy, holy is the Lord God of Hosts: the whole earth is full of His glory!', the sound of their voices echoing from the farthest hills. Then cometh the sound of beating wings, and a silver dove spoke the words, 'It serveth Him whose eye looketh down upon you and seeth naught but the virtues of Man and Angels. Of such shall the Seraphim be made.'

And the light fadeth as the words sang across the forests, meadows, rivers and seas.

And all in the chapel knew that only the most virtuous knight could have asked the question and received the answer. Now all throughout the world should know that evil shall ever fall before the virtuous for they wear the armour of God and carry the shield of Our Saviour and bear the sword of the Holy Ghost. And the Holy Trinity shall reign triumphant throughout all the ages.

At this, King Arthur did set in mind the law that henceforth throughout England all wine at the sacred Eucharist shall be taken from such a chalice in remembrance of that day.

At the end of the Mass, the King asked the man who bore the golden ornament by what name it was known. And the man sayeth that he was the King for whom Gawain had slain the giant, thus winning for him the sword that had struck off the head of Saint John the Baptist and now lay on the altar of the chapel. That King had been baptised in the presence of Gawain and his people had also become Christian. Thereupon, he had become a hermit and had lived by the sea where he saw a ship come ashore that held three priests all named Gregory who had come from the Holy Land. And they sayeth to him that in ancient times King Solomon had three bells to be cast. One bell was for the Saviour of the World, the second was for His Holy Mother, and the third was for all the saints. And God had commanded that the priests bring the third bell to England for no bells were there in that country. And the Hermit King was commanded to show the bell at this castle that others may be cast both great and small. For this all his sins would be forgiven. And King Arthur ordained that all the chapels in England should have bells in memorial of this day.

And Gawain sayeth to the Hermit King, 'Truly, Sire, you are a worthy King, for thy held to your covenant with me.' With this, the Hermit King and all the hermits did depart for their hermitages there to do the work of God.

The King was at meat with Percival and Gawain when the second damsel who was in the company of the Damsel of the Carriage came in to the great hall. On her right arm she bore a great wound as if by a sword or lance. She sayeth to Percival, 'Sire, have mercy upon your poor mother and your sister and on us. Aristor of Moraine, who is cousin to the Lord of the Moors that you did slay, wars upon your mother and hath carried off your sister. He sayeth he will take her to wife but he is of great cruelty and hath the custom of cutting off the head of his wife after the night of the wedding. This he hath done many times before. Sire, I was with your sister when he took her and he wounded me thus. Pray, Sire, that you heed the cry of your mother and go to her aid for great shame will fall upon you should you fail her.'

And Percival sayeth, 'Damsel, there shall be no failing. This very hour shall see my departure.'

And the King sayeth, 'Sire, Gawain and I would count it an honour to be by your side in this endeavour.'

But Percival sayeth, 'Thank you, Sire, but no. Better, Sire, that you repair to Camelot, there to guard the castle and the land for my mother that when she returns she shall find it safe under your protection.'

And to this the King assented.

Part the XXIIIrd

King Arthur and Gawain departed from the Castle of the Holy Grail and rode until they came upon a much ruined castle that once was of great richness. And they lodged therein that night and went to hear Mass in the chapel with the priest that lived alone in the castle. And the priest told them that the castle was named the Castle of Hope, for he prayed in hope for the return of the lord of the castle. They saw that the chapel walls were decorated with fine paintings in bright colours of red, gold, blue and green. And the King sayeth to the priest, 'What know you of these paintings?'

The priest sayeth, 'Sire, the paintings were done by a true and loyal knight who dearly loved the lady and the boy therein. They show the true happenings of that time.'

And Gawain sayeth, 'And what, Sire, is the story they tell?'

The priest then sayeth, 'The good knight Gawain was born in this castle and was given his name in honour of the knight that lived herein. His mother was the wife of King Lot but she did not want it known and she sayeth to the lord of the castle that he should take the child and leave it in the forest to perish or have some other do so. This other Gawain was loathe to do, and had letters that sayeth the child was of royal blood put in his cradle with gold and silver. He then travelled to a far part of the forest and found a humble dwelling wherein lived a worthy man and his wife and he asked them to care for the child. This Gawain then did return to the Castle of Hope and on his death asketh me to remain here until the boy returned. I now hear that the young Gawain is among the best knights in the world and pray God daily that he will return to this castle.'

And Gawain was sore ashamed that he learned of his birth in this manner and that his mother should have sought his death as a child. But King Arthur sayeth, 'Fair nephew, let not your heart be troubled by such tidings. I also have but recently learned of my own coming into this world. None of us can choose how we come or how we depart. You are honoured far and wide for your knightly virtues and none but you hath brought such high esteem.'

The priest, now that he knew to whom he spoke, sayeth to Gawain, 'Sire, you are confirmed in the laws of God and were born of the lawful marriage of King Lot and your mother. Let God be praised that you have come thither.'

Part the XXIVth

It was a hound that led Gawain to the Waste Manor where he found the body of a knight that had been slain by Lancelot. And the knight had a son named Meliant who determined to avenge his father. This Meliant heard that Briant of the Isles had a great and mighty army and he did war upon the land of King Arthur, and many of the King's knights were slain. He journeyed to find Briant and found him in the Castle of the High Rock and there told him of his father's slaying and his desire to find vengeance, and in this told he would help Briant in his war on King Arthur. And Briant received him with joy and made him a knight. Thus raised he wished to find Lancelot and challenge him. But no one knew the whereabouts of Lancelot and some sayeth that he is slain. But he was whole and sound in body yet in great despair at the death of the Queen and deep sorrow did lay heavy in his heart.

Lancelot rode through the forest and came upon a knight and a damsel who did play and laugh with each other. And Lancelot sayeth 'Sire, do you know of any lodging hereabouts?'

And the damsel sayeth, 'You shall not find lodging so good as we have, Sire, for already it is eventide.'

Lancelot sayeth, 'This, damsel, is good tidings indeed for I am greatly wearied.'

'So are all they who come from the land of the Fisher King, Sire, for none may journey from there without suffering as all good knights must.'

And Lancelot sayeth 'Damsel, where is this lodging of which you speak?'

The knight sayeth to Lancelot that he must follow the path before him and he will find it. The knight and the damsel sayeth, however, that they will go another way and meet Lancelot at the lodging.

As Lancelot departed the damsel sayeth, 'That is Lancelot but he knoweth me not. Much do I dislike him for he made a knight that loveth me marry another. And that damsel he loveth not and maketh her sit to eat with the squires and command that none aid nor obey her. But the knight will not abandon her for fear of Lancelot and for his honour.'

Lancelot rode along the path and seeth a large castle strongly walled and at its gate were hung the heads of fifteen knights. And he seeth a knight close by the castle and sayeth to him, 'Sire, what is the name of this castle?' The knight answereth that it is the Castle of the Griffon.

'Why, Sire, do the heads of knights hang there?'

'The daughter of the lord of the castle is the most fair damsel in the land but she will give herself only to the knight that draws a sword from a stone column in the great hall. All knights that lodge there must enter the contest for her hand and try to take the sword from the column. Those that fail must lose their heads. As you may see, Sire, none have succeeded. Now it is said abroad that none but a Grail Knight may draw the sword. But, Sire, take heed of what I say and seek lodging elsewhere for it is an ill adventure that needs place life at risk. No blame will fall on you for leaving, for there also lives in a cavern below the castle a lion and a griffon that have devoured half a hundred knights.'

And Lancelot sayeth, 'Thank you, Sire, but it is evening and I know not the forest. Better I chance the Lord within than the devils without.'

The knight sayeth, 'As you will, Sire, and may God go with you and grant that you depart in safety.'

Lancelot came to the castle gate and entered in to the courtyard where he dismounted and climbed the steps to the hall. Therein he found many knights and damsels but none saluted him or greeted his coming except the lord of the castle who sayeth that he should disarm himself. Lancelot sayeth that it was his wish to be allowed to wear his arms. But the lord of the castle sayeth that none shall sit at meat until he be disarmed and had two squires aid Lancelot in disarming. They dressed him in rich apparel and sat him at the table. Then the damsel of the castle came forth from her chamber and seeth Lancelot and thinketh him most comely. But she also thinketh it would be sore pity for him to have his head struck off.

When they had taken meat the damsel Lancelot had met in the forest came in to the hall and sayeth to the lord of the castle, 'Sire, you have lodging tonight your most deadly enemy, he who slew your brother at the Waste Manor.'

And the lord of the castle sayeth, 'This cannot be! Nor shall it be until it is proven.' He sayeth to Lancelot, 'Sire, ask the question.'

Lancelot sayeth 'Which question, Sire?'

'That you may have my daughter. For if you are worthy you shall have her.'

But the mind of Lancelot is full of the memory of the dead Queen and he hath no desire for neither damsel nor lady. But the custom of the castle was before him and he must follow it if only in courtesy. And he sayeth, 'Sire, any knight would feel himself adorned by such a damsel for his wife should she be willing. Had I thought you would let me take her for a wife I would have asked most willingly.'

And they took him to the column and showed him the sword therein. The lord of the castle sayeth, 'Go, Sire, follow the custom as have other knights.'

Lancelot stepped forward and grasped the hilt of the sword and pulled mightily, and the sword came free of the stone which did shiver at the deed. And the damsel of the castle was much pleased but the damsel from the forest sayeth to the lord of the castle, 'Sire, I tell you plainly that this is the foul knight that did slay your brother. He hath slain many knights and many more will he slay if you allow him to leave the castle alive.'

And the lord of the castle sayeth to Lancelot, 'Sire, I will not be bound by my covenant for you are a mortal enemy who did slay my brother. My daughter will not seek your company lest she be a fool.' But his daughter thinketh she would like to be deep in the forest with Lancelot. The lord of the manor then sayeth to his knights that they should bar the gates to the castle that Lancelot may not depart and they should meet the next dawn full armed for it was intent that Lancelot should have his head struck off and placed above the gate. But the daughter knew of her father's commands and bid haste to send a messenger to Lancelot.

The bearer of the damsel's message came to Lancelot bringing a hound and sayeth, 'Sire, my mistress bids me say to you that her father intends for you to have your head struck off. Twelve knights shall be within the gate and twelve without all armed, and though you be a good knight, this shall be over many for you to contend. There is beneath this castle a cavern which leads to the forest but it is guarded by a most fierce lion and a griffon that hath the beak of an eagle, from which it breaths fire, the eyes of a hawk, the teeth of a wolf, the ears of an owl, the feet of leopard, and the tail of a serpent. There is, Sire, no more hideous beast in the world. My mistress sayeth that you should go this way and she shall meet you with your horse where the cavern reaches the forest.'

'By all that is Holy,' sayeth Lancelot, 'It would be better for me to face the knights than this ill-formed creature.'

And the messenger sayeth, 'Sire, my mistress sayeth that she can aid you no more if you do not do as she directs. She doth it in love for you and sendeth you this hound that you should put before the griffon, for the beast doth love this hound greatly and will not harm it. But for the lion, Sire, you must depend upon God and your own valour.'

'This I shall do,' sayeth Lancelot, 'but the damsel should know by you that it is not cowardice that taketh me from the knights, but her wish.'

And the messenger telleth the damsel and she hath much happiness.

Lancelot armed himself and entered the cavern followed by the hound. And thereon did the cavern grow bright from the fire of the griffon as it came at Lancelot, but the light showed the hound and the griffon lay down and playeth with the hound as the knight went past. Then Lancelot seeth the lion which was of great fierceness. It ran at him but Lancelot moveth not, and the lion opened its jaws wide and in its last leap the knight put aside his shield and ran at the lion and thrust his sword down its throat. And the lion fell slain.

When he came to the forest there he found the damsel with his horse and she asketh him if he is hurt, and he sayeth that he is not. And she looked at him and sayeth, 'Sire, you seemeth not over joyous.'

And Lancelot replieth, 'No, damsel, I am burdened with much sorrow for I have lost that which I love most.'

The damsel sayeth, 'But, Sire, you have won me. It is said that I am the fairest damsel in the kingdom and I have brought you safely from the castle. You, Sire, have my love and much would I have it that you loveth me also.'

Lancelot sayeth, 'Damsel, much would I make of your love and your beauty but my heart owes its loyalty to another who cannot know it. For your service to me, damsel, I can do no more than offer you my protection when I am able so to give it.'

But the damsel was sore at heart and sayeth, 'This, Sire, is betrayal. Better that you were slain in the castle that I may be able to worship your head above the gate.'

And Lancelot commended the damsel to God and rode in to the forest.

The lord of the castle waited for Lancelot that morn and sent his knights to find him, but they found him not. He commanded two knights to enter the cavern where they were devoured by the griffon. The lord of the castle then went to the chamber of his daughter and found her weeping and without consolation. And no knights had the courage to go forth in pursuit of Lancelot.

That day Lancelot came upon a great valley that had forests on both sides and he saw a new and rich chapel upon a hill with a roof adorned with gold Crosses. Nearby were three new houses each facing the chapel. A stream ran by the chapel and fell in to the valley with many waterfalls and a pleasing sound. The knight then heard chanting from the chapel and, alighting, led his horse up the hill. And three hermits came from the chapel and he sayeth, 'Sires, what is this place called?'

And the hermits sayeth, 'It is Avalon, Sire.'

Leaving his sword, lance and shield outside, Lancelot entered the chapel and saw that it was like unto no other chapel that he hath seen. The walls were hung with silk cloths fringed with gold and the ceiling painted with images, and many other images of Our Saviour and His Mother were stood about. In the centre of the chapel were two tombs covered by rich cloths and with candles in gold candlestick at each corner. At each side of the tombs priests knelt and sang psalms. And Lancelot sayeth, 'For whom are these tombs made?'

And the hermits replieth, 'They, Sire, are for King Arthur and Queen Guinevere.'

And he sayeth, 'But King Arthur lives.'

'In truth he doth. But the Queen is herein buried with the head of her son for whom she died in great sorrow. It was the command of the Queen that she be placed by the tomb of her beloved King that he may join her at the side of Our Saviour.'

And the heart of Lancelot was as if torn asunder, but he may not show it at the tomb of the Queen. He goeth to an image of Our Saviour's Mother and knelt down weeping saying, 'It is my greatest desire that I never depart from this place but my honour and the memory of this sweet Lady doth forbid it. I pray therefore that when I die my body may be returned to this place and I might be shrouded and buried close by her. May death come soon for I know no longer the light nor joy of this world.'

And the hermits did come to him and ask him to join them at meat and then to rest. But Lancelot sayeth that he wished to keep a vigil that night by the image of the Saviour's Mother.

As the morning light dimmed the candles Lancelot rose from his prayers and took Mass with the hermits. Before he departed he placed his hands most tenderly upon the tomb of the Queen and commended her soul to the hosts of Heaven, and as he rode from the chapel he turned many times until he could see no more the golden Crosses.

And Lancelot came that night to Castle Cardoil where he seeth the land and manors were spoiled and wasted which angered him greatly. He then saw a knight that had been grievously wounded riding on the path and asketh him, 'Sire, whence have you come?'

And the knight sayeth that he had come from near Castle Cardoil where he had seen Kay and two knights taking as prisoner Yvain le Aoutres, the father of Chaus the squire who had brought the golden candlestick to King Arthur and died so doing.

'Are they far?' sayeth Lancelot.

'No, Sire.' sayeth the knight. 'I will lead you and help you as my wound may allow.'

And they came up to Kay and the knights and Lancelot sayeth loudly, 'Hold, Kay! Be it not enough that you hath slain the son of King Arthur that you now must war upon him?'

Kay replieth not but ran at Lancelot with his lance lowered. But Lancelot was ready to meet him and knocked him hard from his horse. And the knight that led him to the place also tumbled one of the knights of Kay. Lancelot gave the horse of Kay to Yvain as the traitor knight mounted the horse of his fallen knight and rode off to the Castle of the High Rock wherein was Briant of the Isles. Kay telleth Briant of what had happened and Briant sayeth, 'Was the King there?'

But Kay sayeth that he had no time to enquire of such. But Briant and Meliant of the Waste Manor believe that Lancelot is come to Castle Cardoil for the King is slain, and they much rejoiced.

And when Lancelot cometh to Castle Cardoil he telleth the knights there that the King is alive and they have much joy. But many of the knights are sore wounded.

On the morrow Lancelot looked from the castle walls and saw sixty knights on the field below. Among their number was Briant and Meliant but not Kay who was wounded from the buffeting of the day before. And Lancelot did muster seven knights amongst whom was Lucan and sayeth unto them, 'Knights! Nothing can we achieve by skulking behind these walls. Yonder is our foe and with God's will we shall scatter them. Pick your enemy and run at him most mightily, for we do this in the name of our sovereign lord Arthur and the memory of his dear Queen.' And they issued from the gate like arrows newly barbed with steel.

Meliant seeth Lancelot and ran at him so they hurtled with a mighty clash, but Meliant and his horse go to the ground and

Lancelot is minded to alight and run at him with his sword but Briant seeth this and ran at Lancelot. They struck each other so that sparks flew from their armour and their helmets were much buckled. Like lions they fought, and Meliant came to the aid of Briant but Lucan did knock him over again. The knights fought until they were separated by night and Briant returned to the Castle of the High Rock with many knights slain and wounded.

When the knights thereabouts heard that Lancelot had returned to Castle Cardoil and had dealt hard knocks to Briant they began to return. Ere long, Lancelot could muster five and thirty knights and others were mending of their wounds.

Part the XXVth

King Arthur and Gawain had gathered about them five knights within the Castle of Hope when they saw a multitude of knights come to the castle gates. But these knights were loyal to Ahuret the Bastard who had brought them to take vengeance on Gawain for the death of his brother Nabigant of the Rock, whom Gawain had slain on behalf of Meliot of England. For many days the castle was locked from without by these knights, and King Arthur became much angered for it became not a King to avoid combat. Gawain also did think it to be wrong to stay within the castle when the foe was camped outside. And they sayeth one to the other that better to face the foe and die with honour than stay inside to live with shame. And so they gathered their few knights and armoured them all and led them on to the field against the many knights of Ahuret.

The King and Gawain led the charge and they overthrew the knights that came against them, but Ahuret ran at the other knights and they were all slain. Now the King and Gawain commended each other to God, for both knew they were to be slain this day. And Ahuret ran full hard at Gawain and hit his breastplate so forcefully that Gawain lost his stirrups. But Gawain struck back and bent Ahuret back from his saddle. At this, Ahuret saw the King and ran at him but the King did hack at him with his sword and cause him to have a great wound. And the knights of Ahuret were much angered and gathered round to fall upon the King and Gawain. But there was an outcry from the rearmost of the knights for they hath seen more knights come on to the field.

Meliot of England had been given tidings that the King and Gawain were besieged in the Castle of Hope and gathered about him many good knights. Now he fell upon the knights of Ahuret and scattered them until many were slain and the others fled.

And Gawain taketh Meliot by the hand and sayeth, 'Thank you, dear Meliot, for the King and I were sore pressed and may have been very busy this day.'

Meliot replieth, 'Think little of it, Sire, for there was nought else I had in mind to do this day.'

And the King sayeth, 'Then thanks be to God, Sire, that He ordaineth you should rest in quiet this day.'

Then sayeth Gawain to Meliot, 'Meliot, I have need of a good knight to live in this castle and guard it well. Will you undertake so to do?'

And Meliot sayeth that he would right gladly. He sayeth also that as Gawain's man he will come to Gawain's aid without delay for it was proper for a knight to defend his lord without measure.

Gawain thanketh him. And the knight and the King departed as Meliot did build the castle back up.

Part the XXVIth

King Arthur and Gawain rode until they came to a deep forested valley beneath a hill. And the King seeth a rose bush and alighteth from his horse. There he took many roses to the wonder of Gawain, who knoweth not why and why the King is silent thereof. They then rode to the Chapel of Avalon and, after disarming themselves, entered. And the King in great sorrow placed the roses upon the tomb of his Queen. Then Gawain knoweth why the King hath picked the roses, for the knight had not known of the chapel nor of the riches tombs therein. They lodged that night with the hermits and rode to Castle Cardoil after Mass.

At Castle Cardoil the King was greeted with great joy for many thought him to be slain. And the news came to the Castle of the High Rock and Kay is much afeared and taketh him across the sea to Lesser Britain and hideth him in the Castle Chinon. Briant and Meliant stayed at the Castle of the High Rock and doeth much to spoil the land and take plunder where they may. But the knights at Castle Cardoil that came to Lancelot are mended of their wounds and many other knights came there also that the King may soon take vengeance on his foe.

One day the King was sat at meat. With him were sat also Lancelot, Gawain, Yvain the son of King Urien, Sagramors le Desirous and Yvain le Aoutres and other knights. And Lucan brought the King a gold cup that maketh the King think of his Queen. At this, a knight well armed came in to the great hall and bringeth himself before the King and sayeth, 'Sire, I bring you message from my sovereign, King Madeglant of Oriande. He demandeth that you yield up the Round Table for he is close kin and inheritor of the Queen and since she is dead you have no right to hold it. He is also your enemy for you hold to the new laws of God which he sayeth is an abomination. But he sayeth that if you abandon the new laws of God and marry his sister, Queen Jandree, you may hold the Round Table. If you do not do this, such misfortune that comes about will be upon your head.' With this, the knight left the hall and departed the land.

And Gawain sayeth to the King that his knights would follow him to smite his enemy. And he continueth, 'Sire, all Greater Britain is yours and no castles have been taken by your enemies. Only land and houses have been harmed and such shame is lightly mended. King Madeglant is mighty in words only and not in deeds and might easily be vanquished. Indeed, Sire, you need but send one of your best knights against him.'

The King doth order his knights to prepare themselves for conflict and prayeth the Lord God that He should defend that which is right in His eyes. The King also seeth that his ordinance is obeyed, that chalices of the manner of the Holy Grail be used throughout the land for the Eucharist wherein the blood of Our Saviour is taken by the people. And he doeth the same with the bells and seeth that all chapels hath one or more bells according to their means. And the people rejoiced much at the sound of the bells.

One day tidings came to the King that Briant and Meliant were intent on taking Castle Pannenoisance and did take a great army of knights there. At this, the King departed from Castle Cardoil, taking many knights with him, and he came upon Briant upon a field of red clover. And the knights ranged against each other and ran one upon the other with much hurtling. Great was the shock of their meeting and the ground shook with the fury of their combat. Meliant of the Waste Manor sought Lancelot and ran at him so that he pierceth the knight's shield. But Lancelot thrust his lance through Meliant's shoulder. Meliant then turneth and brought his sword down upon the helmet of Lancelot. Then Lancelot brought his sword down upon the shoulder of Meliant and the knight fell from his horse greatly wounded. And many knights fell upon Lancelot but Gawain doth aid him and they drove the knights away. King Arthur hath challenged Briant and they give great blows one to the other and Briant doth stumble, and his knights come to his aid and circle the King. Thereon Yvain and Lucan ride in and bring aid to the King. Sagramors le Desirous met with Briant and knocked him from his horse. He then took his sword and would have slain the knight but the King cried unto him to desist.

With Briant fallen to King Arthur the knights ceased their combat and tended the slain and wounded. Meliant was borne on his shield to the Castle of the High Rock where he died. Briant was taken prisoner to Castle Cardoil and gave his loyalty to King Arthur. Thereon he was made Steward of all the King's lands, and some of the King's knights did think this to be wrong and were downcast, but Briant seemeth to serve the King well. But the King did command that any who did take vengeance on Kay would do so in his name.

One day the King was at Castle Cardoil when a damsel came in to the Great Hall and sayeth to the King, 'Sire, I bear a message from my Lady Queen Jandree. She commandeth me to say to you that she wishes to be Queen of your land, mistress of your household, and your wife. She sayeth that you must give up your obedience to the new laws of God and follow those of the god whom she worships. If you do this not, King Madeglant is ready to fall upon your country. He hath taken oath that he will not end his war upon you until he hath the Round Table which you hold in defiance of him. My Lady would not bring you this message for she cannot look upon any that hold to the new laws of God and hath bound her eyes that she might not see such by mischance. Thus all day and all night she is blind to the world around her.'

And the King sayeth to the damsel, 'Pray say to your Lady that none shall sit here as Queen lest they be as worshipful as Queen Guinevere and the Lord God maketh not her like nor shall He so do. Tell your Lady also that the law given to us by the death of

God upon the Cross shall I never renounce. Further say to her that even though she unbind her eyes she shall not see truth unless she believeth in Our Saviour.'

'Then, Sire,' sayeth the damsel, 'you should prepare yourself for such evil tidings as never before have you known.'

And the damsel goeth to Queen Jandree and telleth to her the King's message. And the Queen sayeth that she would love this king but, as he hath no regard for her and refuses her will and command, he would fall. She sayeth to her brother, King Madeglant, that he should not take his knights to Greater Britain for she would seek her own vengeance on the King.

Part the XXVIIth

Despite the wish of his sister that she might take vengeance on King Arthur, King Madeglant gathered himself a mighty host and came to the shores of England with ten ships. The people defended themselves but cried to King Arthur for aid in their troubles. And his knights sayeth that he must send Lancelot for he was the best among them. Arthur sent for Lancelot and sayeth unto him, 'Sire, there are none that are your measure in knightly virtue and many are they who will follow you. King Madeglant wages war on my kingdom and I have need of a good knight to protect my land. I therefore earnestly pray you will take up my cause and rid England of King Madeglant.'

And Lancelot sayeth, 'Sire, there are many good knights in your court whom you could send. I am but one among many who would willingly serve you thus.'

King Arthur sayeth, 'Sire, modesty is becoming in a knight, but honour is more so. And your honour, Sire, is brighter even than my crown. Such honour have you I know that by it England can be saved.'

That day, Lancelot rode forth with forty knights in search of King Madeglant and discovered him by the coast where he warreth upon the people. And the people were of great joy when they saw Lancelot and joined his company of knights.

And King Madeglant issued forth from his ship and took his knights to do battle with Lancelot. Many of the King's knights were slain and many did run back to the ships but Lancelot had the ships burnt excepting two. King Madeglant took one ship and did flee right willingly and the other ship did follow with conquered knights. And the people sayeth that if King Arthur was willing they would much desire that Lancelot stay to be their king for he was a knight of much goodness and valour.

At Castle Cardoil the King sat to meat when a knight entered the great hall and come before the King without salute and sayeth, 'Sire, where is Lancelot?'

And the King sayeth that Lancelot is elsewhere in the land. The knight then sayeth, 'Sire, wherever he is, he is the mortal enemy of my sovereign King Claudas. And so, Sire, are you if you give this knight aid.'

'Why so? sayeth the King.

'For he hath slain Meliant of the Waste Manor, the son of the sister of King Claudas, as he also slew the father of Meliant. King Claudas grieves much for his nephew and is determined on vengeance against Lancelot.'

And the King sayeth, 'Sire, you should know that I hold not in great honour the name of King Claudas for he hath taken castles from his father and not by conquest. You should further know that I shall stand firm at the side of Lancelot against all the world may send against him. If Lancelot sayeth this demand you make against him is false then the knights of this court and the knights throughout the land shall stand firm by him, for his name in honour is without equal. Should he admit as you accuse him, then his cause for these deaths will be weighed to his advantage for nought would he do in meanness of spirit.'

'That may be, Sire,' sayeth the knight, 'but Lancelot is the enemy of King Claudas and should you aid this knight the consequences will be on your head.' And the knight departeth to return to his king.

The King sent for his knights and held them in council to ask what he should do. And Yvain sayeth that Lancelot had slain Meliant in the service of the King and should not be held to account thereof.'

But Briant of the Isles sayeth, 'Yvain, it is known well that Lancelot did slay the father of Meliant. It is right that he should have sought peace and accord with Meliant. Instead, he did slay him also.

And Gawain sayeth, 'No, Briant, I will not have it. Lancelot is not here to take up his cause for he is on the King's business. It was you who knighted Meliant and loosed him upon his warring against the King. And this whilst the King was far away in pilgrimage of the Holy Grail. It was the King that sent Lancelot to guard his lands that you had under conflict. On the return of the King Meliant knew of it well but did not come to the King nor did he send a messenger to put forth his grievance. Meliant did war against the King who hath never done him a wrong nor rejected a plea. The blame, Sire, doth go to Meliant and to no other. In this matter I will willingly take on the cause of Lancelot and defend his name.'

Briant sayeth, 'In that, Sire, there is no one who will take up your challenge, nor should any of us make enemies of friends but stay our hand for the defence against those kings that make war upon this land. My mind sayeth the King should keep Lancelot far from these lands for a year that King Claudas may see that the King doth not associate with Lancelot. Then will King Claudas seek accord with this court.'

But Sagramors le Desirous then sayeth loudly, 'What? Would you have Lancelot created a coward who hideth from his accusers? Shall we so treat a knight who hath served his King with much honour? No, Sire, we should run upon King Claudas and his knights and send them bruised and limping from this land as would Lancelot were he here.'

Briant sayeth, 'Far better it would be for the King to send Lancelot away for a year than to fight his enemies for the next ten years.'

At this, the good knight Orguelleux entered the hall and heareth what Briant sayeth and himself sayeth, 'Briant, no knight should wish another harm who hath done good service with the King. None are better than Lancelot in this and he is not here to make answer. And so you should not speak ill of him. Much renown hath this court from the works of Lancelot and no braver knight exists in this realm than he. Few enough are the knights in this court who are beyond replace such as he. If King Claudas wars upon this land in the name of hatred of Lancelot, then so be it. For the King and his knights shall suffer warfare on behalf of a good knight in the sight of God. And He shall be pleased.'

And Briant was much angered at this but sayeth nothing for Orguelleux was a hardy knight.

Part the XXVIIIth

When King Arthur learned that King Madeglant had been defeated and the land was quiet he sent to Lancelot and asketh him to return to Castle Cardoil. Though the people in the land where Lancelot had conquered King Madeglant sorrowed that he had returned, the people of Castle Cardoil made great joy. Lancelot was told of the tidings of King Claudas and of Briant but sayeth nothing for in his own mind he thinketh what to do. Briant much disliked Lancelot and wished him away from the place as he had asked the King. Unknown by all, Briant it was that had counselled King Claudas to send his knight.

King Madeglant did hear that Lancelot had returned to Castle Cardoil and he came back and wasted the land and did much plunder. The people asketh the King for the return of Lancelot but the King sendeth Briant and forty knights. And Briant did not protect the land and was defeated by King Madeglant who burned many towns and castles and struck of the heads of those who would not abandon God.

Briant returned to Castle Cardoil as war against the King spread on all sides. He had no liking for the King but pretended to be his loyal servant. Nor had he any liking for Lancelot and the fellowship of knights that gave him company.

On Whitsuntide, the King and the knights were at meat in the great hall when, to their wonderment, an arrow came within and penetrated a stone column. The iron-tipped arrow was made of gold and carried many precious stones. At this, a damsel of great beauty entered the hall on a horse with a squire behind. The horse was attired with gilded harness and the damsel was clothed in the finest silk. And she saluted the King most worthily and sayeth, 'Sire, a favour must I ask of you, nor can I alight from my horse until you grant it.'

'Then alight, damsel,' sayeth the King, 'for no one could refuse to help such a fair one as you.'

And Yvain did lift her from the horse and place her lightly on the ground and take her to sit by him whereon he looked upon her often for she was fair and gentle and of good countenance. And the King sayeth to her, 'Damsel, what is that you wish of me?'

And she sayeth that she hath much need of the knight that could draw the arrow from the column. And the King asketh what the knight should do when he hath drawn the arrow but she sayeth that the arrow must be drawn first.

At this, the King sayeth to Gawain. 'Fair nephew, pull forth the arrow for the damsel.'

But Gawain sayeth, 'Sire, I pray you that you ask the other knights before me. You have here Lancelot who is a great knight than I. No, Sire, I could not take the shame of trying first.'

And the King sayeth, 'Yvain, you try the arrow for you cannot think yourself too humble.'

But Yvain sayeth, 'Sire, nothing in this world would I not do for you, but in this I pray that you excuse me.'

Again the King sayeth, 'Sagramors, or you, Orguelleux, will you do it?'

But they sayeth, 'Sire, we pray you ask us only after Lancelot has tried.'

Now the King sayeth, 'Damsel, pray ask Lancelot that he attempt to remove the arrow that if he fails the others may follow.'

And the damsel sayeth to Lancelot, 'Sire, pray render not my request in vain. In the memory of that you hold most dear, try the arrow that others may follow should you fail.'

But Lancelot sayeth, 'Damsel, there are many knights within this hall and much as I would willingly give you aid I cannot be seen a fool and a braggart by taking first try.'

And the King sayeth, 'No, Sire, you would be seen as a true and courteous knight that giveth aid to a damsel. Pray, sire, do as she asketh.'

Lancelot remembereth the damsel had asked him in the memory of that he held most dear. He held the memory of the Queen most dear and would not bring dishonour upon that memory. At this, he stood up and went to the column wherein was the arrow and pulled it clear with a grasp that caused the column to tremble. And the damsel sayeth to the King, 'Sire, none other could have obtained the arrow but this knight. Now I ask that you honour your covenant and let him give me his aid.'

And the King sayeth, 'Damsel, as Lancelot wishes.'

Lancelot thinketh of the Queen and sayeth, 'Truly shall I do as the damsel requires.'

The damsel sayeth, 'Sire, you must go to the Chapel Perilous wherein you will find the body of a knight shrouded. You shall take the shroud and the sword thereby and take them to the Castle Perilous. Then, Sire, you are to go to the Castle of the Griffon whence you escaped by slaying the lion and return to me at Castle Perilous bringing the head of the griffon. For at that castle lies a knight who cannot be healed but by the shroud, the sword, and the head.'

'It seemeth to me, damsel,' sayeth Lancelot, 'that you care little for my life, but only for the success of your wish.'

'No, Sire,' sayeth the damsel, 'I know full well the dangers you face. But your life you must not lose for the knight who needs to be healed cannot endure without you fulfilling your trial. Also you shall see the damsel most desirous in the world to see you and she is fair beyond all others. Pray go now, Sire, for to tarry will increase the hazard.'

And the damsel departed from the court and sayeth to herself, 'Lancelot, you go to the two most evil and fearful places in the world yet I do not wish for your death. But you I ought to hate above all others for you took away my lover and made him marry another. This I shall never forget.'

Lancelot taketh his leave of the King and his brother knights and issued forth all armed into the forest and commendeth himself to God.

Part the XXIXth

The people who suffered under the slaying and plunders of King Madeglant sent a message to the King and sayeth that they are in sore want of Lancelot to defend them. For Briant did return to the court with but fifteen knights whereof he had taken forty. And the King was troubled for now he hath lost many brother knights and sayeth to Briant, 'How, Sire, did you have so many knights slain?'

And Briant sayeth, 'Sire, King Madeglant hath a mighty force whom none may endure against. No people war so savage as do they. Sire, this land that they war on is far from you and is of little worth. I counsel you to let King Madeglant take it and let it cause you no more trouble.'

'Briant,' sayeth the King, 'both blame and shame would be upon me should I act as you counsel. No man of honour would let another take what is his. A worthy man counts not the value but the honour of what is his. I will not have men say that I have not the heart to defend that which is mine. Already I am at great shame for they bring their ungodly law to my land. If Lancelot were here he would take forty knights and drive King Madeglant and his evil knights back to their own land; Pray God that he returneth soon.'

And Briant sayeth, 'Sire, you should know that the people of that land think nought of you but seek to have Lancelot as their King.'

The King sayeth, 'Sire, they may seek as you say, but Lancelot is my loyal knight and would do nought against my will.'

'Then, Sire,' sayeth Briant, 'I shall say no more on the matter since you choose not to believe me. But I am certain, Sire, that this knight will do great harm to you should you not guard yourself against him.'

Part the XXXth

Lancelot rode through the forest towards the Chapel Perilous and came upon a knight who did bear a grievous wound. And Lancelot sayeth, 'Sire, from whence come you?'

The knight sayeth that he came from Chapel Perilous and Lancelot asketh him of his wound. The knight sayeth, 'Sire, I could not defend myself from the evil people that were there. But for a damsel who came there I would not have escaped alive. She asketh me that, should I come upon a knight they call Lancelot, or another named Percival, or a knight named Gawain, I should ask of them that they go to her straightway for none but such good knights could enter the Chapel Perilous. Indeed, Sire, I marvel much that the damsel there entereth but she oftimes entereth alone. There is inside the chapel the body of a knight that hath of late been slain. He was a strong knight but foul and cruel.'

'What was his name?' sayeth Lancelot.

'He was named Ahuret the Bastard,' sayeth the knight. 'He received a great wound from King Arthur before the walls of Castle Hope and did die thereafter. And his knights did lay siege to Castle Hope and Meliot of England defeated them but was sore wounded by a knight with the sword of Ahuret, which now layeth with him in the Chapel Perilous. Meliot must have the sword and the shroud to save him from death of the wound. May God grant that I meet one of the knights that I might give him the message.'

'Knight' sayeth Lancelot, 'you have found one of the knights for my name is Lancelot. I tell you this that you may leave to restore your wound.'

'Thank you, Sire,' sayeth the knight, 'and may God grant you his protection for you go in great peril. But the damsel hath great desire to see you and will give you what aid she can.'

'Knight, God hath brought me through many a peril and if He so desires He shall bring me through this also.'

With this, Lancelot departed from the knight and came upon the Chapel Perilous at evensong. The chapel standeth in a great forest which pressed hard upon the graveyard walls. At the entrance stood a great Cross and Lancelot did cross himself when he entered the many-tombed graveyard. There also did he see many tall men clothed in black who stand near one to the other and say nothing to him. When he cometh to the chapel he alighteth from his horse and leave his lance and shield outside. He entered the chapel and saw it to be dark but for a small lamp which giveth a poor light. But he seeth therein the coffin in which lay the knight. After kneeling and praying before an image of Our Lady, Lancelot went to the coffin and opened the lid. Therein lay the body of the knight in a shroud all bloody. And Lancelot lifted up the head of the knight to loose the shroud and a great noise issued from the coffin but whence it came he knew not. He teareth away part of the shroud and taketh the sword that lay beside the knight and closed the coffin. And he came to the chapel door and saw that the gate from the graveyard was full barred by many tall knights clothed in black and mounted as if for combat. At this a damsel came running with skirt lifted to aid her haste. And she sayeth to the black garbed knights, 'Do not move until we know who the knight is.'

And she sayeth to Lancelot, 'Sire, lay down the sword and the piece of shroud you have taken from the coffin.'

And he sayeth, 'Damsel, how doth this concern you?'

The damsel sayeth, 'You have taken them without my leave for I have the body of the knight and the chapel in my charge. Tell me, Sire, what is your name?'

And he sayeth, 'My name, damsel, is for the friends that love me, or for the foes that fear me. Tell me, damsel, how would you gain if I give you my name?'

And the damsel sayeth, 'I know not, Sire, whether I would gain or not, for oft I have been deceived.'

He sayeth, 'My name, damsel, is Lancelot of the Lake.'

'Then, Sire,' sayeth she, 'you have right to the sword and the cloth. But, before you depart, come with me to my castle and see the rich tombs I have made for Percival, Gawain, and for you.'

And sayeth Lancelot, 'Damsel, no desire have I to see my sepulchre so early in my life.'

The damsel sayeth, 'If you do not come to my castle, you shall not issue forth from this graveyard, for the knights you see before you are fiends of Hell that guard this graveyard and are at my command.'

But Lancelot sayeth, 'Damsel, no fiend from Hell or from this world can harm a true Christian.'

Then sayeth the damsel, 'Sire, I beg you to come with me to my castle and I shall save your life from these fiends. If you do not come with me, I demand you yield the sword and you may leave in safety.'

And Lancelot sayeth, 'Damsel, I have neither desire nor leisure to enter you castle. Nor shall you have the sword, for it is needed to heal a brother knight and great pity it would be if he were to die at my yielding to you.'

'You, are both vile and cruel to me, for had I the sword you would not escape this graveyard, but with it in your keeping the knights here cannot bar your path. Had I but the sword you would have been taken to my castle there to remain and I would no longer have guardianship of this chapel and graveyard. Now I must come here for ever more.'

But Lancelot is not sorry on her behalf for she was a damsel that caused her own troubles. He took up his lance and shield and mounted his horse and rode slowly to the gate. The knights there, now hideous on being close, moved apart and let him pass and he thanketh God for his deliverance.

Lancelot rode through the forest until the sun rose and came upon a hermit with whom he heard Mass and took a little food.

He rode that day until the sun set and no house nor lodging could he find.

Then he came upon some high walls which surrounded an orchard and gained entrance therein by an unlocked gate. He unbridled his horse and lay down his shield for a pillow and went to sleep. He did not know that the orchard was hard by a castle hidden by the walls and the tall trees. It was the Castle of the Griffon where he had slain the lion and where he was to seek the head of the griffon.

From the castle issued a damsel leading a hound to guard against the griffon. She was come to lock the orchard gate but instead she seeth Lancelot asleep inside. The damsel did run most fast to her mistress and sayeth, 'Rise, Damsel! Lancelot is asleep in the orchard!'

And the damsel ran from her chamber at great pace and came to the orchard and seeth Lancelot but knoweth not what to do. She sat near him and looked at him and sighed and then came more close to the knight. She then sayeth to herself, 'Dear God, what shall I do? Desperately I wish to kiss him, but if I wake him he may not grant me a kiss. If I kiss him whilst he sleeps, he will wake up and perhaps fend me away. Better perhaps that I kiss him now and know that I have done so albeit without his blessing. Such blessed memory will I have of such a kiss.'

And the damsel kneeled by his side and kissed him three times most tenderly on the lips. And Lancelot did leap up and cross himself and say, 'Holy God! Where am I?' And he seeth the damsel.

She sayeth, 'Sweet Sire, you are at the side of her that loveth you. A damsel whose heart is yours for ever.'

But Lancelot sayeth, 'Damsel, truly no one should hate those that love him, but my heart is given to a Lady whose love is beyond this world. This love is deep rooted in my heart and may not be quenched by another although it be the most pure and fine.'

And she sayeth, 'Dearest Sire, come with me to the castle where you may know my thoughts towards you. And where your thoughts of love may turn toward me.'

'Damsel, I seek the healing of a knight that may not be healed but by the head of the griffon.'

'This well I know,' she sayeth, 'for it was my plea that the damsel did send you here that I may see you once more.'

'Then,' sayeth Lancelot, 'I have come in answer to your deception. Now I shall depart, for the head of the griffon is not needed.'

She sayeth then, 'Lancelot, they say you are a good knight, but I say great are your faults. No other knight in the world would have refused my love, but your base heart hath done so. I kept the griffon at bay that he might not harm you. Better I think that it had slain you, or my father came whilst you sleep and put you to death. Better also that I could love you more dead than alive and that your head was put over the gate where I might gaze upon it for ever more. You, Sire, won me by taking the sword from the stone column. I am your prize yet you will not take me.'

And he sayeth, 'Damsel, much have you done for me, but your kisses betray you, for they who doth kiss in like manner may not cause ill against those they kiss.'

And the damsel sayeth, 'Sire, I took only that which never may I have again.'

Lancelot mounted his horse and, after commending the damsel to God, rode from the orchard into the forest. And she looked after him as long as she may, her heart heavy with pain. She then returned to her chamber and wept amongst the silence.

Lancelot rode until noon when he came upon Castle Perilous wherein lay Meliot of England. As he alighted at the mounting stage he met the damsel who had been at the court of King Arthur and she sayeth, 'Welcome, Sire. All here have much joy at your coming.'

And he sayeth, 'Thank you, damsel. May God see your kindness.'

She taketh him to the hall and had him disarm. And he sayeth, 'Damsel, I have here some of the shroud with which the knight was wrapped, and the sword from his side. But you, damsel, did make a fool of me by sending me for the head of the griffon.'

'I did that, Sire,' sayeth the damsel. 'for the sake of the damsel that loved you greatly. Now that she hath seen you, no more shall she place me under her plea.'

The damsel then led him to the place where Meliot lay and sayeth, 'Here, Sire, is Lancelot.'

And Meliot sayeth, 'Much welcome have you Lancelot. How fares Gawain? Is he well?'

'He was most hearty when I departed from him. But had he and King Arthur known of your wounds they would have been most sorrowful.'

And Meliot sayeth, 'The knight that wounded me so is now dead of the wounds I gave him. But the wounds I have rage within me and nothing can I do for them but they are touched by his sword and bound with his shroud all bloody. And only the best knight in the land can find them.'

At this, the damsel sayeth with great joy, 'See, Sire, they are here, brought by Lancelot.'

'By God's mercy!' crieth Meliot. 'Truly they speak of you as the best knight for no other would the coffin open. You would not have had the sword or the cloth and the foul knights that waited in the graveyard would have had you slain. But your goodness and virtue have triumphed and now I may turn away from death's shade.'

They uncovered his wounds and the damsel touched them with the sword and Lancelot bound them with the shroud, and Meliot was comforted and need wait only mending. And Lancelot was with great joy for he knew Meliot to be a good and loyal knight.

And the damsel sayeth unto Lancelot, 'Sire, for long I have hated you for you did take from me the one I loved and gave him to another. Many are the times I have sought to bring you harm for my loss and often I have prayed to God to bring you low. But now, Sire, the time of your offence against me is long gone and the pain has gone from my heart to my fading memory. For that you have done this thing for Meliot you may know that never again shall I seek vengeance upon you, and my grievance against you has withered away.'

Lancelot sayeth, 'Thank you, damsel. May you walk in grace beneath the favour of God.'

That night Lancelot lodged at the castle and departed after Mass the following morning. He returned to Castle Cardoil where he found the King much dismayed, for King Madeglant was despoiling much of his land and the people were turning from God. And Gawain and Yvain had departed from the court for the King trusteth Briant more than he should. And Lancelot thinketh the same and would have departed, for he liketh Briant but little and hath no trust in him. But the King sayeth to him, 'Sire, let your loyalty guide your heart and go on my part and put King

Madeglant to flight for there are none here that might do as you may. Bring the land back to the realm and the people back to God for no better adventure is available to you in this world.'

Lancelot sayeth to the King, 'Sire, I shall not fail you as you would not fail me.'

And the King sayeth, 'Sire, in truth I will not, for to fail you would be to fail myself.'

The King giveth Lancelot forty knights but Lancelot goeth not to find King Madeglant. He goeth instead to the ships which saileth from Oriande bearing King Madeglant's men. And Lancelot doth burn the ships until they be destroyed. He then cometh against King Madeglant and did slay him and his knights. He then rode through the land destroying the copper idols and false images until all the people are brought back to the law of God. And the people sayeth that they need a king and they look to Lancelot to be their ruler, but he sayeth he will not be king for he was a knight of King Arthur and that he would not be against his sovereign.

King Claudas, who still warred against King Arthur, heard that Lancelot had slain King Madeglant and taken King Arthur's land back. And King Claudas sent a secret message to Briant that he should tell the King to keep Lancelot out of his court that King Claudas might take vengeance on King Arthur. And Briant replieth that Gawain and Yvain had gone from the court and that he would put Lancelot at enmity with King Arthur.

Tidings had come to King Arthur that King Madeglant was slain and that the people were back in God's law. He heareth also that the people are want to have Lancelot for their king. At this, Briant sayeth to the King, 'Sire, the lands taken back from King Madeglant have banded together and made treaty that they will attack you under the kingship of Lancelot. This I tell you from my loyalty due to your many kindnesses to me.'

But the King sayeth, 'This cannot be, for Lancelot is my most loyal knight. Such evil would he not do to me.'

And Briant sayeth, 'Sire, long has it been known among many in this court that Lancelot is a traitor to you but none dare to say this to you. I say this from the loyalty of my heart and that I am the most powerful knight in your service and you may depend upon me.'

The King then sayeth, 'For the faith you have shown me I shall send for Lancelot and ask him of this matter. For no worthy king should have disloyal knights about him or in his service.'

The King's messenger found Lancelot in the kingdom of Oriande and, when he had read the letters, he set forth to Castle Cardoil straightway.

And Briant sayeth to the King that he should have forty knights armed beneath their mantles come to the great hall and be ready to take Lancelot and make him prisoner at the King's command. And the King agreed.

These tidings came to Lancelot but only that forty knights were to attend upon the King with arms beneath their cloaks and he came to the hall likewise armed. Briant seeth this and sayeth to the King, 'Look, Sire. Lancelot comes to the hall full armed without your leave so to do. Demand of him why he wishes to do you harm.'

And the King sayeth to Lancelot, 'Sire, why are you full armed within the hall?'

'For I had heard, Sire, that there would be knights within the hall full armed and I feared that they might do you harm.'

'And, Sire,' sayeth the King, 'I have heard right differently for it seemeth that it was you that was intent on harming me.' And the King commanded that Lancelot be taken prisoner.

Briant and his knights fell upon Lancelot who drew his sword and ran at them such that they are all much disconcerted. But there were many of them and the King sayeth that they may not harm him, but they brought him to the ground at cost of seven slain and many others wounded, amongst whom was Briant with a grievous wound. And Lancelot was cast into prison saying to the King, 'This is an evil reward, Sire, for the service I have done you.'

And all they of the court save for Briant and his knights sayeth this must be the end of King Arthur, for Gawain and Yvain have departed and Lancelot is taken prisoner though he hath always done well in the eyes of God. And they knew that this was Briant's doing and they wished him an evil reward and the protection of God upon Lancelot.

Part the XXXIst

Percival rode from the Castle of the Grail with heart full sore at the tidings of his sister brought by the damsel with the wounded arm. The Damsel Dindrane had been taken by Aristor of Moraine to be his wife, whereafter he would strike off her head as was his cruel custom. Percival decided to ask his uncle the King Hermit for guidance in the matter. As he came upon the hermitage he saw three hermits come forth and they sayeth unto him, 'Do not enter, Sire, for a damsel is preparing a body in there.'

'Whose body is it?' sayeth Percival.

'It is the body of the good King Hermit who hath been slain by Aristor of Moraine on account of Percival whom Aristor doth hate with much vigour.'

And Percival is full of sorrow at these tidings for the King Hermit was his uncle and a good and holy man. He staith at the hermitage for the burial of his uncle and intendeth to depart after Mass to find Aristor and take vengeance for his uncle and save his sister. But the damsel who prepared the body of his uncle came to him and sayeth, 'Sire, a full long time I have been seeking you. In a rich box of ivory that hangs at my saddle I carry the head of a knight who ought to be avenged by none other than you. Please help me, Sire, in this matter for I have carried the head for a long time as witnessed by King Arthur and Gawain at court where I asked for you but none knew where you are. My castle is forbidden to me until the knight is avenged.'

'Who is the knight?' sayeth Percival.

'He, Sire, was the son of your uncle Bruns Brandalis. Had he lived, he would have been one of the best knights in the world.'

'And who slew him, damsel?'

'The Red Knight of the Deep Forest that taketh a lion on a lead. He came upon your cousin all unarmed and slew him in cowardly manner.'

'Damsel,' sayeth Percival, 'it greiveth me to know of his slaying as I grieve for my uncle the King Hermit. Him I would avenge more than any in the world for he was slain in my name. This Aristor hath slain a holy man who wished no ill on him, and may God grant that I find him for my vengeance.'

'Sire, he so hateth you that he would come to find you had he tidings of your whereabouts.'

'Then,' sayeth Percival, 'may God grant him the knowledge of my coming, for soon I wish to meet him.'

And the damsel sayeth, 'Sire, pray do not forget your cousin or the foul knight that slew him. To reach the castle of Aristor you must pass through the Deep Forest wherein lives the Red Knight who leads the lion. May God grant that you find him also.'

And Percival departed in haste.

Part the XXXIInd

As Percival rode through the forest he came upon two squires carrying venison and sayeth to them, 'Sires, whence carry you this venison?'

And they sayeth to him, 'To the Castle of Ariste where Aristor is lord.'

Sayeth he, 'Are there many knights at the castle?'

'Not one, Sire, but in four days the castle will throng with thousands for our lord is to marry. He is to take the daughter of the Widow Lady who he hath carried off by force from the Castle Camelot. She is placed in the house of one of our lord's knights until she be married. But we are right sorrowful at this for she is a noble damsel of great beauty, but he shall strike off her head thereafter as is his custom.'

'Might a good knight carry her off to save her from this fate?'

'Yes, if it pleases God for our lord hath such great cruelty. Already he hath slain a good hermit and is greatly desirous of meeting the brother of the damsel, for he sayeth that he is one of the best knights in the world. He sayeth that much pleasure would he have to slay the brother of the damsel.'

'Do you know where he now is?'

'Truly, Sire, we have just left him in combat with a knight.'

'Know you the name of this knight?'

'He is named the Knight Hardy, Sire. He came upon Aristor and telleth him that he is a knight that oweth much to Percival and our lord did run at him with great hurtle. We left them in full fight and could hear the blows of sword upon armour for many a long time. Aristor will surely slay him as he doth all knights he meets in the forest.'

Percival departed at great pace and goeth to the place said by the squires. There he heard the sound of sword and shield and came upon the two knights engaged in combat. Aristor had been wounded in two places but the Knight Hardy hath a lance through his body and blood ran from his armour. At this, Percival gave spur to his horse and cried to God as he lowered his lance and ran at Aristor. Percival hit him hard on the breastplate and bowed him back along his horse. And Percival sayeth in a loud voice, 'Behold, Sire, I am come to my sister's wedding!'

But Aristor came up again and dealt Percival a hard blow on the helmet. With this, Percival drew his horse back and lowered again his lance and hurtled once more at Aristor and tumbled both knight and horse to the ground. Percival alighted and took his sword and removed the helmet of his foe.

And Aristor sayeth, 'what do you intend, Percival?'

'I intend, Sire, to cut off your head which I shall give to my sister whom you have treated in most foul manner.'

'Stay your hand, Sire, I pray you, sayeth Aristor. 'If you let me live, I will forgo my hatred of you.'

'Your hatred, Sire, I can abide, but you are of such foul and cruel manner that neither God nor I will have you in this world!' With that, Percival struck off his head and tied it to his saddle.

He then goeth to the Knight Hardy and sayeth, 'How is it with you, brave Knight?'

And the Knight Hardy sayeth, 'Death comes before me, Sire, but I surrender my life in the good knowledge that I stood and faced fear as you taught me.'

Percival taketh the reins of the Knight Hardy's horse and leadeth him to a hermit where the Knight Hardy did confess his sins before his soul departed his body. And Percival gave the hermit the Knight Hardy's horse and armour that he might have a good and honourable burial. He also giveth him the horse of Aristor.

After Mass there came to the hermitage the damsel who carried the knight's head at her saddle, and she sayeth to Percival, 'Sire, still you have much to do. You have rid this country of the foul Aristor, but you needs must find the Red Knight that slew the son of your uncle. No doubt have I that he you shall conquer, but I have great fear that the lion may be beyond defeat for it is a cruel and savage beast that fights with right hardiness for its lord.'

Percival rode into the forest with the damsel at his side. They had not travelled far when they came upon a knight sore wounded as was his horse. And the knight sayeth, 'Hold, Sire! Do not enter the forest for I have just escaped from a Red Knight who is guarded by a foul lion. And I have to pass by the land of Aristor who wouldst attack any knight that passes that way.'

'Have no fear of that,' sayeth the damsel, 'for his head hangs at the saddle of this knight.'

'Praise God for that,' sayeth the knight.

Percival sayeth unto him, 'Go, Sire, to the hermit that is a little beyond and sayeth to him that he should give you one of the horses I left with him for he hath no use for them.'

And the knight thanked Percival and rode on to the hermitage where he chose the horse of Aristor. This dealing, however, was much to his misfortune for he came upon a knight of Aristor's household who did slay him to retake his master's horse.

Percival and the damsel were deep in the forest when they came upon a glade wherein lay the lion guarding the path of its master and waiting for passing knights. The damsel withdrew in much fear and Percival lowered his lance as the lion came at him with eyes of fire and with jaws wideagape. The knight thinketh to thrust his lance down the throat of the lion but the beast did swerve and jump on the hindquarters of the horse, wounding it much. At this, the horse did kick backwards and break the lion's frontmost teeth whereon it gave a great roar that sounded through the forest. Percival then thrust at the lion with his lance and pierced it through the body and it was slain.

The Red Knight had heard the roar of the lion and came full pace to the place and saw the beast slain upon the ground. And he sayeth to Percival, 'You did falsely slay this lion when it was wounded by your horse.'

And Percival sayeth, 'And you brought about your own death when you slew my uncle's son whose head is borne on the saddle of this damsel.' Without more ado he ran at the knight who came at him with his lance and broke it on the white shield with the red cross. Percival thrust his lance through the breast of the Red Knight and bore him dead to the ground.

Percival then mounted the horse of the Red Knight, for his own was sore wounded by the lion. The damsel sayeth to him, 'Sire, the castle which the Red Knight did steal from me is within this forest and I pray that you accompany me thither that I may take it without conflict from any within.' And Percival sayeth that he will.

When they came to the castle, Percival could see that it was a most fair castle, well walled with battlements and with a many windowed hall. When those inside heard of the death of the Red Knight they yielded the castle most eagerly and accepted the damsel as their mistress. She had the head of the knight buried with great honour and commanded that Mass be said every day for the soul of the dead knight. Percival rested therein until he was ready and departed with the prayers of the damsel for his restoring of the castle to her inheritance.

Percival then returned to the house wherein was held his sister, the Damsel Dindrane. The knight who guarded her for Aristor was of a most kindly nature and had comforted her often when she wept at her fate. Percival came to the gate of the house full armed and the knight came and welcomed him, for he took him to be a knight of Aristor. But he saw the head of Aristor when Percival held it by the hair and marvelled much at the sight. And Percival walked in to the house and seeth his sister that wept in great sorrow. 'Damsel,' he sayeth, 'weep no more for there shall be no wedding. Proof you will have of this token.' And he threw the head of Aristor to her feet.

The damsel looketh at the knight and seeth that it was her brother Percival. Great joy she made of him and thanked Our Saviour that he was alive and had come to her aid. And the knight of the house gave them both much honour for he was joyous at the slaying of Aristor. The Damsel Dindrane took the head of Aristor to the river and threw it in and sayeth, 'Thus may all foul and cruel men be done by, God willing.'

Brother and sister then rode back to Camelot where the Widow Lady was in great sorrow. As she wept in her chamber Percival took the hand of his sister and entered therein saying, 'Dear Lady, look upon what God hath preserved for you.' And she fell to her knees in joy. She then kissed them and sayeth, 'Blessed son and daughter, now my great joy hath returned to me. Thus my life is ended in joy, for I have lived long enough and I am ready to meet Our Saviour.'

'Lady,' sayeth Percival, 'in your life you have harmed no one and deserve tranquillity at your end. You shall live at the Castle of the Holy Grail, and thus when God calls for you, you shall be in the presence of many hallowed and sacred objects.'

And the Widow Lady sayeth, 'It is as you say, fair son, the castle of my good brother hath seen much that is holy.'

Sayeth Percival, 'And I shall see that should my sister wish to marry she shall be honoured as your daughter.'

But sayeth the damsel, 'Thank you brother, but only God will I marry.'

And the Widow Lady sayeth to Percival, 'The Damsel of the Carriage seeks you and will not end her search until she finds you.'

'Narrowly have our paths crossed. She will hear of my whereabouts.'

The Widow Lady then sayeth, 'We have here with us the damsel who was wounded in the arm by the foul knight. She it was that brought news of your sister and now she is healed.'

And Percival sayeth, 'Through her I am well avenged.'

Percival stayed with his mother until the land thereabout was put at peace. The Widow Lady and her daughter led a holy life and placed a chaplain in the chapel between the forest and Camelot that Mass be said therein. In later times the chapel grew to be an abbey which remains to this day.

Percival took leave of his mother and departed from the castle and rode in the forest until he came to a small house wherein he lodged for the night. The house belonged to a knight of simple means who gave Percival great honour but often did he sigh most sorrowfully. And Percival sayeth to him, 'Why, Sire, do you have this downcast countenance?'

And the knight sayeth, 'Sire, my brother was killed but recently by a knight in the service of Aristor, for my brother had been given the horse that had belonged to Aristor. It had been given to him by a hermit for his own horse had been maimed by the lion of the Red Knight. And my brother was a good and worthy knight who harmed no one.'

These tiding were not good for Percival for it was he that had slain Aristor and had given the hermit the horse. He sayeth to the knight, 'Sire, your bother did not deserve his death for he did not slay the knight.'

'I know, Sire, for it was the same knight that slew the Red Knight.'

On the morrow, Percival came upon a hermitage where he heard Mass. The hermit sayeth to him, 'Sire, I counsel great care in this forest for there are knights full armed that waiteth for the knight that slew Aristor and the Red Knight and his lion. Any knight they meet they will slay for the deaths of the two knights.

'Then, Sire,' sayeth Percival, 'may God keep me from such evil knights.'

But he hath not left the hermitage long when he saw two knights, one of whom rode the horse that had belonged to Aristor. And the knights seeth Percival and one sayeth to the other, 'Look, this knight beareth the same shield as he who slew Aristor.'

They came at great pace at Percival who spurred his horse to meet them. Both knights broke their lances upon his shield and Percival pierced the knight that rideth the horse of Aristor and bore him dead to the ground. The other knight returned to the combat but Percival did slay him by the sword. Percival then took the two horses of the slain knights to the hermit and telleth him to give the horses to deserving travellers, 'For it is great courtesy to aid a man when you may.'

And the hermit sayeth to him, 'Sire, I knew of your deed in the forest against the two knights, for three knights came to this hermitage. They did flee from the chance of meeting you and I praised their flight and sayeth unto them that death in combat brings them closer to Hell than to Paradise.'

On the morrow, Percival chanced upon a knight who came fast upon him for the knight knew Percival by his shield. And the knight sayeth, 'Sire, I am come from the Castle of the Black Hermit. There you will find the Damsel of the Carriage who asks you to attend upon her with great pace. Also, Sire, I ask your aid of a most pitiful thing I saw in the forest. There I saw a knight leading a damsel against her will and beating her with a cruel rod. The damsel crieth out for the son of the Widow Lady who hath given her back her castle, and the knight doth hate the son of the Widow Lady and for this intends to put the damsel into a pit of serpents. They were followed by an old knight and a priest who prayed the knight to cease his torment of the damsel but he doth threaten them with death for their pleas.

Percival followed the pointing of the knight and heard the cries of the damsel as he approached the valley, wherein was the pit of serpents. And he heard her cry for mercy whereon the knight did beat her more cruelly. As he rode upon the scene the damsel seeth him and cried out, 'Sweet Sire, please give me your aid for this knight would steal my castle!'

And the knight sayeth to Percival, 'That horse I know. It belonged to the Red Knight of the Deep Forest. I know therefore that it was you who doth slay him!'

'And it was well that I did slay him, for he hath cut off the head of the son of an uncle of mine, and the head was carried by this damsel for many a long time.'

'Then,' sayeth the knight, 'you are my mortal enemy.'

At this, they ran at each other as fast as their horses could carry them and Percival knocked the knight from his horse to the ground. He then alighted and came to stand over the knight who cried him for mercy. And Percival sayeth, 'Have no fear, I shall not slay you, but I shall do to you as you would have done to the damsel.' With this, he commanded the old knight and the priest to carry the knight to the pit of serpents and cast him therein. Thus he died of the serpents biting unmercifully.

And the damsel gave great joy for his mercy. And she returned to her castle never again to be troubled by foul knights for fear of what Percival hath done.

The good knight Percival knew that his Godly labours would be at an end on his visit to the Castle of the Black Hermit and thinketh that he should do more before it endeth. These endeavours would he dedicate to God. He came thus upon a land where he met many strong knights and where the laws of God were not followed but they worshipped false idols and devils. There he met a knight who sayeth to him, 'Turn back, Sire! This land is full of non-believers and I pass through by truce only. The Queen of this land is the sister of King Madeglant of Oriande who was slain by Lancelot, who then turned the land thereabouts back to the true worship. And the Queen hateth God's laws and hath blindfolded herself that she might not gaze upon the true believers. Now her eyes have gone blind of their own accord and she thinketh that the false gods have done such in punishment for the coming of the true faith. Now she prays for the return of the false gods that she may see again. I tell you this, Sire, that you may not face the enemies of God herein.'

But Percival sayeth to the knight, 'Thank you, Sire, but there is no knightly virtue more fair than that which stands by God. This is the greatest knightly endeavour that may be done. As Our Saviour set His body at pain for us, so we should do likewise for Him.' And he departed joyous in the knowledge that Lancelot hath done God's work but he knoweth not that King Arthur hath cast Lancelot in prison.

That nightfall Percival came upon a great castle with many battlements and ancient towers. The castle was guarded by a drawbridge, and at the gate stood a squire with a metal collar around his neck from whence a chain was fastened to a large heavy piece of iron. And the chain length allowed the squire to come to the edge of the drawbridge from whence he sayeth to Percival, 'Sire, do you believe in God and His Son, Our Saviour?'

'Young friend,' sayeth Percival, 'I most certainly believe in God and I do so with all my heart.'

'Then, Sire, for the sake of Our Saviour, do not enter this castle.'

'Why do you thus say?'

And the squire sayeth, 'Sire, I am a Christian and have been enslaved to guard this castle. It is the most cruel place I know and is known as the Raging Castle for within are three young knights who on sight of a Christian knight become raging mad and would slay him. Their hands may be delayed however by a most fair damsel whom they dare not disobey. Full many knights hath she saved thus but many have not escaped this place alive. I live only that I guard the gate.'

'Young friend,' sayeth Percival, 'as a Christian you should know that the power of God is much beyond that of the Devil.' With that he rode across the bridge and entered the courtyard and alighteth from his horse. And a damsel of passing great beauty did see him from a window and came down to the courtyard. There she seeth from his shield that he is a Christian and sayeth, 'Sire, do not go to the great hall for there at table sit three knights that are my brothers. Should they see you they will lose their senses and go mad as they do at the sight of all things from God.'

'Damsel,' sayeth Percival, 'I pray that you are wrong, but it is known that the sight of any Godly matter doth send the non-believers mad.'

With this, Percival doth enter the hall full armed whereupon the three knights saw him and leapt up all maddened. And they took up swords and axes and run upon him but he standeth like a rock before them and they saw that God was in him. At this they fell upon each other and slayeth each other despite the damsel crying for them to cease. And she wept for the loss of her brothers. But Percival sayeth, 'Weep not, damsel, but repent of your false belief for all those with no belief in God die in their madness.'

Then Percival set the squire free of his chain and brought him to the great hall and clothed him in rich robes. At this, the damsel seeth the squire and thinketh that he is of a comely figure and made great honour of him. But still she sorrows for her brothers. And Percival sayeth unto her, 'Damsel, do not sorrow for that which cannot be amended. Comfort yourself instead as you may.'

At this, the damsel thinketh to herself that she may turn Percival from God to her false gods and sayeth, 'Sire, will you renounce your God? For should you so do I would be at your entire commanding.'

And he sayeth, 'Remember, damsel, had you been a man you would have been slain as a non-believer. I hope the lesson will turn you away from such falsehoods.'

The damsel sayeth, 'Sire, then will you promise me that should I accept your God, you will love me as a knight should love a damsel?'

And Percival sayeth, 'Damsel, should you receive baptism you have my word of honour as a Christian that I will love you as a knight who firmly believeth in God should love a damsel.'

'Then no more will I ask of you.'

And they sent for a hermit who came and baptised her with the name Celestre. And those who denied Our Lord were slain that they may soon see their errors. And those remaining in the castle were also baptised, and the hermit did stay with them to teach them the ways of God and the service of the Lord. The damsel became of a good life and did many good works.

Percival departed the Raging Castle praising God that he was able to turn the castle from its cruel ways to those of God's law. He rode a long distance and came to a land that was without cheer and the people said that he was come to destroy their worship for he had already won the strong Raging Castle. And he came upon a great and ancient castle whereat the gate was a great throng of people. From them came a squire, and Percival asked to whom the castle belonged. And the squire sayeth, 'Sire, it is the castle of Queen Jandree, who hath commanded the people to come to her that she may hear of the fall of the Raging Castle and the slaying of the knights therein and the baptising of the damsel. Now that her brother King Madeglant of Oriande is dead she hath no one to defend her and she hath heard that the knight who conquered the castle is the best knight in the world and none may endure against him. She is preparing to go to a stronger castle for her safety.'

And Percival rode to the castle and the people at the gate seeth him come and say to the blind Queen, 'Lady, a Christian knight is come to the castle!'

The Queen sayeth, 'Is it he who is about to overthrow our gods?'

Percival entereth the castle and alighteth and came before the Queen full armed. And the Queen asketh him what he sought. Percival sayeth that he sought nought but what was good for the Queen. She sayeth to him, 'But, Sire, you come from the Raging Castle where there has been much sore loss from the three slain brothers.'

And Percival sayeth, 'True, Lady, I was at the castle, and now it is at the command of Our Lord Jesus Christ as I wish was this castle.'

'And has your God so great a power as it is said?'

'Lady, God hath much greater power than ever it was said.'

'Then,' sayeth the Queen, 'will you stay with me until the power of your God hath been proven?'

'That, Lady, I surely will.'

And Percival taketh her hand and led her in to the great hall of the castle. And the people marvel at this for the Queen would not before allow any Christian knight to be near her. But now she wisheth that she could see, for Percival seemed to her to be a comely and a good knight. And Percival wished that she would turn to God for then the people throughout the land would follow in like manner.

Percival lay the night at the castle. On the morn the Queen sent for all the powerful people of the land to come unto her. She then walked in to the hall where was Percival and all marvelled that she could now see.

When the powerful people had assembled the Queen sayeth to them, 'Well you know of my loyalty and faith to the gods. Last night yet again I prayeth to them to restore my sight but they answereth me that they could not and full sorrowful am I. Then I remembered the God of whom Percival hath spoken and I prayed to Him as sweetly as I may. I asked Him that if He was as powerful and had such virtue of which it was oft said, He would restore my sight for now hath I belief in Him. I then fell asleep and it seemed to me that I saw the fairest Lady in the world who hath with Her a Child that had about Him a light as if from the sun. About the Lady and the Child were a host of angels who were in great joy of Her and Her Son. And an ancient man telleth me that although She was the most worshipful mother ever in the world She was a virgin, for none could surpass Her purity. Then I saw a man bound to a stake and He was beaten right cruelly with rods and scourges and I wept in pity of Him. I then saw the man nailed upon a Cross by evil men and they did thrust a spear in His side until the blood ran therefrom and I wept even more for Him. At the foot of the Cross I saw the Holy Lady and we wept together and she was comforted by a man who had no joy in him. There also was a man who held a vessel to the wound of the man on the Cross and collected the blood therefrom and he bore a shield of white and with the blood he maketh a red cross upon it. This same man then taketh down the body of the man from the Cross and placed it in a simple sepulchre, and such pity did I have that I thought that I would weep forever. And my tears did wash my eyes and made me see again. Such a Lord one ought to believe in for He suffered death when He could have lightly avoided it had He so wished. And this He did for His people. It is now my command that you shall all believe in this Lord and renounce all false gods as devils. And if any do not believe this way they shall be slain or put to a shameful death.'

The Queen was baptised with the name Salubre and she had all non-believers slain or banished. She was a good Lady and believed well in God and led a life so holy that she died in a hermitage. And Percival departed from the castle with joyous heart that the Lady and her people did now believe in the one true God.

Part the XXXIIIrd

Meliot of England had departed from the Castle Perilous with his wounds well healed by virtue of the sword and shroud that Lancelot had brought him. But he was in great sorrow when he heard tidings that Gawain had been cast into prison by two knights who were kin of those who killed each other at the Raging Castle. They had taken Gawain on account of him being a brother knight of Percival who had taken the castle for Our Saviour. And Meliot set his heart on finding Gawain and rode into a dark and gloomy forest. Finding neither house nor hermitage Meliot rode on in the darkness until he saw a damsel sitting alone and much forlorn beneath a tree. He sayeth to her. 'Damsel, why are you here at this hour?'

And she sayeth, 'Sire, I may not depart from here. You may see the reason above me.'

Meliot looked above her and seeth two knights hanging from the branch of the tree. He sayeth, 'Damsel, who hath done so foully of these knights?'

She sayeth, 'Sire, it was the Knight of the Galley that saileth upon the sea.'

'And why?'

'Because they believeth in God and His Holy Mother. I am placed here by command of the knight for forty days to prevent their being cut down for if they are he will lose his castle and would cut off my head.'

And Meliot sayeth, 'Such a watch is shameful for a damsel. Rise, damsel, for you shall not stay here.'

'Then,' sayeth she, 'I am a dead woman for none may face this knight most fearsome.'

'Damsel,' sayeth Meliot, 'I will not take the reproach of good knights for leaving them hanging here. Nor will I take the shame upon myself.'

Thereupon he cut them down and made their graves with his sword.

And the damsel sayeth, 'Sire, the Knight of the Galley will look for me and strike off my head for you have no thought for me.'

But Meliot lifteth up the damsel to his horse and rideth to a hermitage where the Knight of the Galley hath slain the hermit. The damsel and he entered therein and seeth in a great brightness of light a damsel that sitteth by a dead knight. And he sayeth, 'Damsel, when was this knight slain?'

And she sayeth, 'Sire, he was slain by the Knight of the Galley on the sea shore whereof I am commanded to keep watch over him until the Knight of the Galley doth return tomorrow before he attends to the death of Gawain.'

'He hath schemed that Gawain shall die tomorrow?'

'Yes, Sire.'

'But first he will come here?'

'With certainty, Sire.'

'What more do you know of Gawain?'

'He is to face a lion all unarmed, and when he is slain by the beast, the Lady who is mistress of both of us shall be brought to the lion and slain likewise, for she will not renounce the law of God that she accepteth from the knight who took the Raging Castle and through whom her brothers did slay each other. Then the damsel that accompanieth you and I shall be slain by the lion also for you have taken down the hanging knights. Sire, you may save this damsel if you take her away for the knight may not wait for the lion to do its ill, but will cut off her head straightway. For you also have I great fear.'

'Damsel,' sayeth Meliot, 'this Knight of the Galley is a man like any other.'

'No, Sire,' sayeth she, 'He is more strong and cruel than you.'

But Meliot was not afraid and stayed the night at the chapel. In the morning he heard the knight coming from far off for he bringeth the Lady from the Raging Castle and doth loudly and foully revile her. Meliot accordingly was full armed and waiting.

A dwarf that ran behind the Knight of the Galley seeth Meliot and crieth out to his master, 'Look, Sire, it is the knight who hath cost you your castle for he cut down the hanging knights. Haste! and avenge yourself that we may go and attend the death of Gawain!'

And the knight cometh before Meliot and sayeth as a braggart, 'Is it you that hath trespassed on my land and taken down my knights?'

And Meliot replieth, 'They, Sire, were not your knights for they were knights of God. And you have committed an outrage by their shameful death.'

Without more words, Meliot hurtled hard at the knight and pierced his breastplate and wounded him. The knight replieth with a thrust that pierced the shield of Meliot and the dwarf crieth out, 'Go to him, Sire; let him not endure more than the many knights you have slain!'

And the knight ran at Meliot and broke his lance upon his shield in such strong manner that both knight and horse staggered. But Gawain thrust his lance through the knight and he fell dead to the ground. The dwarf thought to escape but Meliot cut off his head and the damsels were both of much joy.

Meliot buried the knight that lay slain in the chapel and sayeth farewell to the damsels. He rode in search of Gawain and came upon a knight full armed and riding at a great pace. And the knight sayeth to Meliot, 'Sire, have you tidings of the Knight of the Galley?'

'Why do you ask?'

The knight sayeth, 'For Gawain is brought to the forest and is to face a lion all unarmed. And they wait for the Knight of the Galley who is to bring two damsels who shall likewise face the lion after Gawain.'

'When will this take place?'

'Soon, Sire, for Gawain is already bound to a stake until such times as the lion comes. He is guarded by two knights meantime. Tell me, Sire, have you tidings of the Knight of the Galley?'

And Meliot sayeth, 'Go on your passage, Sire, and you will hear of him soon enough.'

At a great gallop Meliot came to the part of the forest wherein was Gawain bound to the stake.

There he seeth Gawain and the two knights that guarded him and great pity hath Meliot. He rode hard at the two knights and thrust his lance through one of them. On seeing this, the other knight tried to flee but Meliot did slay him with his sword. Then he went to Gawain and cut his cords and set him free whereof Gawain had great joy.

The tidings came to the land that Queen Jandree was baptised, that a knight had come that was of such might that none may endure against him, that the Knight of the Galley was slain, and that Gawain was set free. And the people of the land that had thought to see Gawain devoured by the lion fled across the sea.

And Gawain and Meliot did depart at great pace and marvelled that none came after them. But their foes had gone away in fear. The knights rode until they came to the sea and seeth a great clashing of arms. And they saw a knight in battle against those who would come on his ship and he keepeth them off with much valour. And they came close and saw that the knight hath a shield of white with a red cross and they knew it to be Percival. But as they went to his aid the ship was blown by the wind from the shore and was set to drift to parts unknown. And they knew great sorrow for they could not aid him nor did they know of the land whence the ship goeth. They watched Percival fending off his foes until they could see him no more and they turned away in sorrow and rode on.

Thereupon they saw a knight who sayeth he was from the court of King Arthur. And they asketh for tidings of the King and the knight sayeth, 'Sires, I have nought but bad tidings for the King neglects his knights for the words of Briant of the Isles, and he hath put one of his best knights in prison.'

And they sayeth, 'Which knight hath he put in prison.'

The knight sayeth, 'Lancelot of the Lake. He had taken back all the lands lost to King Arthur and hath slain King Madeglant and conquered the land of Oriande which he made turn to the Lord God in worship. But the King sent for him and put him in prison on the advice of Briant. Now King Claudas hath assembled a great army to take back Oriande and to fall upon the King on the advice of Briant.'

And Gawain sayeth, 'Surely a king who setteth aside the counsel of good knights for the advice of a traitor must bring his crown to great risk. But to put the good knight Lancelot in prison is to risk all.'

Part the XXXIVth

And King Claudas hath conquered the land of Oriande and now cometh nigh to the lands of King Arthur that was saved from King Madeglant by Lancelot. And the people desired much the return of Lancelot but the King sendeth Briant and nought was gained thereby. Thus the people sayeth that if the King doth not send them aid they will yield up the land and turn away from God. But Lancelot was in prison and Gawain and Yvain and the other good knights did not resort to the court for shame of King Arthur's trust in Briant.

And the King was heavy hearted at this and sat alone in the great hall. At this, Lucan did come to him and sayeth, 'Sire, you seem to be without joy.'

King Arthur sayeth, 'Truly, Sire, I have been without joy since the death of the Queen. Those who may have heartened me come here no longer and I know not their aid yet King Claudas wars upon me and would conquer my lands.'

'Sire,' sayeth Lucan, 'to the blame of no one can you put this save your own. You have done evil to him that hath served you best, and you have honoured the traitor. None will come to your aid whilst you hold Lancelot in prison. He hath served you most honourably and hath faced death many times in your name but your treatment of him keepeth away Gawain and Yvain and the other good knights.'

And the King sayeth, 'You speak truly for I have done a great discourtesy to him. Think you, Sire, that he would ever trust in me again? Lancelot hath a great heart and knows the lesson of forgiveness taught by Our Saviour, yet he would not pause at gaining vengeance where he took his right to be offended.'

'Sire, Lancelot knoweth that you have been ill-advised and loyalty to his King runs through his bones. He pines in prison for service to you. I well believe that you should release him, Sire, that he may take up your cause. The good knights will return and you lands shall be saved. Do otherwise, Sire, and all shall be lost.'

The King thanketh Lucan and had Lancelot brought before him from the prison. And the King sayeth, 'Are you well, Lancelot?'

And the knight sayeth, 'Prison hath made me weak, Sire, but I shall recover soon.'

'Lancelot,' sayeth the King, 'listen to my words for they are the words of a King though no King should have to speak them. I put you in prison for fear of losing my people and my lands. I was ill-advised in this matter and I repent that I did this to you. If your honour has been stained by my deeds I shall do all I can to amend the matter for no better knight could any King have in his court.'

The King would have spoken more but Lancelot sayeth quickly, 'Hold, Sire! I am your loyal knight. All that I do, I do for you. It matters to me none whether your command takes me to the field of battle or to your prison. I know full well that I was not in prison for treason for I have no room in my heart for such evil. I see it not as shame or dishonour to obey my King whatever he commandeth. No, Sire, all I ask is to serve you again that my honour be tested in your cause.'

And the King cometh to Lancelot and taketh his hand saying, 'Sire, my court is rich beyond measure with knights such as you. Get you well with haste for these times doth place us all at hazard.'

But nought made Lancelot well until he encountered Briant in the forest. And Briant tried to flee but Lancelot came upon him with his sword and left the body of the traitor knight for the wild beasts.

Part the XXXVth

Percival hath slain those who would board his ship and only his horse and the pilot remaineth. The pilot, seeing the valour of Percival, did enter in a covenant with him to become a Christian. And for many days the ship was blown by the wind of God until no land could be seen and the pilot knoweth not the stars. Then they came upon an island whereon was a rich castle. At each corner of the castle was a tower which hath a bell within which did make a most pleasing sound across the water.

And the ship came to the castle and took the ground beneath its walls. And Percival did take his horse and the pilot and they go to the castle gate. They entered and saw within the most fair halls and chambers they have ever known. Beneath a tree in the courtyard they seeth a fountain surrounded by tall pillars and thereby a pavement of precious stones. By the fountain sat two Masters with white beards all dressed in white robes whereon the breast thereof was a red cross. When they saw Percival they came to him and knelt in greeting before kissing the shield of white with the red cross. And they sayeth, 'Sire, do not marvel that we do this for we knew full well the good knight who bore this shield before you. Many times did we see him since Our Lord's crucifixion.'

But Lancelot did marvel for they talked of a time long past. And he sayeth, 'Know you the name of this knight?'

'Sire,' sayeth they, 'he was Joseph of Arimathea, but the shield was all white at first. Only upon the death of Christ was the red cross put on with His blood.'

And Percival layeth the shield down and one of the two men placed upon it a wreath of flowers and herbs. Beyond the fountain Percival could see a large ivory vessel wherein stood a knight full armed and he spoke to the knight but reply received him not. And he asketh the two Masters who was the knight and they say he may not yet know. They took him to the great hall and bore his shield before him and all that were in the hall made great joy of his coming. He saw that the great hall was rich indeed and hung with costly cloths of silk. In the centre of the hall was an image of Our Savour in Majesty with His apostles around Him. And in the galleries were many people who all seemed to be of much holiness.

And the two Masters sayeth to Percival, 'This, Sire, is the Royal Hall.'

And he sayeth, 'Such a hall could be nought else but that of a King.'

Percival saw that the hall was full of rich tables of gold and ivory. One of the Masters clapped his hands three times and three and thirty knights entered the hall all of a company. They were clad in white garments and all had a red cross upon his breast. They went to the tables and prayeth to God whereon they put down their cups and washed their hands in a large golden bowl. Then they sat down. The Masters put Percival among them on the Master's table. Thereon they were served with meat and other foods in full worshipful manner.

As they sat at meat Percival seeth a golden crown descend on a golden chain as if from Heaven. At this, the Masters opened a great pit in the floor from whence issued the sound of much sorrowing and all there assembled stretched forth their hands to God in prayer. The crown, the chain, and the sound of sorrow stayed until the meal is finished whereon the Master closed the pit and the crown and chain ascended and could be seen no more. The good knights then gave thanks to God and left the hall.

Percival sayeth to the Master, 'Pray tell me, Sire, of the golden crown and chain.'

But the Master sayeth, 'Sire, until you swear by your honour that you will return to this island when you are called by a ship carrying a white sail which bears a red cross, you can neither leave the island nor be told of the golden crown and chain.'

And Percival sayeth, 'Sire, I promise you faithfully in the name of God that as soon as I have attended to the needs of my mother and my sister I shall return on the ship you send thither.'

'Then, Sire,' sayeth the Master, 'on your return you shall wear upon your head the crown of gold which you saw come down on the chain. And so you shall be seated on a throne and be king of the Isle of Plenty that lacks nought for the good of man. Your uncle, King Hermit, was king of this island and, by his good works, the island is well furnished with all manner of good things. Now he is king in another realm and the people have asked for another worshipful man to be their king. You must continue in a worshipful manner and govern as a true and loyal king as did your uncle. Should you fail in this, the crown will be taken from you and you will be sent to the Isle of Poverty whence you heard the sound of great sorrowing when you sat at the table for meat. They also were kings of the Isle of Plenty but they broke their covenant with the people and were cast out. Also on the Isle of Poverty are many that were not kings but did forget their duties to God and are punished accordingly. And we know not if they should be ever released. One thing more should you know, Sire. Before you return on the ship with the white sail and the red cross, you must obtain the head of a king and queen sealed in gold.'

And Percival sayeth, 'Thank you, Sire. Pray tell me also of the knight full armed that stands in the ivory vessel and also of the name of this castle.'

But the Master sayeth, 'These you may not know until you return. But, tell me, Sire, of the most Holy Grail with which you spoke. Is it still at the chapel of the castle of the good Fisher King?'

'It is, Sire,' sayeth Percival, 'with the sword which struck of the head of Saint John the Baptist, and with many other holy relics also.'

And the Master sayeth, 'I saw the Holy Grail in the hands of Joseph of Arimathea who had used it to collect the precious blood of Our Lord. All your family I know, but you should know that it was your valour and cleanliness of mind that caused God to bring you hither. It is God also that shall choose where the place shall be, and when the time shall come, that you shall see the ship with the red cross.'

Percival sayeth, 'Be assured, Sire, that there is no other place under Heaven where I would rather be than this isle. Were it not for my duty to my mother and sister, I would never depart willingly.'

After a night lodged at the castle where they did him great honour, Percival went to hear Mass in the rich chapel of the castle. The service finished, a Master came to him with a shield of purest white and sayeth unto him, 'Sire, you will leave your shield here as a token of your coming. Instead you will take this shield.'

And Percival sayeth, 'As you wish.'

He goeth on board the ship with the pilot and it sailed from beneath the castle walls with the bells sounding over the water as before. Fast goeth the ship under the guidance of God for within He knew was a good knight.

After many days the ship came to an isle whereon was a castle that once had known greatness but now was in poor condition. They came to the wharf below and Percival entered the castle full armed. On the steps of the castle hall he seeth a lady that hath the bearing of a gentlewoman and two young damsels with her. All were dressed raggedly. And the lady sayeth to Percival, 'Welcome, Sire, for long it hath been since we have seen a knight enter this castle.'

'May God grant you joy and honour, lady,' sayeth Percival.

'We have need of both,' sayeth the lady, 'for none have we seen this many a year.' Then sayeth she, 'Sire, will you lodge in this castle this night?'

Percival sayeth that he would lodge that night. The damsels disarmed him and brought him a robe to wear saying, 'Sire, none better do we have for you than this plain mantle.' And he sayeth that it will do right well.

And Percival seeth that the damsels have by nature been formed well and they have all the sweetness and simplicity of manner that maketh a good woman. And he hath pity on their condition.

'Lady,' sayeth Percival, 'doth this castle belong to you?'

And she sayeth, 'Sire, I am the widow of Calobrutus, a good knight who hath been dead these many years. He is the father of my daughters that you see here. I have also a son who is known as a good knight but hath been taken and put in to prison by the evil knight who hath robbed me of all my land save this castle. My husband was the brother of Alain le Gros but he is dead also and we have no kin nearby to aid us. I have heard that Alain hath a son who is the best knight in the world but he knoweth not of us or I should have my son returned to me. I have also an uncle called King Ban of Benoic. He also is dead, but he hath a son that is also one of the best knights in the world. If either of these knights should come this way, they would return our joy to us.'

The pity Percival hath for the two damsels now grows as they are the daughters of his uncle. And he sayeth, 'Lady, what is the name of your son, and wherein is he prisoned?'

Sayeth she, 'He is named Galobruns, and he is held by Gohaz in the Castle of the Whales.'

Sayeth Percival, 'Is this castle, lady, nearby?'

'It is on the next island, Sire. But none dare to challenge him for he is a mighty knight who hath fear of no one. And he hath come to me and sayeth that I must send him one of my daughters or he hath sworn that he shall rob me of my castle.'

At this Percival sayeth, 'Lady, not all oaths are kept, nor shall this one be. For I am Percival, son of Alain le Gros, and the damsels are daughters of my uncle that is called Calobrutus. And you, Lady, are kin to my brother knight, Lancelot of the Lake, the son of King Ban of Benoic. Neither he nor I will live with this evil that is upon you.'

And the lady and the damsels were overcome with joy and they kisseth his hands and prayeth unto God that he shall find Galobruns and take them from their poverty. Percival sayeth unto them that he shall do all within his powers to help them.

He took his ship until he came to an island whereon he saw a cave above the shore. In the cave he saw a man and took a path from the shore to the cave where he found a most comely knight. And the knight was chained by the neck and foot to the rock from whence he could not depart. Percival sayeth unto him, 'Sire, it seems you are made well fast to this rock.'

And the knight sayeth, 'Truly said, Sire, but I wish it were not so.'

Sayeth Percival, 'Have you food and drink?'

'I have, Sire, for the daughter of the Sick Knight that lives on an island close by brings me meat and drink every day. He that hath prisoned me here hath stolen her castle as he hath those of my mother.'

'Can none free you?'

'Only he that hath prisoned me here for only he hath the key to the lock and he sayeth that I shall never be freed from this place.'

'Does he, Sire? Then he should know that you are the son of my uncle Calobrutus and I am the son of your uncle Alain le Gros. Never would I endure the reproach of leaving you here. Be assured, Sire, that I shall return with the key and you shall be returned to your mother and sisters.'

Percival went to his ship and departed and came upon an island most fair. Near to the shore he saw a small island whereon was a tree. At the top of the tree a knight could be seen and below him on the tree was a damsel who cried out to Percival, 'Sire! Come to the aid of this knight and of me, a damsel.'

And Percival replieth, 'What is it you fear, damsel?'

And she sayeth, 'A great dragon, Sire. It hath driven us up this tree and, in truth, I ought not to be sorry for this knight hath carried me from the house of my father and would have done me shame of my body had it not been for this dragon.'

'What is the name of the knight?'

'It is Gohaz of the Castle of the Whales. This land is his and he hath taken the lands of my father and of others also.'

All this time the knight sayeth nothing for great shame of his deeds and his flight from the dragon. Percival now knoweth that it is he that hath put Galobruns in chains and came ashore with his sword and shield. The dragon came upon him and breathed strong fire but Percival raised his shield and the flame could neither penetrate nor sully the whiteness of the shield. Again the dragon did take breath to send forth more fire but Percival stepped forward and thrust his sword down the throat of the dragon and it fell slain at his feet.

And he sayeth to them in the tree, 'Now, Sire, you may come down and you also damsel.'

The knight sayeth from his place in the tree, 'Sire, one thing more may you do for me. A key hath fallen from me and the dragon did swallow it. Much honour would I give to him that found it for me.'

Percival goeth to the dragon and opened its throat. There lay the key and he taketh it and sayeth, 'I have the key, Sire, now you may come down.'

The knight came down and goeth to Percival with intent to give him good thanks for what he hath done. But Percival doth put him at the point of his sword. And the knight sayeth, 'Have a care, Sire, for I rule all that you see about you.'

'That, Sire, is good for it is with just such a ruler that I would have business. You will come with me.'

And the damsel sayeth, 'Sire, pray do not leave me here but help me return to the castle of my father, the Sick Knight who grieves for me.'

Percival now knoweth that the damsel is she of whom Galobruns gave great praise for her sweet kindness in his troubles. He taketh the knight and the damsel to his ship and goeth to the cave wherein is Galobruns. And much glad is the knight to see him. And Percival put forth Gohaz and sayeth, 'Here, Sire, is your mortal enemy. Do with him as you wish.' Percival taketh the key he had found in the throat of the dragon and unlocked the chains that bind Galobruns and the young knight put them on Gohaz and sayeth to him, 'Look upon this key for the last time, Sire, for you shall not see it again.' At this, he threw the key in to the sea.

Percival took Galobruns and the damsel to the castle of Gohaz and called there all the powerful people and sayeth unto them, 'See here before you your new ruler Galobruns. Before God and before him shall you bow or you heads shall be flung in to the sea.'

And the people of the land made much honour of Galobruns and Percival commended the care of the damsel to Galobruns whereon the young knight looked with much tenderness upon the damsel and calleth her to sit by his side.

Percival then departed and sailed until he came to a shore whereon was a great castle from which issued much flame and smoke. And he went on the shore and came to a hermit and sayeth to him, 'Sire, what is this castle and why doth it burn?'

And the hermit sayeth, 'It is the castle where Joseus, the son of King Pelles, did slay his mother. And it hath been ordained by God that it shall burn for ever and from these flames shall come those that shall cause the world to burn.'

Percival now knoweth that it is the castle of his uncle the King Hermit and he departed at great pace and sailed for many a long time until he saw twelve hermits on the shore. And he goeth to them and asketh them from whence they come and they sayeth. 'Sire, we come from nearby where there are twelve chapels and twelve houses and a graveyard wherein are the graves of twelve knights who are all brothers. We keep watch over them. None of the knights lived for more than twelve years as a knight save one. They all took much land and kingdoms from the misbelievers and they all died under arms. The name of the eldest brother was Alain le Gross who came to this land to avenge the death of his brother Alibans of the Waste City. He had been slain by the Giant King and Alain came from the Valleys of Camelot and avenged him but died of his own wounds after.'

And another hermit sayeth, 'Sire, I was at the death of Alain and to me did he confess his sins. But nought mattered to him more than to see his son, Percival.'

With this, Percival asketh the hermits to take him to the graveyard and they did gladly. Therein did he see the tombs both rich and fair with bright adornments. Then sayeth he, 'Which is the tomb of Alain le Gros?'

And they sayeth, 'The highest, for he was the eldest and the greatest.'

And there goeth Percival who prayed and gave great worship in honour of his father. And when the hermits heard that he was the son of Alain they made great joy. He lodged with the hermits that night and heard Mass in the morning at his father's chapel. Then he departed and came to the shores of Greater Britain where he mounted his horse and sent the pilot and ship away commending him to God.

Percival rode long through the forest until he came upon a house where at the gate he saw a knight lying on a bed where at the top sat a lady of great beauty who hath the head of the knight in her lap and sayeth sweet things to him. But the knight doth revile her and say that he would cut off her head and that he was sick and not well. And the knight seeth Percival and asketh him if he was to lodge the night.

And Percival sayeth, 'If it pleases you, Sire, I would gladly lodge in your house.'

'We should be honoured by your staying,' sayeth the knight, 'but I ask you not to think ill of me for what I may say to my wife.'

'Sire,' sayeth Percival, 'the lady is your wife and you may do as you must, but I would counsel you that courtesy cometh at no cost.'

And the knight commandeth his wife to honour Percival and commanded also that squires take him to his bed in to the house for it is near evensong. And the lady disarmed Percival and gave him a scarlet robe to wear and took him in to the hall of the house. And the knight sayeth to her, 'Be sure you sit with the squires for you shall not sit and eat with me or those that lodge herein.'

Percival asked the lady why her husband reviled and rebuked her in such manner. And she sayeth, 'It is because, Sire, the good knight Lancelot made him marry me. Since that time he hath ever shown me great dishonour. Now he hath become ill on account that his brother is also sick and that Gohaz of the Castle of the Whales hath robbed him of his castle and lands. My husband is of the sort that rages at small things and is overjoyed at small things and always there is something that they desire. For him it is a golden cup he hath heard tell of that is borne by a damsel. It is a golden cup of much richness and the damsel is guarded by a knight and it is said that the cup will go only to the best knight in the world. My husband sayeth that he will treat me lowly until such times he hath the golden cup. But he rages over his brother's lost lands and I have to pay the forfeit for, although I do all that he wills, he giveth me no fair treatment. But, Sire, no churlishness may he bring against me, no ill-manner, and no harsh reviling will set me against him, for he is my husband through the eyes of God and the command of the blessed Lancelot. I have loved my husband in health and I will love him in sickness yet I pray to God to bring him to a better mind towards me.'

'Lady,' sayeth Percival, 'you may set his mind at part ease for I tell you truly that his brother hath both his lands and his daughter back in safety. I was at the reconquering thereof and know this to be true. But of the golden cup I know nothing.'

The lady made Percival sit at the table and when the meat was provided she went to sit with the squires. Percival was ashamed of this but sayeth nothing for he would not provoke the knight.

Percival lodged the night in the castle and departed the next morn after Mass. He thinketh that it would be a good thing to gain the golden cup for the lady but also he thinketh of the ship with the white sail bearing the red cross for at the island castle did he most wish to be. He rode until he came to the forest of the Black Hermit that was a loathly place where grew no green leaves and no birds did sing. There he came upon the Damsel of the Carriage who was changed mightily. 'Sire,' sayeth she to Percival, 'Bald have I been since we first met, but look now upon me.'

And she threw back the hood of her cloak and showeth much hair as golden as the dawn. And Percival sayeth, 'Damsel, before you were indeed comely, now you have beauty surpassing even the whitest lily.'

'Thank you, Sire,' sayeth she, 'also my arm I no longer carry from a cloth of gold about my neck. And the damsel that once walked behind me now rides as she should. And this, Sire, for that you brought about the Holy Grail by the goodness of your heart.'

'No, damsel,' sayeth Percival, 'the Holy Grail was revealed only at the command of God.'

And the damsel sayeth, 'Sire, we come nigh the Castle of the Black Hermit and further I dare not go for there are bowmen at the walls that loose arrows at all who come near them. Only if you live to reach the gate will they stop and then only for they mean to slay you within the walls. You, Sire, need have no fear of those within for they will do you no evil save for the Black Hermit who will gladly slay you.'

And Percival bid the damsel to stay and spurred his horse on to a great gallop. As he came to the castle the bowmen loosed their arrows and he raised his shield and many arrows were lodged therein but he flinched not and rode to the drawbridge which was lowered on his coming and whereon the arrows ceased. The gate was opened, for the knights within thought to slay him but when they saw him they knew him to be Percival and they fell back with great dread.

Percival rode up the steps to the great hall and entered on horse and full armed. And the hall was full of many knights all foul featured. At the far end of the hall was the Black Hermit of great height and seated on his horse full armed also. And the knights cryeth to the Black Hermit saying, 'We have often guarded and defended you, now you defend us from this knight!'

And Percival lowered his lance and raised his shield and ran full hard at the Black Hermit who cometh at him in like manner. And the hall resounded to the clash of steel as the Black Hermit broke his lance on the shield of Percival and was sent to the ground horse and all by the lance of the good knight. When they seeth him fall, the knights of the castle ran upon him and opened a pit from whence came a foul smell and did throw him in. Then all of a company they yielded the castle to Percival and put themselves at his mercy.

With this, the Damsel of the Carriage entered the hall and the knights of the castle gave her the head of a king in a silver box with a golden crown and the head of a queen in a box of lead with a copper crown, which have been robbed of her when she came nigh with Gawain. And she departed joyfully for the Valleys of Camelot.

And Percival put the knights in covenant that they would turn to God and the Holy Mother that they would be saved from the torments of Hell and that they would give courteous lodging to any passing knight that so required. And he departed in full joy that he hath brought the knights to God and for ever after faithful masses were sung in the castle for ever after.

Percival rode until he came upon a damsel and a knight riding through the forest. The damsel carried a golden cup and Percival saluted the knight saying, 'May God be with you this day, Sire.'

And the knight replieth, 'And with you also, Sire.'

Sayeth Percival, 'Is this damsel one of your household?'

And the knight sayeth, 'No, Sire, rather I am one of hers. We go, Sire, to the assembly of knights where they shall contest for this golden cup.'

Percival sayeth, 'That will be a fair sight to see. For now damsel, Sire, I shall depart but mean to meet you again before this day is out.'

With that, Percival rode to the ground of the assembly and seeth there many knights begun in combat and he hurled himself in to the clashing of arms. The assembly continued until evensong when it was time to choose the best knight. All agreed that the Knight of the White Shield did overcome them all in valour and chivalry and the damsel cometh to give Percival the golden cup. She sayeth to him, 'Sire, I present to you this cup of gold for your knightly virtues. You should know, however, from whence it came, for it carries with it a duty which you must discharge.

This cup was given to Gawain by the elder Damsel of the Tent whereat he had defeated the evil custom. But the joy of Gawain was destroyed when that most courteous of knights, Meliot of England, was treacherously slain by Brundans, the son of the sister of Briant of the Isles. Gawain now prays that whosoever should win the golden cup would undertake to avenge the death of Meliot. Brundans carrieth a shield of green and silver.'

Sayeth Percival, 'Damsel, were there no cup of gold, I would willingly do as Gawain requests for both he and Meliot are well deserving of the aid of good knights. Be assured, damsel, that from this moment Brundans lives only with me waiting in his shadow and he shall know soon that treachery brings its own vengeance.'

He then sayeth to the knight with the damsel, 'Sire, I request and charge you that you take this golden cup to the house of the Sick Knight and tell his lady that it was sent thither by the Knight of the White Shield.' And the knight sayeth that he will gladly do as Percival requests.

Percival then rode to Castle Perilous where Lancelot had brought the sword and piece of shroud to cure the wounded Meliot. Therein he found a damsel who was full sorrowful and sayeth that Brundans hath slain the most courteous knight by treachery. As she speaketh another damsel came fast on horse and sayeth to Percival, 'Sire, you must come quickly and give us your aid. You are the only knight in this forest I can find.'

And Percival sayeth, 'How may I aid you?'

Sayeth she, 'A knight is carrying off my lady by force. He hath taken her when she was on her way to the court of King Arthur.'

'Who is your lady?'

'She is the younger Damsel of the Tent where Gawain overthrew the evil custom. For the sake of God, Sire, hasten for he treats her cruelly for her love of Gawain and King Arthur.'

Percival rode as fast as he may with the damsel by his side and come to the forest where they heard the damsel crying for mercy. They heareth also the knight saying that mercy would she have none as he beat her with the flat of his sword. And Percival seeth the damsel and the knight and he seeth also that the knight beareth a shield of green and silver.

Percival cometh up to him and sayeth, 'Hold, Sire! This is too harsh a manner to treat a damsel.'

And Brundans sayeth, 'Hold back. Sire! For this is my affair and I shall treat her as I am content so to do.'

Sayeth Percival, 'No, Sire, you shall not. No knight should treat a damsel thus.'

But Brundans sayeth, 'I have not yet begun to show my treatment of her, ere long she shall be the most sorrowful damsel in the world.' And with this he struck the damsel on the head with the flat of his sword and blood came from her mouth and nose and she fell to the ground.

And Percival sayeth, 'Doubly you hath earned vengeance of me. You hath slain the good Meliot and now you shame this damsel. Mount your horse and prepare to meet me!'

Brundans goeth to his horse and mounteth as Percival goes back apace. They came at each other with a mighty hurtle but Percival thrust his lance through the green and silver shield in to the breast of Brundans and knocked him hard to the ground. And Percival dismounted and went to Brundans and took off his helmet and then struck off his head. He gave the head to the younger Damsel of the Tent and sayeth, 'Damsel, take this with you to the court of King Arthur and salute them for me. Sayeth also to them that this head is the last gift I send them for I shall never see them again in this world. But tell them also they shall remain in my thoughts and never shall I bring to end the love I have for my brother knights. For ever they shall remain the example of knightly virtue to those who would follow.'

And the damsel departed thanking Percival for his aid and he commended her to God. He then rode to the Castle Perilous where the damsel made much joy on hearing of the slaying of Brundans. Percival lodged in the castle that night and heard Mass before parting on the morrow. He then came upon the knight who hath carried the golden cup to the Sick Knight and Percival asketh him how it goeth with the gift. And the knight sayeth, 'Sire, never was a gift received with such goodwill. The knight no longer grudges his wife and she sits at table with him and the household obey her commands.'

Sayeth Percival, 'I am well pleased with this and I thank you, Sire, for doing this on my behalf.'

And the knight sayeth, 'There is nothing I would not do for you, Sire, for you made my brother Knight Hardy that was once Knight Coward.'

And Percival sayeth, 'He was a good and true knight that met a good end, but I think had he been still Knight Coward he would have been alive.'

But the knight sayeth, 'No, Sire, he met death with honour and no more could he ask for otherwise he would have lived with shame. Yet I was not glad of his death for he proved a Knight Hardy and would have done more good had he lived the longer.'

Percival departed from the knight commending him to God and rode to the Castle of the Holy Grail. In his castle he found his mother and his sister brought there by the Damsel of the Carriage. They had brought the coffin from the chapel of Castle Camelot and had laid it in the chapel of the Castle of the Holy Grail also with the coffin from the chapel outside the Castle of the Holy Grail. Never more would they need to open in the presence of the best knight in the world. His sister, Dindrane, hath also brought the piece of shroud that she hath taken from the Chapel Perilous and placed it with the other holy relics.

Percival then stayed in the castle for a long time without any questing for adventure for he gave his loyalty entirely to God and worshiped Him most worthily. He and his mother and his sister did continually pray to Our Saviour and His Sweet Mother that the world should be rid of evil and that the light of God should be seen in every corner of the land. First his mother and then his sister were summoned to God. They were buried by the hermits who sang masses over their tombs. One day Percival was alone in the chapel praying when an angel voice sayeth, 'Percival, you shall not abide here for long. It is the command of God that you spread the relics herein among the hermits. No more shall the Holy Grail appear in this chapel but you shall know soon of the place where it shall be.'

When the voice ceased its speaking all the coffins and tombs within the chapel clattered with sound as the bodies within saluted the speaker.

In obedience to the command of God, Percival called forth the hermits and spread among them the holy relics. The hermits departed and went abroad throughout the land and built churches and abbeys wherein they housed the relics. And those sacred places remain here with us today. Only Joseus, the son of King Hermit, remained with Percival for he knew his time had come.

One day, Percival heard the sound of a bell ringing across the waters. He went to the chapel window and saw a rich ship which bore a white sail whereon was a red cross. In the ship were many good knights dressed in garments of white and with a red cross on their breast. And they came unto the chapel bearing gold and silver vessel which they placed in full reverence on the tombs therein. Percival took his leave of Joseus and the household and went on board the ship. And they watched as the ship departed, the knights standing on the deck with Percival as if to give him great honour. And the ship sailed to a sky red as if of fire and Percival was never seen again in this world.

When Joseus was summoned by God, the castle fell in to decay but the chapel remained as if untouched. No one dare enter the castle for dread of the mighty and virtuous knights that had walked its halls and chambers. But many years on, two young and brave knights came in to the ruined castle. No one knows what they had seen within but they became hermits and lived a hard and good life in the forest. When asked what they had seen therein, they sayeth only, 'We may not tell you, for the knowledge is only for them that hath entered.' They later became Saints.

About the Editor

E. C. Coleman served in the Royal Navy for 36 years, which included time on an aircraft carrier, a submarine, and Nelson's flagship, HMS *Victory*. During that time he mounted four Arctic expeditions in search of evidence from the 1845 John Franklin Expedition. He has written many books on naval, polar, medieval and Victorian subjects and contributed the foreword to two volumes of Captain Scott's diaries. His interest in the Grail legend is longstanding and he is currently researching a new work on the Knights Templar. He lives in Lincolnshire.